"The Cognitive Science of Religion (CSR for short) is often described as a 'new field' but it is rapidly maturing and that is why this introduction is urgently needed. Claire White is exceptionally well placed to provide it, having been among the first cohort of researchers to be trained in the field and now America's first tenure track professor in CSR. This book is essential reading for any student interested in the scientific study of religion."

Harvey Whitehouse, Oxford University, UK.

"This outstanding first-of-its kind introductory text on the cognitive science of religion represents a major step forward for this rapidly growing and high impact discipline. This groundbreaking book, written by one of the field's foremost experts, is authoritative, accessible, and inclusive. I have no doubt that it will become part of the canon of core literature in the cognitive science of religion and will be instrumental in building this fascinating field of study."

Cristine H. Legare, University of Texas at Austin, USA.

An Introduction to the Cognitive Science of Religion

In recent decades, a new scientific approach to understand, explain, and predict many features of religion has emerged. The cognitive science of religion (CSR) has amassed research on the forces that shape the tendency for humans to be religious and on what forms belief takes. It suggests that religion, like language or music, naturally emerges in humans with tractable similarities. This new approach has profound implications for how we understand religion, including why it appears so easily, and why people are willing to fight—and die—for it. Yet it is not without its critics, and some fear that scholars are explaining the ineffable mystery of religion away, or showing that religion is natural proves or disproves the existence of God.

An Introduction to the Cognitive Science of Religion offers students and general readers an accessible introduction to the approach, providing an overview of key findings and the debates that shape it. The volume includes a glossary of key terms, and each chapter includes suggestions for further thought and further reading as well as chapter summaries highlighting key points.

This book is an indispensable resource for introductory courses on religion and a much-needed option for advanced courses.

Claire White is Associate Professor in Religious Studies at California State University, Northridge. She was appointed as the first tenure-track position in the cognitive science of religion at a religious studies department in the United States.

An Introduction to the Cognitive Science of Religion

Connecting Evolution, Brain, Cognition, and Culture

Claire White

LONDON AND NEW YORK

First published 2021
by Routledge
2 Park Square, Milton Park, Abingdon, Oxon OX14 4RN

and by Routledge
605 Third Avenue, New York, NY 10158

Routledge is an imprint of the Taylor & Francis Group, an informa business

British Library Cataloguing-in-Publication Data
A catalogue record for this book is available from the British Library

Library of Congress Cataloging-in-Publication Data
A catalog record has been requested for this book

ISBN: 978-1-138-49924-9 (hbk)
ISBN: 978-1-138-54146-7 (pbk)
ISBN: 978-1-351-01097-9 (ebk)

Typeset in Bembo
by Taylor & Francis Books

One rainy Saturday at the Institute of Cognition and Culture, Belfast in 2006, five scholars deliberated over my academic fate. I am forever grateful for their decision and continued support. This book is dedicated to the members of my Ph.D. Differentiation Committee: Jesse Bering, Emma Cohen, Tom Lawson, Paulo Sousa, and especially my Ph.D. supervisor, Harvey Whitehouse.

Contents

Figures

Tables

Foreword

In 2012, I acquired the first tenure-track position in the cognitive science of religion (CSR) at a religious studies department in the United States. As I soon came to learn, students found the term "cognitive science of religion" vague and daunting. Reading materials on CSR-related topics tended to be targeted towards the specialist, and newcomers felt discouraged in their attempts to learn more.

This book aims to redress this balance by presenting a straightforward overview of CSR, demonstrating the fruitfulness of the approach through research topics and critiques. It is not a comprehensive account of CSR, but chapters are designed to provide the reader with an understanding of many pertinent ideas and research in the subdiscipline. Participation exercises, case studies, key questions, and further reading in the chapters will help students understand and engage with the topics. I hope that this book stimulates the minds of readers from all backgrounds.

Acknowledgements

This book would not have been completed without the help of many individuals at my home institution, California State University Northridge, especially Rick Talbott and Elizabeth Say, who nurtured my professional development. Thanks also to the research assistants at California State University Northridge, especially Adrian Conway, Andrea Velasco, Iliana Mazin, Paul Parrett, Corinne Hummel, Moina Maaz, Sandra Quintana, and students in Huma 620 who proofread the manuscript.

I am also grateful to my family, friends and colleagues whose comments and critiques on aspects of the chapters improved this book. These include Adam Baimel, Ara Norenzayan, Andrew Shtulman, Benjamin Purzycki, Cindel White, David Cooper, Deborah Kelemen, Emma Cohen, Helen De Cruz, Justin Barrett, Jesse Bering, Jeppe Jensen, Jonathan Jong, Justin McBrayer, Jody Myers, John Shaver, Jesper Sorensen, Luther Martin, Larisa Heiphetz, Manvir Singh, Michael Barlev, Mitch Hodge, Nicholas Baumard, Oliver Curry, Paul Bloom, Pascal Boyer, Paul Harris, Robert McCauley, Ryan McKay, Richard Sosis, Rick Talbot, Stewart Guthrie, Shaun Nicholas, Ted Slingerland, and Will Gervais.

I am especially grateful to colleagues who read multiple chapters, including Tom Lawson, Cristine Legare, and Harvey Whitehouse. Special thanks to Armin Geertz, who provided examples of research questions and methodologies, and to Dimitris Xygalatas and another anonymous reviewer for their thorough and helpful feedback on the entire book.

Time was spent on this book in the office and at home. I owe gratitude to my husband, Brian Kravette, for his support as I undertook this writing project. Likewise, thank you to my mother-in-law, Muriel Kravette, who provided me with the time to write.

Given the ambitious nature of providing a short introductory book, it is inevitable that important topics, theories, and researchers have not been given the full treatment they deserve or have been omitted altogether. Any omissions are mine alone. I have tried to provide references throughout the book, and I encourage readers to make use of these and further reading at the end of each chapter.

1 Introduction to the cognitive science of religion

The cognitive science of religion (CSR) was established in the 1990s as a subdiscipline of cognitive science. Today, CSR encompasses scholars from diverse fields such as religious studies, cognitive, cultural, and evolutionary anthropology, evolutionary, developmental, cognitive and social psychology, sociology, philosophy, neuroscience, biology, behavioral ecology, archaeology, and history, among others. While cognitive scientists of religion adopt assumptions and methods from their respective disciplines, they are united by a focus on the role of human cognition in religious thought and behavior. In line with cognitive science, CSR scholars accept that how humans attend and respond to religious representations is not random but influenced and constrained by cognitive processes. In line with evolutionary psychology, CSR scholars concede that these processes are, in turn, shaped by structures that represent our evolutionary history; many evolved to solve recurrent problems in ancestral environments.

How did religion come about? Why is religion so prevalent around the world? What makes religious ideas and practices spread successfully? What are the effects of religious practices on participants? These are some of the questions that CSR scholars are interested in and equipped to answer. Specifically, cognitive scientists of religion are concerned with understanding (a) how the human mind governs which information is attended to, (b) the contexts in which information is attended to, and (c) how information is stored, processed, and acted upon, which gives rise to religious ideas and practices. They are also interested in (d) the effects of religious beliefs and practices on those who engage with them. The ultimate goal of cognitive scientists of religion is to explain how religious ideas, beliefs, and behaviors arise and recur in human populations by integrating knowledge on evolution, cognition, brain, and behavior.

Today, CSR is a flourishing interdisciplinary enterprise, and research is growing at an exponential pace. For instance, the number of publications increased by 314 percent between 2000 and 2011[1] to over 3,000 per year. Publications include articles in leading journals in fields such as cognitive science, psychology, anthropology, and history. They also include edited volumes, journal editions, and book series such as *Advances in the Cognitive Science of Religion series, Religion, Cognition and Culture,* and specialized journals, including the *Journal of Cognition and Culture (JCC), Religion, Brain and Behavior (RBB), Journal of the Cognitive Science of Religion,* and *Journal of Cognitive Historiography*. CSR now boasts a professional society, *The International Association for the Cognitive Science of Religion (IACSR)*, and representation in leading professional organizations on religion such as the *American Academy of Religion, International Association for the History of Religions*, and other disciplines, such as psychology and cognitive science.

The number of institutions dedicated to CSR research has likewise grown. Since the Institute of Cognition and Culture (ICC) was established in Belfast in 2004, many others have followed suit. These include the Religion, Cognition, and Culture research unit (RCC) at Aarhus University; the Centre for Anthropology and Mind (CAM) and the Institute of Cognitive and Evolutionary Anthropology (ICEA) at Oxford University; the International Cognition and Culture Institute, run by the London School of Economics and the Institut Jean Nicod in Paris; the Centre for Human Evolution, Cognition, and Culture (HECC) at the University of British Columbia; the Institute for the Biocultural Study of Religion in Massachusetts; the Center for Mind, Brain, and Culture at Emory University; and the Laboratory for the Experimental Research of Religion (LEVYNA) at Masaryk University in Brno and the Institute for the Bio-Cultural Study of Religion (IBCSR) at the Center for Mind and Culture in Boston.

The allocation of funding to CSR research has also increased, and in recent years includes large projects such as the €2m, three-year "Explaining Religion" (EXREL) project, funded by the European Commission, a £4m, five-year project on "Ritual, Community, and Conflict" (RCC), funded by the UK's Economic and Social Research Council, "Evolution of Religion and Morality," led by UBC with almost CAD $7m in direct and matching funds, and a $2m, three-year "Modeling Religion Project" funded by the John Templeton Foundation.

This pace is likely to continue. As anthropologist Harvey Whitehouse exclaimed in his opening address during a videoconference sponsored by the American Academy of Religion, "these are exciting times for the scientific study of religion." In this chapter, we trace CSR back to its beginnings.

Key points

- CSR began in the 1990s as a subdiscipline of cognitive science.
- CSR continues to expand.
- CSR is a scientific approach to the study of religion.
- CSR Explains how religious ideas, beliefs, and behaviors arise and persist in human populations.

The cognitive revolution as a reaction against behaviorism in the 1950s

Interest in the mental underpinnings of religion was not created by CSR but was reinvigorated by it. As anthropologist Dimitris Xygalatas and psychologist Ryan McKay put it,[2] interest in the role of the human mind in religion:

> Dates back at least to the beginnings of disciplines like psychology, sociology, and anthropology. However, after a long period of drought brought on by the neglect of mental processes during the reign of culturology, behaviorism, and the sui generis view of religion and culture, the cognitive revolution of the 1950s provided the rain that germinated these seeds.
>
> (Xygalatas and McKay, 2013: 2)

The "cognitive revolution" that Xygalatas and McKay refer to above was an intellectual movement in the 1950s. The dominant school in scientific psychology at the time was behaviorism. Behaviorism's central claim was that there was no need to posit mental processes because human and animal behavior could be explained in terms of learned conditioning. Behaviors were construed as reflexes and responses to stimuli in the environment based on past experiences. Behaviorists, therefore, focused on environmental factors to explain human behavior.

The cognitive revolution was primarily the result of a reaction from those who studied the mind, including specialists in anthropology, artificial intelligence, computer science, linguistics, economists, and psychology, against behaviorism. These scholars argued that humans were not "blank slates" without any inbuilt mental content, but that cognitive processes existed and influenced human behavior. They construed the mind as a complex and interacting system that functioned much like a computer, taking inputs and generating outputs. This revolution gave birth to the interdisciplinary study of the mind and its processes, which became known collectively as cognitive science.[3]

Key points

- CSR was foreshadowed by the cognitive revolution, which gave rise to the cognitive sciences.
- The cognitive revolution began as a reaction against behaviorism.
- Behaviorism was the dominant theory in cultural studies in the 1950s and presented humans as though their minds were blank slates.
- The cognitive sciences, by contrast, argued that people were not blank slates, but rather, that the mind was a complex and interacting system.

The cognitive science of religion as a reaction against cultural studies in the 1990s

The cognitive revolution marked a challenge to the principles of behaviorism in the sciences. The cognitive science of religion also marked a revolution, this time against cultural studies of religion in fields such as anthropology and history. Around four decades after the cognitive revolution, a handful of social scientists were working on

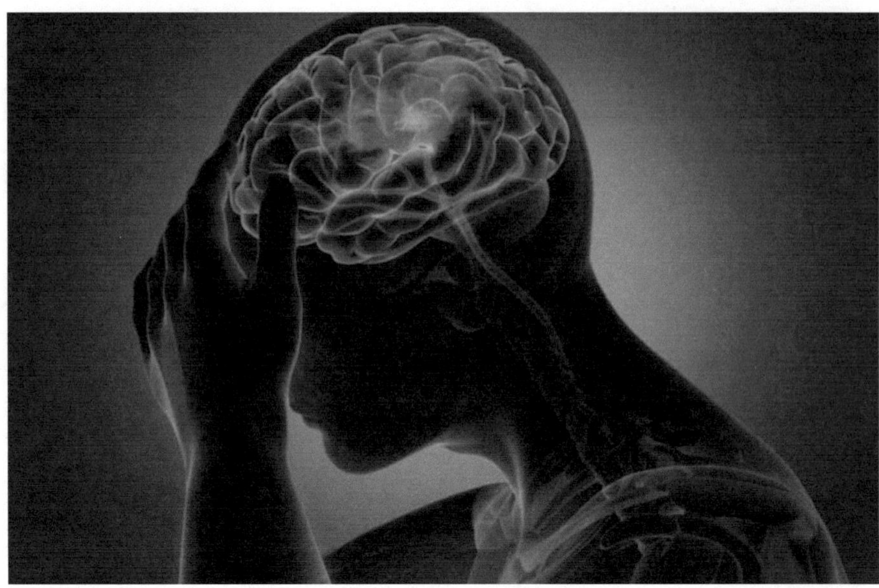

Figure 1.1 CSR was inspired by the cognitive revolution, which aimed to put the human mind back into explanations of human behavior. (Image credit: ESB Professional/Shutterstock.com).

projects concerning religion. These projects occurred at around the same time and were mainly initiated independently of one another. They included:

a) *Rethinking Religion: Connecting Cognition and Culture* (Lawson and McCauley, 1990):[4] A cognitive approach to ritual forms, through applying theories about the principles of language to ritual structure.
b) *Faces in the Clouds: A New Theory of Religion* (Guthrie, 1993):[5] A comprehensive approach to applying cognitive perspectives to the origins of religion.
c) *The Naturalness of Religious Ideas* (Boyer, 1994):[6] Explaining the transmissive success of religious concepts.
d) *Inside the Cult* (Whitehouse, 1995):[7] A theory of religious transmission based on ethnographic fieldwork and findings in cognitive psychology.

Although these works differed on methods, theories, and scope, they were unified by a general dissatisfaction with the dominant views about religion at the time. Much like the cognitive revolution was a reaction against the assumptions of behaviorism in the sciences, CSR was a reaction against the assumptions in cultural studies about religion. The assumptions that these early pioneers took issue with are outlined in detail in the remainder of this section.

Key points

- CSR was a reaction against the methods and approaches of cultural studies of religion.
- CSR began with a handful of scholars who came to similar conclusions.
- One basic conclusion was that current cultural approaches to the study of religion were inadequate to explain how religious ideas and behaviors were learned and transmitted.

Challenges to trends in cultural studies among early pioneers in CSR

1 Principles of postmodernism, cultural determinism, and extreme forms of cultural relativism

(a) Postmodernism

Prior to the formation of CSR, a postmodernist wave swept through anthropology. Postmodernism maintained that humans cannot be objective and construe the world as nothing but a social construct, the result of multiple, competing narratives. For postmodernists, cultures were inherently different, and thus all attempts to capture and compare them were futile.[8]

(b) Cultural relativism

At the time of the formation of CSR, there was an excess of cultural relativism in work on religion. In moderate form, cultural relativism holds that one must understand a culture on its own terms and not to make judgments using the standards of one's own culture. Many cognitive scientists of religion indeed embrace this fruitful perspective. However, the dominant form of cultural relativism in the 1990s was a more extreme version of cultural relativism, which assumed that a person's behavior is only relative to their particular culture and thus can only be understood in light of that specific culture.

(c) Cultural determinism

Cultural determinists widely endorsed an extreme version of cultural relativism. Cultural determinists explained human behavior as more or less determined by culture, and this was the prevailing view at the time in cultural studies. In other words, the behavior of people in groups was construed as the product of environmental inputs. Thus, many scholars, especially social anthropologists, mainly focused on how the sociocultural environment shaped human behavior and primarily ignored how the mind processed those inputs. The ideas of cultural determinism were in stark contrast to research in the cognitive sciences, which demonstrated that humans naturally have cognitive biases and predilections, such as the ability to distinguish between agents and objects, that do not depend upon cultural particulars.

According to the principles of cultural determinism, we cannot explain human behavior in general but only in particular contexts. To understand how and why a person acts a certain way entails an understanding of the particularistic beliefs, values, and practices of each person's culture. Nor can we understand the behavior of one group of people by comparing it to another group because each group is unique. Cultural determinism and extreme versions of cultural relativism had long guided social scientists in their understanding of culture, including the study of religion. Scholars favored a blank slate view of human functioning. The science of human behavior flourished while the science of mental life dwindled.

Early pioneers of the cognitive science of religion were inspired by scholars in relevant fields who challenged these assumptions. One source of inspiration was the writings of French social and cognitive anthropologist Dan Sperber.[9] Sperber had provided a compelling critique of the descriptive methods and interpretative treatments of culture in social anthropology at the time and focused on the role of cognition in the transmission of ideas. Sperber proposed a theory called "the epidemiology of representations," which at its core maintained that some ideas are encoded, stored, and recalled better than others because they exploit specific properties of the human mind.

Just like medical epidemiologists cannot study the incidence and distribution of disease without understanding the host organism's body, Sperber proposed that social scientists could not study the prevalence and distribution of ideas in culture unless they had a better understanding of human minds. More specifically, they needed to understand how humans acquired, processed, and transmitted information privately and in groups, within communities (horizontal transmission) and across generations (vertical transmission). On Sperber's account, the mind was not a blank slate, nor was it like a sponge absorbing all cultural input or even a Xerox machine making identical copies of information in the environment. Instead, humans actively filter and distort information, including religious ideas and behaviors, in the world around them.

Sperber proposed that contemporary understandings of the human mind and the precise methods of scientific inquiry could revolutionize cultural studies in the same way that the cognitive revolution had changed many sciences. Early pioneers of CSR expanded on Sperber's claims about understanding how ideas were transmitted in culture, and they applied similar critiques to the study of religion. These critiques were most extensively outlined by religious studies scholars E. Thomas Lawson, who is widely credited with founding CSR, and his collaborator, philosopher Robert McCauley.[10]

Figure 1.2 Just like epidemiologists in medicine study the incidence and distribution of disease by taking into account what is known about the human body, Sperber maintained that social scientists cannot study the prevalence and distribution of ideas in culture unless they also understood the mind. (Image credit: MarcoVector/Shutterstock.com).

Key points

- CSR scholars reacted against the view that behavior was determined by culture, and extreme versions of cultural relativism, that a person's behavior can only be understood by knowing about their cultural context.
- CSR scholars were influenced by work in the cognitive sciences, which demonstrated that humans naturally have cognitive biases and predilections.

2 The promotion of interpretative accounts of religious ideas and behaviors

One consequence of trends in cultural studies towards postmodernism, cultural relativism and determinism was on how scholars studied religion and the methods they used. Most notably, these consequences led to the rejection of explanatory approaches to culture and the reliance on interpretative accounts of human phenomena. Culture was viewed as a system of signs and symbols (i.e. semiotic) and the task of scholars was to navigate and discover these intricate webs of signs to decipher religion's symbolic meaning. If culture was a form of discourse, then the interpretation of texts became the method of choice. Scholars engaged in explaining with as much detail as possible the reason behind human actions and their meaning, a method known as thick description.

Anthropologist Clifford Geertz, who is well known for his support of symbolic anthropology, used the example of the wink of an eye to clarifying this method.[11] There are many interpretations of this act. Is the person merely rapidly contracting her eyelid? Is she indicating friendship with you? Or faking a wink to deceive you? Attuned to pay attention to the possibilities of the meanings behind actions, religious studies scholars engaged in seemingly endless accounts of cultural practices. Fascinating in their own right, these descriptions were not a reliable basis for explaining religion. Accounts were vague, lacked explanatory power, were unable to be empirically assessed among competing interpretations, and posed more questions about behaviors than they answered.

Many cognitive scientists of religion continue to point out these limitations of previous approaches to the study of religion. For example, as we cover in Chapter 7 (Supernatural Agents), anthropologist Emma Cohen took issue with sociological explanations for spirit possession that dominated social anthropology for decades. The emergence and incidence of possession were often presented as a response to power in class-orientated or male-dominated societies. Theorists had proposed that episodes of trance were an opportunity for the marginalized to express themselves in ways that were not otherwise acceptable in society. In contrast, others maintained that they were a reflection of power, such as an index of their subordinate status.

In her book *The Mind Possessed*, Cohen points out two main weaknesses of these sociological theories that hamper attempts to systematically capture and investigate religion.[12] First, theories are vague. In other words, they lack a clear conceptualization of the causal factors underpinning the participation in possession episodes. These theories do not specify how, precisely, the correlation (i.e. relationship) with social factors was causally significant. They do not delineate carefully between the causes (i.e. independent variables) or effects (i.e. dependent variables) of participating in these episodes. Nor do they outline the sufficient and necessary conditions for participation, including predictions for how factors that affect participation and social outcomes may coalesce, propose methodologies for testing claims or even state what would count as a refutation of their hypotheses.

The second main weakness that Cohen pointed out about many prior sociological explanations of spirit possession was that of competing hypotheses. For example, the theory that trance is a display of power vs. the competing theory that trance is a display against power, make the same predictions. In this example, both hypotheses may well predict that people who are marginalized participate in episodes of trance. Also, these theories focus on single determinants (e.g. raising inequality), most of which apply in some circumstances, while failing to describe many of the features of possession behavior. Additionally, sociological theories say little about the mechanisms through which these states exert their effects. For instance, is participating in a trance-like a form of therapy that alleviates anxiety? Alternatively, is it a form of organized rebellion where communication serves to forward the aims of social change? Some of these issues motivated Cohen to research the cognitive underpinnings of cross-culturally recurrent forms of possession belief.

Participation 1: What is ritual?

1 Imagine that an alien visits earth, and you must describe a ritual (that you have participated in or seen) so that the alien understands the actions involved.
2 Describe your ritual in around 500 words.

Lawson and McCauley took issue with trends towards valuing interpretative treatments of religion and shunning explanatory accounts. They pointed out that the characterization of interpretation vs. explanation among cultural studies' scholars was a false dichotomy. Both interpretation and explanation are invoked to explain human thought and behavior; every explanation depends on the interpretation of data, and interpretation relies on the acceptance of underlying explanatory theories. For example, as Cohen et al. showcase,[13] it is almost impossible to describe a person's actions, such as "Julia is drinking water," without depending upon an implicit, causal theory (i.e. an explanation) of behavior as the result of internal states of belief and desire. In this case, because Julia is thirsty. Using theories about a person's internal states is referred to in psychology as "Theory of Mind" (ToM). In short, interpreting religion entails explaining it.

Participation 2: Descriptions and explanations of ritual

1 Refer back to your description of a ritual in participation 1, where you were instructed to describe the ritual so that an alien visitor could understand the actions.
2 Underline any explanations that you have included in your description. For example, did you include assumptions about why people perform specific actions in the ritual?
3 Discuss with another student: Why do you think it is so tempting to explain religious ideas or behaviors when you describe them?

Alas, even scholars who argued against the use of explanations were already proposing them. Cohen et al.[14] provide examples of this fallacy in the anthropological accounts of historical evidence concerning Hawaiian rituals performed in response to the arrival of Captain Cook in 1779. Cook was first welcomed as a God by the Hawaiians and then later murdered, and there are historical accounts of these events. Even though anthropologists proposed what they considered to be interpretations of the historical accounts, their interpretations depended upon prominent scholarly theories (i.e. explanations) about the rituals. For example, that Captain Cook was treated as a manifestation of a God is in line with the theory of "mythopraxis," in other words, the practice of myth aligns with patterns residing in the collective consciousness of a group of people.

Further, accounts that assumed that he was recruited to help the Hawaiians in a war effort are in line with an altered version of Weber's "practical rationality," the idea that beliefs are rational as a means to an end goal.

Key points

- Scholars in CSR were dissatisfied with the methods of religious studies scholars who described and interpreted aspects of religious traditions.
- These methods often lacked theories and predictions about the causal relationships of aspects of culture and religion.
- Cognitive scientists of religion primarily wanted to develop explanations of religion.

3 Outdated or nonexistent theories of human psychology

As Lawson and McCauley have pointed out, scholars were already proposing explanations of religion. Yet they were often relying on outdated models of human cognition, such as early Freudian psychodynamic theories that view unconscious mental forces (such as fear and desires) as more-or-less exclusively shaping behavior. Others assumed a "black box" theory of human psychology that lacked discussion of the mind and underlying psychological mechanisms altogether.[15] Again, many cognitive scientists of religion continue to point out these limitations of previous approaches to the study of religion (see Figure 1.3).

For example, my work on reincarnation (covered in Chapter 6: The Afterlife), points out the limitations of one widely accepted explanation of reincarnation beliefs in the work of anthropologist Gananath Obeyesekere. Obeyesekere highlighted beliefs about reincarnation that included ideas about the dead returning to

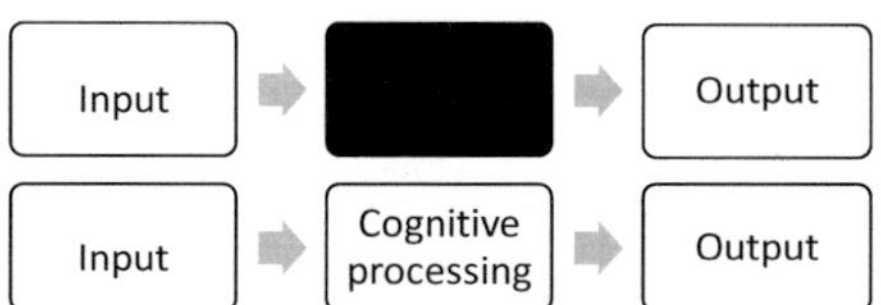

Figure 1.3 Comparison between models that exclude and include the mind to explain human thought and behavior. Models that exclude the human mind (first level of boxes) assume that input (e.g. the stimulus, such as obtaining a reward in the environment) gives rise to outputs (e.g. response, such as repeating the behavior) without any relevant form of active processing in-between (e.g. filtering, distorting information) that would help to explain people's behavior. Hence, they are often deemed as "black box" theories in the social sciences, because there is nothing (i.e. a black box) between input and output, where the mind should be active. By contrast, models that include the human mind (second level of boxes) like those in the cognitive science of religion, include relevant theories about human cognitive processing to explain why and how people respond to their environment.

the human world. These ideas were often accompanied by the idea that people could find their deceased loved one after they were reborn into a new body. He proposed that people believed they could locate reincarnated loved ones because of the desire to identify their loved ones and ensure that they found them.[16] I characterized this type of explanation as a Freudian wish-fulfillment account of reincarnation beliefs, and deemed it an insufficient account.

First, it does not explain why, in very different cultures around the world, people regard the perceived similarity in particular physical and psychological traits between two people as evidence that reincarnation has taken place. Even when specialists decide upon the identity of the newborn child, or when who-was-reborn-as-whom is already culturally prescribed. In these circumstances, people often examine the child for distinctive physical features and indications of a memory of past events as evidence of their former identity. How did the idea that certain features provide better proof of continued identity in reincarnation than others emerge and spread across vastly different cultures? This remaining question led me to conduct systematic cross-cultural research on the topic.[17]

Key points

- Many scholars of religion rejected the idea of trying to explain religion yet proposed explanations themselves.
- Most explanations of religion lacked specificity about how humans tend to think, and often, scholars used outdated explanations of the human mind.

4 Privileging personal accounts over systematic theories of religion

Early pioneers of CSR argued that the study of religion was skewed in favor of personal and interpretative accounts over systematic and explanatory theories. Standard research in the academic study of religion had been concerned with documenting and describing religious diversity. The assumptions of cultural determinism (i.e. a person's behavior is determined by culture) and extreme versions of cultural relativism (i.e. human behavior is only relative to a person's particular culture) had led scholars to construe the behavior of people in groups as the product of environmental inputs. These assumptions had led religious studies scholars to specialize in the knowledge of particular traditions. Most scholars aimed to understand doctrines and behaviors of different groups of people entrenched in their rich, unique, sociocultural contexts, and so area studies approaches to religious traditions became the hallmark of religious studies' departments across the US.

Existing models of culture also privileged religious diversity over cross-cultural patterns and exaggerated the differences between religions. As religious studies scholar Edward Slingerland points out, the field of religious studies was amounting to religion appreciation courses—documenting endless diversity without attempting to situate it in an explanatory framework.[18] Further, what typically passed for a theory of religion was probably better characterized as a philosophy of religion, in the sense that "theories" of religion typically took the form of assertions that were not amenable to empirical testing.[19] Even today, many theory and methods courses proposed in religious studies departments contain very little discussion on methods.

Key points

- The assumptions of cultural determinism and extreme relativism had led many scholars in religious studies to specialize in particular religious traditions.
- Scholars also privileged religious diversity rather than similarity.
- The study of religion became associated with documenting these differences.

5 Assumptions that religion is unique and cannot be reduced

There has been strong resistance in religious studies to those who advocate reductionism. Reductionism involves the practice of describing and analyzing a complex phenomenon in terms of phenomena that are held to represent a simpler or more fundamental level. For instance, chemists may explain the behavior of gases in terms of motions of molecules or biologists may explain the inheritance of traits in terms of genes and replication of DNA. While reductionism is a cornerstone of the scientific method and embraced by cognitive scientists of religion, it is regarded by opponents as a mistaken approach to the study of religion.[20]

There are two main misguided reasons for this disdain of reductionism among many traditional religious studies scholars. First, students of religion were (and are) often taught that religion is sui generis (i.e. unique) and cannot be reduced or compared to anything other than itself. As covered in section 2, *The promotion of interpretative accounts of religious ideas and behaviors* (see pp. 7–8), most discussions of religion already involve a reduction of some sort.

Reduction is inevitable because explanations trace causation from higher to lower levels or uncover hidden relationships. In general, most accounts of religion answer the "why" question by linking the explanandum to another more in-depth, hidden, basic explanation. This was also true of accounts of religion before CSR. As Edward Slingerland put it, allegations of reductionism are "an empty term of abuse—any explanation worthy of being called an explanation involves reductionism of *some* sort.[21]" In short, those in religious studies who argued against reductionism were often already using it. Because they often excluded the role of human cognition or relied on outdated models of the human mind, they often provided poor reductionist explanations of religious thought and behavior.

The second reason against the use of reductionism to explain religion was due to injudicious assumptions about reductionism. While there are many kinds of reductionism, most religious studies scholars who rejected it unfairly equated all scientific endeavors in religion with the most extreme form, ontological reductionism. This extreme form of reductionism often includes the idea that phenomena can be explained *exclusively* by reference to another lower-level entity. For instance, a theory that religious experiences are "all in the mind" or "nothing but" neurocognitive states. While such theories may abound in popular debates on religion, they are virtually nonexistent among cognitive scientists of religion.

Cognitive scientists of religion were using a more moderate form of reductionism in the sciences, describing and analyzing a complex phenomenon in terms of phenomena that are held to represent a simpler or more fundamental level. This process does not involve excluding the other levels of analyses, but in fact, attributes a complementary role to the different levels. For example, we encounter artificial light every day and tend to talk about it in terms of basic ideas such as brightness and color. We could study the fundamental characteristics of light, such as the direction, intensity, contrast, and so on. Physicists also investigate the electromagnetic radiation of any wavelength, whether visible to the human eye or not. These levels of explanation are complementary to a more robust understanding of light.

Similarly, scientists can describe and analyze human phenomena in terms of simpler, or complex, levels. Some of these levels are depicted in Figure 1.4. For example, in many different cultures, people report having religious experiences. Neuroscientists can track and map what happens in that person's brain at the time of the experience (biological explanation), psychologists can investigate the person's motivations, processing and interpretation of information prior to the experience (psychological), and the effects of the experience afterward (behavioral). Other social scientists may focus on explaining other group-level factors that predispose and perpetuate these experiences, such as the support of a religious group, socialization into an environment where people have religious experiences, and so on (social and cultural explanations). These levels of explanation are complementary to a more robust understanding of religious experiences.

Using the method of reduction also provides a method of checks and balances between the levels of explanation. Scholars first separate and then move up the explanatory chain, checking for consistency. The structure of upper levels of explanation emerges out of and depends upon lower levels, so they are inextricably linked. For instance, molecules behave following basic principles of inorganic and organic substances, so if a hypothesis in molecular biology violates these well-established physical chemistry principles, then either the hypothesis is wrong, or we need to rethink physical chemistry altogether.[22]

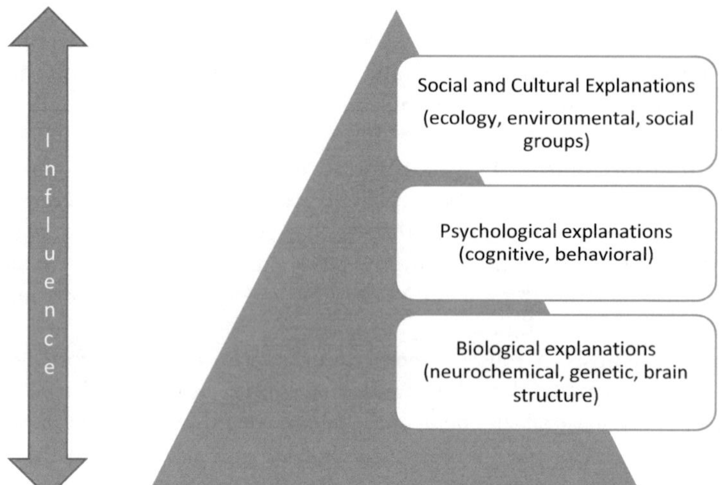

Figure 1.4 Example of reductionism to explain different corresponding levels in human behavior.

Early scholars in CSR were proposing a form of reductionism that first fractionated religion to study its different components. These components included aspects such as the recurrence of ritualized behavior, drawing upon what is known about the biological, psychological, and social consequences of actions. Yet cognitive scientists of religion also acknowledged the complexity and interaction of many levels, such as biological, neurological, cognitive, and cultural. They did not attempt to reduce an explanation of religion to any one level exclusively. In other words, CSR scholars promoted explanatory pluralism. The mutual dependence and interaction of levels of explanation is taken for granted in the natural sciences and is, in fact, one of the guiding principles driving natural scientific inquiry. Yet, the approach was controversial when used to explain religion. Early scholars in the cognitive sciences acknowledged that while religious phenomena have emergent properties, in the sense that the whole is more than the sum of its parts, associated ideas and practices were not outside the scope of scientific inquiry and should be studied.

Key points

- Many scholars of religion were taught that religion was unique and could not be reduced to anything less than the whole.
- CSR scholars were, by contrast, proposing the method of dividing up religion into smaller, meaningful parts in order to study them.

Summary of challenges to trends in cultural studies among early pioneers in CSR

1 Principles of postmodernism, cultural determinism, and extreme cultural relativism

The idea that all reality is subjective, objective research is futile, that human behavior is determined exclusively by culture, and that it is only possible to understand a person's behavior by examining the ideas of their particular culture, underestimates the role of human psychology in religious ideas and behaviors.

2 The promotion of interpretative accounts of religious ideas and behaviors

Descriptions of religious ideas and behaviors without explanatory theories are vague and lack explanatory power.

3 Outdated or nonexistent theories of human psychology

Failure to take account of the role of the human mind in processing and transmitting ideas and contemporary theories about these processes leads to partial, impoverished, and misguided reports of religion.

4 Privileging personal accounts over systematic theories of religion

Idiosyncratic accounts privilege religious diversity over cross-cultural patterns and exaggerate the differences between religions. They lead to philosophies about particular religions rather than explanatory theories of religion.

5 Assumptions that religion is unique and cannot be reduced

If religion could not be reduced or compared to anything else, then it was excluded from scientific and explanatory treatments. Nevertheless, scientists had explained other cultural phenomena using scientific approaches.

The beginnings of a new cognitive approach to the study of religion

The primary objective of the new cognitive approach to the study of religion was not merely to produce a better interpretation of religion but to explain it. Explanations occurred by applying contemporary theories of how the mind works and using scientific methods to test these theories. Not only did early pioneers in CSR advocate for these approaches, but they had begun implementing them. For instance, one of the earliest theories in CSR, proposed by Lawson and McCauley, concerned how people across cultures conceptualized ritual.

Lawson and McCauley were influenced by the work of Linguist Noam Chomsky, which had emerged during the cognitive revolution against behaviorism (described at the beginning of this chapter). Chomsky had noted that people can produce and understand an infinite number of novel sentences, more than they could ever have learned—which he dubbed the "poverty of the stimulus.[23]" Put simply, people know more than they learn. Chomsky theorized that children must have internalized a grammar or set of rules, and they are mentally equipped with an internal preparedness for language acquisition—that he called a "language acquisition device"—which leads to "universal grammar." Put another way, Chomsky proposed that taking account of mental processes, including those that are innate, can explain the stability underlying the seemingly endless array of cultural forms, in this case—language.

Lawson and McCauley applied the approach to the study of ritual (known as "Ritual Form Hypothesis," covered in Chapter 9 (Rituals Part 1). They demonstrated that despite the seemingly endless and distinct varieties of behaviors that have been dubbed as a ritual by social anthropologists, there are discernible patterns that people recognize actions intuitively as a ritual. Again, stated simply, people know more than they learn. Their theory also pinpointed the unique components that led people to dub a ritual as "religious" and led them to predict other features, such as how likely the ritual was to be effective. In other words, by taking account of how people represent actions, Lawson and McCauley argued that it is possible to explain why and predict when people generate assumptions about ritual.

This theory provided a stark contrast to standard research in the academic study of religion, which had been concerned with documenting and describing the diversity of ritual practices. Even systematically comparing traditions was a bold move. Yet, Lawson and McCauley were proposing to explain a feature of religions found across cultures based not on the environment but on how people process actions. This proposal was revolutionary.

Likewise, early pioneers in CSR sought to convince the scholarly community of the explanatory power of a new cognitive approach to the study of religion. Together, the body of work they had initially accumulated showcased how this was possible. This included providing an explicit treatment of current approaches to the study of religion (e.g. *Rethinking Religion: Connecting Cognition and Culture*[24]), proposing broad theories of religion in the hope of showcasing the benefits of a new cognitive approach to religion (e.g. *A cognitive theory of religion*;[25] *Naturalness of Religious Ideas*[26]), and demonstrating the potential of findings from cognitive psychology to enhance explanation in traditional anthropology (e.g. *Inside the Cult*[27]).

These attempts culminated in the refinement of a new approach to the study of religion envisaged as a subdiscipline of cognitive science. In 2000, the approach to the study of religion was well-enough established for the term "cognitive science of religion" to be used.[28] The sentiment of early researchers is expressed in the paper where Lawson first outlined CSR:

> A cognitive science of religion is necessary (in the sense that it is worthy of being done) because it will help lead us to deeper insights about symbolic-cultural systems such as religion. A cognitive science of religion certainly shows every promise of deepening our understanding of the cognitive constraints on the cultural form. Those who are dedicated to cultural relativism and its cousin cultural determinism often give the impression that there are no limits either on the contents of our minds or the cultural products that issue forth from them. We have come to see through the insights of cognitive science that this is not the case. There are limits to cultural (and, a fortiori, religious) variability.[29]

CSR began as a reaction against the dominant social science principles, excessive reliance on philosophy, and the lack of systematic methodological approaches. These principles included the emphasis on religious behavior, the blank slate hypothesis, cultural determinism, and extreme versions of cultural relativism. The contested methodologies included descriptive methods and interpretative treatments of culture to account for the human expression of religion. Early pioneers paved the way for a new cognitive approach to the study of religion, and soon after, developed and refined their ideas. For example, in early 2000, *Bringing Ritual to Mind*[30] followed from *Rethinking Religion: Connecting Cognition and Culture; Religion Explained*[31] followed from *The Naturalness of Religious Ideas*, and *Modes of Religiosity*[32] followed from *Inside the Cult*. As CSR gained scholarly momentum, scholars leveraged cutting-edge philosophies about the human mind and the role of socialization and culture on the development of religious ideas and behaviors to replace what they considered as outdated models.

Key points

- The primary objective of cognitive approaches was to explain religion.
- CSR scholars advocated for the application of contemporary theories of how the mind works and using scientific methods to test these theories.
- One of the earliest theories in CSR concerned how people across cultures conceptualized ritual.

The influence of evolutionary approaches in early formations of CSR

Today, many scholars in CSR use evolutionary approaches to explain human behavior at many different levels. For example, biological, psychological, and cultural. Early evolutionary approaches among CSR pioneers, however, focused on evolution at the level of psychology. In other words, they were interested in how the mind was shaped by recurring problems in the ancestral environment. Evolutionary approaches were apparent in some of the earliest books in CSR, such as anthropologist Stewart Guthrie's *Faces in the Clouds*[33] and later in anthropologist Pascal Boyer's *Religion Explained*,[34] and anthropologist Scott Atran's *In Gods We Trust*.[35] Scholars were also inspired by work focused exclusively on the origins of the human mind by scholars such as Steven Mithen, Merlin Donald, and Terrance Deacon.

One particularly influential book that served as a theoretical foundation for CSR was *The Adapted Mind* in 1992[36] by the anthropologists Jerome Barkow, John Tooby, and psychologist Leda Cosmides. Their book is widely considered the foundational text of evolutionary psychology. The authors argued that philosophies such as cultural determinism were outdated and yet had become part of the "Standard Social Science Model" (SSM) to explain human behavior. They proposed an "Integrated Causal Model" (ICM) to explain human behavior, which took account of the evolution of the human mind and its interaction with the environment. The ICM model contrasted with the SSM on basic philosophies. Like previous proposals in the cognitive sciences, the ICM model rejected the view of the mind as a blank slate, sponge, or Xerox machine.

The "Integrated Causal Model" (ICM) was, however, distinctive because it challenged previous views of the mind held by scientists. Until then, scientists had mainly viewed the mind as a general computer that equally processes all information at the same speed. This view of the mind is often referred to as a domain-general learning mechanism. Barkow, Tooby, and Cosmides proposed that the mind is more like a series of mini-computers or a Swiss army knife, each with specialized devices, which make sense only in light of our evolutionary history. The authors claimed that the reason that the human mind is not like a general computer is that we are born with emotional, motivational, and cognitive tendencies.

For example, some researchers have claimed that language is readily acquired because it evolved to help humans survive. For example, Chomsky and others contend that language may have evolved simply because of how the physical structure of the brain evolved, or because cognitive structures that were used for things like tool making and learning rules were also good for complex communication. These accounts typically propose a language module, which is a hypothetical structure in the brain, which contains innate capacities for language. Debates about the origins of language continue today.[37] Nevertheless, this example helps to illustrate the basic idea that the brain comes equipped to handle problems.

Barkow, Tooby, and Cosmides maintained that cognitive tendencies evolved in an era roughly covering the Stone Age, termed the "Environment of Evolutionary Adaptedness" (EEA), which continues to influence how humans think even today. The tendencies are specialized learning devices—which Barkow, Tooby, and Cosmides dub domain-specific modules. In other words, just like mini-computers can be pre-programmed to deal with particular inputs, or just like a Swiss army knife contains different tools to solve problems encountered in the wild, the mind is pre-programmed to deal with environmental challenges by having swift and intuitive responses. It is important to note that those who endorse this kind of approach do not necessarily assume that there is one anatomical area solely devoted to processing each problem, such as language. The authors proposed that tendencies arise because they helped humans adapt efficiently to their environment. These tendencies explain why humans rapidly acquire aspects of the environment swiftly and in much the same way, like the acquisition of language.

Many cognitive scientists of religion adopted the principal philosophies concerning the mind and culture in evolutionary psychology as outlined in the

Figure 1.5 An evolutionary account views the human mind like a swiss army knife, prepared with tools to deal with different problems based on problems in the past. (Image credit: mkddesign/Shutterstock.com).

ICM. They applied them to religion as a subset of culture. These principles included the idea that religious thought and behavior are the results of interactions between our evolved psychological dispositions and cultural and environmental influences, and that these influences of cognition and culture always constrain religious expression.

Key points

- CSR scholars were influenced by evolutionary psychology, which took account of the evolution of the human mind and its interaction with the environment.
- Cognitive scientists of religion were especially compelled by the idea in evolutionary psychology that the mind is like a series of mini-computers with specialized devices that are pre-programmed to process aspects of the world.
- This evolutionary view of the human mind had the potential to explain why humans rapidly acquire environmental input swiftly and in much the same way.
- This evolutionary view suggested that evolution, cognition, and culture constrain religious expression.

Modern formations of CSR

This chapter tracks the beginnings of an approach that has come to be known as the cognitive science of religion (CSR). There are many methods and theories involved in explaining the presence and persistence of religion today from the perspective of evolution, brain, cognition, and culture. Consequently, there are innumerable researchers and research projects that can be classified as contributing to CSR. This book adopts a principle of generosity, and more scholars are labeled as cognitive scientists of religion here than in other books on the subject. In the chapters that follow, scholars are often identified by their primary discipline, e.g. anthropologist, philosopher, psychologist, sociologist, and yet are also characterized as cognitive scientists of religion.

Key points

- There are many ways to decide which research can be categorized as part of the cognitive science of religion.
- In this book, CSR is construed as an approach to the study of religion that deals with explaining religious phenomena with presumptions about the role of cognition in shaping religious thought and practice, and many scholars fall under this umbrella approach.

Chapter summary

CSR began as a reaction against standard treatments of religion in cultural studies. Most notably, pioneers contested the ideas of cultural determinism and extreme versions of cultural relativism. When taken to extremes, these ideas proposed that culture alone explained how and why people acquired, represented and transmitted religious ideas and behaviors, and that religion could only be understood based on the person's own culture, rather than judged against the criteria of another. In particular, while few would seriously deny that we acquire religion from culture, models at the time examined the environmental inputs (culture) and largely ignored how the mind processed those inputs into (religious) outputs. Given that there are discernible patterns of religiosity across cultures and eras, and given recent work in the cognitive sciences demonstrating that the human mind actively processes ideas, early cognitive scientists of religion argued for scientific research exploring the cognitive foundations of religion.

Discussion questions

1 In your own words, what is the cognitive science of religion?
2 What do you think distinguishes CSR from other approaches to the study of religion?
3 What benefits do you think CSR brings to the study of religion?
4 Which challenges to trends in cultural studies among early pioneers in CSR do you agree and disagree with?

Selected further reading

Articles

1 Bloom, Paul. "Is God an accident?" *Atlantic Monthly* 296, no. 5 (2005): 105.
2 Geertz, Armin, W. (2015). "Religious belief, evolution of." In *International Encyclopedia of the Social and Behavioral Sciences*. 2nd edn, 384–395. Oxford: Elsevier.
3 Xygalatas, Dimitris. (2014). "Cognitive science of religion." In *Encyclopedia of Psychology and Religion*, 2nd edn. D.A. Leeming ed. New York: Springer: 343–347.

Books

1 Boyer, Pascal. *Religion explained: The human instincts that fashion gods, spirits and ancestors*. London: Random House and New York: Perseus, 2002.
2 Stewart, Elliott Guthrie, *Faces in the clouds: A new theory of religion*. New York: Oxford University Press, 1993.

Notes

1 Xygalatas, Dimitris, and Ryan McKay, "Announcing the journal for the cognitive science of religion." *Journal for the Cognitive Science of Religion* 1, no. 1 (2013): 1–4.
2 Xygalatas, Dimitris, and Ryan McKay. "Announcing the journal for the cognitive science of religion." *Journal for the Cognitive Science of Religion* 1, no. 1 (2013): 1–4.
3 For a detailed discussion, see Steven Pinker, *The blank slate*. Southern Utah University, 2005; Armin W. Geertz, "Cognitive science." In *The Oxford handbook of the study of religion*, eds. Michael Stausberg and Steven Engler. Oxford: Oxford University Press, 2016, 97–111.
4 Thomas E. Lawson and Robert N. McCauley, *Rethinking religion: Connecting cognition and culture*. Cambridge: Cambridge University Press, 1990.
5 Stewart Guthrie, *Faces in the clouds: A new theory of religion*. Oxford: Oxford University Press, 1993.
6 Pascal Boyer, *Naturalness of religious ideas: A cognitive theory of religion*. University of California Press, 1994.
7 Harvey Whitehouse, *Inside the cult: Religious innovation and transmission in Papua New Guinea*. Oxford University Press on Demand, 1995.
8 Spiro, Melford E. "Postmodernist anthropology, subjectivity, and science: A modernist critique." *Comparative studies in society and history* 38, no. 4 (1996): 759–780.
9 Dan Sperber, *Explaining culture: A naturalistic approach*. Cambridge, MA: Cambridge, 1996; see also Dan Sperber, "Rethinking Symbolism," *CUP Archive* No. 11 (1975).
10 Thomas E. Lawson and Robert N. McCauley, *Rethinking religion: Connecting cognition and culture*. Cambridge: Cambridge University Press, 1990.
11 Geertz, Clifford. "Thick description: Toward an interpretative theory of culture." In *The interpretation of cultures*. New York: Basic Books, 1973.
12 Emma Cohen, *The mind possessed: The cognition of spirit possession in an Afro-Brazilian religious tradition* (Oxford University Press, 2007).
13 Emma Cohen., Jonathan A. Lanman, Harvey Whitehouse, and Robert N. McCauley, "Common criticisms of the cognitive science of religion—answered." *Bulletin of the Council of Societies for the Study of Religion* 37, no. 4 (2008): 112–115.
14 Emma Cohen., Jonathan A. Lanman, Harvey Whitehouse, and Robert N. McCauley, "Common criticisms of the cognitive science of religion—answered." *Bulletin of the Council of Societies for the Study of Religion* 37, no. 4 (2008): 112–115.
15 Emma Cohen., Jonathan A. Lanman, Harvey Whitehouse, and Robert N. McCauley, "Common criticisms of the cognitive science of religion—answered." *Bulletin of the Council of Societies for the Study of Religion* 37, no. 4 (2008): 112–115.
16 Gananath Obeyesekere, "Foreword: Reincarnation eschatologies and the comparative study of religions." In *Amerindian Rebirth: Reincarnation among North American Indians and Inuit*. Toronto, Canada, 1994.
17 Claire White, "The cognitive foundations of reincarnation." *Method & Theory in the Study of Religion* 28, no. 3 (2016): 264–286.
18 Edward Slingerland, "Back to the future: A response to Martin and Wiebe." *Journal of the American Academy of Religion* 80, no. 3 (2012): 611–617.
19 Edward Slingerland and Joseph Bulbulia, "Introductory essay: Evolutionary science and the study of religion." *Religion* 41, no. 3 (2011): 307–328.
20 See Robert N. McCauley, "The naturalness of religion and the unnaturalness of science." *Explanation and cognition* (2000): 61–85; Edward Slingerland, "Who's afraid of reductionism? The study of religion in the age of cognitive science." *Journal of the American Academy of Religion* 76, no. 2 (2008): 375–411.
21 Slingerland, Edward. "Who's afraid of reductionism? The study of religion in the age of cognitive science." *Journal of the American Academy of Religion* 76, no. 2 (2008): 375–411.
22 Slingerland, Edward. "Who's afraid of reductionism? The study of religion in the age of cognitive science." *Journal of the American Academy of Religion* 76, no. 2 (2008): 375–411.

23 Noam Chomsky, "Rules and representations." *Behavioral and brain sciences* 3, no. 1 (1980): 1–15.
24 Thomas E. Lawson and Robert N. McCauley, *Rethinking religion: Connecting cognition and culture*. Cambridge: Cambridge University Press, 1990.
25 Stewart Guthrie, "A cognitive theory of religion," *Current Anthropology* 21, no. 2 (1980): 181–203.
26 Pascal Boyer, *Naturalness of religious ideas: A cognitive theory of religion*. University of California Press, 1994.
27 Harvey Whitehouse, *Inside the cult: Religious innovation and transmission in Papua New Guinea*. Oxford University Press on Demand, 1995.
28 These two articles were the first time in that the phrase "cognitive science of religion" appeared in print; Thomas E. Lawson, "Towards a cognitive science of religion." *NUMEN-LEIDEN-* 47, no. 3 (2000): 338–348; Justin L. Barrett, "Exploring the natural foundations of religion," *Trends in cognitive sciences* 4, no. 1 (2000): 29–34.
29 Thomas E. Lawson, "Towards a cognitive science of religion." *NUMEN-LEIDEN-* 47, no. 3, p. 342, (2000): 338–348.
30 Robert N. McCauley and Thomas E. Lawson, *Bringing ritual to mind: Psychological foundations of cultural forms*. Cambridge University Press, 2002.
31 Pascal Boyer, *Religion explained: The human instincts that fashion gods, spirits and ancestors*. New York: Vintage, 2002.
32 Harvey Whitehouse, *Modes of religiosity: A cognitive theory of religious transmission*. Lanham, MD, Rowman Altamira, 2004.
33 Stewart, Elliott Guthrie. *Faces in the clouds: A new theory of religion*. New York: Oxford University Press, 1993.
34 Pascal Boyer, *Religion Explained: The human instincts that fashion gods, spirits and ancestors*. New York: Vintage, 2002.
35 Scott Atran, *In gods we trust: The evolutionary landscape of religion*. Oxford: Oxford University Press, 2004.
36 Jerome H. Barkow., Leda Cosmides, and John Tooby, eds., *The adapted mind: Evolutionary psychology and the generation of culture*. USA: Oxford University Press, 1995.
37 Richerson, Peter J., and Robert Boyd. "Why possibly language evolved." *Biolinguistics* 4, no. 2–3 (2010): 289–306.

2 Core assumptions about religion and belief

Since its inception in the 1990s, the cognitive science of religion (CSR) has undergone rapid expansion and continues to grow. Yet, many core aspects of CSR have remained stable throughout these developments. These include axiomatic assumptions from the cognitive revolution that initiated the subfield. For example, the idea that religion is shaped by cognition as well as culture and is amenable to scientific study. CSR is also demarked by its distinctive conceptualization of religion and belief. In this chapter, we consider key questions such as what is religion, according to CSR? How do scholars in CSR define and measure religion? And to what extent does CSR explain religious belief?

Participation 1: What is religion?

1 What is religion? Write down your answer in a few sentences without thinking about it too much.
2 Share and compare your response to another student and note points of similarity or disagreement.

Classic conceptualizations of religion

Religion is a prevalent, potent, and puzzling force. Beliefs about the supernatural world are ubiquitous and resilient features of all known human cultures, and today, millions of people around the world engage in religious practices such as rituals. Many live lives according to religious principles; some fight, and even die for them. It is unsurprisingly, religion has captivated the minds of many of the world's formidable intellects, and their insights on the subject have propelled the study of religion forwards. Perhaps the most common question that scholars of religion ask is, "what is religion?" for instance, is religion a personal spiritual journey? Does it refer to the established religions of the world? Is it an expression of cultural practices? And is it inextricably linked to morality? Is it one of these things, or a combination of some, or all, of them? Indeed, the early study of religion has been characterized by debates and efforts to pinpoint the essential common features of religion.

Table 2.1 summarizes eight theorists who played a formative role in the modern enterprise of studying religion. These exemplary intellectual giants highlight the many differences in how religion can be conceptualized. For instance, Tylor's minimalist definition can be contrasted to Durkheim's all-encompassing view, and James' focus on the individual's experience can be juxtaposed to Geertz's interest at the level of culture. Further, Marx represents religion as a negative force for humanity, Freud as the product of guilt, Tylor as an intellectual attempt to solve problems, and Malinowski as arising from fear and uncertainty. Practically speaking, James' and Tylor's conceptualizations of religion provide a clearer path to studying religion than Eliade.

Table 2.1 Eight classic theories of religion.

#	*Scholar*	*Associated discipline*	*Definition of religion*
1	Edward Tylor	Cultural Anthropology	Religion originated to make sense of puzzling experiences and observations. It is a "belief in spiritual beings.[1]"
2	Bronislaw Malinowski	Cultural Anthropology	Religion is about our greatest fears. It helps individuals and societies deal with emotional stresses that occur, such as death. Religious rituals are performed in times of emotional distress, especially whenever the outcome of human decision making is uncertain.[2]
3	Sigmund Freud	Psychology	Religion originated from feelings of guilt. It is a neurosis of humanity and an illusion of wishful thinking. People are obsessed with religious beliefs because they want them to be true, like the idea of God.[3]
4	Emile Durkheim	Sociology	Religion is a symbolic expression of social order, "religion is a unified system of beliefs and practices relative to sacred things, that is to say, things set apart and forbidden—beliefs and practices which unite into one single moral community called a Church, all those who adhere to them.[4]"
5	Karl Marx	Sociology	Religion emerged as a tool of class oppression. It is the expression of unjust economic restraints and alienation and the protest of this distress. Religion is like a drug. It is "the opium of the people" because it provides the illusion of happiness.[5]
6	William James	Psychology	Religion is a religious experience. It is "the feelings, acts, and experiences of individual men in their solitude, so far as they comprehend themselves to stand in relation to whatever they may consider the divine.[6]"

(*Continued*)

Table 2.1 (Cont.)

#	*Scholar*	*Associated discipline*	*Definition of religion*
7	Mircea Eliade	History of religion	Religion is a response to the sacred. It is a phenomenon in its own right, rather than a group or societal expression. Religion can only be understood from the viewpoint of the believer. It is unique and cannot be reduced to anything other than itself.[7]
8	Clifford Geertz	Symbolic Anthropology	Religion is a cultural system and world view. "Religion is a system of symbols which acts to establish powerful, pervasive, and long-lasting moods in men by formulating conceptions of a general order of existence and clothing those conceptions with such an aura of factuality that the moods and motivations seem uniquely realistic.[8]"

Participation 2: Defining and measuring religion

1. Work with another student to compare, contrast, and group definitions of religion by the classical scholars in Table 2.1 (and optionally, from the book "nine theories of religion[9]") in the ways that they are similar or different. For example, what would qualify as religious? Do they focus on the private experience or group effects of religion? Is their definition broad (incorporating many things) or narrow? Do they see religion as a force for good or harm? Create your own categories. One definition may fit into multiple categories.
2. Write down how your definition of religion in participation 1 compares to the scholars in Table 2.1. Whose definition is most similar and different to yours?
3. Note how you would study religion based on each of the definitions. Consider who you would study, what methods you could use, what you might discover, and how difficult this would be. For example, if religion is based on an individual's private experience, then how would you go about studying that? Would you conduct experiments, historical surveys, analyze data about society? And how easy would it be to make conclusions about religion based on that information?

The conceptualization of religion in CSR

Debates on what constitutes religion continue to abound. Such debates can provide crucial insights into religious thought and behavior, but cognitive scientists of religion point out how fixating upon definitions can stagnate research. Unlike many other approaches, CSR scholars do not concentrate their research efforts on proposing a general theory of what constitutes religion (or a specific religion) or adopt one method that they think best gets at the heart of it. Nor do cognitive scientists of religion use traditions (e.g. Islam, Buddhism, Christianity, Hinduism, Jainism, Sikhism, Zoroastrianism) as units of scientific comparison.

Cognitive scientists of religion realize that religious traditions do not necessarily reveal discrete, bounded entities. Furthermore, many religious ideas and practices pre-date the establishment of organized religion or have been labeled as something else, such as superstition or primal religions (e.g. the Aborigines of Australia, the Yoruba of Africa, the Plain Indians of North America, the Aztecs' religions of Mesoamerica). Therefore, cognitive scientists of religion do not select cultures to study based upon their seeming exoticness as compared to western cultures, but rather, because some theoretically informative aspects of the cultures contrast. For example, one reason why anthropologists Rita Astuti and Paul Harris investigated reasoning about death in a rural Madagascar community was because here children routinely encounter animal death and have greater exposure to death than in the United States, which enables researchers to understand the impact of exposure to death on conceptualizations of death and the after life.[10]

CSR scholars have contributed to important abstract and philosophical issues raised in the scientific study of religion. At the same time, scholars in CSR place a strong emphasis on studies with an empirical basis to collect data on religion, grounding such issues in their cognitive and cultural environments. Cognitive scientists of religion often systematically collect and analyze data on recurrent ideas and behaviors that seem to fall under the general category of religion. One aim of these endeavors is to construct a bottom-up, scientific theory of religion. This bottom-up approach can be contrasted to the top-down approach, where scholars propose a general theory of religion and then examine phenomena that meet that criteria. The following are some core assumptions that underlie the conceptualization of religion in CSR:

1 *Religion is not a singular or naturally occurring phenomenon*

Many religious studies' scholars have noted that religion is not a singular or naturally occurring phenomenon.[11] There are no single or coherent categories of thoughts and behaviors around the world, which scholars can point to and say that "this" demarks religion.[12] Religion is unlike stars or humans. Rather, religion is more like sports or a picnic, because what counts and does not count as a member of these categories is ambiguous. Furthermore, the category of religion may be more of a family resemblance.

Family resemblance describes how people who are genetically related tend to have physical and personality similarities. In this chapter, family resemblance is used in the philosophical sense to describe how things that appear to be similar because of one common shared feature may appear to be that way due to many similar features that overlap. Common examples of a family resemblance include sports or board games. Think about the different types of games—the use of cards, boards, balls, etc. There are many similarities, but not one shared feature that defines them all.

Figure 2.1 Religion is like the category of sport, because there is no single feature that sports share and what is and is not a sport is not clear-cut. (Image credit: GoodStudio/Shutterstock.com).

We may think of religion as being connected by one essential common feature. It may well turn out, however, that what we call religion may be connected by a series of overlapping similarities, where no one feature is common to all phenomena. Yet the term religion is a convenient, general-purpose label that enables scholars to understand particular systems of thought and patterns of behavior. At the core, CSR scholars accept that religion is a product of the mind situated in its cultural environment. In other words, ideas and practices that we deem religious are found in culture and are readily transmitted.

Key points

- CSR recognizes both the value of conceptualizing religion and the danger of becoming transfixed by this task.
- CSR does not adopt a single all-encompassing definition of what counts as religion.
- CSR acknowledges that religion does not occur naturally in the world.
- CSR recognizes that religion is not a single thing.

Participation 3: What's in a name?

In Shakespeare's play, *Romeo and Juliet*, Act II, Scene II, Juliet argues that it does not matter that Romeo is from her family's rival house of Montague, that is, that he is named "Montague."

In the following quote, Juliet implies that Romeo's family name means nothing and that they should be together:

> 'Tis but thy name that is my enemy;
> Thou art thyself, though not a Montague.
> What's Montague? It is nor hand, nor foot,
> Nor arm, nor face, nor any other part
> Belonging to a man. O, be some other name!
> What's in a name? That which we call a rose
> By any other name would smell as sweet; So Romeo would were he not Romeo call'd,
> Retain that dear perfection which he owes
> Without that title. Romeo, doff thy name,
> And for that name which is no part of thee
> Take all myself.[13]

1. What do you think Juliet means when she claims, "What's in a name? That which we call a rose by any other name would smell as sweet"?
2. Do the names of things affect what they are? Explain.
3. Do the names of things affect how we respond to them? Explain.

2 Folk concepts are not a reliable means of constructing scientific theories about religion

Scholarly conceptualizations of religion are often based on how scholars perceive the world to be (i.e. folk concepts). Often scholars propose a definition of what religion is and then provide evidence for this view (i.e. top-down approach) through suggestive anecdotes, ethnographic case studies, among other methods. Of course, theories of the world are shaped to some extent by human cognition, such as intuition and insight. However, these more often reflect phenomenological understandings than taxonomical insights.

Sometimes our intuitions help us develop scientific understandings of the world, and sometimes they hinder them. Most importantly, folk theories are not a reliable means of constructing the boundaries of a phenomenon and should not be attributed explanatory validity (at least not a priori). For instance, evolutionary biological science tells us that the differences among animal species are not accurately portrayed as taxonomic differences in kind but as differences in degree as measured by genetic proximity. Further, species may be more similar than they appear. For example, male capuchinos (birds) can look and sound very different across species, despite being almost identical genetically.[14] Therefore, folk theories do not always provide a useful and accurate conceptual foundation from which to develop scientific theories about how the material world, including religion, works.[15]

Figure 2.2 On the surface, religion appears to be remarkably different, which often cultivates a sense of otherness and intolerance within and between cultures. (Image credit: vector_s/Shutterstock.com).

By labeling a range of phenomena as religious, scholars have designated a package of ideas and behaviors—such as ideas about supernatural agents, rituals, and moral obligations—as being somehow related causally, or even descriptively. However, claims about these relationships have not typically been systematically tested. Folk definitions of religion may tell us more about the perspective humans are inclined to take than denoting meaningful relationships between thoughts, behaviors, traditions, and institutions.[16]

Top-down definitions can easily privilege religious diversity over similarity and emphasize, even exaggerate, the differences between traditions. These definitions are prone to human biases and dispositions, including the tendency to draw from our Western view of the world to explain other religious traditions[17] (i.e. ethnocentrism), and to think that we are privileged over other groups.[18] Just as some birds appear to the untutored mind to be very different while being genetically similar, so too religious traditions may appear so distinct and far removed from that which we are familiar, that we perceive them as not constituting anything like religion.[19]

Alternatively, we may relegate other people's concepts, behaviors, and systems to a "lesser" category, such as paranormal, superstitious, magical, or supernatural.[20] Likewise, the presence of institutionalized religion is a relatively modern phenomenon. Other features of religious ideas and beliefs, such as supernatural explanations of misfortune and ritualized practices, long pre-date the establishment of such institutions. Taking the recurrent features of religious ideas and behaviors into account may well provide a richer understanding of their nature.

Participation 4: Race is a social construct

Religion, like race, is a social construct. Race is a grouping of humans based on perceived shared physical or social qualities into categories generally viewed as distinct by society, defined by markers such as skin color, hair texture, eye shape, ancestry, identity performance, and even name. For example, a person who could be categorized as "Black" in the United States might be considered "white" in Brazil.

Assumptions about genetic differences between people of different races, such as "white" and "Black," have had social and historical repercussions, and they still threaten to fuel racist beliefs today. However, racial categories are weak markers for genetic diversity. The mainstream belief among scientists is that race is a social construct without biological meaning. As Professor of Public Health, Michael Yudell, commented:

> It's a concept we think is too crude to provide useful information, it's a concept that has a social meaning that interferes in the scientific understanding of human genetic diversity, and it's a concept that we are not the first to call upon moving away from.[21]

Scientists have petitioned for the removal of the concept of race from human genetics. Consider the following abstract from a journal article in *Science*:[22]

> In the wake of the sequencing of the human genome in the early 2000s, genome pioneers, and social scientists alike called for an end to the use of race as a variable in genetic research. Unfortunately, by some measures, the use of race as a biological category has increased in the postgenomic age. Although the inconsistent definition and use have been a chief problem with the race concept, it has historically been used as a taxonomic categorization based on common hereditary traits (such as skin color) to elucidate the relationship between our ancestry and our genes. We believe the use of biological concepts of race in human genetic research—so disputed and so mired in confusion—is problematic at best and harmful at worst. It is time for biologists to find a better way.

1 Outline some of the problems with using the concept of race to summarize differences and similarities between groups of people (you may conduct further research on the Internet on this topic).
2 Re-read the sections in this chapter (see pp. 26–27) on how CSR conceptualizes religion. Then answer the following question: To what extent do you think the problems in conceptualizing race also apply to conceptualizing religion?
3 Outline the benefits of using a scientific approach rather than the concept of race to study differences and similarities between people.
4 What are the benefits of using a scientific approach to study religion rather than folk categories?

Key points

- Using what people tend to think of as religious as the means to define religion is not a scientific method.
- Folk concepts of religion are often based upon what is familiar.

3 A bottom-up, fractionation approach is a reliable method to explain religion

Researchers in CSR take the limitations in previous approaches to define religion as the motivation to systematically compare the recurrent features and relationships between aspects of human culture that have been deemed religious. Thus, a scientific approach can refine our understanding. This approach does not mean exhaustively explaining everything that can be subsumed under the label "religion." Instead, CSR scholars construe the term religion as an ideological construction and a general-purpose label that helps to describe specific ideas, behaviors, and systems, such as ideas that life continues after biological death and assumptions about non-human agents that influence the natural world. As Anthropologist Pascal Boyer puts it:

> The study of religion is an 'impure subject,' that is, a subject where the central or official topic is not a scientific object. True, there is 'religion' around, and there may well be 'religions' as well. And there are mountains and giraffes, too. But neither giraffes nor mountains constitute proper scientific objects. Only particular aspects of mountains and giraffes qualify as scientific objects, and those particular aspects are shared with non-mountains and non-giraffes. It follows that there is no privileged 'method' or 'theory' in the study of religion as such. However, there may be particularly adequate theories and methods in the study of specific aspects of religious ideas and practices.[23]

One way that CSR researchers progress empirically is to fractionate religious systems into their constituent components. First, researchers break down aspects that seem to recur across cultures. These include concepts of supernatural agents (e.g. ghosts, gods, ancestors, goblins), ideas about life after death, explanations of misfortune (e.g. death, disease, catastrophe, pain, injustice, loss) by reference to supernatural forces and deities, individual and communal expressions of commitments to supernatural agents (e.g. offering, sacrifice) and ritualized behavior.[24]

Next, researchers break these categories down even further according to the underlying cognitive foundations that give rise to them. These foundations denote panhuman psychological tendencies, biases, and constraints (see Table 2.2). In other words, they describe how humans tend to think (throughout this book, for simplicity they are often referred to jointly as cognitive, or psychological,

Table 2.2 Terms used throughout this book to describe how humans tend to think.

Cognitive foundations		
Psychological propensities	Predispositions	Inherent biases
Predilections	Intuitions	Intuitive biases
Cognitive constraints	Psychological tendencies	Cognitive biases

foundations). For example, concepts of supernatural agents such as gods and ancestors are similar in many ways to concepts of ordinary people. Attributing human characteristics to non-humans is part of a cognitive bias known as anthropomorphism. Thus, ideas about supernatural agents are underpinned by the psychological propensity for anthropomorphism. The underlying assumption in this research method is that recurrent ideas and practices (e.g. supernatural agents) are underpinned by various psychological propensities (e.g. anthropomorphism) that are reassembled in culturally contingent ways.

When applied extensively, this fractionation method is likely to reveal that religious traditions, which appear remarkably different on the surface may be more similar than we think. For example, in the hypothetical example in Figure 2.3, culturally transmitted ideas about supernatural punishment in traditions A "the ancestors are seeking revenge" and B "God is punishing us" are more similar than traditions A and C "it is the result of karma," or B and C. Yet tradition A may appear to the observer to be very different than tradition B. Tradition A presumably engages with ancestors in the immediate environment and tradition B pays homage to an all-powerful God. Likewise, people in karmic tradition C "it is the result of karma" ultimately depend upon intuitions of interpersonal fairness (i.e. proportionality bias) and this may encourage the transmission of cultural information about both karma and moralizing supernatural forces.[25] Again, the scientific re-configuration of religious elements provides more rigorous points of comparison between and across traditions.

This fractionation method has facilitated a deeper understanding of many aspects of religion (see Table 2.3, for examples of topics in this book). These include how and why children reason about and respond to phenomena that are staples of religion, such as gods and supernatural agents,[26] the design and origin of the natural world,[27] and life before, or after, death.[28] Evolutionary and cognitive research has also demonstrated how adults represent and respond to a variety of religious concepts. These include the transmission of religious ideas;[29] gods and supernatural agents,[30] supernatural causes of illness,[31] the origins of the natural world, and a creator deity,[32] prayer,[33] teleological reasoning about life events;[34] continued existence in the afterlife,[35] representations of the self and others during spirit possession,[36] continued personal identity in reincarnation[37] and ritualized actions.[38] In addition to providing accounts of particular types of religious ideas and behaviors, CSR has also proposed broader theories of religion. For example, the

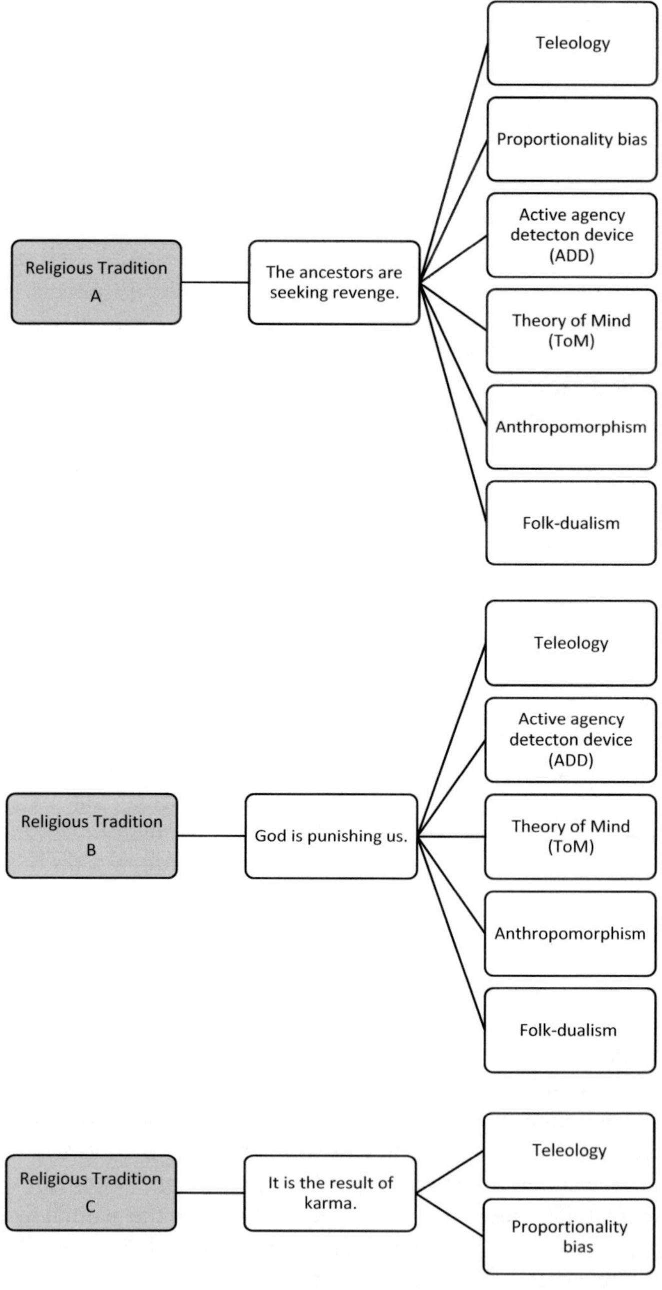

Figure 2.3 Example of the fractionation method showcasing how cultural representations in different religious traditions, such as explanations of misfortune, are triggered and constrained by psychological propensities. For example, the proposition that "the ancestors are seeking revenge" may resonate with intuitions about events happening for a reason (*teleology*), the extent of misfortune being equal to the original misdeed (*proportionality bias*), by agents in the environment (*agency detection device*, ADD) who have the ability to think (*theory of mind*, ToM), much like humans (*anthropomorphism*), except that they are non-visible (*folk-dualism*).

Figure 2.4 By dividing up religious systems into smaller components, a scientific approach can reveal underlying similarities within and between cultures. By showcasing how religions are similar, this scientific approach has the potential to cultivate a sense of togetherness and tolerance within and between cultures. (Image credit: iQoncept/Shutterstock.com.)

relationship between ritual dynamics and socio-political arrangements[39] and the rise of large-scale prosocial religions and moralizing gods.[40]

Participation 5: Comparing definitions of religion

1 Work with another student to compare and contrast the conceptualization of religion in CSR to other classic scholars in Table 2.1. Note the ways that they are similar or different. For example, do they see religion as a force for good or harm? Do they focus on the private experience or group effects? Create your own categories.

Key points

- CSR breaks up the category of religion into different parts that recur.
- These parts can be studied individually and compared across cultures.
- They include supernatural agents and the survival of the mind in the afterlife.

4 Establishing causal relationships between ideas and behaviors is a reliable means of categorizing religion

Cognitive scientists of religion aim to fractionate religious systems into empirically tractable units of analyses, rather than trying to top-down define and then explain religion as a whole. In doing so, they have a better chance of eventually reconstructing and explaining these religious systems in their entirety, namely, as distinct sociocultural packages of ideas and practices.[41]

This explanatory project will include the collaboration of scholars across disciplines and the collection of qualitative and quantitative data. The methodology will entail systematically testing relationships between cognitive predispositions and their expressions within and across cultural systems. At this point, scholars can claim to provide a more robust explanation of a series of constellations that can be deemed 'religious.' This endeavor will become easier with progress in other areas. For example, new theoretical insights in the cognitive and evolutionary

Table 2.3 Examples of research topics in CSR and corresponding chapters.

#	*Topic*	*Chapter*
1	Supernatural causes of illness.	5: The nature of the world.
2	The origins of the natural world, and a creator deity.	5: The nature of the world.
3	Teleological reasoning about life events.	5: The nature of the world.
4	Continued existence in the afterlife.	6: The afterlife.
5	Continued personal identity in reincarnation.	6: The afterlife.
6	Prayer.	7: Supernatural agents.
7	The transmission of religious ideas.	7: Supernatural agents.
8	Gods and supernatural agents.	7: Supernatural agents.
9	Representations of the self and others during spirit possession.	7: Supernatural agents.
10	The rise of large-scale prosocial religions and moralizing gods.	8: Morality.
11	Ritualized actions.	9, 10: Rituals.
12	The relationship between ritual dynamics and socio-political arrangements.	9, 10: Rituals.

sciences, the advancement of mapping human cognition and culture, and the development of methodological tools.

Crucially, however, CSR scholars are prepared for the eventuality that what they have characterized as religious is merely a family resemblance of words and ideas with causal relationships that differ from what they predict. As psychologist Justin Barrett explains, scholars embrace this possibility because they aim to understand how cognition interacts with culture to produce ideas and behaviors, not to justify the existence of religion as a category.

> (CSR) avoids the age-old problem of defining 'religion.' Rather than specify what religion is and try to explain it in whole, scholars in this field have generally chosen to approach 'religion' in an incremental, piecemeal fashion, identifying human thought or behavioral patterns that might count as 'religious' and then try to explain why those patterns are cross-culturally recurrent. If the explanations turn out to be part of a grander explanation of 'religion,' so be it, if not, meaningful human phenomena have still been rigorously addressed.
>
> (p. 768[42])

In sum, the concept of religion is a useful starting point in CSR because it appears to characterize a cluster of recurring features across and within cultures. It is thus a convenient, non-technical pointer to what we can study scientifically.[43] In other words, it is the start, rather than the endpoint, of research. In the next section, we consider a series of key research questions, methods, and critical assumptions that underpin CSR.

Participation 6: Can CSR increase religious tolerance?

1. Imagine that you have been appointed as head of a new national task force to promote tolerance among religious groups across the world. Drawing upon the core assumptions of CSR in this chapter, write your opening five-minute speech to convince the public to be more tolerant of people from other religions.
2. In groups of around four students, take turns reading your speech to the other members of your group.
3. Each member will vote for the speech they found most convincing.

Key points

- CSR aims to deconstruct religion into parts that recur across cultures, and eventually, to map relationships between the elements and reassemble them scientifically.

- Once the parts within and across religions are mapped, we will have a more robust scientific explanation of religion, or more specifically, of cross-culturally recurrent phenomena that can be dubbed "religious."

Summary of core assumptions underlying the conceptualization of religion in CSR

1 Religion is not a singular or naturally occurring phenomenon

There are no single or naturally occurring categories of thoughts and behaviors around the world that demarks religion. The term religion is a convenient, general-purpose label.

2 Folk concepts are not a reliable means of constructing scientific theories about religion

Scholarly conceptualizations of religion are based on how scholars perceive the world to be (i.e. folk concepts). They are not a reliable means of constructing the boundaries of a phenomenon that often differ from scientific theories and models of the world.

3 A bottom-up, fractionation approach is a reliable method to explain religion

CSR fractionates religious systems into their constituent components and then systematically compares the recurrent features and relationships between them.

4 Establishing causal relationships between ideas and behaviors is a reliable means of categorizing religion

One reliable means of explaining a series of constellations that can be deemed "religious" is to systematically test relationships between cognitive predispositions and their expressions within and across cultural systems.

The conceptualization of belief in CSR

Belief is another thorny concept that has been widely debated throughout the history of the study of religion. Generally speaking, the term belief is often used to refer to a propositional commitment to the truth value of an idea. For example, the idea that supernatural agents interact with the world, or that ritual practices bring about intended consequences, and so on. CSR has a distinctive perspective on the concept of belief based on cognitive science understandings of how the mind processes information. The following core assumptions underlie the conceptualization of belief in CSR:

1 Intuitive assumptions draw upon different cognitive processes than propositional beliefs

CSR scholars tend to adopt a dual-process model of the mind.[44] Dual-process models distinguish between two kinds of processes (see Table 2.4). The first are called intuitive processes (often called system 1 or "non-reflective" beliefs). These are quick, automatic, and implicit. In other words, we are not consciously aware of our intuitive expectations. These inherent assumptions about the world are generated automatically and without conscious reflection and draw on system 1.

For instance, you do not necessarily reflect on the assumption that an object will fall downwards if you drop it. This assumption is based on principles of intuitive physics that ordinary people develop from childhood with minimal instruction (for more examples of intuitions, see Table 7.1 in Chapter 7: Supernatural Agents). From the perspective of CSR, this kind of reasoning emerges from our intuitive ideas. In other words, system 1 ideas showcase how humans tend to often think. Alas, CSR scholars are very interested in these ideas because they often reveal how the human mind shapes religious ideas and behaviors.

The second kind of processes in the dual-process model of the mind are known as reflective processes (often called system 2). These are slow, deliberate, and explicit. For instance, if someone asks you whether or not you believe in fate, you may pause and consider your answer and then continue to explain the reasoning behind your stance. From the perspective of CSR, this kind of reflective response is belief proper. In other words, belief is a high-level, conscious, metarepresentational state of mind.[45] Therefore, belief typically draws on system 2 processing.[46] CSR scholars are also interested in these beliefs because they tend to also reveal how the human mind interacts with culture to shape religious beliefs and behaviors.

For convenience, think about the distinction between ideas and beliefs as between intuitions (system 1 ideas) and reflections (system 2 beliefs) about the world. Both systems 1 and 2 are involved in motivating and sustaining people's thoughts and behaviors that have been labeled as 'religious.' Yet researchers, such as anthropologists and psychologists, have tended to rely upon methods such as self-report and questionnaires that tap into propositional beliefs (system

Table 2.4 Characteristics of the dual-process model of the mind.

System	*Mental processes*	*Characteristics*	*Convenience label*
1	Intuitive processes.	Quick, automatic, implicit.	Intuitive ideas.
2	Reflective processes.	Slow, deliberate, explicit.	Propositional beliefs.

2). If used as the only method of understanding how and why belief develops, then these measures reveal little about other influences. Anthropologist Dimitris Xygalatas describes coming to this realization during the two years he spent as a doctoral student conducting ethnographic fieldwork in Southern Europe. Xygalatas asked hundreds of people why they participated in painful and stressful activities such as fire-walking. Yet, most of them could provide no specific answer other than that it was their tradition.[47]

And who can blame people for their answers? Consider how you would respond to a person from another culture asking the following: How does knocking on wood prevent harm? Why are ghosts more active at night? Why do bad things happen on Friday the 13th? Asking people to explain why they believe relies on insight that may not be available or accessible to them. Indeed, in some cultures, such as the Akhan-speaking people of Northern Thailand, locals consider the idea of belief irrelevant because the focus is on religious practices.[48] In scientific approaches to the study of religion, the exclusive reliance on explicit reasoning (system 2) leaves gaps in our understandings of how and why people adopt and perpetuate religion.

Consider, for example, that belief is often a poor predictor of behavior. In other words, what people say they believe (system 2) and how they behave (system 1) differ. Take the popular folklore story in Ireland that trees house

Figure 2.5 Belief is a high-level, conscious, metarepresentational state of mind and arises from system 2 processing. (Image credit: ONYXprj/Shutterstock.com.)

fairies (known as the sídhe). Most natives know that if you damage or cut down one of these trees then you will be faced with a lifetime of bad luck, although few farmers in Ireland would actually confess to believing that fairies exist.

Yet when traveling through Ireland, you will often see a perfectly cultivated field and, in the middle, an untouched fairy tree. To explain the behavior of farmers requires an understanding of intuitive biases against harm, even when the probability (of fairy-induced bad luck) is low when the costs of performing such actions (not cutting down fairy trees) are also low. These behaviors are based on intuitions evolved to solve problems in our ancestral history. An understanding of evolutionary psychology can provide us with a more satisfying explanation of practice in this instance than questioning farmers alone.

Consider another example: do you believe in ghosts? Either way, you would be unlikely to volunteer to spend the night alone at an allegedly haunted house, such as the Château de Trécesson in France (supposedly haunted by a young woman who was believed to be buried alive on the premises) or Morgan House in India (said to still be visited by the spectral, tortured wife who once lived there). Even if you mustered up the courage to stay after dark, it is likely that you would be highly vigilant in your new quarters and experience a set of cold shivers down the spine to things that go bump in the night.

Your experiences in the haunted house scenario are likely grounded in assumptions about ghosts. For example, even though you cannot physically see them, you are likely to view the dead as occupying a specific location in space. Of course, these ideas have been communicated. They are accepted in the culture—hence the popularity of ghostly movies—but they are accepted more quickly, without conscious reflection, because they are grounded in intuitive expectations of spatiality and physicality that we hold for agents generally. These are ideas based on intuition. Again, these intuitions often evolved to solve problems in our ancestral history. Scholars in the cognitive science of religion use an array of theories in the evolutionary sciences and methods to tap into people's intuitions as well as their explicit beliefs.

For these aforementioned reasons, CSR scholars are most interested in examining how intuitive processes give rise to religious ideas. Many cognitive scientists of religion use methods to tap into these implicit processes, such as asking people to make judgments under time constraints, or without thinking too much about them, and measuring people's behaviors in different circumstances.

Key points

- CSR distinguishes between propositional beliefs and implicit ideas.
- Propositional beliefs (system 2) are reflective and often captured by what people say they believe.
- Implicit ideas (system 1) are often less obvious to us and reveal themselves when we are under time constraints and do not have time to reflect.

Figure 2.6 Intuitive expectations about the world are based on system 1. They are quick, automatic, and implicit. Many assumptions underlying popular ideas about religion are the result of these processes, such as ghosts, like people, occupying a specific location in space. (Image credit: Vladimir Mulder/ Shutterstock.com).

2 CSR explains the transmission potential of religious ideas

Cross-culturally recurrent religious ideas and behaviors are, of course, culturally transmitted. Yet CSR proposes that many popular beliefs and practices are successful because people find them intuitively plausible. CSR scholars are also interested in the formation of beliefs, and there are many combinations of cognitive and cultural inputs that lead to them. For example (see Figure 2.7), when intuitive ideas become explicit, cognitively elaborated upon, and moderately supported by others, they become beliefs. For instance, the idea that consciousness continues after death is common among religious traditions does not arise from weighing the evidence for and against the existence of religious concepts. Instead, these ideas are often reflective elaborations on unquestioned intuitions about the world.

Sometimes, however, beliefs are formed that counter panhuman intuitions about the world (i.e. counter-intuitive), but these require much more support at the cognitive (e.g. rehearsal, elaboration) and cultural (e.g. socialization, reinforcement) level to spread. Consider the example of the Buddhist doctrine of non-self (i.e. *anatta* or *anātman*) in some Buddhist traditions. The idea that there is no unchanging, permanent self runs counter to our basic intuitions about people. To explain why many Buddhists endorse this belief requires an

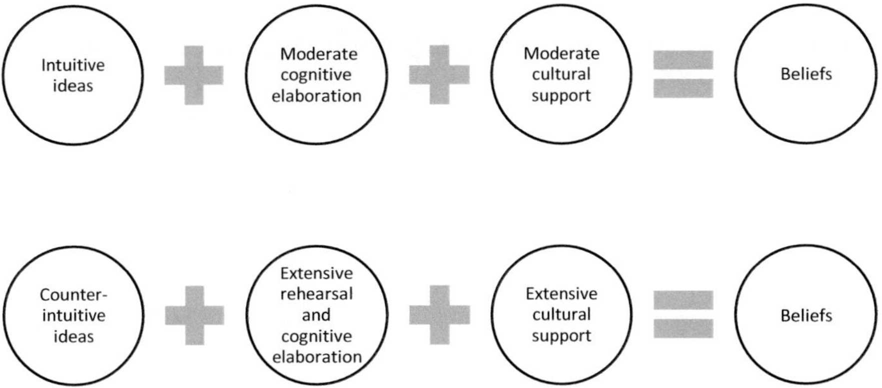

Figure 2.7 Examples of different cognitive and cultural routes from ideas to beliefs.

explanation that takes into account historical and context-dependent factors of that particular tradition. In sum, cognition (i.e. intuitions, reflections) and culture (e.g. socialization, environment) create religion, but the exact configuration of each of these components differs according to beliefs and practices. There are, however, disagreements in CSR about the optimal amount of intuitiveness that it takes for an idea to spread rapidly. We consider some of these debates in more detail in Chapter 7 (Supernatural Agents).

Cognitive scientists of religion have focused most on pinpointing how intuitions about the world underpin ideas about religion, and why this makes certain beliefs—that depend to some extent on these intuitions—spread more successfully in and across religious traditions. As we will encounter throughout the book, general theories in CSR purport to explain why (all else being equal) religious ideas become widespread, based on what is known about the human mind. These theories are about the transmission potential of religious views. A more comprehensive explanation of religious beliefs occurs when scholars take these theories and apply them to specific contexts with an understanding of the cultural and historical context within which religious ideas are communicated.

Key points

- Propositional beliefs and implicit ideas about religion are sometimes similar, and sometimes they are different, but what people say they believe does not mean uncovering their intuitive assumptions.
- CSR scholars have focused primarily on pinpointing how intuitions about the world underpin ideas about religion, and why this makes certain beliefs spread more successfully than others.

Summary of core assumptions underlying the conceptualization of belief in CSR

1 Intuitive assumptions can be distinguished from propositional beliefs

Propositional beliefs are conscious, and metarepresentational states. Beliefs can be separate from intuitive assumptions about the world, which are often automatically generated without conscious reflection. Some beliefs spread more quickly because they are based on intuitive assumptions about the world; others require more social support, such as opportunities for rehearsal.

2 CSR explains the transmission potential of religious ideas

CSR explains the transmission potential of religious ideas. Cross-culturally recurrent beliefs are often based on reflective elaborations on intuitions. These types of beliefs are the most obvious candidates to study from a cognitive perspective.

Chapter summary

CSR is also characterized by its distinctive conceptualization of religion and belief. In this chapter, we considered how debates about what religion is do not derail CSR scholars in their empirical attempts to capture recurrent ideas and behaviors. Cognitive and evolutionary scientists categorize beliefs as propositional ideas about the world, which can be contrasted to inherent ideas that all normally developing humans adopt with minimal instruction.

Discussion questions

1 What is religion, according to CSR?
2 How does the approach to conceptualizing religion in CSR differ from others?
3 To what extent do you think CSR explains why people believe in religion?

Selected further reading

Articles

1 McCauley, Robert N., and Emma Cohen. "Cognitive science and the naturalness of religion." *Philosophy Compass* 5, no. 9 (2010): 779–792.
2 McKay, Ryan, and Harvey Whitehouse. "Religion and morality." *Psychological Bulletin* 141, no. 2 (2015): 447.

3 Pyysiäinen, Ilkka. "Intuitive and explicit in religious thought." *Journal of Cognition and Culture* 4, no. 1 (2004): 123–150.

Books

1 Jensen, Jeppe Sinding. *What is religion?* Routledge, 2019.
2 Pals, Daniel L. *Nine theories of religion* Oxford: Oxford University Press, 2015.

Notes

1 Tylor, Edward Burnett, *Primitive Culture: Researchers into the Development of Mythology, Philosophy, Religion, Language, Art, and Custom*, 2 vols., 4th edn, rev. (London: John Murray, [1871], 1903), 1:424.
2 Malinowski, Bronislaw, *Magic, science and religion* (Garden City, NY: Doubleday, 1954 [1925]).
3 Freud, Sigmund, *The Future of an Illusion. The Standard Edition of the Complete Psychological Works of Sigmund Freud* (translated from the German under the General Editorship of James Strachey). (London: Hogarth Press, 1961).
4 Durkheim, Emile. *The elementary forms of the religious life*, tr. Joseph Ward Swain (New York: The Macmillan Company, 1915), p. 47.
5 Marx, Karl, "Critique of Hegel's philosophy of right" in Niebuhr, Marx and Engles on Religion, (New York: Schocken Books, 1964), p. 42.
6 James, William. *The varieties of religious experience: A study in human nature,* The Modern Library. (New York: Random House, 1936 [1902]), pp. 31–32.
7 Eliade, Mircea. *Patterns in comparative religion.* tr. Rosemary Sheed (New York: Meridian Books [1949] 1963). University of Nebraska Press, 1996.
8 Geertz, Clifford. "Religion as a cultural system." In *The interpretation of cultures: selected essays* (New York: Basic Books, 1973) p. 90.
9 Pals, Daniel L. *Nine theories of religion.* Oxford: Oxford University Press, 2015.
10 Astuti, Rita, and Paul L. Harris. "Understanding mortality and the life of the ancestors in rural Madagascar." *Cognitive science* 32, no. 4 (2008): 713–740.
11 Lindeman, Marjaana, and Annika M. Svedholm. "What's in a term? Paranormal, superstitious, magical and supernatural beliefs by any other name would mean the same." *Review of General Psychology* 16, no. 3 (2012): 241–255; Smith, Jonathan Z. (2004). *Relating religion: Essays in the study of religion.* IL: University of Chicago Press; Taylor, Mark C. (Ed.). (2008). *Critical terms for religious studies.* IL: University of Chicago Press.
12 E.g. see Atran, S. (2002). *In gods we trust: The evolutionary landscape of religion.* New York, NY: Oxford University Press; Boyer, P. (2013). "Explaining religious concepts. Lévi-Strauss the brilliant and problematic ancestor." In D. Xygalatas & W. W. McCorkle (Eds.) *Mental culture, classical social theory and the cognitive science of religion* (pp. 164–175).
13 Act II, Scene II, Page II. Shakespeare, William. *Romeo and Juliet.* Cambridge University Press, 2003.
14 Retrieved 12 April 2020, from: www.allaboutbirds.org/news/how-can-9-species-look-so-different-yet-be-genetically-almost-identical/.
15 Cohen, E. (2008). *'Out with religion': A novel framing of the religion debate.* Proceedings of the Oxford Amnesty lectures. Manchester University Press.
16 McCauley, Robert N., and Emma Cohen, "Cognitive science and the naturalness of religion." *Philosophy Compass*, 5, no. 9 (2010): 779–792.
17 McKay, Ryan, and Harvey Whitehouse, "Religion and morality." *Psychological Bulletin*, 141, no. 2 (2015): 447.

18 E.g. Willard, Aiyana K., and Ara Norenzayan, "Cognitive biases explain religious belief, paranormal belief, and belief in life's purpose." *Cognition*, 129, no. 2 (2013): 379–391; Gelman, Susan A., and Cristine H. Legare, "Concepts and folk theories." *Annual Review of Anthropology*, 40 (2011): 379–398; Kelemen, Deborah, and Cara DiYanni, "Intuitions about origins: Purpose and intelligent design in children's reasoning about nature." *Journal of Cognition and Development*, 6, no. 1 (2005): 3–31; Atran, Scott, "Folk biology and the anthropology of science: Cognitive universals and cultural particulars." *Behavioral and brain sciences*, 21, no. 4 (1998): 547–569.

19 Franek, J. (2014). "Has the cognitive science of religion (re) defined 'religion'"? *Feedback,* 22, no. 1; McCutcheon, R. T., *Manufacturing religion: The discourse on sui generis religion and the politics of nostalgia.* New York, NY: Oxford University Press, 1997.

20 Lindeman, Marjaana, and Annika M. Svedholm. "What's in a term? Paranormal, superstitious, magical and supernatural beliefs by any other name would mean the same." *Review of General Psychology*, 16, no. 3 (2012): 241–255.

21 Retrieved 1 February 2020 from: www.scientificamerican.com/article/race-is-a-social-construct-scientists-argue/.

22 Yudell, Michael, Dorothy Roberts, Rob DeSalle, and Sarah Tishkoff, "Taking race out of human genetics." *Science* 351, no. 6273 (2016): 564–565.

23 Boyer, Pascal. "Religion as an Impure Subject: A Note on Cognitive Order in Religious Representation in Response to Brian Malley" *Method & theory in the study of religion* 8, no. 2 (1996): p. 212.

24 E.g. see Boyer, Pascal. (2003). Religious thought and behaviour as by-products of brain function. *Trends in cognitive sciences,* 7 (3): 119–124.

25 White, Cindel J.M., Ara Norenzayan, and Mark Schaller. "The content and correlates of belief in Karma across cultures." *Personality and Social Psychology Bulletin* 45, no. 8 (2019): 1184–1201; See also here: (forthcoming) https://psyarxiv.com/39egn.

26 Barrett, Justin L., and Rebekah A. Richert. "Anthropomorphism or preparedness? Exploring children's God concepts." *Review of Religious Research* (2003): 300–312; Knight, Nicola. "Yukatek Maya children's attributions of belief to natural and non-natural entities." *Journal of Cognition and Culture* 8, no. 3–4 (2008): 235–243; Piazza, Jared, and Paulo Sousa. "Religiosity, political orientation, and consequentialist moral thinking." *Social Psychological and Personality Science* 5, no. 3 (2014): 334–342.

27 Evans, E. Margaret. "Cognitive and contextual factors in the emergence of diverse belief systems: Creation versus evolution." *Cognitive psychology* 42, no. 3 (2001): 217–266; Kelemen, Deborah. "Are children 'intuitive theists'? Reasoning about purpose and design in nature." *Psychological Science* 15, no. 5 (2004): 295–301.

28 E.g. Astuti, Rita, and Paul L. Harris. "Understanding mortality and the life of the ancestors in rural Madagascar." *Cognitive Science* 32, no. 4 (2008): 713–740; Bering, Jesse M., and David F. Bjorklund. "The natural emergence of reasoning about the afterlife as a developmental regularity." *Developmental Psychology* 40, no. 2 (2004): 217; Harris, Paul, and Rebekah Richert. "The ghost in my body: Children's developing concept of the soul." *Journal of Cognition and Culture* 6, no. 3–4 (2006): 409–427; Emmons, Natalie A., and Deborah Kelemen. "The development of children's prelife reasoning: Evidence from two cultures." *Child development* 85, no. 4 (2014): 1617–1633.

29 Boyer, Pascal, and Charles Ramble. "Cognitive templates for religious concepts: Cross-cultural evidence for recall of counter-intuitive representations." *Cognitive Science* 25, no. 4 (2001): 535–564.

30 Barrett, Justin L. "Cognitive constraints on Hindu concepts of the divine." *Journal for the Scientific Study of Religion* (1998): 608–619; Bering, Jesse. "Intuitive conceptions of dead agents' minds: The natural foundations of afterlife beliefs as phenomenological boundary." *Journal of Cognition and Culture* 2, no. 4 (2002): 263–308; McKay, Ryan, Charles Efferson, Harvey Whitehouse, and Ernst Fehr. "Wrath of God: Religious primes and punishment." *Proceedings of the Royal Society B: Biological Sciences* 278, no. 1713 (2011):

1858–1863; Purzycki, Benjamin Grant. "The minds of gods: A comparative study of supernatural agency." *Cognition* 129, no. 1 (2013): 163–179.

31 Legare, Cristine H., and Susan A. Gelman. "Bewitchment, biology, or both: The co-existence of natural and supernatural explanatory frameworks across development." *Cognitive Science* 32, no. 4 (2008): 607–642; Legare, Cristine H., E. Margaret Evans, Karl S. Rosengren, and Paul L. Harris. "The coexistence of natural and supernatural explanations across cultures and development." *Child development* 83, no. 3 (2012): 779–793.

32 Järnefelt, Elisa, Caitlin F. Canfield, and Deborah Kelemen. "The divided mind of a disbeliever: Intuitive beliefs about nature as purposefully created among different groups of non-religious adults." *Cognition* 140 (2015): 72–88.

33 Barrett, Justin. "How ordinary cognition informs petitionary prayer." *Journal of Cognition and Culture* 1, no. 3 (2001): 259–269.

34 Heywood, Bethany T., and Jesse M. Bering. "'Meant to be': How religious beliefs and cultural religiosity affect the implicit bias to think teleologically." *Religion, Brain & Behavior* 4, no. 3 (2014): 183–201.

35 Bering, Jesse M. "The folk psychology of souls." *Behavioral and brain sciences* 29, no. 5 (2006): 453–462.

36 Cohen, Emma. *The mind possessed: The cognition of spirit possession in an Afro-Brazilian religious tradition*. Oxford University Press, 2007; Cohen, Emma, and Justin Barrett. "When minds migrate: Conceptualizing spirit possession." *Journal of Cognition and Culture* 8, no. 1–2 (2008): 23–48.

37 White, Claire. "Establishing personal identity in reincarnation: Minds and bodies reconsidered." *Journal of Cognition and Culture* 15, no. 3–4 (2015): 402–429; White, Claire. "Cross-cultural similarities in reasoning about personal continuity in reincarnation: Evidence from South India." *Religion, Brain & Behavior* 6, no. 2 (2016): 130–153; White, Claire, Robert Kelly, and Shaun Nichols. "Remembering past lives." *Advances in Religion, Cognitive Science, and Experimental Philosophy* (2016): 169–195; White, Claire. "Who wants to live forever?: Explaining the cross-cultural recurrence of reincarnation beliefs." *Journal of Cognition and Culture* 17, no. 5 (2017): 419–436.

38 Atran, Scott. *In gods we trust: The evolutionary landscape of religion*. Oxford University Press, 2002; Cohen, Emma, Roger Mundry, and Sebastian Kirschner. "Religion, synchrony, and cooperation." *Religion, Brain & Behavior* 4, no. 1 (2014): 20–30; Fischer, Ronald, Dimitris Xygalatas, Panagiotis Mitkidis, Paul Reddish, Penny Tok, Ivana Konvalinka, and Joseph Bulbulia. "The fire-walker's high: Affect and physiological responses in an extreme collective ritual." *PloS one* 9, no. 2 (2014); Legare, Cristine H., and Rachel E. Watson-Jones. "The evolution and ontogeny of ritual." *The handbook of evolutionary psychology* (2015): 1–19; Konvalinka, Ivana, Dimitris Xygalatas, Joseph Bulbulia, Uffe Schjødt, Else-Marie Jegindø, Sebastian Wallot, Guy Van Orden, and Andreas Roepstorff. "Synchronized arousal between performers and related spectators in a fire-walking ritual." *Proceedings of the National Academy of Sciences* 108, no. 20 (2011): 8514–8519.

39 Whitehouse, Harvey. *Modes of religiosity: A cognitive theory of religious transmission*. Lanham, MD, Rowman Altamira, 2004.

40 Norenzayan, Ara. *Big gods: How religion transformed cooperation and conflict*. Princeton University Press, 2013.

41 Boyer, P. "Religious thought and behaviour as by-products of brain function." *Trends in Cognitive Sciences* 7 No. 3 (2003): 119–124; McKay, Ryan, and Harvey Whitehouse. "Religion and morality." *Psychological Bulletin* 141, no. 2 (2015): 447.

42 Barrett, J. "Cognitive science of religion: What is it and why is it?" *Religion Compass* 1, No. 6 (2007): 768–786.

43 E.g. see Taves, Ann. "2010 Presidential Address: 'Religion' in the Humanities and the Humanities in the University." *Journal of the American Academy of Religion* 79, no.

2 (2011): 287–314; Whitehouse, H. (2008). "Cognitive evolution and religion"; "Cognition and religious evolution". In J. Bulbulia, R. Sosis, E. Harris, R. Genet, C. Genet & K. Wyman (eds.) *The Evolution of Religion: Studies, Theories, and Critiques*. Santa Margarita, CA: Collins Foundation Press; Boyer, P. (2013). "Explaining religious concepts. Lévi-Strauss the brilliant and problematic ancestor." In D. Xygalatas & W. W. McCorkle (Eds.) *Mental Culture, Classical Social Theory and the Cognitive science of religion* (pp. 164–175). McCauley, Robert N., and Emma Cohen. "Cognitive science and the naturalness of religion." *Philosophy Compass* 5, no. 9 (2010): 779–792; "Cognitive science of religion: What is it and why is it?" *Religion Compass*, 1, No. 6 (2007): 768–786.

44 Tversky, Amos, and Daniel Kahneman. "Prospect theory: An analysis of decision under risk." *Econometrica* 47, no. 2 (1979): 263–291.

45 Sperber, Dan. *Explaining culture: A naturalistic approach*. Cambridge, MA: Cambridge, 1996; Baumard, Nicolas, and Pascal Boyer. "Religious beliefs as reflective elaborations on intuitions: A modified dual-process model." *Current Directions in Psychological Science* 22, no. 4 (2013): 295–300.

46 Pyysiäinen, Ilkka. "Intuitive and explicit in religious thought." *Journal of Cognition and Culture* 4, no. 1 (2004): 123–150.

47 https://items.ssrc.org/insights/strong-interdisciplinarity-and-explanatory-pluralism-in-social-scientific-research/.

48 Tooker, Deborah E. "Identity systems of Highland Burma:'belief', Akha zan, and a critique of interiorized notions of ethno-religious identity." *Man* (1992): 799–819.

3 Research questions

One aspect that makes the cognitive science of religion (CSR) a distinctive approach to the study of religion is the kinds of questions that scholars tend to ask. Namely: Why do some religious ideas and behaviors persist? What kind of mind does it take to represent these ideas? What is the source of these cognitive foundations? And, how does culture interact with cognition to produce religion? Sometimes scholars state these questions explicitly in their writings, but more often than not, they remain implicit in their work. We consider these questions in this chapter.

1 Why do some religious ideas and behaviors persist?

CSR has focused on explaining why particular kinds of ideas and behaviors persist in relatively stable forms throughout history, within and across different cultural environments. Explaining the recurrence of specific ideas and practices is especially important when there may be many versions that can be constructed.[1] Think for a moment about the many different configurations of supernatural agents in the world that could exist. Yet, despite the potential for diversity in religious ideas across cultures, some concepts, such as representations of supernatural agents as having human-like features, recur. This is in part because ideas are constrained by our experience of the world.

Often, these particular sets of ideas and behaviors that appear to be cross-culturally recurrent have coalesced to form systems that resemble what scholars have tended to label "religious." As discussed in Chapter 2 (Core Assumptions), CSR typically fractionates religion into cross-culturally recurrent forms of ideas and practices. These include concepts of non-visible agents as punitive deities, continued consciousness in the afterlife, and ritualized behavior.[2] Explaining why particular forms of these ideas and actions emerge and persist is what CSR scholars mean when they say that we can explain "religion." To ascertain the types of beliefs and behaviors that are recurrent and across religious systems, researchers often collect or draw upon existing archaeological, historical, ethnographic, and experimental data. This data is then analyzed for recurrent patterns.

Key points

- CSR is concerned with explaining why specific ideas and behaviors are found in similar forms across cultures and throughout history.

(a) Popular and theological versions of religion

CSR focuses on explaining the cultural transmission of religious ideas but distinguishes between theological versions of religion and those employed by ordinary people every day. Cognitive scientists of religion are particularly interested in explaining ideas that emerge relatively easily, with little instruction, established at an early age. These kinds of ideas tap into intuitive processes (i.e. system 1). As covered in Chapter 2 (Core Assumptions), ideas emerging from system 1 are quick, automatic, and implicit. Philosopher Robert McCauley calls the types of religious ideas that emerge relatively easily "maturationally natural." Maturationally natural ideas tend to characterize many every day lay understandings of religion (for more examples of intuitions that underpin maturationally natural ideas, see Table 7.1 in Chapter 7 (Supernatural Agents).

If theological concepts counter our assumptions about the world, then how do experts recite theological doctrines with ease? McCauley calls these abilities "practiced naturalness." Practiced naturalness arises not through the ordinary course of physical and psychological development and with minimal instruction, but rather, through consistent training. Think about learning to play a musical instrument, or driving a car, for example. These ideas require support for people to adopt them, such as frequent rehearsal. Theological ideas that counter our intuitions are explicitly held and consciously accessible concepts. That is to say; people tend to recite them accurately only when they have time to think or when they stick to the rehearsed script.

Key points

- Ideas that emerge easily and with little instruction are called maturationally natural.

Table 3.1 Characteristics of religious ideas.

Associated system	*Mental processes*	*Characteristics*	*Often found in …*
1	Maturationally natural.	Emerge easily from a young age with minimal instruction.	Popular religion.
2	Practiced naturalness.	Are reinforced through cognitive effort and cultural support.	Theological religion.

CSR scholars are interested in the sociocultural conditions that give rise to the formation of theological beliefs when these explanations also include a role for human cognition. Cognitive scientists of religion also acknowledge that many theological concepts are complicated and differ from our intuitions about the world. For example, the Christian doctrine of the Trinity presents God as three distinct persons (i.e. the Father, Son, and Holy Spirit) yet of the same substance,[3] which counters our intuition that a person is singular. CSR scholars are most interested in the relationship between theological versions of religion and popular versions of these ideas because they tell us much about the role of cognition in processing religious concepts.

Key points

- Ideas often rehearsed and quickly accessible are called practiced naturalness.

(b) Theologically correct and incorrect ideas

Cognitive scientists of religion have focused more on explaining the persistence of ideas in popular religion, espoused by ordinary people, rather than formal religion articulated by theologians. Yet often ordinary people draw upon theological sources when constructing beliefs. For instance, people often profess to believe in theological versions of religious ideas, such as the concept of karma in the Buddhist tradition. Cognitive scientists of religion call these "theologically correct"[4] ideas. By labeling certain ideas as theologically correct, CSR scholars are not making judgments about what is the true, or correct, version of a given doctrine. Rather, the term refers to people's explicit reference to theological versions of religious ideas. There are, of course, many versions of theological correctness. What matters for cognitive scientists of religion is what people say they believe when they have time to reflect.

Sometimes people's theologically correct ideas are consistent in different contexts. People claim they believe in certain ideas based on religious teachings. Yet, they often unconsciously revert to versions of these ideas that are more straightforward and intuitive (i.e. closer to maturationally natural ideas). For example, many Buddhists hold a belief in luck despite the incompatibility with the doctrine of karma.[5] CSR scholars deem these "theologically incorrect"[6] ideas.

The discrepancy between professed beliefs and everyday reasoning occur in different contexts but are especially likely under two conditions. The first is during real-time cognitive processing, such as when under time constraints to provide an answer. For example, as we discuss in Chapter 7 (Supernatural Agents), one study found that Christian participants explicitly represented the

Abrahamic God as omnipotent[7] (theologically correct). Yet when under pressure, they tended to represent God as having limited abilities and preferences, just like an ordinary person (theologically incorrect).

The second condition where discrepancies are likely to occur is when people are in strong emotional states, such as distress. For example, many Christians feel that it is morally unacceptable to be angry with God (theologically correct). Nevertheless, when they experience an adverse event, such as a diagnosis of cancer, some report experiencing bouts of anger towards God[8] (theologically incorrect). Again, CSR scholars are most interested in discrepancies between what people say they believe at different times and under different conditions because this informs us about the role of cognition in processing religious concepts.

So far in this chapter, we have covered many aspects of research in CSR. Although CSR overlaps with other disciplines that study the mind and culture, aspects of CSR are different. For instance, CSR is similar to the field of psychology of religion in many ways, such as applying theories and methods of the psychological sciences to explain religious thought and behavior. Yet cognitive scientists of religion tend to be less concerned with explaining individual psychology, for example, answering questions like "why does a specific *individual* become religious?" Instead, CSR scholars tend to be more concerned with accounting for cross-cultural patterns in what people tend to believe, for example, answering questions like "why do *people* intuitively represent God as a human-like agent with special powers?"

Key points

- There are often differences between what people say they believe (theologically correct) and how they reason every day (theologically incorrect).
- These discrepancies often occur when people do not have time to think or are in an emotional state.
- CSR is more concerned with explaining how people reason every day than what people say they believe.

Table 3.2 Characteristics of religious ideas.

Associated system	*Label*	*Definition*	*Often found in circumstances …*
1	Theologically correct.	Ideas consistent with espoused religious beliefs.	When people have time to reflect.
2	Theologically incorrect.	Ideas inconsistent with espoused religious beliefs.	When people do not have time to reflect or are in an emotional state.

2 What kind of mind does it take to represent these ideas and behave accordingly?

One key endeavor in CSR is to explain the limited and recurrent repertoire of religious ideas and behaviors by appealing to what is known about how humans tend to think, especially as there is a vast number of alternative ideas and practices that may be adopted and transmitted. As we discussed earlier in this chapter, human minds and cultures may give rise to a seemingly endless variety of ideas, but only some enjoy transmissive success. For instance, why do many people think that everything happens for a reason rather than by chance? Why assume that life continues, rather than ends, at biological death? Why are supernatural agents, such as ghosts, typically represented as invisible persons with minds rather than as mindless? How come God is depicted as interested in moral behavior rather than the mundane details of life? Why do people engage in rituals in different cultures and not some other behavior? These and many more questions guide the research described in this book.

Key points

- To answer questions about why some ideas about religion are cross-culturally recurrent, CSR scholars draw upon an understanding of how humans tend to think.

(a) Identifying cognitive foundations

At the heart of most cognitive science of religion queries is the question: what kind of mind would it take to represent these ideas, and behave accordingly? In technical terms, this involves identifying the psychological predispositions, cognitive and content biases, and constraints necessary for representing ideas or displaying behaviors. To identify these cognitive or psychological foundations, scholars draw from existing research in the cognitive sciences. They often engage in new research with children and adults within and across cultures that differ meaningfully from one another.[9] This methodology allows researchers to investigate whether, and how, natural responses emerge. If cultures differ in their accepted views, yet people tend to think similarly, then it suggests that cognitive foundations underpin ideas.

As we will cover throughout the chapters, fundamental cognitive foundations have been identified or proposed as underpinning religious ideas and behaviors. These include teleology, a bias towards seeing things in the world as having a purpose and being made for that purpose;[10] folk dualism, the intuition that minds are separate and independent from bodies;[11] anthropomorphism, the tendency to attribute human-like properties, including mental states and characteristics, to non-human things[12] fairness or proportionality bias, the tendency to represent our actions and consequences as having proportionate consequences;[13] kinship detection and identity fusion, the ability to recognize and calibrate kinship—and by extension, fuse identity with imagined kin[14] (see Table 3.3 for a more extensive list).

For an example of how to identify cognitive foundations of religion, take the seemingly simple act of praying to God for help (i.e. supplication, or petitioning), something millions of people do every day. In performing this action, people often automatically, and without reflection, assume that God:

a Exists.
b Can access the request.
c Understands the request.
d Can affect an outcome.
e Is willing to affect an outcome.

We can break down these assumptions about God even further. For instance, (b) that God can access the request and (c) understands the request, take for granted that God has mental states such as beliefs, desires, and intentions. It also assumes that God has different mental states than ours so that what the petitioner is thinking is not the same as what God is thinking, and what the petitioner desires, believes, and intends is not necessarily the same as what God desires, believes, and intends.

Holding these assumptions during prayer is an example of *anthropomorphism*, attributing human-like properties, including mental states and characteristics, to non-human things. The tendency to attribute others with mental states and represent these states as different from our own is often referred to as a "*Theory of mind*" (ToM), or more generally, mentalizing.

If humans could not represent agents as possessing mental states such as desires and intentions, then the act of asking a deity to change an outcome would presumably not have appeared so readily in human culture.[15]

We can identify cognitive predispositions when they emerge early among children with minimal instruction, even though cultural environments shape the specific forms they have taken.[16] They give rise to maturationally natural ideas and form cognitive biases that are not unique to religious ideas. For example, as we discussed in Chapter 2 (Core Assumptions), it is difficult to think of examples where these mentalizing abilities are not evoked. Individuals who are impaired in the ability to represent others' desires and intentions, such as people with autism spectrum disorders,[17] often have difficulty navigating the social world. These cognitive predispositions, which underpin religious actions, readily appear in other domains and everyday social interactions.

Key points

- CSR scholars identify the cognitive and behavioral biases necessary for representing common religious ideas and behaviors.
- These cognitive biases are not found exclusively in religion and emerge in other domains.

Table 3.3 Examples of some psychological foundations that underpin and impact religious ideas and a chapter where they are discussed in more detail. These are illustrative, not exhaustive.

#	*Cognitive foundation*	*Description or example*	*Example chapter*
1	Teleology	Seeing things in the world as having a purpose and being made for that purpose.	5: The nature of the world.
2	Psychological essentialism	Members of a category share deep commonalities that make them what they are.	5: The nature of the world.
3	Immanent justice reasoning	Reasoning as though good things happen to good people and, conversely, that bad things tend to happen to bad people.	5: The nature of the world.
4	Folk-dualism	Perceiving minds are separate and independent from bodies.	6: The afterlife.
5	Simulation constraint	The inability to imagine something. For example, imagining not having mental states, because imagination depends upon thinking.	6: The afterlife.
6	Offline social reasoning	The ability to think about a person as continuing in another realm when they are not physically present.	6: The afterlife.
7	Embodiment	The tendency to think about people as physically embodied, even when represented as in a supernatural sphere of existence.	6: The afterlife.
8	Anthropomorphism	Attributing human-like properties, including mental states and characteristics, to non-human things.	7: Supernatural agents.
9	Minimally counter intuitive transmission advantage	Attending to, and remembering, ideas that meet most of our default expectations about the world and counter a few others.	7: Supernatural agents.
10	Proportionality bias	Representing actions and consequences as having proportionate consequences.	8: Morality.
11	Imitative fidelity	A social learning strategy where we imitate some behaviors more closely than others.	9: Rituals: Part 1.
12	Action representation system	Ritual actions are handled by the same cognitive system that processes everyday actions.	9: Rituals: Part 1.
13	Mnemonic effects	The frequency of ritual performance impacts how the behaviors are processed.	9: Rituals: Part 1.

(*Continued*)

Table 3.3 (Cont.)

#	*Cognitive foundation*	*Description or example*	*Example chapter*
14	Hazard precaution system	Spontaneous ritualized behavior occurs when people threats are detected in the environment.	10: Rituals: Part 2.
15	Emotional effects	Ritual performance reduces anxiety.	10: Rituals: Part 2.
16	Affiliative effects	Experiencing pain in a ritual setting makes people more amenable to group bonding.	10: Rituals: Part 2
17	Kinship detection and identity fusion	Recognizing and calibrating kinship, and by extension, fusing identity with imagined kin.	10: Rituals: Part 2.

(b) Religion emerges as a result of typically developing cognition

There are many examples of psychological foundations that underpin both ideas and behaviors in religion and other domains. For example, consider the following cases:

- The feeling of transcendence induced by hallucinogenic drugs at a music festival.
- The state of awe experienced from staring at a natural wonder of the world, such as the vastness of the Grand Canyon.
- The sense of collective effervescence among team members playing a sport.
- The stereotyped, rigid movements of dancers in a theatre.
- The precision with which children meticulously leave out cookies and milk for Santa Claus on Christmas Eve.
- Sacred values of patriotism that serve to inspire or legitimize violence.

If the psychological tendencies that underpin religious concepts and behaviors are not distinct from those that underpin their non-religious counterparts, then there is no need to posit a unique domain reserved for religious cognition or behavior. For example, although there is something particular about the actors and the actions performed in religious ritual, the basic structure of these agents' actions does not fundamentally differ from what we find in everyday acts. As anthropologist Pierre Lienard and religious studies scholar, E. Thomas Lawson put it, "Ritual drummers ritually drumming on ritual drums are still drummers drumming on drums.[18]" Given what we know about the persuasiveness of particular forms of thought, which underpin much of religion in different contexts, religious ideas are part and parcel of our typically developing cognition. These ideas and behaviors emerge with minimal instruction and spread when introduced in social environments; much like music, art, or language, religion is cognitively natural.[19]

Key points

- The cognitive biases that underpin religious ideas emerge with little instruction. Ideas spread rapidly when introduced to other environments.
- Other non-religious ideas and behaviors also emerge with little instruction, such as music, art, and language.
- Religion, like music, art, and language, is cognitively natural.

(c) Religious traditions may have distinctive configurations of religious ideas and behaviors, but they draw upon the same pool of psychological tendencies

The psychological foundations that make up religion do not differ from those that constitute non-religious domains. However, these tendencies may join together in specific ways to form components that make up religious traditions. For instance, certain kinds of altered states of consciousness underpin many types of religious experiences, and the compulsion to act in repetitive ways in groups of like-minded people undergirds many types of religious rituals. Yet CSR acknowledges that the individual components within religious traditions may appear distinctive; for example, rituals may be performed with different explanations about the meaning related to specific sacred values.

Furthermore, religious traditions may have distinctive configurations of these components. For instance, some religious groups may emphasize individual altered states of consciousness, whereas others may be centered on group-ritualized action. Religious systems draw upon the same pool of psychological tendencies. They tend to have similar components (e.g. continued consciousness after biological death, ritualized actions, altered states of consciousness).

For illustration, consider those fun plastic construction toys, Legos. You can build two different objects, like those in Figure 3.1. They look completely different, but upon closer inspection, you come to realize that some of the colored blocks (e.g. white and brown) appear in both objects. Ultimately, the blocks are drawn from the same bag, and so there cannot be endless configurations of shapes; overlap is inevitable.

These fundamental similarities in the psychological building blocks of religion are one reason why early pioneers of CSR took issue with some mainstream assumptions in religious studies. Namely, that religion is unique (i.e. sui generis[20]), and that religions are so different that they cannot be compared to each other (i.e. extreme versions of cultural relativism).

These psychological biases explain not only why some ideas and behaviors are possible in the first place, but also why they are probable, given what we know about the human mind. For example, as we cover in Chapter 7 (Supernatural agents), supernatural agents such as ghosts, ancestors, and gods tend to be represented as special kinds of persons. On the one hand, we hold many of the same default expectations for supernatural agents that we also hold for ordinary people,

Figure 3.1 Just like Legos make different objects from the same pool of blocks; religious traditions have distinctive configurations with some overlap, and they are underpinned by the same suite of psychological propensities. (Image credit: HeinzTeh/Shutterstock.com).

such as the assumption that they can hear and communicate with us. On the other hand, supernatural agents also tend to violate a few other default expectations that we hold for ordinary people. For instance, they can move through walls.

To some extent, these culturally successful concepts enjoy transmissive success across and within cultures because they depend upon meeting and tweaking intuitive expectations about different categories of objects in the world. These categories are known as intuitive ontological categories,[21] such as persons, animals, and human-made objects[22] (for illustration, see Table 7.1 in Chapter 7: Supernatural Agents). In other words, they have more significant transmission potential than other concepts that do not meet and then minimally violate our intuitive expectations for agents. CSR scholars refer to the transmission potential of different concepts as content biases.

Another important consideration in identifying cognitive predispositions and biases is the effects that ideas and behaviors have on people. For example, ideas about supernatural agents exert important effects on those who hold such beliefs; they are often construed as providing prescriptions or guidelines for how humans should behave, typically with perceived negative consequences for those who do not comply. As we discuss in Chapter 10 (Rituals: Part 2), one especially cross-culturally recurrent form of compliance is the participation in cultural rituals. Ritual participation also serves essential functions, such as an

Figure 3.1 Continued

honest signal of a person's commitment to the group, and the belief that the gods are watching is a means of social surveillance. These ideas and behaviors enhance cooperative group living, particularly in large-scale societies.[23]

Key points

- The tendency for humans to engage in cognitive biases partly explains the spread of religious ideas.
- Similar biases may make up different features of religious traditions.
- The combination of biases is unique to each tradition.
- Each concept has the potential to become widespread. These are known as content biases.

3 What is the source of these cognitive tendencies?

A related question concerns the source of these cognitive tendencies; in other words, why do these aspects of human thought and behavior emerge so readily?

(a) Cognitive accounts

The early emergence of ideas is an indication of cognitive naturalness. That is to say, given minimal instruction, humans are predisposed to represent the world in specific ways. One indication that cognitive predispositions underpin ideas is similarities in how people tend to think about concepts, including religion. One important point to keep in mind is that predispositions exist even though cultural environments can modify ideas.[24]

For example, consider again the theory of language acquisition that we covered in Chapter 1. Chomsky noted that people can produce and understand an infinite number of novel sentences, more than they could ever have learned. Consequentially, he theorized that we are mentally equipped with an internal preparedness for language acquisition. Taking account of mental processes and internalized rules like grammar can explain the stability underlying the seemingly endless array of language. This cognitive account also assumes that different forms of language exist and are learned. Likewise, a cognitive account can explain the stability underlying the diversity of religious representations and behaviors by highlighting predispositions and biases as criteria of what makes certain features of religion natural. This cognitive account of religion also takes as a starting point the fact that different forms of religious ideas and practices exist and are acquired by cultural learning.

Key points

- CSR scholars acknowledge that content biases depend upon on how humans tend to think.
- A focus on content biases is mostly a cognitive account of religious ideas and behaviors.

(b) Cognitive-evolutionary accounts

In Chapter 1 (Introduction), we considered the influence of evolutionary approaches in the early formations of CSR. Today, an extension of the cognitive account in CSR draws upon the evolutionary sciences to explain *why* aspects of human thought and behavior emerge so readily. These cognitive-evolutionary accounts locate the source of these intuitions to evolved domain-specific systems. The systems themselves, which are a product of human evolution, are responsible for these early emerging biases.

Consider the example of praying to a deity again. Representations of the concept of God can be understood as an expression of a more general and intuitive bias in the domain of psychology: that of attributing human characteristics to non-human things and events (i.e. anthropomorphism[25]). This tendency may well have emerged as an adaptive response to increasingly complex primate social interaction in our ancestral past.[26] In other words, it was adaptive to be able to infer people's intentions and desires, and more broadly, make predictions about their future behavior. In modern society, it is adaptive to reason about the intentions and desires of our conspecifics. In religious contexts, this tendency has been merely extended to special kinds of agents.

Drawing on the evolutionary sciences and formulating testable hypotheses to explain religion demarks CSR from most other approaches to the study of religion. All evolutionary accounts attempt to get at the ultimate causality behind the origins and persistence of religious ideas. Research on the human mind helps to explain the proximate mechanisms (i.e. the event immediately responsible) for causing the recurrent features of religion. Evolutionary explanations also focus on the ultimate mechanisms, or causes, of the recurrent features of religion (i.e. a distal cause, often referred to as the ultimate cause). Put another way, ultimate explanations address evolutionary functions (the "why" question), and proximate explanations address how that functionality is achieved (the "how" question).

To illustrate, take a simple example of an event, why did the ship sink? (Figure 3.2) One proximate cause is that it had a hole, and water entered the ship, and it could not stay afloat (the "how" question). One ultimate cause is that the ship was on autopilot, which was inaccurate, and caused the ship to hit a rock (the "why question"). Likewise, evolutionary scientists use proximate and ultimate mechanisms to understand religious ideas and behaviors.

Consider another example from the cultural domain. Why do people participate in high-ordeal community rituals, such as walking barefoot through burning coal fires? One proximate explanation is that fear of social ostracism from the community motivates people to participate in the ritual. One ultimate explanation is that in our ancestral history, characterized by small groups of people dependent on each other for survival, social ostracism would have meant death to the individual, and lack of cooperation, the death of humans as a species. There were fitness benefits to conforming to displays of commitment to the group, for individuals and groups. So those who have survived (i.e. modern individuals) are strongly motivated to avoid social ostracism. Both proximate and ultimate explanations are valuable and complementary in explaining religious dispositions.

These two broad kinds of questions, proximate and ultimate, can be subdivided into two questions each (see Table 3.5). This subdivision was an attempt in 1963 by the ethnologist Niko Tinbergen to expand and clarify the distinction between proximate and ultimate questions to explain animal behavior. It is now known as "Tinbergen's four questions.[27]" These questions guide the research agendas of many cognitive-evolutionary scholars of religion. The first two

Figure 3.2 Why did the ship sink? Answering this question draws on both proximate causes (it had a hole in the deck) and distal causes (faulty autopilot steered the ship into a rock). (Image credit: Astarina/Shutterstock.com).

Table 3.4 Characteristics of cognitive-evolutionary accounts.

Type	*Characteristics*	*Often found in …*	*Source*
Proximate explanation.	Focus on the cause immediately responsible.	"How" questions	Cognitive
Ultimate explanation.	Focus on the ultimate cause.	"Why" questions	Evolutionary

questions (mechanism and ontogeny) are proximate (how) explanations That CSR scholars often employ. The second two questions (phylogeny and adaptive significance) require ultimate or evolutionary (why) kinds of explanations, and these are the kinds of questions that cognitive-evolutionary scholars also explore.

Seeking answers to all four of Tinbergen's questions expands explanations beyond mechanisms to also describe the development, evolutionary history, and adaptive significance of features of religious thought and behavior.

For example, one observation is that people in different cultures often reason about God as human-like. For instance, God is assumed to be constrained even though they may subscribe to a theological view of God as all-powerful and knowing. Why have anthropomorphic concepts of God emerged and proliferated in human culture when they are introduced to populations rather than other concepts of God? One account in CSR is outlined below and developed in Chapter 7 (Supernatural Agents):

- **Mechanism:** What is the structure of the tendency?

  Adults tend to reason about God as human-like when they are under cognitive load, or during time constraints. This finding indicates that it is less cognitively effortful to think of supernatural agents, like God, as similar to humans than to think that God is different. In other words, people have a natural tendency to anthropomorphize God.

- **Ontogeny:** How does the tendency develop in individuals?

  Young children also anthropomorphize God, which supports the claim that people have a natural tendency to anthropomorphize God.

- **Phylogeny:** What is its evolutionary history?

  People are constrained in their representations of supernatural agents by how they represent human agents generally.

- **Adaptive significance:** How have the variations influenced fitness?

  These anthropomorphic biases are part of a constellation of adaptations for detecting, reasoning, and making decisions about intentional agents, which would have aided predator evasion and prey capture throughout our evolutionary history. We also, however, can acquire concepts that were not targets of natural selection. We draw inferences about extra-ordinary agents from our concepts of agents in general. This tendency is a by-product that does not serve an adaptive function in the context of reasoning about extraordinary agents.

Cognitive-evolutionary scholars in CSR aim to provide answers to all four questions to explain religion. This includes accounting for why aspects of religious cognition and behavior make them likely to recur in similar forms across cultures, and how these predispositions interact with the environment to produce variations of similar forms. Hence, the subtitle of this book: Connecting evolution, brain, cognition, and culture.

In practice, cognitive scientists of religion often focus on one or several of the four questions based on their expertise and the question. For instance: (a) brain: neurocognitive and cognitive scientists tend to focus on uncovering the mechanism (what is the structure?); (b) cognition: developmental psychologists tend to track ontogeny (how does it develop in individuals?); those also versed in the evolutionary sciences (a, b, c), such as evolutionary biologists, anthropologists and psychologists, ask additional questions about the phylogeny (what is the

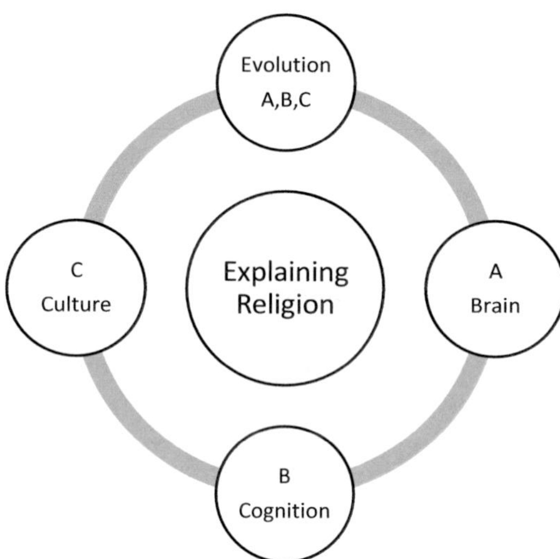

Figure 3.3 The goal of CSR is to explain religion by connecting four domains of knowledge. Note that evolutionary theory can be applied to the other levels of brain, cognition, and culture, which is why many scholars label evolutionary theory as unifying approaches within the subdiscipline.

evolutionary history?) and adaptive significance of traits (how have variations influenced fitness? how has culture shaped it?)

Given the growing number of interdisciplinary institutes dedicated to cognitive-evolutionary research on religion, it appears that the next generation of graduate students in training will come to inherit a wide range of methodologies and perspectives. Interdisciplinary research and methodological pluralism will continue to be important because together, researchers can provide answers to these four questions, explain and map religious predispositions, and their cultural expression. Not all questions have been given equal attention, and progress has been made for some aspects of religion on some questions and not others. There are also more disagreements on the answers to some questions. Eventually, it will be possible to provide a list of predispositions and data to inform answers to all four questions. To date, this endeavor is a work in progress.

Key points

- Evolutionary accounts attempt to get at the ultimate causality behind the origins and persistence of religious ideas.
- Evolutionary accounts focus on the ultimate mechanisms, or causes, of the recurrent features of religion (i.e. a distal cause, often referred to as the ultimate cause).
- Ultimate explanations address evolutionary functions (the "why" question).

- Adaptationist theories explain religion as adaptations that enhanced fitness.
- By-product theories explain religion as by-products of predispositions and biases.
- Four questions guide cognitive-evolutionary accounts. These are related to mechanism, ontogeny, phylogeny, and adaptive significance.

So far, in this section, we have discussed evolutionary accounts as ultimate explanations that address evolutionary functions (the "why" question). Considerations such as ontogeny, phylogeny, and adaptive significance of the trait provide explanations beyond mechanisms and are pursued by many cognitive scientists of religion. Cognitive scientists of religion sometimes disagree over the answers to Tinbergen's four questions for aspects of religious concepts and behaviors. They may also disagree on the level of selection of the trait, namely, whether this occurs at the genetic, individual, or group level as well as the historical origins and current function.

Answers about the historical origin and current function of a trait give rise to two main accounts of the precise role of evolution in the emergence and spread of religion in the cognitive-evolutionary sciences. One takes the form of adaptationist arguments, explaining at least some aspects of religious systems as biological and/or cultural adaptations that enhanced the fitness of individuals or groups. Some scholars argue that natural selection has favored the psychological propensity for religious practices and representations about the afterlife, intelligent design, and moral obligations because they provide benefits that increase the fitness of the individual or group. Some of these postulated benefits include encouraging socially advantageous attitudes and behaviors and promoting better physical health.[28] For example, religious commitment and ritual participation are associated with marked improvements in physical well-being, including less coronary artery disease, hypertension, stroke, immune system dysfunction, cancer, and overall mortality as well as mental health benefits.[29]

Another account proposes that standard features of religious systems are by-products (i.e. unintended consequences) of cognitive predispositions and biases, rather than biological and/or cultural adaptations that enhance fitness. These predispositions and biases give rise to standard features of religion. However, they are ultimately by-products of cognitive machinery that evolved for reasons that have nothing to do with religion. They evolved because of their success in other non-religious domains. For example, construing the tendency to represent invisibly but monitoring supernatural agents in the environment as an unintended consequence of the inclination of humans to perceive agency in the environment. This tendency is known as hyperactive agency detection device (HADD), or more recently, agency detection device (ADD).[30] This inclination may have evolved to help support the detection of predators and prey, but not ghosts or gods.

While the adaptationist and by-product perspectives contrast, they do not necessarily contradict one another, even when they refer to the same trait. This state of affairs is because the origins of a trait (Table 3.6) and the trait's function may well change over time. In other words, a trait's current use (function) does not necessarily explain its origin.

For instance, like biological traits, most adaptations start as by-products or spandrels (i.e. traits that are not especially adaptive but are retained because they are not harmful). They can be co-opted (i.e. have a use other than the one for which natural selection has built it) because of their benefits, and are then selected. For instance, the earliest feathers belonged to dinosaurs not capable of flight, so they must have evolved for something else, like attracting mates or keeping warm.[31] Later on, feathers became essential for modern birds' flight. Similarly, ritualization might emerge as a by-product, but if it helps reduce anxiety, it can be selected for. Another important consideration in evolutionary accounts of religion is the level of selection; in other words, the heritable variation underpinning differential fitness. In CSR, the levels are typically genetic, individual, and group.

Table 3.5 Tinbergen's four questions commonly expressed today.

#	*Object of explanation*	*Question*	*Kind of explanation*
1	Mechanism	What is the structure of the trait?	Proximate
2	Ontogeny	How does the trait develop in individuals?	Proximate
3	Phylogeny	What is the trait's evolutionary history?	Ultimate (evolutionary)
4	Adaptive significance	How have the trait variations influenced fitness?	Ultimate (evolutionary)

Table 3.6 Example of accounts of the origin and function of religion. Note that there are many combinations of possibilities related to the historical origins and current functions.

Type	*Historical origin*	*Current function*	*Example of theory*
Adaptation	Adaptations that enhanced the fitness of individuals or groups.	Enhance the fitness of individuals or groups.	Ritual participation enhances well-being.
By-product	Unintended consequences of an adaptation.	None, or neutral: do not enhance or detract from the fitness of individuals or groups.	Ability to infer the presence of intentional agents favors the spread of religious ideas about agents.

For example, consider ritual participation again. One adaptationist account, covered earlier in this section, proposed that religious commitment and ritual participation increase physical well-being and were selected for at the individual level because of the individual benefits. Another adaptationist account at the group level proposes that rituals are culturally successful because they enhanced the survival of the group. In small-scale and traditional societies, being part of a group was essential for survival, and yet group-living also brings the risk of free-riders, who are not committed but reap the benefits of group living. Rituals may serve as costly signals and credibility enhancing displays to convey one's commitment to the group and facilitate their acceptance as a reliable and collaborative group member. This explanation is at the group-level, because of the group benefits. Of course, aspects of ritual behavior may have both individual and group benefits. Likewise, some may be adaptive and others, by-products, so the explanatory picture of religion can become complicated.

While the by-product account came to influence early conceptualizations of CSR, today, scholars differ according to their endorsement of particular theories and research on the evolutionary origins of religious ideas and behaviors. This evolutionary approach includes fundamental questions such as whether, and to what extent, religion is a by-product of cognitive processes and practices that evolved for other purposes and because of their success in other non-religious domains.

So far, in this section, we have considered examples mainly where the mechanism of selection can be described as "natural selection"—that differential survival and reproduction of individuals is due to differences in heritable traits characteristic of a population over generations. It is important to note, however, that this is not the only possible mechanism of selection. For example, another is sexual selection, differences in reproductive rates, and cultural selection, differences in rates of cultural transmission of ideas and behaviors.

After natural selection, cultural selection is the second most popular school of evolutionary theorizing about religion in CSR. This model of cultural selection very much resembles natural selection. The key difference is that while natural selection concerns genetic inheritance, cultural selection deals with cultural inheritance not necessarily connected with human reproduction. For example, a behavior can be transmitted to others who are genetically unrelated.

Cultural evolution is faster than genetic evolution and thus influences it. For example, by age five, most children cannot break down the sugars in milk; they are lactose intolerant. Lactase persistence, which allows drinkers to access milk's nutrition, is very much under genetic control. Yet one culturally involved package that influenced the emergence of lactase persistence was the domestication of cattle around 10,000 years ago, which permitted people to extract nutrients from milk into adulthood. In short, culture influences genes. Proponents of cultural selection advocate for the role of culture beyond the genetic level to the individual and group level also. An example of cultural evolution as the mechanism of selection in religion (at the group-level) is the theory encountered earlier in this section, that ritual participation cultivates cooperation to benefit the group.

In sum, evolutionary theories deal with ultimate questions about the emergence and persistence of religious phenomena. Still, they sometimes differ in terms of the mechanism of selection proposed the level of selection and the origins and function of the mechanism (Table 3.7). The goal of this chapter is to enable students to identify the basic differences in evolutionary explanations for religion. A more thorough discussion of the intricacies and relationships between and within evolutionary accounts is beyond the scope of a general introduction to CSR. Still, students can refer to the citations of scholars cited in Table 3.7 for further reading on the topic.

Although there is an ongoing debate about the origin, function, and exact role of evolution in religious ideas and behaviors,[33] most scholars agree that understanding the evolutionary causality behind the origins of ideas and behaviors leads to a better explanation of religion overall.[34] Most cognitive scientists of religion assume that evolutionary sciences are, or should be, essential to a cognitive

Table 3.7 Mechanism of selection often featured in evolutionary explanations of religion.[32]

#	*Mechanism of selection*	*Explanation*	*Example*	*Example of scholars who endorse view*
1	Natural	*Adaptation:* Some features of religions are straightforward adaptations for individuals resulting from the process of natural selection.	Religious commitment and participation increase adherent's fitness benefits, such as physical well-being.	a) Bulbulia. b) Sosis.
		By-product: Some features of religions are by-products of cognitive predispositions and biases.		a) Boyer. b) Lawson & McCauley.
2	Sexual	Religions aid humans in the successful propagation of their genes.	Religiosity serves as a cultural signal about values such as fidelity. Religion enables individuals to appeal more to members of the opposite sex and ensure a good pool of prospective mates.	a) Slone and Van Slyke. b) Weeden, Cohen and Kendrick.
3	Cultural	Cultural selection impacts the differential transmission of cultural ideas and practices	Religion cultivates cooperation among members to benefit the individuals and group overall.	a) Henrich. b) Norenzayan.

explanation of religious phenomena. Some[35] have argued the case that the evolutionary sciences are distinct and complementary, often referring to "cognitive and evolutionary approaches to the study of religion" to capture both.[36]

Key points

- Many CSR scholars acknowledge that to explain religion, we also need to take account of the ultimate mechanisms shaping ideas and behaviors.
- These scholars propose that evolutionary processes explain how humans tend to think.
- These are cognitive-evolutionary accounts of religious ideas and behaviors.
- Scholars in CSR differ on the origin, function, and exact role of evolution in religious ideas and behavior.

4 How does culture interact with cognition to produce religion?

As we covered in Chapter 1 (Introduction), early pioneers in CSR argued that the study of religion was skewed in favor of personal and interpretative accounts of religion over systematic and explanatory theories. Their endeavors aimed to redress this balance by including explanatory accounts. As McCauley points out, the aim of CSR was never to dismiss the insights provided by interpretative accounts, but rather, to enrich them by including explanations of religion.[37] This endeavor includes specifying how cognitive predispositions interact with the environment, which often entails an understanding of sociocultural particulars. The historical and culturally situated character of religion is, correspondingly, emphasized, even by early works in the area, such as those by anthropologists Harvey Whitehouse (1995)[38] and Stewart Guthrie (1993).[39] As Trigg and Barrett put it, the cognitive science of religion "draws upon the cognitive sciences to explain how pan-cultural features of human minds, interacting with their natural and social environments, inform and constrain religious thought and action.[40]"

Key points

- CSR aimed to explain religion by taking account of how cognition interacts with culture.
- Some scholars in CSR, especially anthropologists, have dedicated much of their research to understanding religious ideas and behaviors in particular contexts.

(a) Content and context biases

To answer questions about the interaction between cognition and culture, researchers build on their knowledge of cognitive biases (which give rise to content biases) by evoking the cultural environments that give rise to recurrent ideas and practices. As we cover in Chapter 10 (Rituals: Part 2), evolutionary anthropologist Joseph Henrich and colleagues have proposed that content biases are necessary to explain the stability and change of religious ideas and behaviors over time and across cultures. However, they are not sufficient.[41] Henrich proposed the need to evoke context biases to explain such things.[42] Context biases are not related to the content of specific ideas but rather, to the context in which they are transmitted, such as the perceived reliability of the person transmitting the information and the sociocultural context within which they occur.

Consider the following examples from Chapter 7 (Supernatural Agents). First, think about popular agents in western culture, such as the Tooth Fairy or Santa Claus. These agents are depicted as having similar properties of gods, yet they are not believed in as gods, nor do they evoke the same level of commitment that they would if they were represented as gods. After all, no wars have been fought over whether the Tooth Fairy is real. Second, consider other agents such as Zeus, who contains all the features of a successful god but is no longer believed to be a god.[43] Why do children tend to endorse the beliefs of their parents? Why does belief change over time? Moreover, why do people not believe in other people's gods if they all employ content biases that enjoy transmissive success?

To answer these questions, Henrich and colleagues urge us to consider various contextual factors, including context biases. These factors include understanding the history of ideas that have been labeled religious, including an understanding of how ideas originated and the cultural context within which they spread and changed over time. For instance, philosopher Helen De Cruz and colleagues have outlined the relationship between theological ideas and intuitions (i.e. natural theology) and the historical development and transmission of theological concepts over time.[44] Another series of contextual considerations include questions of how intergroup conflict exacerbates or emphasizes differences within religious traditions. For example, Theologian Hugh Nicholson provides an account of the emergence of the Buddhist doctrine of no-self and the Christian doctrine of the Trinity that takes into consideration both cognitive biases and intergroup conflict at critical points during the emergence of these doctrines.[45]

A great deal of human knowledge comes through cultural learning. Some concepts are more readily endorsed than others because the source of information influences us. For example, people are more likely to endorse ideas about God from a prestigious individual with traditional authority, such as the Catholic Pope, than those without authority, such as a stranger during Mass. Likewise, as we cover in Chapter 10 (Rituals: Part 2), the convictions of individuals who engage in credibility enhancing displays (i.e. literally walk the walk) are more likely to be believed, in so far as their behavior is connected to authentically living out professed religious beliefs. Accounting for context-dependent factors enhances the explanatory power of CSR over and above content biases alone. As we cover in Chapter 11 (Conclusion), recent developments in CSR include an appreciation that human cognition is a result of dual inheritance from interacting genetic and cultural streams of evolution, which broadens the scope of traditional evolutionary accounts.[46]

Cognitive scientists of religion have attempted to understand how these biases manifest themselves in particular sociocultural contexts, thus endorsing context biases and other features of the environment at the time of their research. This understanding is achieved by drawing on their specialist knowledge and often spending extended periods in the field conducting ethnographic research.[47]

Key points

- Content biases refer to biases that direct our attention to the content of representations.
- Context biases are related to the context in which ideas are transmitted, such as the reliability of the source.
- Scholars have proposed that content biases are necessary, but not sufficient, to explain the popularity of some religious ideas and behaviors.
- Scholars propose that context biases, such as the perceived reliability of the person transmitting the information and the sociocultural context within which they occur, enhance the explanatory power of CSR.

Summary of standard research questions

1 Why do some ideas and behaviors persist?

Of all the possible types of religious ideas and behaviors that could be possible, we find some that recur. First, scholars identify what these popular ideas and behaviors are, and then they ask what makes these ideas and behaviors especially common?

2 What kind of mind does it take to represent these ideas?

One reason why these ideas and behaviors are especially prevalent within and across cultures is that they relate to how humans tend to think. They may also have important individual and societal effects, which makes them more likely to be remembered and passed on.

3 What is the source of these biases?

One way of identifying how humans tend to think is by looking at early emerging biases in children and adults in different cultures, and to examine our evolutionary history for possible origins and adaptive functions of these biases and behaviors.

4 How does culture interact with cognition to produce religion?

These ideas and behaviors are especially prevalent within and across cultures because they fit well with the environment. Other ideas seem very different in different contexts or may change depending on the sociocultural conditions. Understanding how culture interacts with cognition provides a more fruitful explanation of religion.

Overview summary of basic assumptions in CSR as outlined in this chapter

1 Religion is cognitively natural

Cognitive biases that underpin religious ideas and actions emerge early among children with minimal instruction. Religious ideas are part and parcel of our normally developing cognition and rapidly spread when introduced in social environments.

2 Religion is not unique

Some religious systems are distinctive, but all contain fundamental psychological biases.

The cognitive biases that underpin religious ideas and actions readily appear in other domains.

3 Religion can be explained scientifically

Religion is not a singular, naturally occurring phenomenon. It can be fractionated into cross-culturally recurrent forms of ideas and practices to explain why certain forms of these ideas and behaviors emerge and persist. Theories about religion can be tested using scientific methods such as formulating falsifiable hypotheses and performing statistical analyses.

4 Religion can be explained through a better understanding of cognition and culture

To explain how and why specific ideas emerge and are recurrent within and across cultures entails taking account of cognitive biases and how they are manifested and shaped by different cultural contexts.

Chapter summary

According to CSR, to successfully explain religion involves two things: the first draws on what is known in the cognitive and evolutionary sciences about panhuman cognition; that is, how humans attend to, process, and remember information, to explain why these patterns persist (content biases). The second draws on a specialist understanding of particular sociocultural environments in which these ideas and behaviors operate, to explain how these predisposed patterns of thinking and behaving manifest themselves in particular contexts (context biases and other sociocultural conditions[48]). This perspective demarks CSR from disciplines such as the sociology of religion, which tends to focus more on how social dynamics shape religious ideas and behaviors rather than specifying the interaction between the environment and cognitive mechanisms to account for such variation.

Discussion questions

1 What is CSR? Draft a response using your own words and compare it to your answer from Chapter 1.
2 Based on Chapters 1–3, outline the distinguishing features of CSR.
3 Based on Chapters 1–3, what do you think are the strengths and weaknesses of CSR?

Selected further reading

Articles

1 Barrett, J. L. "Cognitive science of religion: What is it, and why is it?" *Religion Compass* 1, No. 6 (2007): 768–786.
2 Boyer, Pascal. "Religious thought and behaviour as by-products of brain function." *Trends in Cognitive Sciences* 7, no. 3 (2003): 119–124.

Books

1 Evans, Dylan, and Oscar Zarate. *Introducing evolutionary psychology: A graphic guide*. Icon Books Ltd, 2015.
2 McCauley, Robert N. *Philosophical foundations of the cognitive science of religion: A head start*. Bloomsbury Publishing, 2017.
3 Whitehouse, Harvey, and James Laidlaw, eds. *Religion, anthropology, and cognitive science*. Durham, NC: Carolina Academic Press, 2007.

Notes

1 Sperber, Dan. *Explaining culture: A naturalistic approach*. Cambridge, MA: Cambridge, 1996.

2 McKay, Ryan, and Harvey Whitehouse. "Religion and morality." *Psychological Bulletin* 141, no. 2 (2015): 447.
3 Nicholson, Hugh. *The spirit of contradiction in Christianity and Buddhism*. Oxford: Oxford University Press, 2016.
4 Barrett, Justin L. and Frank C. Keil. "Conceptualizing a nonnatural entity: Anthropomorphism in God concepts." *Cognitive Psychology* 31, no. 3 (1996): 219–247.
5 Slone, Jason. *Theological incorrectness: Why religious people believe what they shouldn't*. Oxford: Oxford University Press, 2007.
6 Slone, Jason. *Theological incorrectness: Why religious people believe what they shouldn't*. Oxford, Oxford University Press, 2007.
7 Shtulman, Andrew. "Variation in the anthropomorphization of supernatural beings and its implications for cognitive theories of religion." *Journal of Experimental Psychology: Learning, Memory, and Cognition* 34, no. 5 (2008): 1123.
8 Exline, Julie Juola, and Alyce Martin. "Anger toward God: A new frontier in forgiveness research." In *Handbook of Forgiveness*, Routledge, 2007, 97–112.
9 White, Claire, Maya Marin, and Daniel M.T. Fessler. "Not just dead meat: An evolutionary account of corpse treatment in mortuary rituals." *Journal of Cognition and Culture* 17, no. 1–2 (2017): 146–168; Emmons, Natalie A., and Deborah A. Kelemen. "Young children's acceptance of within-species variation: Implications for essentialism and teaching evolution." *Journal of Experimental Child Psychology* 139 (2015): 148–160; Cohen, Emma, Emily Burdett, Nicola Knight, and Justin Barrett. "Cross-cultural similarities and differences in person-body reasoning: Experimental evidence from the United Kingdom and Brazilian Amazon." *Cognitive Science* 35, no. 7 (2011): 1282–1304; Astuti, Rita, and Paul L. Harris. "Understanding mortality and the life of the ancestors in rural Madagascar." *Cognitive Science* 32, no. 4 (2008): 713–740; Malley, Brian. *How the Bible works: An anthropological study of evangelical biblicism*. Rowman Altamira, 2004; Whitehouse, Harvey. *Inside the cult: Religious innovation and transmission in Papua New Guinea*. Oxford University Press on Demand, 1995.
10 Kelemen, Deborah. "Are children 'intuitive theists'? Reasoning about purpose and design in nature." *Psychological Science* 15, no. 5 (2004): 295–301.
11 Chudek, Maciej, Rita McNamara, Susan Burch, Paul Bloom, and Joseph Henrich. "Developmental and cross-cultural evidence for intuitive dualism." *Psychological Science* 20 (2013).
12 Barrett, Justin L. *Why would anyone believe in God?* United Nations Publications, 2004; Guthrie, Stewart, Joseph Agassi, Karin R. Andriolo, David Buchdahl, H. Byron Earhart, Moshe Greenberg, Ian Jarvie et al. "A cognitive theory of religion [and comments and reply]." *Current Anthropology* 21, no. 2 (1980): 181–203.
13 Baumard, Nicolas, and Pascal Boyer. "Explaining moral religions." *Trends in Cognitive Sciences* 17, no. 6 (2013): 272–280.
14 Swann Jr, William B., Michael D. Buhrmester, Angel Gomez, Jolanda Jetten, Brock Bastian, Alexandra Vazquez, Amarina Ariyanto et al. "What makes a group worth dying for? Identity fusion fosters perception of familial ties, promoting self-sacrifice." *Journal of Personality and Social Psychology* 106, no. 6 (2014): 912; Atran, Scott. *Talking to the enemy: Violent extremism, sacred values, and what it means to be human*. Penguin UK, 2010; Hamilton, William D. "The genetical evolution of social behaviour. II." *Journal of Theoretical Biology* 7, no. 1 (1964): 17–52.
15 Norenzayan, Ara, Will M. Gervais, and Kali H. Trzesniewski. "Mentalizing deficits constrain belief in a personal God." *PloS One* 7, no. 5 (2012); Johnson, Dominic, and Jesse Bering. "Hand of God, mind of man: Punishment and cognition in the evolution of cooperation." *Evolutionary Psychology* 4, no. 1 (2006).
16 McCauley, Robert N. *Why religion is natural and science is not*. Oxford University Press, 2011.

17 Baron-Cohen, Simon. *Mindblindness: An essay on autism and theory of mind*. MIT Press, 1997.
18 Liénard, Pierre, and E. Thomas Lawson. "Evoked culture, ritualization and religious rituals." *Religion* 38, no. 2 (2008): 158, 157–171.
19 McCauley, Robert N. *Why religion is natural and science is not*. Oxford University Press, 2011; Barrett, Justin L. "Exploring the natural foundations of religion." *Trends in Cognitive Sciences* 4, no. 1 (2000): 29–34.
20 Idinopulos, Thomas A., and Edward A. Yonan, eds. *Religion and eductionism: Essays on Eliade, Segal, and the challenge of the social sciences for the study of religion*. Vol. 62. Brill, 1994.
21 Boyer, Pascal, and H. Clark Barrett. "Domain specificity and intuitive ontology." In *The handbook of evolutionary psychology* 2005, 96–118.
22 De Cruz, Helen. "Religious concepts as structured imagination." *International Journal for the Psychology of Religion* 23, no. 1 (2013): 63–74; Nyhof, Melanie, and Justin Barrett. "Spreading non-natural concepts: The role of intuitive conceptual structures in memory and transmission of cultural materials." *Journal of Cognition and Culture* 1, no. 1 (2001): 69–100; Boyer, Pascal. *The naturalness of religious ideas: A cognitive theory of religion*. University of California Press, 1994; Ward, Thomas B. "Structured imagination: The role of category structure in exemplar generation." *Cognitive Psychology* 27, no. 1 (1994): 1–40.
23 Norenzayan, Ara, Azim F. Shariff, Will M. Gervais, Aiyana K. Willard, Rita A. McNamara, Edward Slingerland, and Joseph Henrich. "The cultural evolution of prosocial religions." *Behavioral and Brain Sciences* 39 (2016); Sosis, Richard, and Eric R. Bressler. "Cooperation and commune longevity: A test of the costly signaling theory of religion." *Cross-cultural Research* 37, no. 2 (2003): 211–239.
24 McCauley, Robert N. *Why religion is natural and science is not*. Oxford University Press, 2011.
25 Stewart, Guthrie. *Faces in the clouds: A new theory of religion*. New York: Oxford University Press, 1993.
26 Brüne, Martin, and Ute Brüne-Cohrs. "Theory of mind—evolution, ontogeny, brain mechanisms and psychopathology." *Neuroscience & Biobehavioral Reviews* 30, no. 4 (2006): 437–455.
27 Tinbergen, Niko. "On aims and methods of ethology." *Zeitschrift für tierpsychologie* 20, no. 4 (1963): 410–433.
28 E.g. Bering, Jesse M. "The folk psychology of souls." *Behavioral and Brain Sciences* 29, no. 5 (2006): 453–462; Bulbulia, Joseph. "Nature's medicine: religiosity as an adaptation for health and cooperation." *Where God and science meet* 1 (2006): 87–121.
29 Koenig, Harold G., Michael E. McCullough, and David B. Larson. "Religion and health." New York: Oxford University Press 1 (2001): 276–291.
30 Barrett, J. *Why would anyone believe in God? (Cognitive Science of Religion)*. Walnut Creek, CA: Altamira, 2004.
31 Retrieved 4th June, 2020, from: https://www.livescience.com/25948-dinosaurs-feathered-tails-shake.html.
32 Adapted from Figure 2: Robert N. McCauley, "Recent trends in the cognitive science of religion: Neuroscience, religious experience, and the confluence of cognitive and evolutionary research"; Connor Wood, "Antistructure and the roots of religious experience …" *Zygon®* 55, no. 1 (2020): 97–124.
33 Bering, Jesse M. "The folk psychology of souls." *Behavioral and Brain Sciences* 29, no. 5 (2006): 453–462; Bloom, P. (2009). "Religious belief as an evolutionary accident." In *The believing primate: Scientific, philosophical, and theological reflections on the origin of religion*, 118–127; Bulbulia, Joseph, Richard Sosis, Erica Harris, R. Genet, Cheryl Genet, and Karen Wyman. *The Evolution of Religion Studies, Theories, & Critiques*. 2008; Henrich, Joseph, and Richard McElreath. "The evolution of cultural evolution." *Evolutionary Anthropology: Issues, News, and Reviews: Issues, News, and Reviews* 12, no. 3 (2003): 123–135; Richerson, Peter J., and Robert Boyd. *Not*

by genes alone: How culture transformed human evolution. University of Chicago Press, 2008; Sosis, Richard. "The adaptationist-byproduct debate on the evolution of religion: Five misunderstandings of the adaptationist program." *Journal of Cognition and Culture* 9, no. 3–4 (2009): 315–332; Wilson, David. *Darwin's cathedral: Evolution, religion, and the nature of society*. University of Chicago Press, 2010.

34 Bloom, Paul. "Religious belief as an evolutionary accident." In *The believing primate: Scientific, philosophical, and theological reflections on the origin of religion* (2009): 118–127; Sosis, Richard. "The adaptationist-byproduct debate on the evolution of religion: Five misunderstandings of the adaptationist program." *Journal of Cognition and Culture* 9, no. 3–4 (2009); Bulbulia, Joseph, Richard Sosis, Erica Harris, R. Genet, Cheryl Genet, and Karen Wyman. *The Evolution of Religion Studies, Theories, & Critiques*. 2008; Henrich, Joseph, and Richard McElreath. "The evolution of cultural evolution." *Evolutionary Anthropology: Issues, News, and Reviews* 12, no. 3 (2003): 123–135.

35 Barrett, Justin L. "Cognitive science of religion: Looking back, looking forward." *Journal for the Scientific Study of Religion* 50, no. 2 (2011): 229–239.

36 Barrett, Justin L., and Roger Trigg. *The roots of religion: Exploring the cognitive science of religion (Ashgate Science and Religion Series)*. Ashgate Publishing Group, 2014; Watts, Fraser, and Léon P. Turner, eds. *Evolution, religion, and cognitive science: Critical and constructive essays*. Oxford: Oxford University Press, 2014.

37 McCauley, Robert N. *Philosophical foundations of the cognitive science of religion: A head start*. Bloomsbury Publishing, 2017.

38 Whitehouse, H. *Inside the cult: Religious innovation and transmission in Papua New Guinea*. Oxford University Press on Demand, 1995.

39 Stewart, Guthrie. *Faces in the clouds: A new theory of religion*. New York: Oxford University Press, 1993.

40 Barrett, Justin L., and Roger Trigg. *The roots of religion: Exploring the cognitive science of religion (Ashgate Science and Religion Series)*. Ashgate Publishing Group, 2014: 4.

41 Peter J. Richerson and Robert Boyd, *Not by genes alone: How culture transformed human evolution*, 1st edn. University of Chicago Press, 2006; Henrich, Joseph. "The evolution of costly displays, cooperation, and religion." *Evolution and Human Behavior* 30, no. 4 (2009): 244–260.

42 Gervais, Will M., and Joseph Henrich. "The Zeus problem: Why representational content biases cannot explain faith in gods." *Journal of Cognition and Culture* 10, no. 3–4 (2010): 383–389.

43 Gervais, Will M., and Joseph Henrich. "The Zeus problem: Why representational content biases cannot explain faith in gods." *Journal of Cognition and Culture* 10, no. 3–4 (2010): 383–389.

44 De Cruz, Helen, and Johan De Smedt. *A natural history of natural theology: The cognitive science of theology and philosophy of religion*. MIT Press, 2014.

45 Nicholson, Hugh. *The spirit of contradiction in Christianity and Buddhism*. Oxford University Press, 2016.

46 Henrich, Joseph, and Richard McElreath. "The evolution of cultural evolution." *Evolutionary Anthropology: Issues, News, and Reviews* 12, no. 3 (2003): 123–135.

47 Cohen, Emma. *The mind possessed: The cognition of spirit possession in an Afro-Brazilian religious tradition*. Oxford University Press, 2007; Whitehouse, Harvey. *Inside the cult: Religious innovation and transmission in Papua New Guinea*. Oxford University Press on Demand, 1995; Whitehouse, Harvey, and Luther H. Martin, eds. *Theorizing religions past: Archaeology, history, and cognition*. Rowman Altamira, 2004; Xygalatas, Dimitris. *The burning saints: Cognition and culture in the fire-walking rituals of the Anastenaria*. Routledge, 2014.

48 Gervais, Will M., and Joseph Henrich. "The Zeus problem: Why representational content biases cannot explain faith in gods." *Journal of Cognition and Culture* 10, no. 3–4 (2010): 383–389; Henrich, Joseph, and Richard McElreath. "The evolution of cultural evolution." *Evolutionary Anthropology: Issues, News, and Reviews* 12, no. 3 (2003): 123–135.

4 Methods

The cognitive science of religion (CSR) is characterized by the diversity and flexibility in methods employed. There are, however, core assumptions that bind the seemingly endless varieties of research methodologies in CSR together. These include the conviction that (a) religion can be studied using scientific methods and commitments to (b) methodological naturalism and (c) methodological pluralism. We consider these assumptions in more detail below.

Methodological assumptions

1 Religion can be studied using scientific methods

As we discussed in previous chapters, one conviction of early cognitive scientists of religion was that religious ideas and behaviors, like other kinds of human phenomena, can be studied scientifically. Cognitive scientists of religion formulate theories about religious ideas and behaviors and make predictions about the past, present, and future state of affairs. What makes these theories scientific is that they are (or can be) tested using formal methods of the sciences. CSR scholars often generate testable predictions (i.e. hypotheses) using formalized methods, such as statistical analyses, which is the interpretation of numerical facts and data using mathematical theories of probability. These predictions about religion are subject to verification or revision based on the principles of testability and goodness-of-fit of existing data.

For instance, many CSR scholars invite critique from an array of specialists in multiple disciplines on topics such as ritual behavior[1] or ideas about the afterlife.[2] In some cases, entire research agendas have been shaped and modified based on collaboration, testing, and feedback. For instance, anthropologist Harvey Whitehouse teamed with experimental psychologists to formulate his theory of Modes of Religiosity (MoR) in ways that could be empirically tested against competing alternatives.[3] He also sought out historians of religion to apply his theory to prehistorical, Graeco-Roman, and Christian religions to test the model,[4] and modified his theory in light of evidence.[5]

Key points

- CSR is a scientific approach to religion.
- Scholars formulate theories about religious ideas and behaviors and make predictions about the past, present, or future state of affairs.
- These theories are tested using formal methods of the sciences, such as the generation of testable predictions using formalized methods, including statistical analyses.
- CSR has enriched our understanding of many aspects of religion.

2 Methodological naturalism

Previously, we considered the assumption (1) that "religion can be explained using scientific methods." It would be more accurate to state that CSR scholars hold the opinion that "*some aspects* of religion can be studied using scientific methods." This is because CSR researchers are bound together by a commitment to methodological naturalism, the basic idea that only the "human side" of religious ideas and experiences can be studied in naturalistic terms. This boundary has implications for what cognitive scientists of religion study.

Cognitive scientists of religion are interested in understanding how and why humans respond to ideas that are deemed religious, rather than to decipher whether or not those ideas are true or false (i.e. ontological status). Scholars in CSR tend to see questions about whether or not religious concepts such as God exist as outside the scope of scientific research both methodologically (how would we test it?) and theoretically (why would we test it?). Thus, religious concepts such as "transcendence" and "holy" are significant to the extent that they can be operationalized and studied empirically.

Neuroscientists, in particular, are often asked about the implications of their work on religion. For example, neuropsychologist Uffe Schjoedt and his research team found that informal types of prayers directed to the Christian God activate primary areas of social cognition in the brain. In his work, Schjoedt is explicit that his research aim is to describe the basic neural processing employed by participants in religious practices.[6] Regardless, he often has to clarify in interviews that these findings say nothing about the reality of God or religion, only the corresponding areas of the brain that are activated in this specific type of practice.[7] We return to these issues in more detail in the conclusion of this book (Chapter 11).

Key points

- CSR scholars espouse a commitment to methodological naturalism, which is the basic idea that only the "human side" of religious ideas and experiences can be studied in naturalistic terms.

3 Methodological pluralism

If religion is not a singular entity, then it follows that no one method will provide ample insight. CSR scholars thus adopt a range of methods to answer research questions (i.e. methodological pluralism). Examples of the kinds of research methods CSR scholars use to answer research questions are provided in Table 4.1. These examples are illustrative, not exhaustive.

Participation 1: Identifying research

1 Working in pairs, obtain one of the original research articles from the following research topics in Table 4.1 using your resources, such as a the college library, Google Scholar, or Academia (the references are in endnotes).

Answer the remaining questions with your partner.

1 Summarize some of the research questions about this topic based on the introduction (or start) of the chapter, using your own words. For example, do people in different cultures believe in reincarnation? Why are these ideas about how to identify someone who has died similar?
2 Outline the methods that the author used to investigate these questions (e.g. large historical databases, cross-cultural experiments).
3 In your own words, summarize the author's conclusions.

Key points

- CSR scholars adopt multiple methods, to address questions in the study of religion.

4 Interdisciplinarity integration in CSR

The assumption that the human side of religion can be studied scientifically creates a boundary around the type of research that CSR scholars conduct. Within this scientific and naturalistic framework, research in the evolutionary and cognitive sciences is diverse and is characterized by the integration of disciplines and methods. By contrast, research in most academic institutions tends to be compartmentalized, and scholars tend to stay within their own perspectives. For example, sociologists talk largely about the global, cultural anthropologists focus on describing diversity, and cognitive psychologists are more interested in human universals than particulars.

Table 4.1 Examples of research questions and methodologies employed in CSR.

#	*Question*	*Methods*	*Summary*	*Findings*
1	What is cognition?	Philosophy of science analysis, ethnographic data and experimental evidence.	There is disagreement between earlier and later generations of cognitive scientists.	CSR scholars disagree on what cognition is. Some claim that it is primarily formal-logistic mental representations while others expand it to include emotions, embodiment, contexts, and culture.[8]
2	Which cognitive biases help explain religious belief, paranormal belief, and belief in life's purpose?	Statistical modeling.	A path model testing the various relationships between cognitive biases and different types of supernatural belief.	Extensions of theory of mind (anthropomorphism, mind body dualism, and teleology) mediate the impact of theory of mind on a variety of supernatural beliefs. Anthropomorphism predicts increased paranormal belief but not belief in God. Anthropomorphic tendencies are also negatively impacted by living in a religious area, but belief in God is increased.[9]
3	How do people represent spirit possession?	Ethnography. Participant-observation and interviews.	18 months of participant-observation and interviews in an Afro-Brazilian religious tradition in northern Brazil.	Intuitive ideas about bodies and minds facilitate the spread and appeal of popular ideas about spirit possession.[10]
4	How do people integrate natural and supernatural explanations for the same events?	Experiments, studies, ethnography.	Experiments with individuals and groups in multiple settings, vignette studies, surveys, focus group discussion, key informant interviews, ethnography.	People reconcile natural and supernatural explanations by using them to understand multiple levels of causality. Natural explanations are often used to explain how something happened; supernatural explanations are often used to explain why something happened.[11]

5	Why do shamans observe costly taboos?	Field experiments. Present participants with stories about shamans who do and do not self-deny and measure their inferences.	Mentawai (Siberut Island, Indonesia) participants were presented stories about shamans to measure their inferences.	Mentawai people infer that self-denying shamans are more cooperative, supernaturally powerful, and sincere in their belief.[12]
6	Why do gods care about the things we do?	Surveys in naturalistic contexts. Free-list data, a variety of metric scaling techniques, cross-cultural comparisons.	Surveys and interviews with American Christian students and Buddhist-animist Tyvans from southern Siberia.	Cross-culturally, gods care about and punish a relatively narrow set of concerns. When directly asked, however, locally salient deities appear to care about and punish moral transgressions.[13]
7	How does the human cognitive system process ritualized actions?	Experimental studies. Participants watched videos of various functional and non-functional (ritual) action sequences and pressed a response button for each segment they could identify.	Two different experiments were conducted on Danish undergraduates to study how participants divide up and represent actions when observing functional and non-functional (ritual) behavior.	People process ritual behaviors in a way that heightens cognitive load and hampers memory encoding. Thus, stimulating expectations (predictive processing).[14]
8	Why do people subject themselves to painful religious rituals and what effects do they have?	Experiments in the lab and the field using physiological measures (heartbeat, blood pressure, impedance cardiography and respiration), videos of facial expressions, painful electrical stimulation, pre-scan tests and post-scan interviews and economic games.	Various experiments were conducted on Danish, Spanish and Mauritian participants to determine the psychological and sociocultural functions of painful religious rituals.	Painful and extreme religious rituals promote prosociality, not only in participants undergoing the ritual but also among observers of high-ordeal participants. Painful rituals can cause analgesic states and dissociative symptoms, which are sometimes experienced as divine presence. They also affect memory by cognitive depletion. Prayer seems to modulate the expectations, intensity and unpleasantness of pain.[15]

(*Continued*)

Table 4.1 (Cont.)

#	*Question*	*Methods*	*Summary*	*Findings*
9	How do the special features of ritual influence memory formation?	Field experiments.	Field experiments involving online measurement of excitement, video-recording and post hoc recollection by participants.	Participants' memory encoding of highly exciting ritual action is impeded, which facilitates post hoc social (re-) construction of events as well as potential meaning.[16]
10	Does participation in extreme religious rituals send costly signals?	Ethnographic fieldwork and experiments in the field, economic games, interviews, and statistical analyses of historical documents.	Various experiments performed in various parts of the world to determine the costly signal hypothesis.	Basically, they do. However, field studies indicate that extreme ritual behavior is not enough, whereas together with regular temple or church attendance it is more effective.[17]
11	How do emotionally intense "imagistic" rituals bond groups?	Mathematical models, online experiments.	Mathematical models generated predictions that a team of psychologists then tested in collaboration with experts on highly fused groups (e.g. military, extreme sports, twins) and via online experiments.	Sharing personally transformative (memorable, meaningful, and self-defining) experiences with other group members produce identity fusion (a visceral sense of oneness motivating strong forms of pro-group action).[18]
12	What are the functions of ritual?	Developmental and cross-cultural research.	Experiments with individuals and groups in multiple settings, vignette studies, surveys, focus group discussion, key informant interviews, ethnography.	Rituals serve a variety of functions; practical (e.g. solving problems), psychological (e.g. reducing anxiety), and social (e.g. cooperation, initiation).[19]

13	What are the neural correlates of religious experiences?	Neuroscience. Pre-scan psychological tests, functional magnetic resonance imaging (fMRI) using various experimental conditions, followed by post-scan interviews.	Three different experiments were conducted on Danish participants from various denominations (mostly Inner Mission Lutherans and Pentecostals) and a secular control group (mostly BA students in the humanities).	There are no specific neural mechanisms dedicated to religious experiences. Even simple phenomena such as prayer draw on various areas and mechanisms in the brain and are influenced by individual expectations (predictive processing).[20]
14	How do assumptions about speakers' charismatic abilities change how information is processed?	Neuroscience, questionnaires.	Functional magnetic resonance imaging (fMRI) in response to speakers who Christian participants believed had healing abilities.	Participants' recognition of charismatic authority enhances their susceptibility to charismatic influence by down regulating their executive system.[21]
15	Can religious experiences (sensed presence, healing, miracles) and paranormal beliefs be induced experimentally?	Card games, interviews, hypnosis, sensory deprivation, Virtual Reality, eye tracking and fMRI.	A variety of experiments with and observations of Dutch and Danish participants.	Tests indicate that the use of suggestion can induce religious and paranormal experiences. When manipulating with the senses, predictive processes take over in the brain and meet the cultural and individual expectations of the participants.[22]
16	Must young children think of God the same as a human being?	Developmental cross-cultural research: knowledge-ignorance Theory of Mind (ToM) task.	Three- to six-year-old children in four different countries (the UK, Israel, Dominican Republic, and Kenya) participated in a version of the classic "false-belief" task.	Though preschoolers may mistake God for a human being, they do not have to. Children in four different cultures distinguished between God's knowledge and their mother's even before they had a stable understanding of what their mom knows and does not know.[23]

(*Continued*)

Table 4.1 (Cont.)

#	*Question*	*Methods*	*Summary*	*Findings*
17	Do people more easily remember minimally counterintuitive ideas (MCI)?	Recall and memory experiments using 15 coded types of MCI.	A variety of recall and memory experiments have been conducted on Western and non-Western participants.	The results are mixed. Results contradict each other, and cognitive architecture is often more complex than assumed.[24]
18	Do people have a hypersensitive agency detection device (HADD)?	Biological motion perception tasks, point-light displays, ethnographic evidence, threat-inducing experiments and Virtual Reality experiments.	Experiments to test whether American, Dutch and Danish participants show illusory agency detection.	Studies show that people do occasionally detect agents in ambiguous situations, but threatening situations do not intensify agent detection. Thus, the term "hypersensitive" is unwarranted.[25]
19	Why do people look for physical marks and behaviors that imply continued memory?	Cross-cultural experiments using imaginative perspective-taking tasks.	Series of experiments with participants in the UK and India. The distinctiveness of physical marks and memories were manipulated.	People regard physical marks and behaviors that imply a memory from a past life as strong evidence that a person has been reborn, but for different reasons. They also implicitly assume the body continues, even though they say it changes.[26]
20	What is the cultural evolutionary history of modes of religiosity?	Ethnographic, historical, and archaeological data.	Quantitative analysis of data from regional and global samples of ethnographic, historical, and archaeological sources.	Imagistic practices are associated with small-scale group bonding, whereas doctrinal practices are associated with increasing agricultural intensity and the rise of larger and more complex social formations.[27]
21	How can we understand ancient initiation rituals in the Roman cults of Mithras (2nd to 4th century CE)?	Historical texts and images.	Review of the description of Mithraic initiation rituals based mostly on depictions, such as images.	Initiation rituals documented throughout history show that initiates are subject to "rites of terror." These rites are memorable, but their significance is locally construed.[28]

22	Do prehistorical and ancient religions support the modes of religiosity theory?	A combination of historical texts, images, and archaeological data.	A number of studies have been published by historians and archaeologists on the pros and cons of the modes theory.	The results are mixed. The problem of causality (do cognitive constraints cause modes of ritual organization) is intractable. There is, however, a general acceptance of the theory.[29]
23	Is mind-body dualism present in China?	Philosophical analysis, qualitative and quantitative textual analyses.	Three different machine-based techniques—word collocation, hierarchical clustering, and topic modeling analysis of ancient Chinese texts.	Chinese thought is often portrayed as radically different from Western thought. Textual evidence provides support against strong mind-body holism.[30]
24	Can math be used to analyze myths?	Phylogenetic analysis of big data.	Conceptual mapping, bioinformatics, component analysis, and social networks analyses of mythical and folklore corpuses.	Phylogenetic analyses of various textual corpuses divulge relationships and patterns that are difficult or even impossible to find by traditional methods. They can also resolve conflicting theories of myths.[31]
25	Can we test evolutionary theories of religion?	Developing large databases consisting of all relevant information in particular parts of the world from the deep prehistorical past to the present in order to statistically test competing hypotheses of the evolution of religion.	Two prominent databases, Database of Religious History[32] and Seshat: Global History Databank[33] have been developed to test competing hypotheses. Such as: 1) that moralizing gods play a causal role in the development of complex societies and 2) that complex societies developed before the belief in moralizing gods.	The results are inconclusive. Each of the two databases support the hypotheses of their own research teams. The disagreement rests on very complex statistical procedures.[34]

(*Continued*)

Table 4.1 (Cont.)

#	*Question*	*Methods*	*Summary*	*Findings*
26	Can computer simulations model religious change and religious evolution?	Agent-based statistical modeling.	A statistical analysis of data from the International Social Survey Programme Religion Module (ISSP) and the Human Development Report (HDR).	The modeling provides an accurate forecast of changes in existential security and religiosity in a very large number of countries and periods of time.[35] It also can simulate religions as adaptive systems.[36]
27	Can computer simulations test religious studies theories?	Computer models and computer simulations.	A number of modeling studies have been applied to CSR theories such as Lawson & McCauley's ritual competence theory and theories in the general study of religion such as Rodney Stark's theory of religious movements and Robert Bellah's Axial Age theory.	The procedures necessary to develop computer models requires careful, detailed thought about the intermediate assumptions in particular theories of religion. The modeling can indicate which theories are most robust and can also lead to further unforeseen research questions.[37]

Much of the discrepancy in disciplines is due to philosophical and ideological differences, as well as the history of the approaches. Yet early proponents of a cognitive approach to the study of religion had been trained in a variety of methods across many disciplines: including religious studies, philosophy, anthropology, and psychology, and the subdiscipline has continued to study religion from an interdisciplinary perspective. The ultimate goal of CSR is to connect what is known about evolution, brain, cognition, and culture to explain religion by integrating disciplinary approaches. There are four key dimensions of interdisciplinary integration in CSR:[38]

1 *Unit of integration*

The unit of integration refers to the level at which integration takes place. Interdisciplinarity in CSR means multiple things. First, individual researchers master skills and methods in more than one discipline. This kind of interdisciplinary research, where one scholar increases knowledge across disciplines, provides insights but is not the only way that CSR is interdisciplinary. After all, this approach alone risks CSR becoming a jack of all trades and master of none. CSR is also integrated at a higher unit, beyond individual scholars, by promoting the team-based research paradigm. This is evidenced through the many multi-authored papers published in the cognitive and evolutionary sciences today.

In the following illustration, consider how this team-based approach works by imagining that an interdisciplinary team of cognitive scientists of religion is addressing the question, "why and how do ideas and behaviors that have been deemed religious, spread?" This particular team consists of an evolutionary psychologist, a neurocognitive scientist, a cognitive psychologist, and other social scientists.

(1) EVOLUTIONARY PSYCHOLOGIST

The evolutionary psychologist is interested in questions about whether and how intuitive responses emerge. Intuitive responses are likely to be based on universal mechanisms, constraints, traits, etc., which may have been selected for during evolution. To understand whether a response is based on an intuitive mechanism, the researcher conducts experiments in different cultures, especially those that differ. If cultures differ in their accepted views, yet people tend to think similarly, then it suggests that evolutionary processes also influence responses.

(2) NEUROCOGNITIVE SCIENTIST

The neuroscientist wants to understand better how cognitive functioning and emotional states are activated in the brain, as well as the connections between them. These gesture towards the neurobiological, and even evolutionary deep-rooted, basis of ideas and behaviors. This researcher uses methods such as neuroimaging to see which brain areas are activated in religious activities.

(3) COGNITIVE PSYCHOLOGIST

The cognitive psychologist is interested in cognition and wants to seek out conditions that make it possible to tap into intuitive processes. For example, by designing nifty experiments where people respond based on their off-the-cuff, gut-like reactions rather than relying on people's carefully thought through responses.

(4) OTHER SOCIAL SCIENTISTS

Many other social scientists involved in this hypothetical example are also equipped to study the distribution and stability of religious concepts. These include anthropologists, cognitive scientists, historians, psychologists, philosophers, sociologists, and religionists. These researchers use a combination of methods including archaeological surveys, historiographical analyses, textual analyses,[39] self-reports, interviews, narrative recall tasks, behavioral tasks, economic games, experimental and quasi-experimental fieldwork,[40] and computer modeling.

For example, those vested in cultural processes also take into account the role of the environment to understand how socialization and cultural input modifies and shapes both intuitive and reflective thought—for example, comparative research with children and adults and large-scale cross-cultural and historical surveys. Unfortunately, the vast amount of what we know about

Figure 4.1 CSR scholars often work in interdisciplinary teams to conduct research on religion. (Image credit: fizkes/Shutterstock.com).

human psychology comes only from WEIRD traditions (i.e. Western, Educated, Industrialized, Rich, and Democratic).[41] CSR conducts cross-cultural research, often in other non-WEIRD traditions, to address questions about the recurrence of religious concepts in many different cultures.[42]

Social scientists also draw upon existing archaeological, historical, ethnographic data, and large-scale social surveys to test goodness-of-fit with their theories.[43] Others conduct secondary analyses of existing massive ethnographic and historical databases, such as the Standard Cross-Cultural Sample (SCCS) and the Human Relations Area Files (HRAF),[44] and the Database of Religious History (DRH[45]). Such databases make possible analyses of aspects across cultures and throughout time while controlling for effects of historical contact between societies (i.e. Galton's problem). These databases also enable scholars to formally test probabilistic models of aspects of religious ideas and behaviors.

Probabilistic models deal with statistical trends in data, enabling researchers to make claims about the frequency of ideas and behaviors in the world. In other words, they can reasonably make claims about how the world tends to be. These include the tendency to engage in physical contact with the corpse by kin during ritual preparation for disposal,[46] the co-occurrence of ritual dynamics and particular socio-political arrangements,[47] and the representation of high gods as interested in moral behavior.[48]

Together, these areas of inquiry and associated methods enable teams of scholars to understand how and why ideas and behaviors that have been deemed religious, spread. Of course, the examples of methods provided here are not exhaustive. For example, many researchers have engaged in the philosophical, historical, archaeological and theological treatment of CSR theories.[49]

This interdisciplinarity and methodological pluralism result in fluidity and a lack of clear demarcation of who is a CSR researcher and who is not, and throughout this book, scholars are referred to by their primary field of training (e.g. anthropologist, psychologist). As discussed in Chapter 1 (Introduction), the criteria for inclusion is their commitment to some of the main principles outlined in Chapters 1–4 of this book, as well as the nature of research, which typically reflects this commitment.

Participation 2: Create a new research topic

Based on what you have read so far in this book:

1 Come up with a research topic about religion that is typical in CSR. This can be about a religious idea, belief, or behavior, and it could have been asked before or be unique. For example, life after death, goblins, ghosts, fairies, fate, rituals to prevent harm.
2 Write down a list of 3–4 scientific questions about this topic. For example, have people always believed in life after death? Do people in

different cultures believe in life after death? How are these ideas about life after death modified by the cultural environment?

3 Outline the methods that you would use to answer each of these questions (e.g. archaeology, large historical databases, neuroimaging, ethnography, field studies, cross-cultural experiments, large databases).
4 Based on the methods you would use, write down who you would want in your research team (e.g. archaeologist, historian, anthropologist, psychologist).
5 Swap your response to another student, give, and receive, feedback. Provide feedback on how they could improve based upon your understanding of CSR.
6 Modify your answers in light of their feedback.

Key points

- Interdisciplinary integration is the level at which integration takes place.
- Integration takes place in CSR at the level of the individual scholar, and in teams of scholars.

2 Scope of integration

The scope of integration refers to the degree of similarity between participating fields. A narrow form of interdisciplinarity involves collaboration between closely related fields, for example, archaeology and history. By contrast, CSR adopts a broad form of interdisciplinarity because collaboration occurs between fields whose key ideas, commitments, and methods tend to differ, such as literature and neuroscience.

Key points

- The scope of integration refers to the degree of similarity between participating fields.
- CSR integrates fields that are both similar and different.

3 Type of integration

The type of integration refers to the ways in which core theories about the nature of the world in different fields are brought together. In multidisciplinary research, scholars address problems from different disciplinary perspectives. These collaborative efforts often divide up labor and result in the culmination, but not necessarily the integration of knowledge. Religious Studies is an example of a multidisciplinary field. Here, students are often taught different perspectives on religion, while the contributing areas may benefit from added perspectives; they usually remain unchanged by it. By contrast, cognitive scientists of religion also borrow methods, concepts, and theories from one another. This type of interdisciplinarity leads to a pluridisciplinarity form of interaction.

CSR aims to go even further and produce a synthesis of methods, concepts, and theories that is qualitatively different than any single disciplinary approach. This ultimate aim is still a work in progress, but existing examples of the most influential forms of interdisciplinarity in other areas have led to new fields that cut across disciplinary boundaries such as behavioral economics and cognitive science itself.

Key points

- The type of integration refers to the ways in which core theories about the nature of the world in different fields are brought together.
- CSR is a multidisciplinary and pluridisciplinary approach.

4 Methodological integration

One unfortunate consequence of distinctive disciplinary approaches is the reluctance to go outside them, and scholars who focus on specific aspects of religion are often left with a narrow range of tools. As the saying goes, if the only tool you have is a hammer, it is tempting to treat everything as if it were a nail.[50] Strong interdisciplinarity requires methodological integration.

While many researchers who study religion talk about interdisciplinarity as a way to increase knowledge, they often construe interdisciplinarity as obtaining and exchanging more data from different scholars. This approach will result in more data, of course, but conducting the same protocol in different contexts also means that any design errors will also be replicated. As anthropologist Dimitris Xygalatas notes, "the problem is not that you won't get data; it is that you won't really know what those data mean.[51]"

Cognitive scientists of religion concede that there is no one right predetermined way to study religion. Religion can be considered at different levels, such as neurochemistry, brain, and culture. CSR scholars use methods that are most appropriate to the types of questions they ask concerning the persistence and prevalence of "religious" ideas and behaviors. To extend the previous analogy, if scholars who remain in their disciplinary boundaries tend to approach problems in the study of religion with a hammer, then cognitive scientists come equipped with a tool kit.

Figure 4.2 CSR scholars come equipped with a methodological tool kit to solve problems in the study of religion. (Image credit: Emojoez/Shutterstock.com).

Research in the cognitive and evolutionary sciences on religion involves teamwork, collaboration, and continuous interaction between and within groups of specialists rather than uncoordinated efforts by isolated generalists. This results in methodological pluralism and integration. In this format, researchers often combine these methodologies from different epistemological traditions into a single research agenda. Figure 4.3 showcases how interdisciplinary perspectives offer a better explanation of religious phenomena. Table 4.2 provides examples of how interdisciplinary research provides a better account of ritual by answering Tinbergen's four questions (covered in detail in Chapter 3: Research Methods) about the mechanism, ontogeny, phylogeny, and adaptative significance of ritual behavior.

Key points

- CSR adopts methodological pluralism and methodological integration.

Summary of methodological assumptions and approaches in CSR

1 Scientific methods

A commitment to scientific methods binds scholars. This commitment includes the formulation of testable hypotheses and the performance of statistical tests to determine trends in religious ideas and behaviors.

2 Methodological naturalism

CSR researchers are bound together by a commitment to methodological naturalism, which is a basic stance that scientists can study the emergence and effects of religious ideas and behaviors. However, they cannot determine whether these ideas are true or false.

3 Methodological pluralism

Cognitive scientists of religion employ a diverse array of methods to answer questions about religion. Researchers use methods that are appropriate for the type of questions they ask. Often scholars use approaches common to the neurosciences (e.g. brain imaging), evolutionary sciences (e.g. cross-cultural studies), psychological sciences—including developmental psychology (e.g. behavioral experiments), and anthropology (e.g. ethnographic fieldwork).

4 Interdisciplinary integration

Scholars from a diversity of disciplines work together in CSR to answer questions about religion. They include archaeologists, anthropologists, psychologists, philosophers, scholars of religion, and historians. Integration in CSR is characterized by the unit, scope, and type of interdisciplinarity.

Chapter summary

Nowadays, CSR has come to be characterized by its diversity in theories (interdisciplinarity) and methods (methodological pluralism). This combination is rare, but, in some ways, it is hardly surprising that it has characterized CSR;

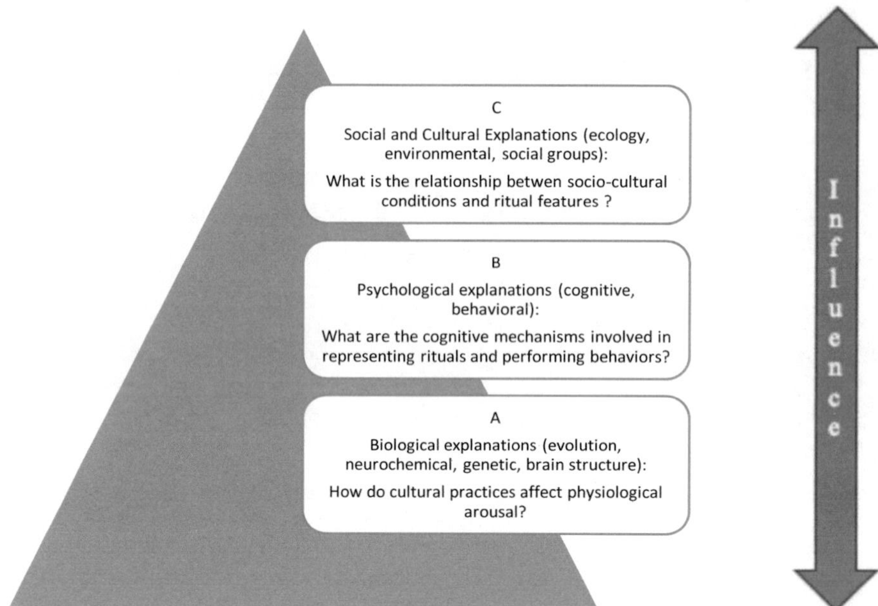

Figure 4.3 Example of how different levels of analyses and corresponding methods provide a better explanation of rituals. For example, researchers measured the physiological responses of participants and spectators during real-time in a ritual performed in the field[52] (a). Other research has focused on the cognitive representation of the effectiveness of ritualized action,[53] while various studies have investigated ritual synchrony (b).[54] Others have investigated the relationships between the features of ritual and the socio-political dynamics of religion (c).[55]

after all, many scholars study the mind and how humans think, yet they each bring to the table a variety of theories, methods, and approaches, which enhances the research. Generally speaking, cognitive scientists of religion tend to have a specialty in an understanding of evolution, the human mind, cognition, and culture, with the ultimate aim of drawing on all four areas to explain the stability and diversity in religious forms.

Discussion questions

1 What are the strengths and weaknesses of the methodological approach used by CSR?
2 What aspects of religion do you think are outside the scope of scientific inquiry?

Table 4.2 Example of how interdisciplinary research provides a better account of ritual by answering Tinbergen's four questions.[56]

#	*Object and kind of explanation*	*Tinbergen's question applied to rituals*	*Example of research findings and informed theories and conclusions on this question*	
1	Mechanism (proximate)	What are the mechanisms underlying ritual?	Rituals decrease anxiety. Ritual synchrony increases cohesion. Effects depend upon context.	Bio-psycho-social mechanisms undergird the effects of rituals.
2	Ontogeny (proximate)	How does ritual behavior develop in individuals?	By engaging in rituals, children learn how to segregate their social world into those who are trust-worthy and have high status and those who do not.	Learning rituals are motivated by a drive to affiliate with social groups.
3	Phylogeny (ultimate)	What is the evolutionary history of ritual?	Traces of ritual behavior observed in Wild Guinea baboons and white-faced capuchin monkeys but not the great apes. Evidence of ritual in archaic human history from the archaeological record.	Rituals are not a product of the modern environment, and humans have a psy-chological propensity to engage in rituals.
4	Adaptive significance (ultimate)	What are the functions of ritual?	Rituals promote trust and have psy-chological benefits such as reducing the anxiety of individuals and groups.	Rituals identify group members, ensure commitment to the group norms, facil-itate cooperation with coalitions and maintain group cohesion.

Selected further reading

Articles

1 Legare, Cristine. H., and M. Nielsen. "Ritual explained: interdisciplinary answers to Tinbergen's four questions." *Philosophical Transactions of the Royal Society of London. Series B, Biological Sciences* 375, no. 1805: (2020).

Books

1 McCauley, Robert N. "Recent trends in the cognitive science of religion: Neuroscience, religious experience, and the confluence of cognitive and evolutionary research." *Zygon* 55, no. 1 (2020): 97–124.
2 Whitehouse, Harvey., "Twenty-five years of CSR: A personal retrospective." In Luther H. Martin & Donald Wiebe (eds.). *Religion explained? The cognitive science of religion after twenty-five years.* London and New York: Bloomsbury Academic, 2017, 43–55.
3 Xygalatas, Dimitris. "Bridging the gap: The cognitive science of religion as an integrative approach." In *Evolution, cognition, and the history of religion: A new synthesis.* Leiden and Boston: Brill, 2018, 255–272.

Notes

1 Boyer, Pascal, and Pierre Liénard. "Why ritualized behavior? Precaution systems and action parsing in developmental, pathological and cultural rituals." *Behavioral and Brain Sciences* 29, no. 6 (2006): 595–613; Schjoedt, Uffe, Jesper Sørensen, Kristoffer Laigaard Nielbo, Dimitris Xygalatas, Panagiotis Mitkidis, and Joseph Bulbulia. "Cognitive resource depletion in religious interactions." *Religion, Brain & Behavior* 3, no. 1 (2013): 39–55; Norenzayan, Ara, Azim F. Shariff, Will M. Gervais, Aiyana K. Willard, Rita A. McNamara, Edward Slingerland, and Joseph Henrich. "The cultural evolution of prosocial religions." *Behavioral and Brain Sciences* 39 (2016).
2 Bering, Jesse M. "The folk psychology of souls." *Behavioral and Brain Sciences* 29, no. 5 (2006): 453–462.
3 Atkinson, Quentin D., and Harvey Whitehouse. "The cultural morphospace of ritual form: Examining modes of religiosity cross-culturally." *Evolution and Human Behavior* 32, no. 1 (2011): 50–62; Barrett and Lawson 2001; Cohen and Barrett 2008; Richert et al. 2005.
4 Whitehouse, Harvey, and Luther H. Martin, eds. *Theorizing religions past: Archaeology, history, and cognition.* Rowman Altamira, 2004.
5 Whitehouse, Harvey, and Robert N. McCauley, eds. *Mind and religion: Psychological and cognitive foundations of religiosity.* Rowman Altamira, 2005.
6 Schjoedt, Uffe. "The religious brain: A general introduction to the experimental neuroscience of religion." *Method & Theory in the Study of Religion* 21, no. 3 (2009): 310–339.
7 Schjoedt, Uffe, Hans Stødkilde-Jørgensen, Armin W. Geertz, and Andreas Roepstorff. "Highly religious participants recruit areas of social cognition in personal prayer." *Social Cognitive and Affective Neuroscience* 4, no. 2 (2009): 199–207.
8 Boyer, P. *The naturalness of religious ideas: A cognitive theory of religion.* Berkeley, LA, London: University of California Press, 1994; Boyer, P. "Cognitive tracks of cultural inheritance: How evolved intuitive ontology governs cultural transmission."

American Anthropologist 100 no. 4 (1999): 876–889; Donald, M. "The slow process: A hypothetical cognitive adaptation for distributed cognitive networks." *Journal of Psychology* 101 (2007): 214–222; Donald, M. "The first hybrid minds on earth." In A. W. Geertz and J. S. Jensen eds., *Religious narrative, cognition and culture: Image and word in the mind of narrative*. Sheffield & Oakville: Equinox Publishing, 2011, 67–96; Geertz, A. W. "Brain, body and culture: A biocultural theory of religion." *Method and Theory in the Study of Religion* 22, no. 4 (2010): 304–321; Jensen, J. S. "The complex worlds of religion: Connecting cultural and cognitive analysis." In I. Pyysiäinen & V. Anttonen eds., *Current approaches in the cognitive science of religion*. London & New York: Continuum, 2002, 203–228; Jensen, J. S. "Normative cognition in culture and religion." *Journal for the Cognitive Science of Religion* 1, no. 1 (2013): 47–70; Kundtová Klocová, E. & Geertz, A. W. "Ritual and embodied cognition." In R. Uro, J. J. Day, R. E. DeMaris, and R. Roitto eds., *The Oxford handbook of early Christian ritual*. Oxford: Oxford University Press, 2019, 74–94; Lawson, E. T. "Counterintuitive notions and the problem of transmission: The relevance of cognitive science for the study of history." *Historical Reflections/Reflexions Historiques* 20, no. 3 (2013): 481–495; Lawson, E. T., and McCauley, R. N. *Rethinking religion: Connecting cognition and culture*. Cambridge: Cambridge University Press, 1990; McCauley, R.N. *Why religion is natural and science is not*. Oxford: Oxford University Press, 2011; Newen, A., de Bruin, L., & Gallagher, S. eds. *The Oxford Handbook of 4E Cognition*. Oxford: Oxford University Press, 2018.

9 Willard, Aiyana K., and Ara Norenzayan. "Cognitive biases explain religious belief, paranormal belief, and belief in life's purpose." *Cognition* 129, no. 2 (2013): 379–391.

10 Cohen, E. *The mind possessed: The cognition of spirit possession in an Afro-Brazilian religious tradition*. Oxford: Oxford University Press, 2007.

11 Gelman, S., & Legare, C. "South African children's understanding of AIDS and flu: Investigating conceptual understanding of cause, treatment and prevention." *Journal of Cognition and Culture* 9, no. 3–4 (2009): 333–346.

12 Singh, M., & Henrich. J. (2020). "Why do religious leaders observe costly prohibitions? Examining taboos on Mentawai Shamans." *Evolutionary Human Sciences* 2 (e32). https://doi.org/10.1017/ehs.2020.32.

13 Purzycki, B. G. "The minds of gods: A comparative study of supernatural agency." *Cognition* 129, no. 1 (2013): 163–179; Purzycki, B. G. "The evolution of gods' minds in the Tyva Republic." *Current Anthropology* 57, no. S13 (2016): S88–S104.

14 Nielbo, K. L., & Sørensen, J. "Spontaneous processing of functional and non-functional action sequences." *Religion, Brain & Behavior* 1, no. 1 (2011): 18–30.

15 Jegindø, E.-M. E., Vase, L., Jegindø, J., & Geertz, A. W. "Pain and sacrifice: Experience and modulation of pain in a religious piercing ritual." *International Journal for the Psychology of Religion* 23, no. 3 (2013): 171–187; Jegindø, E.-M. E., Vase, L., Skewes, J. C., Terkelsen, A. J., Hansen, J., Geertz, A. W., … Jensen, T. S. "Expectations contribute to reduced pain levels during prayer in highly religious participants." *Journal of Behavioral Medicine* 36, no. 4 (2013): 413–426; Konvalinka, I., Xygalatas, D., Bulbulia, J., Schjødt, U., Jegindø, E.-M., Wallot, S., … Roepstorff, A. "Synchronized arousal between performers and related spectators in a fire-walking ritual." *Proceedings of the National Academy of Sciences* 108, no. 20 (2011), 8514–8519; Xygalatas, D., Mitkidis, P., Fischer, R., Reddish, P., Skewes, J., Geertz, A. W., … Bulbulia, J. "Extreme rituals promote prosociality." *Psychological Science* 24, no. 8 (2013): 1602–1605; Xygalatas, D., Schjoedt, U., Bulbulia, J., Konvalinka, I., Jegindø, E.-M., Reddish, P., … Roepstorff, A. "Autobiographical memory in a fire-walking ritual." *Journal of Cognition and Culture* 13, no. 1 (2013): 1–16.

16 Xygalatas, Dimitris, Uffe Schjoedt, Joseph Bulbulia, Ivana Konvalinka, Else-Marie Jegindø, Paul Reddish, Armin W. Geertz, and Andreas Roepstoff. "Autobiographical memory in a fire-walking ritual." *Journal of Cognition and Culture* 13, no. 1–2 (2013): 1–16.

17 Bird, R. B., & Power, E. A. "Prosocial signaling and cooperation among Martu hunters. *Evolution and Human Behavior* 36 (2015): 389–397; Bulbulia, J. "Charismatic signalling." *Journal for the Study of Religion, Nature and Culture* 3, no. 4 (2019): 518–551; Bulbulia, J., & Sosis, R. "Signalling theory and the evolution of religious cooperation." *Religion* 41, no. 3 (2011): 363–388; Carl Brusse "Signaling theories of religion: Models and explanation." *Religion, Brain & Behavior* 10, no. 3 (2020): 272–291; Power, E.A. "Discerning devotion: Testing the signaling theory of religion." *Evolution and Human Behavior,* 38 (2017): 82–9; Sosis, R. "Religious behaviors, badges, and bans: Signaling theory and the evolution of religion." In P. McNamara ed., *Where God and science meet: How brain and evolutionary studies alter our understanding of religion. Volume 1: Evolution, genes, and the religious brain.* Westport & London: Praeger Publishers, 2006, 61–86; Sosis, R., and Bressler, E.R. "Cooperation and commune longevity: A test of the costly signaling theory of religion." *Cross-Cultural Research* 37, no. 2 (2003): 211–239; Sosis, R., & Ruffle, B.J. "Religious ritual and cooperation: Testing for a relationship on Israeli religious and secular kibbutzim." *Current Anthropology* 44, no. 5 (2003): 713–722.

18 Whitehouse, Harvey, Jonathan Jong, Michael D. Buhrmester, Ángel Gómez, Brock Bastian, Christopher M. Kavanagh, Martha Newson et al. "The evolution of extreme cooperation via shared dysphoric experiences." *Scientific Reports* 7 (2017): 44292.

19 E.g. Wen, Nicole J., Aiyana K. Willard, Michaela Caughy, and Cristine H. Legare. "Watch me, watch you: Ritual participation increases in-group displays and out-group monitoring in children." *Philosophical Transactions of the Royal Society B*375, no. 1805 (2020): 20190437; Watson-Jones, Rachel E., Harvey Whitehouse, and Cristine H. Legare. "In-group ostracism increases high-fidelity imitation in early childhood." *Psychological Science* 27, no. 1 (2016): 34–42.

20 Schjødt, U., Stødkilde-Jørgensen, H., Geertz, A. W., & Roepstorff, A. "Rewarding prayers." *Neuroscience Letters* 443 (2008): 165–168; Schjødt, U., Stødkilde-Jørgensen, H., Geertz, A. W., & Roepstorff, A. "Highly religious participants recruit areas of social cognition in personal prayer." *Social Cognitive and Affective Neuroscience,* 4 (2009): 199–207; Schjødt, U., Stødkilde-Jørgensen, H., Geertz, A. W., Lund, T. E., and Roepstorff, A. "The power of charisma—perceived charisma inhibits the frontal executive network of believers in intercessory prayer." *Social Cognitive and Affective Neuroscience,* 6 (2011): 119–127; Bulbulia, J., & Schjoedt, U. "The neural basis of religion." In F. Krueger & J. Grafman eds., *The neural basis of human belief systems.* Hove & New York: Psychology Press, 2013, 169–190.

21 Schjoedt, Uffe, Hans Stødkilde-Jørgensen, Armin W. Geertz, Torben E. Lund, and Andreas Roepstorff. "The power of charisma—perceived charisma inhibits the frontal executive network of believers in intercessory prayer." *Social Cognitive and Affective Neuroscience* 6, no. 1 (2011): 119–127.

22 Andersen, M. "Predictive coding in agency detection." *Religion, Brain & Behavior* 9, No.1 (2019): 65–84; Andersen, M., Nielbo, K. L., Schjoedt, U., Pfeiffer, T., Roepstorff, A., & Sørensen, J. "Predictive minds in ouija board sessions." *Phenomenology and the Cognitive Sciences* 18 (2018): 577–588; Andersen, M., Pfeiffer, T., Müller, S., & Schjoedt, U. "Agency detection in predictive minds: A virtual reality study." *Religion, Brain & Behavior* 9, no. 1 (2009): 52–64; Andersen, M., Schjoedt, U., Nielbo, K. L., & Sørensen, J. "Mystical experience in the lab." *Method and Theory in the Study of Religion* 26 (2014): 217–245; Deeley, Q., Walsh, E., Oakley, D.A., Bell, V., Koppel, C., Mehta, M.A., and Halligan, P.W. "Using hypnotic suggestion to model loss of control and awareness of movements: An exploratory fMRI study." *PloS ONE* 8, no. 10 (2013): e78324. Deeley, Q., Walsh, E., Oakley, D.A., Bell, V., Koppel, C., Mehta, M.A., and Halligan, P.W. "Modelling psychiatric and cultural possession phenomena with suggestion and fMRI." *Cortex* 53 (2014): 107–119; Hoogeveen, S., Schjoedt, U., & van Elk, M. "Did I do that? Expectancy effects of brain stimulation on error-related negativity and sense of agency." *Journal of Cognitive Neuroscience* 30, no. 11 (2018): 1720–1733; van Elk, M.

"An EEG study on the effects of induced spiritual experiences on somatosensory processing and sensory suppression." *Journal for the Cognitive Science of Religion* 2, no. 2 (2014): 121–157; van Elk, M. (2017). "The self-attribution bias and paranormal beliefs." *Consciousness and Cognition* 49: 313–321.

23 Burdett, E.R.R., Wigger, J.B., & Barrett, J.L. "The minds of god, mortals, and in-betweens: Children's developing understanding of extraordinary and ordinary minds across four countries." *Psychology of Religion and Spirituality* (2019, September 2nd). Advance online publication. https://doi.org/10.1037/rel0000285.

24 Barrett, J.L. "Coding and quantifying counterintuitiveness in religious concepts: Theoretical and methodological reflections." *Method and Theory in the Study of Religion* 20 (2008): 308–338; Barrett, J.L., Burdett, E.R., & Porter, T.J. "Counterintuitiveness in folktales: Finding the cognitive optimum." *Journal of Cognition and Culture* 9 (2009): 271–287; Boyer, P., & Ramble, C. "Cognitive templates for religious concepts: Cross-cultural evidence for recall of counter-intuitive representations." *Cognitive Science* 25 (2001): 535–564; Purzycki, B.G., & Willard, A.K. "MCI theory: A critical discussion." *Religion, Brain & Behavior* 6, No. 3 (2016): 207–248; Gonce, L.O., Upal, M.A., Slone, D.J., & Tweney, R.D. "Role of context in the recall of counterintuitive concepts." *Journal of Cognition and Culture* 6 (2006): 521–547; Gregory, J., Barrett, J.L. "Epistemology and counterintuitiveness: Role and relationship in epidemiology of cultural representation." *Journal of Cognition and Culture* 9, no. 3 (2009): 289–314; Norenzayan, A., Atran, S., Faulkner, J., & Schaller, M. "Memory and mystery: The cultural selection of minimally counterintuitive narratives." *Cognitive Science* 30, (2006): 531–553; Upal, M.A., Owsianiecki, L., Slone, D. J., & Tweney, R.D "Contextualizing counterintuitiveness: How context affects comprehension and memorability of counterintuitive concepts." *Cognitive Science* 31 (2007): 1–25.

25 Andersen, M. "Predictive coding in agency detection." *Religion, Brain & Behavior* 9, no. 1 (2019): 65–84; Andersen, M., Pfeiffer, T., Müller, S., & Schjoedt, U. "Agency detection in predictive minds: A virtual reality study." *Religion, Brain & Behavior* 9, No. 1 (2019), 52–64; Barrett, J.L. (2000). "Exploring the natural foundations of religion." *Trends in Cognitive Sciences* 4, no. 1 (2000): 29–34; Barrett, J.L. *Why would anyone believe in god?* Walnut Creek, Lanham, MD: AltaMira Press, 2004; Barrett, J.L., & Burdett, E.R. (2011). "The cognitive science of religion." *Psychologist* 24, no. 4 (2011), 252–255; Barrett, J.L., & Lanman, J.A. "The science of religious beliefs." *Religion* 38, no. 2 (2008): 109–124; Guthrie, S.E. *Faces in the clouds: A new theory of religion.* Oxford & New York: Oxford University Press, 1995; Guthrie, S.E. "Animal animism: Evolutionary roots of religious cognition. In I. Pyysiäinen & V. Anttonen eds., *Current approaches in the cognitive science of religion.* London & New York: Continuum, 2002, 38–67; Guthrie, S.E. "Prediction and feedback may constrain but do not stop anthropomorphism." *Religion, Brain & Behavior* 9, no. 1 (2019): 89–91; Maij, D.L.R., van Schie, H.T., & van Elk, M. "The boundary conditions of the hypersensitive agency detection device: An empirical investigation of agency detection in threatening situations." *Religion, Brain & Behavior* 9, no. 1 (2019): 23–51; van Elk, M. "Paranormal believers are more prone to illusory agency detection than skeptics." *Consciousness and Cognition* 22 (2013): 1041–1046; Van Leeuwen, N., & van Elk, M. "Seeking the supernatural: The interactive religious experience model." *Religion, Brain & Behavior* 9, no. 3 (2019): 221–275.

26 White, C. "Cross-cultural similarities in reasoning about personal continuity in reincarnation: Evidence from South India." *Religion, Brain & Behavior* 6, no. 2 (2016): 130–153.

27 Atkinson, Quentin D., and Harvey Whitehouse. "The cultural morphospace of ritual form: Examining modes of religiosity cross-culturally." *Evolution and human behavior* 32, no. 1 (2011): 50–62; Whitehouse, Harvey, Pieter Francois, Patrick E. Savage, Thomas E. Currie, Kevin C. Feeney, Enrico Cioni, Rosalind Purcell et al.

"Complex societies precede moralizing gods throughout world history." *Nature* 568, no. 7751 (2019): 226–229; Gantley, Michael, Harvey Whitehouse, and Amy Bogaard. "Material correlates analysis (MCA): An innovative way of examining questions in archaeology using ethnographic data." *Advances in Archaeological Practice* 6, no. 4 (2018): 328–341.

28 Martin, L.H. "Ritual competence and mithraic ritual." In L.H. Martin ed., *The mind of mithraists: Historical and cognitive studies in the roman cult of Mithras*, London: Bloomsbury, 2015, 41–56; Panagiotidou, O., & Beck, R. *The Roman Mithras cult: A cognitive approach.* London: Bloomsbury Academic, 2017.

29 Martin, L.H., & Pachis, P. eds. (2009). *Imagistic traditions in the Graeco-Roman world: A cognitive modeling of history of religions research. Acts of the panel held during the XIX Congress of the International Association for the History of Religions (IAHR), Tokyo, Japan, March 2005.* Thessaloniki: Vanias Editions; McCauley, R.N., & Lawson, E.T. *Bringing ritual to mind: Psychological foundations of cultural forms.* Cambridge: Cambridge University Press, 2002; Whitehouse, H., & Martin, L.H. *Theorizing religions past: Archaeology, history, and cognition.* Walnut Creek, Lanham, MD: AltaMira Press, 2004.

30 Slingerland, E. "Body and mind in Early China: An integrated humanities-science approach," *Journal of the American Academy of Religion* 81, no. 1 (2013): 6–55; Slingerland, E., Nichols, R., Nielbo. K., & Logan, C. "The distant reading of religious texts: A 'big data' approach to mind-body concepts in early China" *Journal of the American Academy of Religion* 85, no. 4 (2017): 985–1016.

31 Berezkin, Y.E. "Peopling of the new world from data on distributions of folklore motifs." In R. Kenna, M. MacCarron, & P. MacCarron eds., *Maths meets myths: Quantitative approaches to ancient narratives.* Bern, Switzerland: Springer International Publishing, 2017, 71–89; Gramsch, R., MacCarron, M., MacCarron, P., & Yose, J. "Medieval historical, hagiographical and biographical networks." In R. Kenna, M. MacCarron, & P. MacCarron eds., *Maths meets myths: Quantitative approaches to ancient narratives.* Bern, Switzerland: Springer International Publishing, 2017, 45–69; Kenna, R., & MacCarron, P. (2017). "A networks approach to mythological epics." In R. Kenna, M. MacCarron, & P. MacCarron eds., *Maths meets myths: Quantitative approaches to ancient narratives.* Bern, Switzerland: Springer International Publishing, 2017, 21–43; Thuillard, M., Quellec, J.-L. L., d'Huy, J., & Berezkin, Y. "A large-scale study of world myths." *Trames. A Journal of the Humanities and Social Sciences* 22, no. 4 (2018): 407–424; Weiss, D. "How quantitative methods can shed light on a problem of comparative mythology: The myth of the struggle for supremacy between two groups of deities reconsidered." In R. Kenna, M. MacCarron, & P. MacCarron eds., *Maths meets myths: Quantitative approaches to ancient narratives.* Bern, Switzerland: Springer International Publishing, 2017, 213–228.

32 https://religiondatabase.org/landing/.

33 http://seshatdatabank.info/.

34 Beheim, B., Atkinson, Q.D., Bulbulia, J., Gervais, W.M., Gray, R.D., Henrich, J., … Willard, A.K. "Corrected analyses show that moralizing gods precede complex societies but serious data concerns remain." (2019): 1–30. doi:10.31234/osf.io/jwan2n; Lang, M., Purzycki, B. G., Apicella, C. L., Atkinson, Q. D., Bolyanatz, A., Cohen, E., … Henrich, J. "Moralizing gods, impartiality and religious parochialism across 15 societies." *Proceedings of the Royal Society B*, (2019): 286, 1–9. doi:10.1098/rspb.2019.0202; Norenzayan, A. *Big gods: How religion transformed cooperation and conflict.* Princeton & Oxford: Princeton University Press, 2013; Savage, P.E., Whitehouse, H., Francois, P., Currie, T.E., Feeney, K.C., Cioni, E., … Turchin, P. "Reply to Beheim et al.: Reanalyses confirm robustness of original analyses. (2019): 1–17; Turchin, P., Whitehouse, H., Francois, P., Hoyer, D., Nugent, S., Larson, J., … Squitieri, A. "Explaining the Rise of Moralizing Religions: A Test of Competing Hypotheses Using the Seshat Databank." *SocArXiv Preprint*, (2019): 1–28. doi:10.31235/osf.io/2v59j; Whitehouse, H., Francois, P., Savage, P.E., Currie, T.E., Feeney, K.C., Cioni, E., …

Turchin, P. "Complex societies precede moralizing gods throughout world history." *Nature* 568, (2019): 226–229.

35 Gore, R.J., Lemos, C.M., Shults, F.L., & Wildman, W.J. "Forecasting changes in religiosity and existential security with an agent-based model." *Journal of Artificial Societies and Social Simulation* 21, no. 1 (2018): 1–26; Shults, F.L., Gore, R.J., Wildman, W.J., Lynch, C.J., Lane, J.E., & Toft, M.D. "A generative model of the mutual escalation of anxiety between religious groups." *Journal of Artificial Societies and Social Simulation* 21, no. 4 (2018): 1–25.

36 Sosis, R. "Why cultural evolutionary models of religion need a systemic approach." In A.K. Petersen, I.S. Gilhus, L.H. Martin, J.S. Jensen, & J. Sørensen eds., *Evolution, cognition, and the history of religions: A new synthesis. Festschrift in honour of Armin W. Geertz*. Leiden and Boston: Brill, 2019: 45–61; Sosis, R. "Four advantages of a systemic approach to the study of religion." *Archive for the Psychology of Religion* 42, no. 1 (2020): 142–157; Wood, C., & Sosis, R. "Simulating religions as adaptive systems." In S.Y. Diallo, W. J. Wildman, F.L. Shults, & A.Tolk eds., *Human simulation: Perspectives, insights, and applications*. Cham, Switzerland: Springer Nature, 2019, 209–232.

37 Czachesz, I., & Lisdorf, A. "Computer modeling of cognitive processes in biblical studies: The primacy of urban christianity as a test case. In I. Czachesz & R. Uro eds., *Mind, morality and magic: Cognitive science approaches in biblical studies*. Durham: Acumen, 2013, 77–97; Lane, J.E., Shults, F.L., & McCauley, R. N. (2019). "Modeling and simulation as a pedagogical and heuristic tool for developing theories in cognitive science: An example from ritual competence theory." In S. Y. Diallo, W. J. Wildman, F. L. Shults, & A. Tolk (Eds.), *Human simulation: Perspectives, insights, and applications* (pp. 143–154). Cham, Switzerland: Springer Nature; Nielbo, K. L., Braxton, D. M., & Upal, A. (2012). "Computing religion: A New tool in the multilevel analysis of religion." *Method and Theory in the Study of Religion* 24, no. 3: 267–290; Shults, F. L., Wildman, W. J., Lane, J. E., Lynch, C. J., & Diallo, S. (2018). "Multiple axialities: A computational model of the axial age." *Journal of Cognition and Culture,* 18: 537–564; Taves, A. "Modeling theories and modeling phenomena: A humanist's initiation." In S.Y. Diallo, W.J. Wildman, F.L. Shults, & A. Tolk eds., *Human simulation: Perspectives, insights, and applications*. Cham, Switzerland: Springer Nature, 2019, 83–94.

38 See Xygalatas, Dimitris. "Bridging the gap: The cognitive science of religion as an integrative approach." In *Evolution, cognition, and the history of religion: A new synthesis*. Leiden and Boston: Brill, 2018, 255–272.

39 Slingerland, Edward. "Body and mind in early China: An integrated humanities-science approach." *Journal of the American Academy of Religion* 81, no. 1 (2013): 6–55.

40 Xygalatas, Dimitris. *The burning saints: Cognition and culture in the fire-walking rituals of the Anastenaria*. Routledge, 2014.

41 Henrich, Joseph, Steven J. Heine, and Ara Norenzayan. "The weirdest people in the world?" *Behavioral and Brain Sciences* 33, no. 2–3 (2010): 61–83.

42 Harris, Paul L., and Rita Astuti. "Learning that there is life after death." *Behavioral and Brain Sciences* 29, no. 5 (2006): 475–476; Cohen, Emma. *The mind possessed: The cognition of spirit possession in an Afro-Brazilian religious tradition*. Oxford University Press, 2007; Emmons, Natalie A., and Deborah Kelemen. "The development of children's prelife reasoning: Evidence from two cultures." *Child development* 85, no. 4 (2014): 1617–1633; White, Claire. "Cross-cultural similarities in reasoning about personal continuity in reincarnation: evidence from South India." *Religion, Brain & Behavior* 6, no. 2 (2016): 130–153; Whitehouse, Harvey. *Inside the cult: Religious innovation and transmission in Papua New Guinea*. Oxford University Press on Demand, 1995.

43 Baumard, Nicolas, and Pascal Boyer. "Explaining moral religions." *Trends in cognitive sciences* 17, no. 6 (2013): 272–280; Norenzayan, Ara. *Big gods: How religion transformed cooperation and conflict*. Princeton University Press, 2013; Norenzayan, Ara, and Azim

F. Shariff. "The origin and evolution of religious prosociality." *Science* 322, no. 5898 (2008): 58–62; Norenzayan, Ara, and Azim F. Shariff. "The origin and evolution of religious prosociality." *Science* 322, no. 5898 (2008): 58–62; Purzycki, Benjamin Grant. "The minds of gods: A comparative study of supernatural agency." *Cognition* 129, no. 1 (2013): 163–179.

44 Slingerland, Edward, and Brenton Sullivan. "Durkheim with data: The database of religious history." *Journal of the American Academy of Religion* 85, no. 2 (2017): 312–347.

45 Slingerland & Sullivan, 2015; Baumard & Boyer, 2013; Norenzayan, 2013; Purzycki, 2013; Atkinson & Whitehouse, 2011; Turchin et al., 2012; Norenzayan & Shariff, 2008; Johnson, 2005.

46 White, Claire, Maya Marin, and Daniel MT Fessler. "Not just dead meat: An evolutionary account of corpse treatment in mortuary rituals." *Journal of Cognition and Culture* 17, no. 1–2 (2017): 146–168.

47 Atkinson, Quentin D., and Harvey Whitehouse. "The cultural morphospace of ritual form: Examining modes of religiosity cross-culturally." *Evolution and Human Behavior* 32, no. 1 (2011): 50–62.

48 Johnson, Dominic D.P. "God's punishment and public goods." *Human Nature* 16, no. 4 (2005): 410–446.

49 E.g. De Cruz and De Smedt 2010; Geertz and Jensen, 2014; Hodge 2011; Nichols 2007; Nicholson 2014; Pyysiäinen 2001; Schloss and Murray 2011; Whitehouse and Martin, 2004.

50 Abraham H. Maslow (1966). *The psychology of science*. p. 15. Joanna Cotler Books,

51 https://items.ssrc.org/insights/strong-interdisciplinarity-and-explanatory-pluralism-in-social-scientific-research/.

52 Konvalinka, Ivana, Dimitris Xygalatas, Joseph Bulbulia, Uffe Schjødt, Else-Marie Jegindø, Sebastian Wallot, Guy Van Orden, and Andreas Roepstorff. "Synchronized arousal between performers and related spectators in a fire-walking ritual." *Proceedings of the National Academy of Sciences* 108, no. 20 (2011): 8514–8519.

53 Barrett, Justin, and E. Thomas Lawson. "Ritual intuitions: Cognitive contributions to judgments of ritual efficacy." *Journal of Cognition and Culture* 1, no. 2 (2001): 183–201.

54 Mogan, Reneeta, Ronald Fischer, and Joseph A. Bulbulia. "To be in synchrony or not? A meta-analysis of synchrony's effects on behavior, perception, cognition and affect." *Journal of Experimental Social Psychology* 72 (2017): 13–20.

55 Atkinson, Quentin D., and Harvey Whitehouse. "The cultural morphospace of ritual form: Examining modes of religiosity cross-culturally." *Evolution and Human Behavior* 32, no. 1 (2011): 50–62.

56 Table based upon: Legare, C.H., and M.Nielsen. "Ritual explained: Interdisciplinary answers to Tinbergen's four questions." *Philosophical Transactions of the Royal Society of London. Series B, Biological Sciences* 375, no. 1805 (2020): 20190419–20190419.

5 The nature of the world

Anyone who has spent time with children will know that they ask many questions. They especially delight in asking "why" questions: "Why is the sky blue?" "Why did the dog pee on the carpet?" "Why did my sister get a cookie?" Researchers have provided evidence that this type of constant questioning is not merely a bid by young children to keep the conversation going. Rather, they are legitimate requests for causal explanations.[1] Causal explanations uncover how one event, process, or state contributes to another; in other words, the conditions and circumstances that bring the outcome about. As developmental psychologist Cristine Legare points out, the capacity to use questions flexibly and efficiently is a sound strategy. It allows children to acquire new information, increase their understanding, and solve problems.[2] Even preschool children will continue to ask questions until they have what they believe is a satisfactory answer from a reliable source.[3,4]

Children also tend to find some types of explanations more compelling than others. For instance, they are attuned to the consistency of current accounts with their prior knowledge. If children receive information that is inconsistent with what they currently know, then they are motivated to seek out and construct an explanation.[5] Adults also tend to find some types of answers more inherently satisfying than others. For example, they tend to privilege patterns in explaining behaviors and make generalizations based on these perceived patterns rather than on individual examples.[6] It appears that while seeking and providing explanations supports the remarkable human capacity to discover information about the world around us, the capacity is also biased towards particular kinds of explanations.

Cognitive scientists of religion have proposed that cognitive biases towards particular types of explanations often make religious views of the world more compelling than scientific or other views. Conversely, intuitions often impinge on the scientific understanding of the world. As cognitive scientist Andrew Shtulman has argued, we are biased towards a misunderstanding of how the world works more generally—in stark contrast to what science has revealed. Shtulman claims, we are, in fact, "scienceblind." Similarly, philosopher Robert McCauley has concluded that religion—at least, as popularly construed in the minds of ordinary people—is cognitively natural and science is not.[7] As we covered in Chapter 3 (Research Questions), scholarly endeavors in the cognitive science of religion (CSR) focus on identifying cognitive biases that predispose us towards religious explanations.

In this chapter, we consider religious explanations for the origins and development of the natural world, species, and the cause of natural events and illnesses. We cover research that showcases why the idea of an ordered, purposeful world intentionally created by a designer inherently provides a more compelling explanation for the development of the world than the processes of evolutionary change. We then move onto other ideas about events in the world, such as thinking that good people are rewarded with good fortune rather than luck, that terminal illness and natural disasters happen to people for a reason rather than morally neutral processes. We will also encounter research on how people typically reason when natural and supernatural explanations collide. We will also consider how these findings challenge popular misconceptions throughout the history of academia that acquiring scientific knowledge replaces religious beliefs. First, we turn to competing explanations of the world through the controversial debate on intelligent design versus evolution by natural selection that is especially prominent in the US.

Explaining the origins and development of the natural world

There is overwhelming scientific evidence supporting evolution by natural selection, the underlying biological theory that species change over time, give rise to new species, and share a common ancestor. However, around 39 per cent of adults in the US reject the very idea of evolution, and about 40 per cent accept it—a relatively low rate when compared to other economically prosperous nations.[8] Researchers have proposed that the comparatively low acceptance of evolution in America (as compared to other countries) is due in part to widespread religious fundamentalism.[9]

Religious groups often present evolution by natural selection as incompatible with religious ideas about the origins and development of the natural world, such as intelligent design. Intelligent design includes the underlying assumption that the universe and living things are designed and created by an intelligent entity. Those who endorse intelligent design often identify as creationists. Creationists hold the view that the universe and life originated from specified acts of divine creation, such as through the work of God. For instance, scientists estimate the world to be 4.5 billion years old and maintain that species evolve through mutation and selection, which are processes that involve a degree of randomness, and genetic error. By contrast, many young-earth creationists believe that God intentionally created the world and all species between 6,000 to 10,000 years ago. This is an example of a conflicting account because the purported relationship between science, or more specifically, biological evolution and religious accounts of the world, is viewed as incompatible.

Others construe the relationship between biological evolution and religious accounts of the origin and development of the world as compatible. For example, those who endorse "theistic evolution" (also known as "evolutionary creationism") hold views that regard religious teachings about God as compatible with modern scientific understandings of evolution. The list of proponents of theistic evolution includes a list of established religious figures, including Pope Benedict XVI. When people reason that these accounts are compatible, they often adopt a form of coexistence reasoning referred to by cognitive scientists as integrated thinking, in which evolutionary and religious explanations are combined into a single account. For example, many proponents of theistic evolution point out that while evolutionary theory explains how life and species evolve gradually, it is neutral on the question of how life began on earth in the first place.

Many instances of integrative thinking about religion and evolution provide a single explanation of the origins and development of the world that includes a causal chain of proximate and distal causes. As we discussed in Chapter 3 (Research Questions), distal causes are the most distant, or ultimate causal explanation of the event. For instance, that God creates the conditions under which evolution can occur. Proximate causes are the closest causal explanations to the event, for example, how life and species evolve. This type of integrative thinking includes the view that a deity guides evolution by specifying the laws that govern it (i.e. distant cause). The outlook also leaves species to evolve according to the conditions they experience as time goes by (i.e. the proximate cause).[10] Even school-age children, who may not have an accurate understanding of evolutionary biology, will nonetheless exhibit this type of integrative thinking, reasoning that God created the first monkeys, and then humans evolved from them.[11] Nevertheless, many subpopulations in the US hold views about the nature of the world that are not construed as compatible with scientific accounts of biological evolution, and they reject evolutionary theory in favor of creationist explanations.

Participation 1: Case study: Should public schools teach students about evolution and present intelligent design as an alternative?

Background

The perceived conflict between scientific and religious views of the origins and development of the world and its inhabitants is apparent in the debate over whether, and how, public schools should teach students about evolution and present intelligent design as an alternative. These issues have been debated in many states and at all levels of state government. Currently, whether or not intelligent design is taught in public schools, and indeed, whether schools opt out of teaching evolution altogether, differs by state.[12] Science and education communities have sought to provide reassurance that scientific knowledge does not contradict religious beliefs because it says nothing about religious realities or values. Despite these efforts, many continue to believe that the theory of evolution threatens and is in direct conflict with their religious beliefs.

Kitzmiller v. Dover Area School District

In September 2005, 11 parents of public-school children sued the Dover Area School District in Pennsylvania because the school board changed its biology-teaching curriculum to require that intelligent design is taught as a scientific alternative to evolution by natural selection. The case was the first direct challenge in the US federal courts testing a public-school district policy that required teaching intelligent design. Much of the trial featured testimonies from theologians, professors, and other specialists arguing for and against the explanatory power of evolution and the relevance of intelligent design as a scientific alternative. The case was the first direct challenge in the US federal courts testing a public-school district policy that required teaching intelligent design. The judge ruled that intelligent design was a religious theory and should not be taught in science class.

Assignment

- After researching this case on the internet, outline at least four arguments in total, including those for and against the explanatory power of evolution and the relevance of intelligent design as a scientific alternative.
- Label these arguments as either conflict or compatibility accounts of the relationship between biological evolution and supernatural explanations of the world.
- Rank these arguments concerning how convincing you find them on a scale of 1–4.
- Explain in a few sentences why you find the top-ranked argument most convincing and the lowest-ranked argument least compelling.
- Do you think public schools teach students about evolution and present intelligent design as an alternative? Explain your answer.

Key points

- Children and adults find some types of explanations intuitively more compelling than others.
- Cognitive scientists of religion have proposed that biases towards particular types of explanations often make religious views of the world more compelling than scientific or other views.

- Intuitions may impinge on the scientific understanding of the world, especially the origins and development of the natural world and its inhabitants.
- Religious groups often present evolution by natural selection as incompatible with religious ideas about the origins and development of the natural world and species, such as intelligent design.
- Sometimes religion and science are construed as compatible, and people integrate supernatural and natural explanations to explain the origins and development of the world and species.

Why do people reject evolutionary theory and endorse creationism?

One obvious question is the extent to which aspects of cognition and culture explain the rejection of evolutionary theory and endorsement of creationism. Is this due to cognition, culture, or both? In this section, we review some of the main factors that contribute to people's ideas about evolution and creationism, including, but not limited to, the cognitive factors that cognitive science of religion (CSR) scholars have identified.

1 Worldview

The rejection of evolutionary theory and endorsement of creationism is shaped to some extent by a person's worldview. Two aspects in particular predict the rejection of evolutionary accounts and acceptance, of creationism, as part of a worldview.

Enculturation

The first aspect that helps to explain the rejection of evolutionary theory and endorsement of creationism is enculturation into a group. Children are socialized into conventional ways of thinking about the world. They receive information about the nature of the world from in-group members whom they regard as reputable sources of authority, such as parents and religious leaders. As locally accepted ideas are repeated often, they become highly accessible to children. Children are repeatedly exposed to ideas through their parents, social reference groups, and subculture. For instance, a child who is brought up in a fundamentalist Christian community is likely to say that God created the universe. Furthermore, enculturation into the western world may also have an impact on the accessibility of ideas; the idea of nature as being purposefully made is prevalent in Christian and Abrahamic theistic traditions and discourse in the US.[13,14]

While researchers accept that culturally accepted ideas are more accessible to children, they differ, however, on the extent to which they think enculturation influences beliefs. The extreme enculturation view maintains that beliefs are determined exclusively by social learning. This perspective is part of the broader view of human cognition and behavior as a cultural construct. As we covered in Chapter 1 (Introduction), early pioneers of CSR disliked the theory of cultural determinism because it negated the role of humans as active in processing the world around them.

Several findings provide a reason to reject the extreme version of the enculturation hypothesis. As we review in the next section, preferences for creationist types of explanations are found among young children and adults, across religious traditions and cultures. Scholars in CSR tend to endorse a more moderate version of the enculturation hypothesis. This version rightly grants that exposure and socialization are essential in the development of children's reasoning about the world. The difference between those who endorse the extreme version of the exposure hypothesis and those who accept a more moderate view is where they place causal weight. Those who support the extreme version of the enculturation hypothesis assume that exposure to ideas is the causal mechanism of children's tendency to reason in ways that reinforce religious views of the world. According to this view, exposure enables the understanding and availability of ideas about creationism. That is, children are quick to access these ideas when reasoning about the nature of the world. This process leads to the internalization, acceptance, and commitment of these ideas as facts (i.e. belief).

By contrast, those who endorse a moderate view of enculturation accept the role of early socialization in the salience (i.e. accessibility) of ideas about nature, such as the idea that the world was created for a purpose. They also grant a role for socialization in explaining how people come to endorse views about the world, such as the belief in creationism. What they take issue with, however, is a single causal chain model between exposure to ideas on the one hand and reasoning about the world on the other. This simplistic equation misses a crucial component in children's thinking, the role of cognitive biases, and the processing of information (Figure 5.1).

To illustrate this point, consider again the example of the child who is brought up in a fundamentalist Christian community. Scholars agree that the child is likely to say that God created the universe. Cultural determinists propose that this is because the child has received repeated exposure and socialization about creationism, and cognitive scientists agree that socialization has an impact. However, CSR scholars would add that a creationist view of

Figure 5.1 The extreme version of the enculturation hypothesis is a form of the "black box" theories (see Figure 1.3, Chapter 1) because they do not allocate a role for human cognitive processing in belief formation.

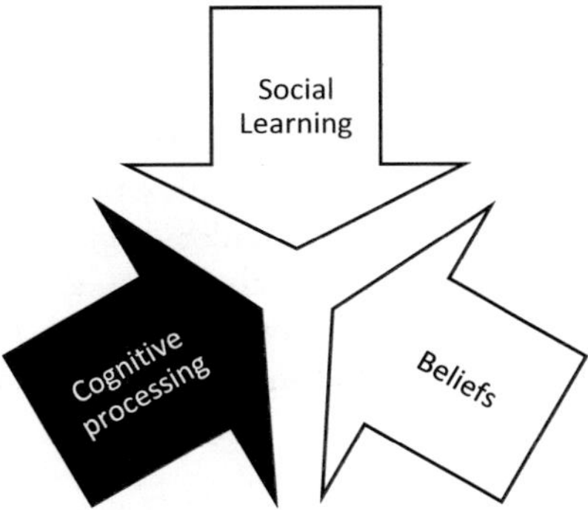

Figure 5.2 The moderate version of the enculturation hypothesis allocates an interactive role for human cognitive processing in the development of beliefs.

the world emerges early and is rapidly developing also because it satisfies default cognitive biases in children (Figure 5.2). A child who receives repeated exposure to evolutionary theory, which is not well supported by early emerging cognitive biases, might find it difficult to internalize this view. For example, they may well endorse evolution but are likely to make predictable errors when reasoning about the process of natural selection. These errors are anticipated in the sense that they reflect assumptions more compatible with the creationist or intentional views that other children find quite easy to endorse. By comparison, the child who receives repeated exposure to ideas about creationism, which is well supported by early emerging cognitive biases, might find it easier to internalize these views.

Group identification

The second aspect that helps to explain the rejection of evolutionary theory as part of a worldview is group identification. Group identification includes identification by demographics, politics, and of course, religious affiliation. A large-scale demographically representative survey of the American public's understanding of, and attitudes towards, evolution reveals essential insights. Psychologist Deena Weisberg and colleagues found that participants who had higher levels of religiosity were more likely to reject the idea of evolution.[15] Levels of religiosity and identification with a religious group, more specifically, are influenced by enculturation. Of course, children may change their opinions as they become older. Encountering information about evolution as adults may trigger a type of motivated reasoning known as identity-protective cognition.[16] Rather than weighing up the likelihood of evolution, people automatically respond to the group's values. If the group rejects evolutionary theory (i.e. they hold a conflicting account of the relationship between evolution and religion), then the individual will also reject it.

Group identification and worldview affect the processing of new ideas. As discussed at the start of the chapter, children are attuned to the consistency of current explanations with prior knowledge. Information that is inconsistent with what they currently know is judged differently than information that is consistent with what they know. In particular, if children receive information that is inconsistent with what they currently know, they are motivated to seek out and construct an explanation.[17] This tendency may lead to the rejection of evolutionary theory if it is perceived as inconsistent with conventional religious interpretations of the world.

2 Understanding evolution

Another reason why people reject evolutionary theory and thus are more likely to endorse alternative views of the origins and development of the world is that they do not understand it. People often struggle to grasp critical concepts such as inheritance, variation, natural selection, and adaptation.[18,19] There are two main reasons why people find it especially challenging to understand the theory of evolution.

Lack of knowledge

One reason why people do not understand evolutionary theory is that they lack knowledge about it, often referred to as a knowledge-deficit hypothesis.[20] This is the view adopted by Weisberg and colleagues, who conducted a large-scale survey on attitudes towards evolution. They found that knowledge about evolutionary theory predicts levels of acceptance in the US to a greater extent than demographics, political identification, and even religiosity.[21]

Cognitive obstacles

Cognitive scientists of religion have outlined some of the cognitive obstacles that people face when they encounter evolutionary theory. These obstacles are a product of the fact that the fundamental tenets of evolutionary theory often conflict with our cognitive biases about what makes an explanation of the world cognitively compelling. These biases tend to predispose people towards favoring religious explanations for the world, such as creationism. Some of these biases are outlined in the next section.

Key points

- CSR scholars propose that a creationist view of the world emerges early and is rapidly developing because it satisfies default cognitive biases in children.
- These biases often make religious views about the nature of the world more compelling than scientific or other views.

- These biases also create cognitive obstacles to understanding evolutionary theory and partially explain why many people reject it in favor of creationist explanations of the world.
- Belief in creationism emerges readily when cognitive biases are coupled with cultural information that supports religious views about the origins and development of the natural world.

Cognitive biases that impede understanding evolution and favor creationism

Almost all scientists accept the theory of evolution by natural selection, yet the American public is divided.[22] By contrast, the basic idea that a being or beings created the universe or natural order recurs throughout cultures.[23] These facts bring us to two questions: Why is evolutionary theory so poorly understood in the US? Moreover, why are supernatural ideas about the origins of the universe so widely accepted among different cultures? Research in the social cognitive sciences points to cognitive obstacles that impede the understanding of evolution by natural selection and make religious ideas about the origins and development of the world and species, such as creationism (the idea that divine intervention created the universe) a compelling alternative. In this section, we focus on three cognitive biases that affect reasoning about the world: promiscuous teleology, anthropomorphism, and psychological essentialism.

Figure 5.3 Many cultures endorse the idea that a supernatural being such as God created the universe and humans. The Creation of Adam painting by Italian artist Michelangelo illustrates the Biblical creation narrative from the Book of Genesis in which God gives life to Adam. (Image credit: doom.ko/Shutterstock.com).

Promiscuous teleology

Evolution by natural selection involves the component of blind chance variations (mutations), which are selected for by consequences. Chance is described here as blind because there is no forward-looking component, such as a designer (e.g. God). It is difficult to accept that the inhabitants of the world emerge and change as a result of chance. Even Charles Darwin (who is regarded as the father of evolutionary theory), had trouble accepting this component because it contradicted the commonsense view that everything happens for a reason.[24] By contrast, the tendency to see things in the world as having a purpose (and being made for that purpose) is readily endorsed. This tendency is often referred to as teleology, and it helps to explain the appeal of religious views that depict the world as ordered and purposeful. Indeed, developmental psychologists Deborah Kelemen and Cara DiYanni[25] found that children's preferences for teleological explanations of nature's origins were associated with the endorsement of a non-human intelligent design of nature. They also found this association between purpose and agency in Chinese children. Thus, their findings extend beyond individuals raised in a non-Abrahamic and officially secular culture.[26]

People are especially adept at adopting teleological reasoning with artifacts, and here it often proves useful. Consider an episode in Season 2 of Game of Thrones, for example, when Grenn, Edd, and Samwell Tarly found an object buried in the snow in a landmark in the wilderness.[27] The men reasoned that the sharp object was a spear, made of dragon glass, and they immediately asked questions about the intentions of the person who left it. The men reasoned that the person who left the spear must have been a ranger of the Night's Watch—a military order that guards a wall that serves as a border between lands. Nevertheless, the men concluded that the person wanted someone else to find the weapon, so it must be of great importance. On the basis of this reasoning, the men decided to keep the artifact, much to their advantage later when it turns out that the spear kills monsters known as White Walkers. This fictional example of teleological reasoning demonstrated an instance when teleology was correctly applied. Namely, the spear was made for a purpose. When this reasoning extends to things that were not prepared for a purpose, teleological thinking becomes "promiscuous."

Kelemen first coined the term promiscuous teleology and she has conducted the most extensive research on the development of teleological thought to date. In one of her studies, Kelemen asked US children and adults a series of questions about living and nonliving natural objects. These included questions about objects to which teleology applies (e.g. artifacts, parts of organisms such as teeth to chew food). They also included questions about objects to which teleology does not apply (e.g. whole organisms such as tigers and nonliving entities). She found that children were much more likely than adults to explain the properties of living kinds like lions in teleological terms, including nonliving natural kinds like clouds. Compared to adults, preschoolers were much more likely to say that living things, artifacts, and non-living natural objects are "for" something.[28]

Further, when given options such as asking whether rocks were pointy because of a physical process (i.e. "bits of stuff piled up for a long period of time") or because they performed a function, children (in contrast to adults) attributed a function to almost every kind of object. For example, they reasoned that rocks were pointy "so that animals wouldn't sit on them and smash them" or that "animals could scratch on them when they got itchy." In other words, children assumed that the pointiness of the rocks, like the properties of other objects, had a function.

The cognitive basis of promiscuous teleology

Kelemen explains children's preferences for teleological explanations as rooted in deep-seated biases that favor intentions and purpose-based explanations more generally. As we covered at the start of this chapter, children like to explain things, and this tendency spills over to all domains. This theory implies that, in line with the naturalness-of-religion thesis in CSR, reasoning about nature as purposefully designed is cognitively natural. On this account, the tendency to see things in the world as having a purpose is a by-product of the tendency to see agents as having goal-directed behavior and to see artifacts as designed by agents with specific goals.

As we will cover over the next two chapters (Chapter 6: The Afterlife, Chapter 7: Supernatural Agents), humans are naturally inclined to privilege intentional explanations for agents' behavior. In other words, people's behavior is not represented by children as random action sequences. Instead, they represent behavior as governed by a set of non-observable mental states. These states include beliefs (drinking water will stop me from being thirsty), desires (I would like to quench my thirst), and intentions (I will drink the glass of water to quench my thirst). The desire to explain agents' behavior is a core component of human cognition, emerges early, and continues to develop throughout childhood. For example, by 12-months, children will attribute goals to computer-generated shapes;[29] moreover, 15-month-olds infer the goals of a nonhuman agent to make predictions about their future behavior.[30]

The tendency to reason about people as intentional agents is often referred to as mentalizing. This tendency may well be evolutionarily adaptive because it helps people to predict others' future behavior and respond accordingly. Nevertheless, this tendency sometimes leads to error. For instance, we often think that there exists intention behind ambiguous events, even when social entities or forces cause them. For example, children and adults are likely to say that an unusually positive event (such as a woman who suddenly recovers from cancer) is due to supernatural causes such as good character, God, or luck than natural causes.[31] In high stakes situations, the tendency also leads to actual behavioral consequences in children and adults. For example, after observing an adult unwittingly give one of two children a lesser reward for a task, children will avoid that adult just as much as they avoid an adult who intentionally gives one of two children a smaller award for a job.[32]

Although it may seem less obvious, reasoning about the intention behind the creation of artifacts, another early emerging tendency, may also serve similar mentalizing functions. Throughout much of human history, understanding the intentions behind actions involved in artifact manipulation (i.e. ultimately to create something useful) would have facilitated efficient strategies to reproduce the tool or something like it that served the same purpose. For instance, when 15, 18-month-old children see a demonstrator fail to produce what they had intended (based on previous successful attempts by the demonstrator), they do not precisely copy what the demonstrator does. Instead, they produce the result that the demonstrator intended to create and even come up with their actions along the way.[33] Promiscuous teleology starts to robustly display itself around the same time that children explicitly understand artifact design.

Research supports the interpretation that teleology is a naturally emerging cognitive bias. First, the tendency of children in Kelemen's studies, in contrast to the adults, was to endorse teleological explanations for all types of things. If this tendency were a product of enculturation, then we would expect the bias to attribute purpose to natural kinds as increasing, not decreasing, with age and repeated exposure to ideas. Second, the developmental psychologist Margaret Evans found that all children preferred creationist accounts of the origins of natural kinds over alternative accounts. This finding was regardless of whether parents in Christian fundamentalist and non-fundamentalist communities taught evolution-based origins.[34] Finally, other research has demonstrated the tendency for children and adults to reason teleologically about living and nonliving kinds and to embrace a design stance in different cultures. This includes cultures with a comparatively lower degree of religiosity, such as children from Britain[35] and China,[36,37] and Finnish adults.[38] These findings suggest that the tendency for teleological reasoning is not an exclusive product of the level of religiosity endorsed by the broader population. Nor is it due to exposure to the worldview of Western Abrahamic culture.

Reasoning about the intended purpose of the world and things in it is cognitively natural, and some versions of this tendency (such as reasoning about the intentions behind artifact production) served humans well. However, the tendency to reason about nature as having an intended purpose may not serve us so well in the contemporary western world, where the mainstream scientific community endorses evolution by natural selection as fact.

Anthropomorphism

As previously discussed, evolution by natural selection involves the component of blind chance. No forward-looking deity designs the world or its inhabitants; rather, variations of species occur by chance and are selected for in biology by their consequences. By contrast, proponents of intelligent design view the universe and living things as designed and created by an intelligent entity. As per the creation story in Genesis, creationists believe that this entity is God. The general idea that an agent intentionally created the world is not exclusively found in the modern western world and recurs across history and throughout cultures in creation stories. Versions include the idea among Australian Aborigines that the Maker of Many Things brought up living things from underground, the Mayan idea that agents thought aspects of the world into existence, and the Scandinavian tradition that gods made the earth from the flesh of a giant.[39] Research in CSR suggests that the tendency towards anthropomorphism may help to explain the appeal of religious views that depict the world as designed and brought into existence by an agent.

Anthropomorphism is the tendency to attribute human features (e.g. agency, emotional states, intentions) to nonhuman things. Classic scholars, including Spinoza, Hume, Feuerbach, Nietzsche, Tylor, Horton, and Levi-Strauss, have long noted the importance of anthropomorphism in religion. Following these scholars, the anthropologist Stewart Guthrie made a cognitive theory of anthropomorphism central to a modern cognitive theory of religion. Guthrie argued that the tendency to anthropomorphize was initially established as a perceptual strategy.[40,41] The crux of this cognitive theory is that when people face chronic uncertainty about the nature of the world, they are sensitive to the detection of intentional agency, such as a person, and are biased to attribute deliberate action as the cause of things and events. One specific consequence of this tendency is that people project human-like characteristics onto nonhuman agents and objects, such as supernatural agents, clouds, and chairs.

Guthrie and others have argued that this tendency to project human-like features everywhere results in the tendency to see human-like beings everywhere. It gives rise to animism and to interpret ambiguous evidence as being caused by an agent. Consider the case of "crop circles." (Figure 5.4) In many parts of the world, people have reported intricate patterns or geometric shapes emerging overnight in grain fields. On closer inspection, the stalks of the plants have been flattened to create these shapes. These events could be due to natural processes, such as the weather, magnetism on the earth's surface, deformities in the grain, or the unintended consequence of an agent, such as animals consuming the plants. However, people commonly attribute these patterns to an agent with the intention to produce the visual effect. For example, as though a person was trying to make it seem as though a supernatural agent has created the patterns or the work of a superhuman agency (such as dancing fairies, extra-terrestrial life, or God).

Those who endorse intelligent design propose an anthropomorphic account of the universe, namely, that design implies a designer. Proponents of intelligent design sometimes use the "watchmaker analogy" to illustrate this point, proposing that if you stumbled upon a correctly functioning watch on the ground, you are likely to assume that someone designed it and placed it there at some point in time. Proponents of creationism often point out that intricacy, and the perfection of complex systems, such as the universe and species, is the result of the work of God.

Figure 5.4 Crop circles in field in Alsace, France. (Image credit: Sahara Prince/Shutterstock.com).

The cognitive origins of anthropomorphism

People are biased to attribute the intentional action of an agent as the cause of affairs when information is ambiguous. Psychologist Justin Barrett posited a mental tool that he called a hyperactive agency detection device (HADD).[42] From an evolutionary perspective, scholars have argued that this bias was adaptive. Mistakenly interpreting a noise in a bush as a tiger when it is wind (a false positive) has no costs. Nevertheless, failing to detect a tiger in a bush when our ancestors heard a noise (a false negative) would have been detrimental to fitness. These implications facilitated the development of belief in supernatural agents. In the modern environment, HADD is triggered and produces beliefs in unseen agents who are assumed to be the cause of the stimuli. Thus, people are likely to see meaning in the stars, faces in the clouds, and even Jesus Christ in a slice of toast.[43] This anthropomorphic tendency is heightened when there is perceived intricacy and perfection of complex systems (when considering the universe, for example).

Psychological essentialism

Developmental psychologist Susan Gelman coined the term psychological essentialism, and she has conducted the most extensive research on psychological essentialism to date.[44] Psychological essentialism is an implicit belief that members of a category, such as species of animals, share deep commonalities that make them what they are. For example, when asked what causes a tiger to have stripes and to roar children often claim, "there is something about tigers" that leads to those characteristics.[45] The idea of a tiger's essence also leads children to assume that it makes them different from other animals, such as zebras. These commonalities among category members are often characterized as determined by a true underlying nature that cannot be observed directly (i.e. an "essence"). The essence remains stable even when the animals physically change and it is also perceived as responsible for similarities that members share.[46,47]

The tendency to engage in psychological essentialism creates problems for learning the scientific theory of evolution and enhances the likelihood of endorsing creationist explanations of the world. First, a fundamental principle of evolutionary theory is that all existent life forms share a common ancestor. This principle is mostly inconsistent with the idea that a unique and discrete essence undergirds species. Second, if species are perceived to be bounded, fundamentally unchanging and homogeneous, then construing relations within and among species is difficult to comprehend. This essentialist bias makes grasping the selective survival and reproduction of particular individuals within populations—another critical component of evolutionary theory—challenging. As cognitive scientists Andrew Shtulman and Laura Schulz have shown, adults typically think of evolution as the gradual transformation of an entire population (e.g. the moths become darker over time). They are less likely to endorse explanations about the selective survival and reproduction within populations (e.g. darker moths are more likely to reproduce than lighter moths).[48]

Shtulman and Schulz found that those who tend to endorse essentialism in biology also tend to have a poor understanding of evolutionary theory.[49] Around one-third of the US population rejects evolutionary theory because they find it implausible that one species can transform into another.[50] In other words, species are unchanging and stable, which lends to design-based thinking. This bias enables an even easier acceptance of creationism. If species are fixed and created, then it lends easily to the idea that God created species. Many Christian fundamentalists maintain that God created species between 6,000 and 10,000 years ago. They further maintain that only God can create new.[51]

The cognitive origins of psychological essentialism

The tendency for psychological essentialist reasoning emerges early. From around the age of two, children reason about animal species as having immutable essences. This bias is part of early emerging folk biology; in other words, pre-scientific, naïve theories about how people tend to classify and reason about the natural world.[52] These folk theories provide children with a way to categorize living things and to explain their behavior.[53,54] As Legare and colleagues propose, essentialist thinking about species is likely to be evolutionarily adaptive because it enables people to make inferences about the biological world that would have facilitated their survival.[55] For instance, viewing predators such as snakes as having unchanging inherent hazardous properties motivates people to avoid them. However, extending essentialist reasoning to all category members impedes understanding of the relationships between and within species through the process of evolution.

Key points

- Cognitive biases emerge early in children.
- Cognitive biases help to explain why evolutionary theory is poorly understood in the US and the inherent appeal of creationism as an alternative explanation of the world.
- Biases can be traced to our evolutionary history as directly aiding survival (e.g. essentialism), or alternatively, as a by-product of reasoning that helped survival when applied to the correct domain for which it was intended (e.g. teleology, anthropomorphism).
- These biases include promiscuous teleology (which favors intentions and purpose-based explanations of the world), anthropomorphism, (the tendency to project human-like features everywhere, which results in interpreting ambiguous evidence as being caused by an agent), and psychological essentialism, (the tendency to view members of a species as having a fixed essence of innate being that determines their observable properties).

When intuitions and scientific facts about the world collide

Research in the social cognitive sciences has illustrated that people have a deep-rooted tendency to view nature as designed by an agent and species as having immutable essences. These biases may function in ways that are beneficial in some domains. For example, reasoning about the intention behind the maker of an object. However, they are less helpful when they interfere with understanding the processes of biological evolution. One obvious question is whether, and how, people can override these tendencies to understand evolutionary processes better?

Science and education communities are motivated in part by the view that increased knowledge leads to increased understanding of evolution (i.e. the knowledge-deficit hypothesis). Consequentially, they have increased efforts to help young children, students, and the broader public understand the theory of evolution by providing more information about it. These are worthy endeavors. Providing more information about biological processes is an essential first step, but it does not, however, guarantee the understanding or acceptance of evolution. As outlined at the start of the chapter, people's worldviews also partially determine how they respond to the theory of evolution. As we have also covered in the chapter, cognitive scientists of religion have outlined the cognitive obstacles that all people face when they encounter evolutionary theory. Scholars in CSR paint a more complicated picture of the relationship between knowledge and belief formation than a straightforward knowledge-deficit hypothesis or enculturation account would predict. They propose strategies that take account of critical time periods of theory formation in children as well as cognitive biases that continue to adulthood, for increasing the likelihood of understanding evolution.

Research in CSR has demonstrated that cognitive biases are deeply entrenched and resistant to change. In order to build a scientific understanding of the world, children need to undergo conceptual change. They need to understand the concepts that are fundamental to evolution (such as heritable characteristics, common ancestry, and selective survival), and to comprehend how these concepts cohere to form the theory of evolution by natural selection—yet conceptual change is challenging to initiate and complete. To achieve conceptual change, children must overhaul their intuitive theories constructed in the absence of a scientific theory.

Conceptual change requires restructuring knowledge, not just enriching it. As Shulman explains, scientific theories never entirely overwrite intuitive theories. He likens the outcome of conceptual change to a palimpsest, an old manuscript typical in the Middle Ages. During this period, because of the scarcity of materials, one document was physically recorded on top of another.[56] Thus, even though people have knowledge of the correct answers, when they are under pressure, they revert to heuristics about the nature of the world and often make incorrect judgments.

Figure 5.5 Just like the new ink doesn't completely cover up words written earlier; Shulman explains how intuitive theories about the world lurk below scientific ones. (Image credit: Ann Baldwin/Shutterstock.com).

The early emerging intuitive construal of the nature of the world is more likely to be a lifelong bias. Even though such inherent tendencies may be inhibited or concealed by later constructed beliefs—such as science education—they are never entirely displaced. Thus, theories about purposeful design and evolutionary principles often coexist. People can override their intuitions by effortful processing, such as the explicit answers given by participants concerning nature when they have time to reflect. However, intuitions often re-emerge when participants are forced to make speed judgments about nature and do not have time to reflect.[57,58] These findings can be understood from a dual-process model of the mind covered in Chapter 3 (Research Questions). There seems to be a discrepancy between adults' reasoning about the origin of nature when they have time, energy, and motivation (and can access System 2) and how they respond quickly (and must default to System 1).

For example, as Kelemen and other developmentalists have shown, when given time to reflect on an answer to a question, for example, asking what things are "for," adults tend to reject teleological explanations for the world more often than children. When adults do not have time to reflect (for example, when they had to make a speeded judgment), they tend to revert to the default intuition that natural phenomena are purposefully made.[59,60] Researcher Elisa Järnefelt and colleagues conducted a series of these types of speeded judgment studies.[61] The researchers found that, as expected, religious adults' baseline tendency to endorse nature as purposefully created was higher than non-religious participants. Nevertheless, even the non-religious participants tended to default back to understanding natural phenomena as purposefully made when under time pressure.

While being educated is a protective factor, being a scientist is not—at least not to the degree that we might expect. Those with little to no formal schooling tend to endorse more teleological explanations than those with formal schooling science training.[62] Indeed, those who have received an extensive education, such as college professors, tend to have less teleological explanations for natural phenomena than those who have received tertiary education, such as undergraduates. Even professional physical scientists accept as many scientifically unwarranted teleological explanations as those in the humanities who lacked this training.[63] Importantly, the degree of the speeded effects (i.e. the tendency to default to teleological ideas under time pressure) is the same regardless of education. For instance, even though physical scientists understand the cause of metabolic processes of plants, when under timed conditions, many judged the statement "trees produce oxygen so that animals can breathe" as "true."

There are individual differences in the extent to which adults can override their intuitive biases against evolutionary theory by engaging in effortful processing. Psychologist Will Gervais found that the tendency to engage in analytic thinking predicted endorsement of evolution among US college students, even when taking into account other things that predict evolutionary beliefs, like belief in God. Analytic thinking is a step-by-step methodological approach to thinking where a complex problem is broken down into single and manageable components. When this method is used, it often conflicts with intuitive responses.[64]

Gervais has proposed that individuals who engage in the form of analytic or reflective thinking are more likely to be able to override the instinctive reaction against evolution to endorse it. Given that analytic thinking is a crucial skill facilitated in higher education, this may well explain the correlation between education level and rejection of purposeful design in nature when participants have the chance to think without time pressure before answering. Yet other research has suggested that some of these findings do not always replicate cross-culturally, and relationships between cognitive reflection and beliefs also depend upon cultural exposure to relevant ideas.[65] Belief is a much more complicated process than one's cognitive style. Yet, Gervais' findings provide a reason to encourage analytic thinking among those of us who do not always want to accept our instinctual responses.

Recent research has suggested that a more effective method to ensure that adults come to understand evolutionary theory is to teach them about evolution while they are young. For example, science education standards recommend a comprehensive explanation of adaptation by natural selection in grades 8 and 12;[66] in part, due to the assumption that children are incapable of understanding the theory at an earlier age. Yet by this stage, children's intuitive ideas (such as viewing the world as intentionally designed and imbued with hidden essences), act as impediments to learning about evolution. This tendency is in part because they have not received information on alternative coherent theories to challenge prior beliefs. They have not received information on the theory of evolution because of the assumption that they are not capable of understanding it before this age.

As Shtulman has pointed out, educators then have to help students not only to learn accurate theories but also to unlearn their naïve (i.e. pre-scientific) theories about the world.[67] Some scholars have challenged the assumption that younger children are incapable of understanding evolutionary theory. Researchers Emmons, Smith, and Kelemen have demonstrated that even children as young as five years old are capable of understanding complex biological ideas. They created a storybook specifically to aid the understanding of evolutionary theory.[68] These scholars advocate for introducing age-appropriate tools, such as storybook depictions of evolution, to enhance children's early understanding of evolution. Also, cognitive scientists of religion propose that arming educators with an awareness of these biases can inform pedagogical strategies to improving evolution understanding and help them to teach evolution to students more effectively. For instance, Legare and colleagues have produced a guide for teaching evolution in the social sciences that outlines both biases and teaching strategies.[69]

Key points

- CSR scholars have demonstrated that cognitive biases that serve as obstacles to understanding evolutionary theory are profoundly entrenched and resistant to change, and they are never entirely displaced by scientific knowledge.

- To build a scientific understanding of the world, children need to undergo conceptual change. Educators must help students to learn scientific theories about the world but also unlearn naïve assumptions about the world.
- Informing educators about these biases can inform pedagogical strategies to improving evolution understanding and help them to teach evolutionary theory to students more effectively.

The rationality of religious and scientific thinking

In the previous section, we covered research demonstrating that cognitive biases towards creationist explanations for the world exist despite increasing age and advanced education. These findings and the research of CSR, more generally, have implications for the academic study of religion. They relate specifically to the idea that science is rational, and faith is irrational, referred to here as the science-as-rational and religion-as-irrational theses. These theses have roots in early nineteenth-century anthropologists, often referred to as intellectualists, such as Edward Tylor and James Frazer. Among other endeavors, they were preoccupied with uncovering the origins of religious and magic beliefs. An era of rationalism profoundly influenced these Victorian scholars, and they worked within what was then construed as an evolutionary framework, where religion was interpreted as the misapplication of scientific principles, and science was construed as the highest level of rational thinking.

According to these early intellectualist theories, as thinking becomes more sophisticated, cultures pass through a series of stages, from magic to religion and finally to science. Eventually, more knowledge will eradicate religion. They favor a displacement theory and would predict that increasing scientific knowledge supplants religious ideas. This prediction has not been borne out, and research in the cognitive-evolutionary sciences provides a much more complicated picture than is often depicted in popular accounts. Yet, versions of the argument have appeared throughout history by some of the world's most famous thinkers (e.g. Nietzsche, Marx, and Freud). These ideas are also regurgitated in different forms in the writings of new atheist thinkers, most notably the "four horsemen": Richard Dawkins, Daniel Dennett, Sam Harris, and the late Christopher Hitchens. It seems that religious thinking, which tends to favor creationist explanations, is not replaced by scientific reasoning and that religion is not going to be eliminated.

Other theorists espouse a different view of the relationship between science and religion. For instance, evolutionary biologist Stephen Jay Gould advocates for a view called "non-overlapping magisterial" (NOMA), that science and religion represent different areas of inquiry, so there is a difference between the aspects they have legitimate authority, or magisterium, over. He describes the NOMA principle as the following,

> Science tries to document the factual character of the natural world and to develop theories that coordinate and explain these facts. Religion, on the other hand, operates in the equally important, but utterly different, realm of human purposes, meanings, and values—subjects that the factual domain of science might illuminate, but can never resolve.[70]

Of course, Gould is discussing the epistemological relationship between science and religion in the world. This view is related in many ways to the corresponding psychological models of these two phenomena, as showcased in this chapter by cognitive science researchers, such as Kelemen, Legare, and Shulman, among others. These scholars suggest that scientific explanations do not replace religious ones but rather coexist with them. In other words, tendencies towards creationist reasoning about nature are not supplanted by increased knowledge and elaboration of ideas about science. This theory is known as a coexistence model.

Coexistence models are used to explain how people reason about natural and supernatural phenomena more generally.[71,72] They account for how people can accommodate and reconcile multiple explanations for the same kind of event or outcomes. These could be scientific and lay theories, for example, or natural and supernatural theories. People do this by using different types of explanations to explain different levels of causality. We visit coexistence models between natural and supernatural explanations in more detail in the next section.

Participation 2: Increasing the understanding of evolutionary theory

1 Imagine that you have been appointed as head of a new national task force to assign funds to increase the understanding of evolutionary theory. Draft a brief (5-minute) rebuttal to members on the task force, based on what you have read in this chapter.

   (A) Commentator A claims that the only way to increase understanding of scientific theories about the world is to prove that religion is false. He proposes spending 100 percent of the funds on materials to discredit religious ideas such as intelligent design.

   (B) Commentator B claims that the only way to increase understanding of scientific theories about the world is to increase understanding about evolution. She proposes spending 100 per cent of the funds on materials to teach children about evolution.

2 Next, outline how you would spend the funds to increase the understanding of evolutionary theory. You can allocate funds to multiple strategies (e.g. public policy, education, advertising, recruiting groups, and so on).

Key points

- CSR scholars have demonstrated that cognitive biases that serve to facilitate belief in creationist understandings of the world are never entirely displaced by scientific knowledge.
- These findings do not support a displacement theory of how people represent scientific and religious explanations of the world, which predicts that increasing scientific knowledge supplants religious ideas.
- The findings support a coexistence model of how people represent scientific and religious explanations of the world because people accommodate and reconcile biological and supernatural accounts.

Summary of explaining the origins and development of the natural world

- Many adults in the US outwardly reject evolutionary theory as an explanation of the origins and development of the world and species, and many accept creationist ideas as an alternative explanation.
- There are many aspects of cognition and culture that explain these trends.
- CSR has outlined cognitive obstacles to understanding evolutionary theory and biases that favor creationist accounts. These include promiscuous teleology, anthropomorphism, and essentialism.
- These biases are never entirely displaced by scientific knowledge, and supernatural and scientific explanations often coexist in people's minds.

Explaining events in the world: Coexistence reasoning

Thus far, we have learned that cognitive scientists of religion endorse a coexistence account of theory change to explain cognitive biases about the origins and development of the world among adults. That is to say, naïve theories about nature are not displaced by increased knowledge about science, but rather, are concealed by later constructed beliefs, so ultimately naïve and learned theories coexist in the minds of people. Cognitive scientists have demonstrated that coexistence reasoning exists across cultures and throughout development. This is especially prominent when people reason about events in the world, such as the origins of species, misfortune, illness, and death.[73,74] These scholars have also proposed that people are much more likely to employ coexistence reasoning to explain highly significant events.

We have already covered examples of coexistence reasoning about the origins of species at the start of the chapter. As you may recall, some people construe the relationship between biological evolution and supernatural accounts of the origin and development of the world are compatible, often adopting integrated thinking. For example, reasoning that evolutionary theory explains how life and species evolve gradually but that God created life on earth in the first place. We also cover examples of coexistence reasoning about death in Chapter 6 (The Afterlife). Here, research reveals that people are sensitive to aspects of the context in their explanations. For example, when presented with a narrative highlighting the biological aspects of death (e.g. the unsuccessful efforts of doctors to save the dead person), people are likely to assert that living functions (and mainly bodily functions) have ceased. By contrast, when the same people are presented with a narrative highlighting the spiritual aspects of death (e.g. a religious figure or ceremony), they are more likely to assert that living functions (and particularly spiritual or mental functions) continue. In what follows in this section, we concentrate on coexistence reasoning about misfortune and illness.

Misfortune

One of the most well-known examples of coexistence reasoning about misfortunate events was in the 1930s by the British anthropologist Evans-Pritchard. Evans-Pritchard disagreed with his intellectualist predecessors who viewed science as the highest form of thought and religion and magic as the misapplication of science. Evans-Pritchard's grounds for disagreement was spending an extended time conducting ethnographic fieldwork—observing and interacting—with the Azande people in North Central Africa, with the goal of understading the people in their terms. He argued that the Azande used both natural and supernatural explanations to explain events.

Evans-Pritchard provided what is now a famous example of a collapsing granary (i.e. a massive structure of beams and clay to store for grain where people also gather under the shade). This unfortunate event happened frequently, he observed, so there was nothing at all remarkable about it. Sometimes, however, the granary would collapse, and people were injured as a result. Evans-Pritchard explained that people are not ignorant of natural laws. They understand that termite damage and decay make the eventual demise inevitable. Yet the Azande were not so much concerned with the question of how the granary collapsed as with why it collapsed at that particular moment on those specific people.[75] Thus, Pritchard claimed that the Azande supplemented naturalistic explanations of the collapse of the granary with supernatural forces of witchcraft. Witchcraft caused the granary to collapse at that particular moment in time when specific individuals were underneath it.

One of the main contributions of Evans-Pritchard's work was to make a seemingly exotic belief in witchcraft seem easy to relate to when considered in context. To extend Evans-Pritchard's observations, consider how Azande's beliefs relate to people's thinking in the modern western world today. We too make a host of assumptions about the world's reality because we cannot trace all causal pathways, and they remain hidden from our perception. We fill these "black boxes" of causal pathways with all sorts of laws when probed, just like the Azande. The following quote from the pioneer in cybernetics, Ross Ashby, sums up this idea:

> The child who tries to open a door has to manipulate the handle (the input) so as to produce the desired movement at the latch (the output), and he has to learn how to control the one by the other without being able to see the internal mechanism that links them. In our daily lives, we are confronted at every turn with systems whose internal mechanisms are not fully open to inspection, and which must be treated by the methods appropriate to the Black Box.[76]

Few people can explain the internal mechanism that links a handle to the latch, or how flipping a light switch results in electricity and light, yet we blindly trust these aspects of our environment. In part, this is due to context biases because it is easier to learn from others we trust than to practice a behavior only when we understand the inner workings of causality. Thus, for a child growing up in the modern West, a belief in electricity is no more rational than Azande's belief in magic.

Illness

Access to natural and supernatural explanations is not confined to the Azande. Developmental psychologist Cristine Legare (whose research we encountered earlier in the chapter), investigated how children and adults reasoned about the cause and spread of AIDS in South Africa.[77] Just like Evans-Pritchard reported that the Azande used different types of explanations for the collapsing granary, Legare and colleagues also found a difference between the type of cause of AIDS that participants endorsed.

As we discussed at the start of the chapter, scientists often categorize questions, and explanations, as either proximate or distal. Distal causes are the most distant, or ultimate, causal explanation of the event, and proximate is the closest causal explanation. Legare and colleagues found that people endorsed witchcraft as providing an answer to the "why" question of illness (the distal cause), whereas biology offers a response to the "how" question of disease (the proximate cause). For instance, participants tended to identify a proximate natural cause for contracting AIDS, such as having unprotected sex, and a distal cause as supernatural, such as reasoning that the witches distorted people's sense of good judgment or put an HIV infected person in a person's path. We discuss this research in more detail in the case study at the end of the chapter.

Combining both natural and supernatural explanations about illness is not only found in Africa. Legare and colleagues have also found similar types of coexistence reasoning about illness in Vanuatu, a Melanesian island nation in the South Pacific.[78] There are also many instances of coexistence reasoning in the modern western world, especially when it comes to the diagnosis of life-threatening illness.

Consider the devastating scenario of a woman hearing for the first time from the oncologist that she has cancer. The oncologist may well preempt the "how" (i.e. proximate) question by explaining the risk factors that make people susceptible to diseases, such as genetics. She may even explain to the patient that the exact cause of cancer is unknown.

Most people have a rudimentary understanding of the underlying mechanisms of disease, just enough knowledge to justify protective behavior. For example, most Americans know that the coronavirus (COVID-19) spreads from person to person, and that avoiding social contact is the safest way to avoid contamination. Yet even those who have expertise in the biological model of disease do not find this model a satisfying explanation of misfortune. More often than not, the question that is most pressing in the mind of a newly diagnosed individual with a life-threatening disease, such as metastatic cancer, is "why me?"[79] This has been dubbed as "the question with no answers".[80,81] This term refers to the fact that, in the mind of the individual, there are no satisfactory answers from a medical model of disease that adequately explain the ultimate cause of their cancer, and why they have to endure the condition rather than someone else.

Many people who are diagnosed with a chronic illness, such as cancer, are likely to employ a non-biological framework to make sense of their plight.[82] These frameworks are generally referred to in the coping literature as "meaning-making." This refers to the representation or restoration of possible meaningful relationships between events, and people frequently employ teleological reasoning, such as the idea that their suffering is for a purpose.[83] Unsurprisingly, research in the psychology of religion suggests that at least in non-life-threatening stages of cancer, patients report becoming more religious following diagnoses.[84] Drawing upon religion may be especially prevalent in the early stages following diagnoses because it may provide people with reassurance and certainty to an otherwise uncertain outcome, for instance, that God has a purpose for them or can help them cope. Certainty reduces anxiety about consequences, and studies report overall better mental health outcomes for believers suffering from chronic illness relative to non-believers.[85]

Other studies report a decline in religious belief in terminal illnesses when patients are closer to death. This finding is commensurate with the interpretation that drawing upon religious frameworks helps people make sense of uncertainty.[86] The psychologist Julie Exline and colleagues found that many cancer survivors—especially those who reported belief in God—reported being angry at God for their disease.[87] Appealing to a sense of divine order in the world to explain suffering may be more cognitively appealing than the alternative, which is to explain one's suffering as deserved (i.e. immanent justice) or just misfortune. Indeed, of all the possible causes for good health, people rate luck as the least important factor.[88]

Just like the Azande drew upon their culturally salient model of witchcraft to explain why the granary collapsed at a particular moment injuring specific individuals, believers are likely to draw upon their existing beliefs and culturally dominant representations of God and divine order to make meaning from their suffering. On the one hand, cancer survivors have an understanding of cancer from a biomedical model. Yet, on the other, they employ other non-biological frameworks to answer questions about why they got the disease. Both cases depict the coexistence of natural and supernatural explanations that again serve to dispel the idea that has permeated many discussions about the rationality of religion, that greater scientific knowledge displaces religious thinking.

In sum, converging evidence from diverse contexts demonstrates that supernatural beliefs are not replaced by scientific knowledge but instead coexist and are often employed to explain different types of causes. This coexistence reasoning is not unique to the domain of the supernatural or religious but applies to many naïve theories of how the world works.[89,90] In the next section, we continue to focus on how intuitive biases predispose us towards specific explanations for events in the world. As will become apparent, these tendencies favor religious over secular accounts.

Key points

- Supernatural beliefs are not replaced by scientific knowledge but instead coexist and are often employed to explain different types of causes.
- Cognitive scientists have demonstrated that coexistence reasoning exists across cultures and throughout development when reasoning about events in the world, such as the origins of species, illness, and death.
- One of the most well-known examples of coexistence reasoning was the description of the Azande people in North Central Africa in the 1930s by the British anthropologist Evans- Pritchard.
- The Azande were concerned with the question of how the granary collapsed, and they used naturalistic examples to explain this. They were also concerned with the question of why the granary collapsed at a particular time when certain people were sitting under it, and they used supernatural forces of witchcraft to explain this.

Explaining events in the world: reasoning about moral justice

Previously in the chapter, we covered research by cognitive scientists of religion, who showcased how people are cognitively biased to explain naturally occurring events in terms of an inherent purpose, known as teleology. How many times have you heard the following phrases employed by people to explain an event? "It was meant to be," "everything happens for a reason," "what goes around comes around," "you reap what you sow." You may have even uttered the words to yourself on occasion. Chances are that when you utter these phrases, they are not being used to explain mundane, insignificant events, such as realizing that your spouse did not tighten the lid on the jam jar properly.

As people often think that significant events happen for a reason, they are also motivated to uncover the reason for the event. Consider the endowment of the disaster with purpose; to communicate something to the people affected. On 11 March, 2011, a powerful magnitude-9 earthquake in Northeastern Japan initiated a series of massive tsunami waves that wreaked havoc on many coastal areas of the country. Around 150,000 evacuees lost their homes, and approximately 16,000 people lost their lives. The damage of property was estimated to be in the region of $235 billion, making it the costliest natural disaster in world history.[91] On 14 March, Tokyo Governor Shintaro Ishihara told reporters that the disaster was "divine punishment" because the Japanese people had become egoistic and greedy.[92] His comments sparked many public criticisms—most notably from the governor of Miyagi Prefecture, north of Tokyo on the east coast of Honshu island, where the death toll was expected to be around 10,000. Shintaro later retracted his remarks and apologized.[93]

On the one hand, we can attribute Shintaro's comments about the tsunami to the unfiltered thoughts of a 78-year old conservative politician with a history of making offensive remarks. On the other hand, while Shintaro was the most vocal, he was not the only public figure to have offered such explanations.[94] A poll conducted by the Public Religion Research Institute (PPRI) in April 2011 reported that 38 percent of Americans surveyed believed that natural disasters, such as the Tsunami in Japan, were a sign from God.[95] What differed in the accounts between the Eastern and Western cultures was the mechanism through which they proposed the tragedy occurred; Ushihara, a follower of Buddhism and Shinto, attributed it to a supernatural force, whereas many Americans attributed it specifically to the will of a monotheistic God. What was similar to both Buddhist and Christian explanations was the assumption that the tragedy was purposefully intended to communicate something to the people affected. This is a prototypical example of teleological reasoning.

In addition to reasoning that the event had a purpose, Shintaro was also assuming that bad things tend to happen to bad people. The tendency to reason this way, and conversely, that good things happen to good people is common among ordinary people as well as political leaders. It is part of a tendency known as immanent justice reasoning. We may find Shintaro's comments morally offensive, yet we would find it more cognitively perplexing if he had commented that the disaster was a divine reward (rather than divine punishment) because the Japanese people had become self-centered and greedy.

Immanent justice reasoning

Immanent justice reasoning refers to the tendency to reason that good things happen to good people and, conversely, that bad things tend to happen to bad people—even when there are no plausible naturalistic causal links between the actions and outcome. Consider the following example of immanent justice reasoning from Northern Ireland. A charity called the "Kevin Bell Repatriation Trust" is run by a modest retired couple, Mr. and Mrs. Bell, who set up the charity when their son died unexpectedly in the US in 2013. Vowing never to let another family deal with the stress and hardship of arranging and paying to have their family members returned home, they spent their years working hard on fundraising and helping hundreds of families who had lost a loved one abroad. The couple is famously admired in Northern Ireland for their charity work.

In 2017, news broke all over Ireland that the Bells had won £1 million in the UK lottery.[96] Immediately news and social media platforms like Twitter and Facebook were inundated with well-wishers who advocated teleological explanations for the event. Local celebrities, news reporters, and the public delighted in how good things happen to good people and that they were rewarded for their generosity. Some said that it was a gift from God, while others explained it as karma. During that time, it was tough not to attribute their success to some force of nature. Consider the alternative explanation that their fate was merely down to good fortune. In the UK National lottery, six numbers are drawn at random from the set of integers between 1 and 49, which means that there is a vast, but limited, combination of numbers. Statisticians have calculated that the jackpot chance is approximately 1 in 14 million. Their fate was improbable, but not impossible. Were they just lucky?

Let's consider a counterexample. In 2004, Iorworth Hoare, a 52-year-old felon in England convicted of sex attacks including raping a retired schoolteacher, was on day release from his life imprisonment sentence when he decided to buy a lottery ticket. Hoare hit the jackpot and scooped a 7.2 million win. He was released in 2005. The retired policeman who arrested Hoare in 1966 said that he could not think of a "less deserving person" to win the money. Despite public outcry, the government could not stop Hoare from collecting latter his prize.[97]

In this latter example, you are likely to feel a deep sense of unease. You may even search for something to compensate for this event, such as "well maybe the victims can seek more compensation money," or "the man can never be seen in public now because the win made his face recognizable." I doubt that you would interpret this event as "meant to be" or "the will of God" or "karma." You are more likely to say that Hoare's lottery win was due to chance than the Bells'. Yet when you sit down and think about it in the cold light of day, there is nothing causally linking the Bells' good deeds with their lottery win more than Hoare's atrocious crimes to his good financial fortune—yet the explanation of fate, rather than chance, is more cognitively appealing in the Bell case. Your assumptions are based on immanent justice reasoning: good things happen to good people and conversely, that bad things happen to bad people.

The cognitive basis of immanent justice reasoning

Why do we tend to reason as though good things happen to good people and, conversely, that bad things tend to happen to bad people, even when there are no plausible naturalistic causal links between the actions and outcome? This tendency is a product of both cognition and culture. Ideas about immanent justice reasoning recur throughout large-scale societies. Scholars have pointed to the many examples in the Judeo-Christian culture of people suffering for their sins.[98] Moreover, the many western cases of good deeds attracting good outcomes and bad deeds attracting adverse results can be found in popular media.[99] Thus, ideas about immanent justice are likely to be strengthened with enculturation. For instance, adults tend to engage in immanent justice reasoning more than elementary school children,[100,101] and the relationship between the extent to which people watch fictional television (whose narratives often represent the world as just) positively correlates with the extent to which they employ immanent justice explanations.[102]

Cognitive biases and motivational beliefs enable the rapid endorsement of immanent justice reasoning. Research has repeatedly shown that children engage in immanent justice reasoning to make sense of the world, and notably when entailing judgments of fairness.[103] The tendency has been reported cross-culturally, including in Eastern traditions,[104] suggesting that this form of reasoning is not a product of Judeo-Christian or WEIRD traditions (i.e. Western, Educated, Industrialized, Rich, and Democratic), but is likely to have cognitive foundations. For instance, scholars in the cognitive and social sciences have argued that the underlying tendency to think that things happen for a reason is a by-product of universal social-cognitive biases, specifically, the tendency to reason about the intention behind artifacts and people's behaviors. As we covered in the last section of this chapter, these tendencies spill over to other domains, leading us to see the world as a product of agency, purpose, and design (i.e. promiscuous teleology).

Against the baseline tendency to reason about events as happening for a reason, immanent justice involves reasoning that links actions and outcomes—good deeds lead to good results, and bad deeds lead to adverse outcomes. One prominent theory in social psychology explains the motivation behind immanent justice reasoning as stemming from a "just-world hypothesis," a sense that the world is purposefully ordered and just, and thus a safe place to live. Hence the sense that people's actions are inclined to bring morally fair and fitting consequences. Indeed, immanent justice reasoning can bring a sense of control over the world and is often used to explain events for which we do not have control over or comprehend.

Cognitive scientist Nicolas Baumard and colleagues have proposed an evolutionary explanation for immanent justice reasoning. He suggests that it is derived from our evolved sense of fairness.[105] In a series of studies, they found that people who do not claim to believe in immanent justice are implicitly influenced by it. Most importantly, all participants were likely to evoke notions of fairness when the misdeed is followed by misfortune, but not when the misfortune is disproportionate to the crime. For example, when they heard a story about a man who insulted a beggar and then was hit by a car and died, participants were likely to say that the cause of the man's death was not because he insulted the beggar.

On the other hand, when they heard a story about a man who insulted a beggar and then tripped on his shoelace and fell, they were likely to say that the cause of the fall was because the man insulted the beggar. In other words, our evolved sense of fairness construes misfortune as a way of compensating for the misdeed. This sense of fairness was adaptive. In our species' development in cultural evolution, cooperation was crucial for survival; few would cooperate with a social group member who did not abide by and enforce a sense of fairness. In other words, the group punishes those who do wrong, and those who do right are rewarded.

Related, and as we will cover in Chapter 8 (Morality), the general tendency to construe the world as fair serves to deter those who would not otherwise abide by the rules. This effect is stronger if the moral policing agent dishing out fairness is a supernatural agent or divine force, such as God, or karma.[106,107] Of course, immanent justice reasoning is found without the appeal to divine order or intervention, with dire consequences. For example, many Germans living under the Nazi regime were persuaded that those who were sent to the concentration camps were members of an impure race who did something wrong to deserve their fates.[108] Still, many popular versions of religion have been influenced by the tendency to reason about good fortune as a reward for adhering to moral rules and ill fortune as imposed for violation of regulations.[109]

As we covered earlier in the chapter, people tend to engage in attributing the intentional action of an agent as the cause of affairs in the world. Thus, the idea of an agent or sense of agency as evoked in the causal process between deed and outcome is cognitively appealing. Indeed, many theologians have sought to justify why bad things happen to good people, and good things happen to bad people in western Christianity where a monotheistic God is sovereign (a conundrum often referred to as the problem of evil, or theodicy). Developmental psychologist Paul Bloom and colleagues have turned their attention to how ordinary people reason about deeds and outcomes. They found that the relationship between religious belief and immanent justice reasoning may be mediated by mentalizing ability, which, as we covered in the previous section, refers to the tendency to reason about agents as intentional beings. Specifically, they found that higher mentalizing is related to the tendency to engage in immanent justice explanations.[110] This finding supports the view that immanent justice reasoning is a by-product of the human inclination to reason about the intention behind people's behaviors.

Research has demonstrated that while both religious and non-religious adults provide teleological explanations for the causes of life-altering events, theists give significantly more of these explanations than atheists and they tend to hold stronger teleological beliefs.[111,112] The relationship may not be solely about religious beliefs but rather, the tendency of religious individuals to reason about the goals, intentions, and beliefs of their deities or cosmic order. Even though most contemporary religious doctrines state that punishment occurs only in the afterlife, many people are automatically tempted to explain adverse events regarding immanent justice. Thus, natural disasters like the 2011 tsunami are interpreted as divine warnings or cautions to sinful behavior. Likewise, in India, vast differences in inequality and the caste system are justified by the laws of karma, the accumulation of deeds over lifetimes. It appears that immanent justice reasoning is a naturally emerging tendency that is often supported by cultural ideas about the nature of the world.

Participation 3: Cognitive biases

1 Provide a brief definition of the following cognitive foundations: (a) promiscuous teleology (b) anthropomorphism (c) psychological essentialism, and (d) immanent justice reasoning.

   Table 3.3 in Chapter 3 (Research Questions) provided examples of the cognitive foundations of religious ideas. Based on this table and chapter:

2 Table 3.5 in Chapter 3 (Research Questions) outlines four questions to enrich explanations of religion. Go through this chapter and find one answer to each of the questions for the selected biases.

   1 Mechanism or bias 1: What is the structure of immanent justice reasoning?
   2 Ontogeny: How does promiscuous teleology develop in individuals?
   3 Phylogeny: What is the evolutionary history of anthropomorphism?
   4 Adaptive significance: How has psychological essentialism influenced fitness?

3 Explain (in a few sentences for each) how each bias enriches the understanding of how people reason about the natural world.

Key points

- People often think that significant events happen for a reason, and they are motivated to uncover the reason for these events.
- People tend to reason that good things happen to good people and conversely, that bad things tend to happen to bad people, even when there are no plausible naturalistic causal links between the actions and outcome.
- Cognitive scientist Nicolas Baumard and colleagues have proposed that immanent justice reasoning is derived from our evolved sense of fairness.
- Cognitive biases (such as promiscuous teleology, anthropomorphism, and a sense of fairness), and cultural worldviews enable the rapid endorsement of immanent justice reasoning.

Summary of explaining events in the world

- People employ coexistence reasoning across cultures and throughout development to explain events in the world, such as the origins of species, misfortune, illness, and death.
- People often adopt integrated thinking when reasoning about accounts of the origins of species and illness.
- Integrated thinking is a type of coexistence reasoning where people construe the relationship between natural and supernatural accounts as compatible, and they integrate both into a single explanation.
- Evans-Pritchard and Legare and colleagues found that people in Africa endorsed supernatural causes to explain "why" misfortune occurred (the distal cause). In contrast, natural causes told "how" misfortune occurred (the proximate cause). Similar types of coexistence reasoning about illness are present in other parts of the world, such as Melanesia and the modern West.
- People often explain events in the world by endorsing ideas about moral justice. They are likely to reason concerning immanent justice, that good things happen to good people, and conversely, that bad things tend to happen to bad people.
- Cognitive biases and enculturation facilitate the widespread endorsement of immanent justice reasoning.

Research case study: The coexistence of natural and supernatural explanations for illness

Developmental psychologist Cristine Legare was intrigued by Evans-Pritchard's early observations about how the Azande reason about the causes of events. Drawing from her background in cross-cultural and developmental psychology, Legare noted that access to natural as well as supernatural explanations is not confined to the Azande. Legare noted the distinct parallels between Evans-Pritchard's observations of reasoning about misfortune in Zandleland and the presence of both biological and supernatural explanations for the transmission and cure of illnesses in parts of the world where serious diseases are prevalent. For example, in parts of South Africa, although people have access to information about the transmission of the AIDS virus, supernatural accounts of infection based on witchcraft are also disseminated.

Legare wondered whether biological knowledge supplants supernatural explanations. In other words, one possibility is that people use supernatural explanations until they acquire an adequate understanding of biological reasons. Another option is that people use both supernatural and natural frameworks, but here, little was known about how people used these types of explanations. For instance, supernatural and natural frameworks may remain distinct and alternative views of the world that are recruited to explain specific types of events, or they may be used jointly to explain the same phenomenon. Based on Evans-Pritchard's observations and the research on chronic illness, Legare expected the latter. Yet only a detailed and systematic series of studies, which compared different ways of coexistence thinking, would provide concrete evidence for this and information about how, precisely, they coexist at the same time.

Legare and colleagues thus investigated how children and adults reasoned about the cause and spread of AIDS among two communities in South Africa, where discourse about AIDS is prevalent.[113] The communities Legare worked with had both knowledge of biomedical explanations for AIDS (e.g. contaminated blood) and supernatural frameworks of understanding (e.g. bewitchment). Also, research with communities other than the Azande would speak to the question of whether, and to what extent, coexistence reasoning appears cross-culturally. Furthermore, by conducting studies with children and adults, Legare and her colleagues were able to understand the development of coexistence reasoning over time.

In one series of studies, Legare and her team asked children and adults to reason about the likelihood of different types of explanations for the contraction of AIDS. They found that all participants gave biological explanations, and almost all (93 percent) gave at least one bewitchment explanation throughout the study. Based on these findings, they concluded that bewitchment explanations were more flexible and idiosyncratically employed than biological explanations. Importantly, they also found a difference between the type of cause that participants endorsed. Proximate explanations are like the "why." In the case of the granary, this was the termites eating the wood, and in the case of cancer, this is the cell dividing at an alarming rate. They focus on the closest causal explanation to the event. By contrast, distal accounts concentrate more on the "how" questions; they focus on the most distant, or ultimate, causal explanation of the event. In other words, witchcraft caused the termites to eat the wood at that precise time, or that by getting cancer, God had a purpose for the individual.

In Legare's study, most participants identified a proximate natural cause for contracting AIDS, (e.g. having unprotected sex), and the distal cause was supernatural (e.g. reasoning that witches distorted your sense of sound judgment). Furthermore, participants often combined both types of statements in a precise fashion to explain contracting AIDS, referred to as integrated thinking. For example, participants provided reasons such as "a witch can make a condom weak and break," "jealousy and spells, people sent someone with AIDS to sleep with him," and "the people that hated her paid the witches to put the virus in her path."

Both children and adults reasoned about the causes of AIDS similarly, and adults were even more likely than children to cite supernatural causes.

From her research, Legare argued that bewitchment explanations were neither the result of ignorance nor replaced by biological explanations. Instead, they coexist to explain particular aspects of illness. Furthermore, the combination of biological and natural reasoning about events are not naïve ways of thinking that we grow out of, but rather, are robust default explanatory frameworks that are supported by enculturation. As she and others who have studied the development of causal reasoning have discovered both biological and supernatural explanations are found in many different cultures on diverse topics, including evolutionary and creationist accounts of the origin of species among Americans and Europeans.

Discussion questions

1 In your own words, summarize the claims Legare is making.
2 What are the differences and similarities between Legare's research and previous research (e.g. Evans-Pritchard's research) on coexistence reasoning?
3 What do you think demarks this research as typical of the CSR approach to religion?
4 What are the implications of this research on the religion-as-irrational thesis proposed by new atheists (covered earlier in the chapter)?

Further reading

1 Legare, Cristine H., and Susan A. Gelman. "Bewitchment, biology, or both: The coexistence of natural and supernatural explanatory frameworks across development." *Cognitive Science* 32, no. 4 (2008): 607–642.
2 Watson-Jones, Rachel E., Justin T.A Busch, and Cristine H. Legare. "Interdisciplinary and cross-cultural perspectives on explanatory coexistence." *Topics in Cognitive Science* 7, no. 4 (2015): 611–623.
3 Busch, Justin TA, Rachel E. Watson-Jones, and Cristine H. Legare. "The coexistence of natural and supernatural explanations within and across domains and development." *British Journal of Developmental Psychology* 35, no. 1 (2017): 4–20.
4 C.H. Legare and A. Shtulman (2017). "Explanatory pluralism across cultures and development." In J. Proust and M. Fortier, eds. *Metacognitive Diversity*. Oxford, UK: Oxford University Press.

Chapter summary

Developmental and cross-cultural research provides evidence that people have cognitive biases that predispose them towards understanding and endorsing particular ideas about the world. These biases often make religious views more appealing to people than scientific explanations, including the idea that an intelligent agent purposefully designed the world and its inhabitants; that events happen in the world for a reason; that good deeds lead to good outcomes, and evil deeds lead to adverse outcomes. Indeed, even when adults receive sophisticated science education, they cannot help but fall back on intuitive pre-scientific theories when pressured or burdened. Perhaps we can educate children about evolution at a younger age, thinking harder as adults will encourage us to override our naïve assumptions about the world. Yet as research has shown, both natural and supernatural explanations tend to coexist. It seems to be the case that natural explanations suffice in certain circumstances. Still, when it comes to an understanding of tragic and significant events, people find supernatural explanations more satisfying as ultimate explanations.

Discussion questions

1. Can you think of examples of coexistence reasoning about significant events (including from your personal experience or those you have encountered in the media) not listed in the chapter?
2. If cognitive biases favor supernatural explanations for events, then what are the implications for believers and non-believers?
3. What are the practical implications of the research on cognitive biases that favor religious explanations? (e.g. child-rearing, education, debates on science as rational and religion as irrational).

Selected further reading

Articles

1. Banerjee, Konika, and Paul Bloom. "Why did this happen to me? Religious believers' and non-believers' teleological reasoning about life events." *Cognition* 133, no. 1 (2014): 277–303.
2. Kelemen, Deborah. "Why are rocks pointy? Children's preference for teleological explanations of the natural world." *Developmental Psychology* 35, no. 6 (1999): 1440.
3. Legare, Cristine H., E. Margaret Evans, Karl S. Rosengren, and Paul L. Harris. "The coexistence of natural and supernatural explanations across cultures and development." *Child Development* 83, no. 3 (2012): 779–793.

Books

1. McCauley, Robert N. *Why religion is natural and science is not.* Oxford University Press, 2011.
2. Shtulman, Andrew. *Scienceblind: Why Our Intuitive Theories About the World are So Often Wrong.* Hachette UK, 2017.

Notes

1 Frazier, Brandy N., Susan A. Gelman, and Henry M. Wellman. "Preschoolers' search for explanatory information within adult-child conversation." *Child Development* 80, no. 6 (2009): 1592–1611.

2 Legare, Cristine H., Candice M. Mills, André L. Souza, Leigh E. Plummer, and Rebecca Yasskin. "The use of questions as problem-solving strategies during early childhood." *Journal of Experimental Child Psychology* 114, no. 1 (2013): 63–76.

3 Mills, Candice M., Cristine H. Legare, Meridith G. Grant, and Asheley R. Landrum. "Determining whom to question, what to ask, and how much information to ask for: The development of inquiry in young children." *Journal of Experimental Child Psychology* 110, no. 4 (2011): 539–560.

4 Ronfard, Samuel, Imac M. Zambrana, Tone K. Hermansen, and Deborah Kelemen. "Question-asking in childhood: A review of the literature and a framework for understanding its development." *Developmental Review* (2018).

5 Legare, Cristine H. "Exploring explanation: Explaining inconsistent evidence informs exploratory, hypothesis-testing behavior in young children." *Child Development* 83, no. 1 (2012): 173–185.

6 Williams, Joseph Jay, Tania Lombrozo, and Bob Rehder. "The hazards of explanation: Overgeneralization in the face of exceptions." *Journal of Experimental Psychology: General* 142, no. 4 (2013): 1006.

7 Robert N McCauley, *Why Religion is Natural and Science is Not*. New York: Oxford University Press, 2011.

8 Jon D. Miller, Eugenie C. Scott, and Shinji Okamoto, "Public acceptance of evolution." *Science* 313, no. 5788 (2006): 765.

9 Jon D. Miller, Eugenie C. Scott, and Shinji Okamoto, "Public acceptance of evolution." *Science* 313, no. 5788 (2006): 765.

10 Mivart, St George Jackson. *On the genesis of species*. Cambridge: Cambridge University Press, 1871.

11 Evans, E. Margaret. "The emergence of beliefs about the origins of species in school-age children." *Merrill-Palmer Quarterly (1982-)* (2000): 221–254.

12 Pew (2014: February 3). "Fighting over Darwin, state by state." www.pewforum.org/2009/02/04/fighting-over-darwin-state-by-state/. Downloaded October 5, 2018.

13 Arthur McCalla, "Creationism." *Religion Compass* 1, no. 5 (2007): 547–560.

14 Scott, E.C., Miller, J.D., and Okamoto, S., "Public acceptance of evolution." *Science*, 313, No. 5788 (2006): 765–766.

15 Weisberg, Deena Skolnick, Asheley R. Landrum, S. Emlen Metz, and Michael Weisberg. "No missing link: Knowledge predicts acceptance of evolution in the United States." *BioScience* 68, no. 3 (2018): 212–222.

16 Cohen, Geoffrey L., Joshua Aronson, and Claude M. Steele. "When beliefs yield to evidence: Reducing biased evaluation by affirming the self." *Personality and Social Psychology Bulletin* 26, no. 9 (2000): 1151–1164.

17 Legare, Cristine H. "Exploring explanation: Explaining inconsistent evidence informs exploratory, hypothesis-testing behavior in young children." *Child Development* 83, no. 1 (2012): 173–185.

18 Rosengren, Karl S., Sarah K. Brem, E. Margaret Evans, and Gale M. Sinatra, eds. *Evolution Challenges: Integrating Research and Practice in Teaching and Learning about Evolution*. Oxford: Oxford University Press, 2012.

19 Andrew Shtulman, "Qualitative differences between naïve and scientific theories of evolution." *Cognitive Psychology* 52, no. 2 (2006): 170–194.

20 Weisberg, Deena Skolnick, Asheley R. Landrum, S. Emlen Metz, and Michael Weisberg. "No missing link: Knowledge predicts acceptance of evolution in the United States." *BioScience*, 68, no. 3 (2018): 212–222.

21 Weisberg, Deena Skolnick, Asheley R. Landrum, S. Emlen Metz, and Michael Weisberg. "No missing link: Knowledge predicts acceptance of evolution in the United States." *BioScience* 68, no. 3 (2018): 212–222.
22 Pew Research Center. "Religious landscape study." Washington, DC, 2014.
23 David Adams Leeming, *Creation Myths of the World: An Encyclopedia*, Vol. 1. Santa Barbara: ABC-CLIO, 2010.
24 Darwin, Charles. *Life and Letters of Charles Darwin*. Vol. 1. Krill Press via PublishDrive, 2016.
25 Deborah Kelemen and Cara DiYanni, "Intuitions about origins: Purpose and intelligent design in children's reasoning about nature." *Journal of Cognition and Development* 6, no. 1 (2005): 3–31.
26 Schachner, Adena, Liqi Zhu, Jing Li, and Deborah Kelemen. "Is the bias for function-based explanations culturally universal? Children from China endorse teleological explanations of natural phenomena." *Journal of Experimental Child Psychology* 157 (2017): 29–48.
27 *Game of Thrones* "The Prince of Winterfell." Episode 8, Season 2. Directed by Alan Taylor. Written by David Benioff and D.B. Weiss. HBO, Air Date, 2012.
28 Deborah Kelemen, "The scope of teleological thinking in preschool children." *Cognition* 70, no. 3 (1999): 241–272.
29 Susan C. Johnson, Amy Booth, and Kirsten O'Hearn, "Inferring the goals of a non-human agent." *Cognitive Development* 16, no. 1 (2001): 637–656.
30 Csibra Gergely and György Gergely, "The teleological origins of mentalistic action explanations: A developmental hypothesis." *Developmental Science* 1, no. 2 (1998): 255–259.
31 Jacqueline D. Woolley, Chelsea A. Cornelius, and Walter Lacy, "Developmental changes in the use of supernatural explanations for unusual events." *Journal of Cognition and Culture* 11, no. 3–4 (2011): 311–337.
32 Donovan, Elizabeth, and Deborah Kelemen. "Just rewards: Children and adults equate accidental inequity with intentional unfairness." *Journal of Cognition and Culture* 11, no. 1 (2011): 137–150.
33 Malinda Carpenter, "Instrumental, social, and shared goals and intentions in imitation." In *Imitation and the Social Mind: Autism and Typical Development*. 2006: 48–70.
34 E. Margaret Evans, "Cognitive and contextual factors in the emergence of diverse belief systems: Creation versus evolution." *Cognitive Psychology* 42, no. 3 (2001): 217–266.
35 Deborah Kelemen, "British and American children's preferences for teleo-functional explanations of the natural world." *Cognition* 88, no. 2 (2003): 201–221.
36 Järnefelt, Elisa, Liqi Zhu, Caitlin F. Canfield, Marian Chen, and Deborah Kelemen. "Reasoning about nature's agency and design in the cultural context of China." In *Religion, Brain & Behavior*. 2018: 1–23.
37 Rottman, Joshua, Liqi Zhu, Wen Wang, Rebecca Seston Schillaci, Kelly J. Clark, and Deborah Kelemen. "Cultural influences on the teleological stance: Evidence from China." *Religion, Brain & Behavior* 7, no. 1 (2017): 17–26.
38 Järnefelt, Elisa, Caitlin F. Canfield, and Deborah Kelemen. "The divided mind of a disbeliever: Intuitive beliefs about nature as purposefully created among different groups of non-religious adults." *Cognition* 140 (2015): 72–88.
39 Pag Clark, Kelly James. *Religion and the Sciences of origins: Historical and Contemporary Discussions*. Springer, 2014: 1–2.
40 Guthrie, S. "A cognitive theory of religion." *Current Anthropology* 21, no. 2 (1980): 181–203.
41 Stewart, Elliott Guthrie. *Faces in the Clouds: A New Theory of Religion*. New York: Oxford University Press, 1993.
42 Barrett, Justin L. *Why Would Anyone Believe in God?* Walnut Creek: AltaMira Press, 2004.

43 www.buzzfeed.com/arielknutson/people-who-found-jesus-in-their-food?utm_term=.biWVxyoee#.hs4Y5xVoo.
44 Gelman, Susan A. *The Essential Child: Origins of Essentialism in Everyday Thought.* Oxford Series in Cognitive Development, 2003.
45 Gail M. Gottfried and Susan A. Gelman, "Developing domain-specific causal-explanatory frameworks: The role of insides and immanence." *Cognitive Development* 20, no. 1 (2005): 137–158.
46 Douglas L. Medin and Andrew Ortony, "Psychological essentialism." *Similarity and Analogical Reasoning* 179 (1989): 195.
47 Susan A. Gelman and Henry M. Wellman, "Insides and essences: Early understandings of the non-obvious." *Cognition* 38, no. 3 (1991): 213–244.
48 Andrew Shtulman and Laura Schulz. "The relation between essentialist beliefs and evolutionary reasoning." *Cognitive Science* 32, no. 6 (2008): 1049–1062.
49 Andrew Shtulman and Laura Schulz. "The relation between essentialist beliefs and evolutionary reasoning." *Cognitive Science* 32, no. 6 (2008): 1049–1062.
50 Pew (2013: December 30). "Public's views on human evolution." www. pewforum.org/2013/12/30/publics-views-on-human-evolution/. Downloaded March 27, 2018.
51 Alice B. Kehoe, "Scientific creationism: Worldview, not science." *Cult Archaeology and Creationism* (1987): 11–20.
52 Gelman, Susan A. "Psychological essentialism in children." *Trends in Cognitive Sciences* 8, no. 9 (2004): 404–409.
53 Douglas L. Medin and Scott Atran, eds. *Folkbiology*. Massachusetts: MIT Press, 1999.
54 Susan A. Gelman, John D. Coley, and Gail M. Gottfried, "13 Essentialist beliefs in children: The acquisition of concepts and theories." In *Mapping the Mind: Domain Specificity in Cognition and Culture* (1994): 341.
55 Legare, Cristine, John Opfer, Justin Busch, and Andrew Shtulman. "A field guide for teaching evolution in the social sciences." *Evolution and Human Behavior* 39, no. 3 (2018): 257–268.
56 Andrew S. Shtulman, *Scienceblind: Why Our Intuitive Theories About the World are So Often Wrong*. New York: Basic Books, 2017.
57 Kelemen and Rosset, "The human function compunction," 138–143.
58 Andrew Shtulman and Joshua Valcarcel, "Scientific knowledge suppresses but does not supplant earlier intuitions." *Cognition* 124, no. 2 (2012): 209–215.
59 Robert F. Goldberg and Sharon L. Thompson-Schill, "Developmental 'roots' in mature biological knowledge." *Psychological Science* 20, no. 4 (2009): 480–487.
60 Deborah Kelemen and Evelyn Rosset, "The human function compunction: Teleological explanation in adults." *Cognition* 111, no. 1 (2009): 138–143.
61 Elisa Järnefelt, Caitlin F. Canfield, and Deborah Kelemen, "The divided mind of a disbeliever: Intuitive beliefs about nature as purposefully created among different groups of non-religious adults." *Cognition* 140 (2015): 72–88.
62 Krista Casler and Deborah Kelemen, "Developmental continuity in teleo-functional explanation: Reasoning about nature among Romanian Romani adults." *Journal of Cognition and Development* 9, no. 3 (2008): 340–362.
63 Deborah Kelemen, Joshua Rottman, and Rebecca Seston, "Professional physical scientists display tenacious teleological tendencies: Purpose-based reasoning as a cognitive default." *Journal of Experimental Psychology: General* 142, no. 4 (2013): 1074.
64 Jonathon M. Seidl, "Over 50% of Harvard, Princeton and MIT students get this simple logic question wrong," last modified November 14, 2013.
65 www.nature.com/articles/s41562-018-0426-0.
66 Achieve, Inc. (2013). "Next-generation science standards."
67 Shtulman and Valcarcel, "Scientific knowledge," 209–215.
68 Kelemen, Deborah, Natalie A. Emmons, Rebecca Seston Schillaci, and Patricia A. Ganea. "Young children can be taught basic natural selection using a picture-storybook intervention." *Psychological Science* 25, no. 4 (2014): 893–902.

69 Legare, Cristine, John Opfer, Justin Busch, and Andrew Shtulman. "A field guide for teaching evolution in the social sciences." *Evolution and Human Behavior* 39, no. 3 (2018): 257–268.

70 Gould, Stephen Jay. *Rocks of Ages: Science and Religion in the Fullness of Life*. Ballantine Books, 2011: 31.

71 Cristine H. Legare, E. Margaret Evans, Karl S. Rosengren, and Paul L. Harris, "The coexistence of natural and supernatural explanations across cultures and development." *Child Development* 83, no. 3 (2012): 779–793.

72 Kevin Dunbar, J. Fugelsang, and Courtney Stein, "Do naïve theories ever go away? Using brain and behavior to understand changes in concepts." *Thinking with Data* (2007): 193–206.

73 Legare, C.H., Evans, E.M., Rosengren, K.S., and Harris, P.L. (2012). "The coexistence of natural and supernatural explanations across cultures and development." *Child Development* 83, no. 3: 779–793.

74 Busch, Justin T.A., Rachel E. Watson-Jones, and Cristine H. Legare. "The coexistence of natural and supernatural explanations within and across domains and development." *British Journal of Developmental Psychology* 35, no. 1 (2017): 4–20.

75 Edward E. Evans-Pritchard, *Witchcraft, Oracles and Magic Among the Azande*. Vol. 12. London: Oxford, 1937.

76 Ashby, W. Ross, "Chapter 6: *The black box*." In *An Introduction to Cybernetics*. London: Chapman & Hall, 1956, 86–117.

77 Cristine H. Legare and Susan A. Gelman, "Bewitchment, biology, or both: The co-existence of natural and supernatural explanatory frameworks across development." *Cognitive Science* 32, no. 4 (2008): 607–642.

78 Busch, Justin T.A., Rachel E. Watson-Jones, and Cristine H. Legare. "The coexistence of natural and supernatural explanations within and across domains and development." *British Journal of Developmental Psychology* 35, no. 1 (2017): 4–20.

79 Tori Tomalia, "The Why Me of Cancer." *Cure*, last modified December 12, 2014.

80 Conrad Eamonn, "Why me? The question with no answers." *The Huffington Post*, last modified February 13, 2013.

81 Comment on "Why Me?" *Cancer Survivors Network* (weblog). https://csn.cancer.org/node/294615.

82 Juliet M. McMullin, Israel De Alba, Leo R. Chavez, and F. Allan Hubbell, "Influence of beliefs about cervical cancer etiology on Pap smear use among Latina immigrants." *Ethnicity & Health* 10, no. 1 (2005): 3–18.

83 Crystal L. Park, "Making sense of the meaning literature: An integrative review of meaning-making and its effects on adjustment to stressful life events." *Psychological Bulletin* 136, no. 2 (2010): 257.

84 Richard N. Eidinger and David V. Schapira, "Cancer patients' insight into their treatment, prognosis, and unconventional therapies." *Cancer* 53, no. 12 (1984): 2736–2740.

85 Simon Dein and J. Stygall, "Does being religious help or hinder coping with chronic illness? A critical literature review." *Palliative Medicine* 11, no. 4 (1997): 291–298.

86 Robert J. Baugher, Candice Burger, Roberta Smith, and Kenneth Wallston, "A comparison of terminally ill persons at various periods to death." *OMEGA – Journal of Death and Dying* 20, no. 2 (1990): 103–115.

87 Julie J. Exline, Crystal L. Park, Joshua M. Smyth, and Michael P. Carey, "Anger toward God: Social-cognitive predictors, prevalence, and links with adjustment to bereavement and cancer." *Journal of Personality and Social Psychology* 100, no. 1 (2011): 129.

88 Adrian Furnham, "Explaining health and illness: Lay beliefs on the nature of health." *Personality and Individual Differences* 17, no. 4 (1994): 455–466.

89 Legare, Evans, Rosengren, and Harris, "The coexistence of natural and supernatural," 779–793.
90 Shtulman, *Scienceblind*.
91 Becky Oskin, "Japan earthquake and tsunami of 2011: Facts and information." *LiveScience*. September 13, 2017.
92 Jackson, Andy, "Tokyo mayor: Tsunami was 'divine punishment.'" Asian Correspondent, last modified March 15, 2011.
93 Justin McCurry, "Tokyo governor apologizes for calling tsunami 'divine punishment,'" last modified March 15, 2011.
94 McCurry, "Tokyo governor."
95 Robert P. Jones and Daniel Cox, "Few Americans see natural disasters a sign from God." *PRRI*, last modified 2011.
96 "Kevin Bell Trust founders win £1m in UK lottery." RTE News, last modified June 29, 2017.
97 "UK | England | West Yorkshire | 'Lottery rapist' freed from jail." BBC News, last modified March 31, 2005.
98 Lakshmi Raman and Gerald A. Winer, "Evidence of more immanent justice responding in adults than children: A challenge to traditional developmental theories." *British Journal of Developmental Psychology* 22, no. 2 (2004): 255–274.
99 Markus Appel, "Fictional narratives cultivate just-world beliefs." *Journal of Communication* 58, no. 1 (2008): 62–83.
100 Konika Banerjee and Paul Bloom, "'Everything happens for a reason': Children's beliefs about purpose in life events." *Child Development* 86, no. 2 (2015): 503–518.
101 Raman and Winer, "Evidence of more immanent justice," 255–274.
102 Appel, "Fictional narratives cultivate just-world beliefs," 62–83.
103 Paul E Jose, "Just-world reasoning in children's immanent justice judgments." *Child Development* 61, no. 4 (1990): 1024–1033.
104 Zick Rubin and Letitia Anne Peplau. "Who believes in a just world?" *Journal of Social Issues* 31, no. 3 (1975): 65–89.
105 Nicolas Baumard and Coralie Chevallier, "What goes around comes around: The evolutionary roots of the belief in immanent justice." *Journal of Cognition and Culture* 12, no. 1–2 (2012): 67–80.
106 Ara Norenzayan, *Big Gods: How Religion Transformed Cooperation and Conflict*. New Jersey: Princeton University Press, 2013.
107 Cindel White, Adam Baimel, and Ara Norenzayan, "What are the causes and consequences of belief in karma?" *Religion, Brain & Behavior* (2017): 1–4.
108 Robert Nevitt Sanford and Craig Comstock, *Sanctions for Evil. Sources of Social Destructiveness*. [By] *Nevitt Sanford, Craig Comstock, and Associates*. New Jersey: Jossey-Bass, 1971.
109 R. Shweder, N. Much, Manamohan Mahapatra, and Lawrence Park, "Divinity and the 'big three' explanations of suffering." *Morality and Health* 119 (1997): 119–169.
110 Banerjee and Bloom, "Why did this happen to me?" 277–303.
111 Konika Banerjee and Paul Bloom, "Why did this happen to me? Religious believers' and non-believers' teleological reasoning about life events." *Cognition* 133, no. 1 (2014): 277–303.
112 Bethany T. Heywood and Jesse M. Bering, "'Meant to be': How religious beliefs and cultural religiosity affect the implicit bias to think teleologically." *Religion, Brain & Behavior* 4, no. 3 (2014): 183–201.
113 Cristine H. Legare and Susan A. Gelman, "Bewitchment, biology, or both: The co-existence of natural and supernatural explanatory frameworks across development." *Cognitive Science* 32, no. 4 (2008): 607–642.

6 The afterlife

The belief that something extraordinary happens to people when they die is cross-culturally ubiquitous. Across the dazzling array of ideas about the afterlife, there are a few underlying assumptions in common depictions: that the person survives biological death, retains his or her mental processes and identity, embarks on a journey to the next life, and resides in a physical location. In this chapter, we will consider three types of theories in the cognitive evolutionary sciences about why these ideas are so prevalent.

First, we consider cognitive theories of afterlife beliefs. These theories propose that we are cognitively predisposed to represent people as continuing in some form after biological death. Second, we turn to contextual approaches of afterlife beliefs. These theories also tend to endorse cognitive predispositions and biases as underpinning ideas about the afterlife. Still, they tend to place more emphasis on context and the role of cultural transmission and cultural learning on the development and endorsement of these ideas than cognitive accounts. Third, we consider motivational theories of afterlife beliefs, which focus on the motivation to believe that life exists after biological death. These include terror management theorists who propose that belief in an afterlife is driven by the need to control the fear of death. The chapter ends by considering the implications of cognitive science of religion (CSR) theories on the truth, rationality, and justification of afterlife beliefs.

Cognitive theories of afterlife beliefs

Cognitive scientists of religion have argued that cognitive predispositions help to explain why people find it relatively easy to accept the idea of an afterlife, and why specific ideas about the afterlife—for example, that mental process such as thinking, continue—are cross-culturally recurrent. In what follows, we review research that investigates children's and adults' representations of death and the afterlife, before turning to contextual theories.

Immortality in the afterlife as cognitive default

Psychologist Jesse Bering conducted a series of studies in the United States and Europe designed to investigate how children and adults intuitively reason about death. In one set of studies, Bering asked adults to reason about the states of a protagonist named Richard. In the story, they read that Richard was in a bad mood because he suspected that his wife had an affair; hungry, so he sucked on a fresh breath mint; accidentally pressed on the accelerator instead of the break, hit another car, and died in the crash. Participants were asked, now that Richard is dead, can he experience certain states? Bering categorized each of the states. They included psychobiological (e.g. is he still *hungry*?), perceptual (e.g. can he *see* the paramedics trying to resuscitate him?), epistemic (e.g. is he *thinking* about his wife?), emotional (is he still *angry* at his wife?), and desire (does he *want* to be alive?). Bering found that participants were more likely to say that Richard's emotional and epistemic (i.e. thinking) states continued while his psychobiological (e.g. hunger) and perceptual states ceased at death. This effect occurred mostly regardless of what participants said they thought happens to a person after death (i.e. their explicit afterlife belief).

Along with psychologist David Bjorklund, Bering presented a modified version of this original study to children between 4- and 12-years-old and adults using a puppet show. Children witnessed a toy alligator eating a stuffed brown mouse.[2] Again, participants (both adults and children) were asked to reason about brown mouse's states now that he was no longer alive. They found that as children got older (around 8–12 years old), they tended to say that emotional, desire and epistemic (i.e. thinking) states continued. In contrast, psychobiological state, (e.g. hunger) and perceptual states no longer existed. Thus, older children and adults in this study were reasoning similarly to how adults reasoned in the original research. Bering found that in this new study, young children were likely to say that all states continued; after his demise, the brown mouse was still thinking and feeling thirsty, and so on. In other words, they did not discriminate between the states but instead had a default stance that all states continue after death.

Bering and colleagues replicated the puppet studies with Spanish school children. They also investigated the role of religious instruction on representations of death by comparing the responses of children who attended a Catholic vs. secular school. Overall, Catholic school children were more likely to reason that all states continue after death than children attending secular school.[3] In short, religiously schooled children were more likely than non-religiously schooled children to attribute states to the dead, most likely because of the increased exposure to afterlife beliefs. This finding is not surprising. Children grow up in traditions that support the notion of life after death. Hence, repeated exposure to the idea that life continues after death is likely to strengthen the belief that life continues after death.

Although participants differ in their representations of death according to the extent of their religious indoctrination, the findings of Bering's research team cannot be explained as exclusively determined by instruction. Younger children were more likely to assume that all states continue, whereas older children privileged certain types of psychological states. This trend is precisely the opposite of what we would expect if the origins of such beliefs could be traced exclusively to religious indoctrination. If religious instruction was driving children's ideas about the afterlife, then increased exposure (which comes with age) to religiously endorsed ideas about life after death in school should lead to older children representing all states as continuing.

Yet it was younger children (who have less exposure to theologically accepted ideas about life after death) who asserted that all states continue. Nor can the results of the studies be explained exclusively as a product of enculturation in America. Bering and colleagues found fundamental similarities in reasoning about the afterlife among Spanish and American schoolchildren. With both sets of participants, they found that older children were more likely to say that fewer states continued and that all children were more likely to say that the mouse continued to think, desire, and love than to see, feel hungry or need to use the bathroom. These findings suggest that cognitive predispositions may also influence how participants conceptualize death.

The studies of Bering's research team revealed that children and adults were aware of the fact that the body stops working at death, but they viewed the mind as active. Researchers concluded that states tied to the body are therefore easy to represent as ceasing to continue at the point of death. Bering also concluded that we have a natural predisposition towards immortality and psychological immortality especially, since even with increasing age, children were more likely to say that mental states continued after death. According to Bering, we are naturally inclined to be immortalists, and this explains how ideas about life after death spread so quickly once introduced into a population. Further, we are especially prone to thinking that mental states continue after biological death, and this explains why ideas about the afterlife (that depict the person after death as a psychological being) enjoy widespread cultural success.

Other studies further support Bering's claim that psychological immortality is cognitively natural, and that when supported by cultural ideas, rapidly develop into beliefs about the afterlife. Psychologist Natalie Emmons and colleagues investigated how children reasoned about their existence before they were conceived.[4] Specifically, Emmons and her team asked children about their states before they existed in their mother's belly.

They found that children reasoned about their existence before this life (i.e. prelife beliefs) just like children reasoned about their existence after death. With increasing age, children reasoned as though their emotions and desires were present before their birth but that their bodily states were not. This study is particularly important because it took place in two non-Western cultures in Ecuador, where cultural scripts about prelife were not as available as afterlife scripts. Bering's studies have also been replicated in other non-Western countries, including China.[5] The results of these studies also offer support for the theory that we are predisposed to represent people as immortal, and especially, continuing psychologically after biological death.

This research presented in CSR thus far concludes that the cognitive default is to represent psychological states as continuing to exist, with the implication that this tendency facilitates belief in the afterlife. Others have argued that early emerging representations of death are not as consistent or static as the psychological immortality account implies; and that enculturation and context affect people's reasoning about death much more than this research acknowledges.

Key points

- Bering and colleagues conducted studies with children and adults in the US and Spain.
- Even though adults had different beliefs about the afterlife, they tended to reason similarly about a person who had died. This finding suggests that the results are not merely due to an explicit belief or disbelief in an afterlife.
- Adults reasoned that a person's mental states (such as remembering and feeling) were more likely to continue after death than states related to the person's physical body (such as seeing the paramedics or being hungry).
- Younger children in the US and Spain assumed that all states continued after death, whereas older children, like adults, thought that only mental states continued. This finding suggests that the results are not merely due to a view of life after death endorsed by the USA or Spain.
- Catholic schoolchildren were more likely to assume that all states continue after death than children attending a secular school. This finding suggests that religious instruction increases the belief that all states continue after death.
- Bering concludes that the idea of immortality comes naturally to us. Furthermore that psychological immortality is exceptionally intuitive and resistant to change and that this explains why afterlife beliefs spread so quickly once introduced to a population.

Contextual theories of afterlife beliefs

Like cognitive theories, contextual theories also tend to endorse the possibility that cognitive predispositions underpin ideas about the afterlife. Still, they place more emphasis on the role of cultural transmission and cultural learning on the development of these ideas. Researchers who propose contextual accounts of afterlife beliefs often conduct cross-cultural research. Contextual theories depict representations of death and the afterlife as more fluid and nuanced than cognitive approaches.

Immortality in the afterlife as culturally learned

Developmental psychologist Paul Harris, social anthropologist Rita Astuti, and psychologist Marta Giménez conducted a series of cross-cultural studies with children and adults. These studies aimed to assess the extent to which there are cultural similarities and variability in children's and adult's reasoning about death and the afterlife. The researchers thus selected two cultures that differed according to people's exposure to death and culturally endorsed views on the afterlife. First, Harris and Giménez conducted studies in Madrid, Spain,[6] where Catholicism is the predominant religious affiliation, and a belief in Christian Heaven is apparent. Next, Astuti and Harris conducted a follow-up study in rural Madagascar, a country off the southeast coast of Africa, where a belief in ancestors is culturally endorsed. Ancestors are dead relatives who are said to affect the living, and people often behave in ways that aim to please their ancestors.[7]

The study in rural Madagascar is especially crucial for understanding how variation in cultural input may affect the development of afterlife beliefs for three reasons.

First, Madagascar is a non-western culture. The context enables researchers to assess whether the findings of their studies are a product of western ideas about death and the afterlife or whether they generalize across cultures. Second, children in Madagascar have many more experiences of death than is typical of western cultures because they participate in the killing of animals. This context enables researchers to investigate the impact of the first-hand experience on concepts of the afterlife. Third, ancestral beliefs and practices are widespread in Madagascar. These beliefs would allow researchers to assess the extent to which culturally accepted ideas influence people's concepts of death and the afterlife.

Harris and colleagues found that children were mostly unsystematic in their responses to questions about life after death before the age of seven. Thus, the researchers did not focus on pinpointing the cognitive default view of young children's reasoning about death because their research indicates that young children do not exhibit any consistent patterns. Instead, they are interested in explaining ideas about death that appear to be increasingly consolidated in older children. These findings are in contrast to the results of Bering's studies. As you may recall, Bering and colleagues found that younger children (from around age five) tended to say that all states continued; in other words, they were immortalists. These findings led Bering to propose that the cognitive default view is personal immortality, which helps to explain the widespread endorsement of afterlife beliefs.

Harris and colleagues found that children became more systematic in their reasoning about death from around age seven. At this age, they characterize children as extinctivists, tending to deny the continuity of all states to people after death. Harris and colleagues propose that children are essentially espousing a predominantly biological view of death. This emerging biological view of death is likely to be a product of both children's increasing understanding of biology and in some circumstances, such as in the context of Madagascar, their personal experience of death. As they come to understand that the cessation of biological functions characterizes death, children assume that the processes that sustain life (including cognitive and emotional states) cease at death.

The research of Harris and colleagues also suggest that while children's earliest systematic view of death is extinctivist, they gradually come to view some aspects of a person as continuing to exist. Like Bering, they found that older children and adults are more likely to claim that mental processes continue after death than younger children. Bering asked participants questions about the physical and mental processes of characters in his studies. In the studies in Madagascar, Astuti and Harris also included questions about the continuity of the soul after biological death. While participants responded that the mind was more likely to continue than the physical body, results demonstrated that they also thought that the soul was more likely to continue than the mind.

When interpreting their research findings, Harris and colleagues did not rule out the possibility that intuitive biases underpinned participants' reasoning. They placed more emphasis, however, on the role of cultural learning about the afterlife to explain their findings, as children get older, they are exposed to afterlife beliefs and rituals in the community. Ideas about life after death, therefore, become more accessible through frequent activation, and children come to adopt them. For instance, in Madagascar, people often talk about the intentions and desires of the ancestors who are said to be lurking around. They also participate in rituals designed to honor their ancestors.

Psychological and physical continuity in the afterlife

A later series of studies with children and adults suggests that in certain cultures, at least, people represent the body as continuing after death. These studies were conducted by Harris and psychologists Rachel Watson-Jones, Justin Busch, and Cristine Legare in Tanna, Vanuatu (a Melanesian island in the South Pacific).[8] Vanuatu maintains indigenous supernatural beliefs but also increasingly embraces Christian doctrine. In particular, participants in Vanuatu often adopt a literal interpretation of scripture. They are exposed to the Christian concept of resurrection, the belief that bodies will be raised from the grave at the time of Final Judgment. Researchers also conducted the studies in Austin, Texas, which is characterized by diversity in religious affiliation with a majority of liberal Christians. Participants were asked whether or not different biological and psychological processes continue to function after death, and these questions were framed in a theistic (e.g. "now that David is with God") and non-theistic (e.g. "now that David is dead") narrative.

Commensurate with previous studies, younger children did not discriminate between biological and psychological processes and were likely to say that both continued after death. From age seven, participants reasoned in the non-theistic narrative that living processes ceased at death, and in the theistic framed question, those processes continue after death. Further, US adolescents and adults were likely to endorse the continuation of psychological processes over biological processes. Participants in Vanuatu, however, provided more physiological than mental processes following the theistic framed question. In other words, when people were told that David was with God, they tended to assume that David's eyes and ears still worked, that his legs could move, his heart could beat, and so on.

Participants also tended to offer as many supernatural types of explanations for the continuation of biological and psychological processes, for instance, claiming that God gives his legs the power to work. From their results, the authors concluded that the participants in Vanuatu were reasoning as though the people in heaven were not disembodied, but rather, required their bodies to be with God. They propose that in specific contexts, at least, the representation of people in the afterlife as physically embodied is as intuitive as the representation of people as psychologically immortal.

In summary of the chapter thus far, Bering proposes that children's intuitive stance is towards psychological immortality and that with increasing age, they become more efficient at materialist reasoning. For instance, they are better able to incorporate their acquired scientific knowledge about the relationship between the brain and mind into their views about psychological functioning after death. When intuitions about life after death are culturally elaborated upon, they produce beliefs in the afterlife. Thus, psychological immortality of the dead is the natural stance, and this enables beliefs about the afterlife to be quickly adopted. By contrast, Harris and colleagues propose that older children first come to understand death in terms of the breakdown of biological processes. Thus, their first systematic theory of death is extinctive. With increasing exposure to ideas and practices surrounding the afterlife, children come to adopt a view of people as existing elsewhere. The afterlife includes beliefs about personal immortality but is also characterized by the continuity of the soul and in specific contexts, continuity of the physical body. Both accounts explain why particular ideas about the afterlife (e.g. that the mind and soul continue), are readily endorsed by ordinary people. Harris and colleagues also propose that people do not abandon their biological concepts of death in favor of culturally learned ideas about the afterlife. Instead, they hold two parallel concepts of death.

Biological and religious conceptions of death

The experimental designs of Harris and colleagues enabled them to investigate the possibility that people have more than one concept of death. While Bering and colleagues presented participants with a single narrative or depiction and then asked about the fate of this person after death, Harris and colleagues created two stories. These narratives highlighted either the biological or religious aspects of a person's death, and then researchers asked about the person's fate. In one study, researchers asked children and adults about the outcome of a person when the person was described as a corpse.

This description elicited a common secular conception of death—i.e. when biological functions cease, the person dies. In another narration, the person was characterized according to the prevailing afterlife beliefs. For example, in the study in Spain and Vanuatu, the person was described as with God. In Madagascar, the person was described as in the tomb, like all ancestors. These descriptions elicited religious conceptions of death—i.e. that the person survives death. In the context of the religious narrative, however, participants tended to claim that most mental processes continued after death. Thus, adults were more, not less likely, to endorse the afterlife.

In Chapter 5 of the book (The Nature of the World), we covered the theory by Legare and colleagues that people use coexistence reasoning when they think about why things happen, including biological and supernatural explanations for events. When it comes to thinking about death, people also reason, according to more than one view of the world. Harris and colleagues (including Legare) proposed that older children and adults are inclined to adopt two parallel concepts of death. One is a biological conception of death, in which people think of the deceased as a corpse. This conception corresponds to many secular understandings of death, where the person ceases to exist when their biological functions cease.

The second is a religious conception of death, in which people think of the deceased as someone who has departed this life but lives on somewhere in some form. This conception corresponds to concepts of the afterlife in many cultures. These ideas coexist and can be individually elicited depending upon the context within which questions are framed. Their findings present a more nuanced and context-dependent account of afterlife beliefs than cognitive theories had previously acknowledged. More importantly, Harris and colleagues propose that people hold two concepts of death, biological and religious, which are elicited in different contexts. Thus, people can endorse the idea of an afterlife, but in other settings, to accept that death brings an end to biological functions.

So far, in the chapter, we have covered cognitive and contextual theories of death and the afterlife. While similar in many aspects, they differ according to the default or early emerging, cognitive view of death, and the extent to which cultural learning affects this conceptualization. As we will see in the next section, it is not only the research teams of Bering and Harris that disagree over the cognitive default view of death. Scholars have proposed many predispositions that they claim bias people towards the belief in an afterlife.

Participation 1: Theories about children's concepts of death

1. Divide up into groups of about 3–4 students. Work together as a group.
2. Briefly summarize the work so far in this chapter on children's concepts of death and the afterlife, a few sentences for each theory is sufficient.
3. Explain differences in the claims that the researchers are making.
4. Consider why these differences exist (e.g. theoretical background, methods etc.).
5. Decide which theory you agree with most.

Key points

- Harris and colleagues conducted studies with children and adults in Spain and the non-western country, Madagascar.
- They found a few patterns to children's reasoning before the age of seven. At around age seven children tended to deny the continuity of all states at death, but older children and adults tended to view mental states as continuing after death.
- Contrary to Bering, Harris, and colleagues concluded that young children do not start as immortalists, but gradually become extinctivists—as they come to understand the biology of death. They later adopt a biological view of death, and eventually, in part due to the influence of culturally endorsed ideas about the afterlife, come to view the person as continuing to exist. They suggest that enculturation has a significant impact on cognitive intuitions about death.
- Based on studies in Spain, rural Madagascar, and Vanuatu, Harris, and colleagues proposed that people hold multiple ideas about the fate of the person after death, one based in biology—where states cease at death, and one based in culturally endorsed beliefs about the afterlife—where the person exists in some form after death. These ideas can be activated in different contexts.
- Based on studies in Vanuatu and Texas, Harris and colleagues claimed that in specific contexts, people also assume a default view of people in the afterlife as embodied.
- Cognitive and contextual theories of the afterlife differ on what they take to be the early emerging cognitive view of death, and the extent to which they propose context and cultural learning impact this conceptualization.

Summary of cognitive and contextual theories of afterlife beliefs

- Researchers agree that adults tend to assume that the afterlife entails immortality for people.
- They differ, however, according to whether they consider personal immortality as the cognitive default view, endorsed by young children, or whether the idea of psychological immortality is acquired later through exposure to beliefs about the afterlife.
- While all acknowledge that cognitive constraints are embedded in cultural norms, scholars differ in the extent to which they think that religious indoctrination and enculturation impact intuitive assumptions about the fate of the person after death.

Intuitions that favor afterlife beliefs

In the previous section, we discovered that across cultures, people tend to assume that a person continues to survive after biological death. In this section, we consider theories about intuitive biases that cognitive scientists of religion claim facilitate the spread of afterlife beliefs.

Simulation constraints

Recall the studies by Bering and colleagues covered earlier in the chapter. They found that older children and adults reasoned that a person's mental states were more likely to continue after death than states related to the person's physical body. While we can imagine what it is like not to have psychobiological states, not to feel hungry, or not need to use the bathroom, other states like thinking and feeling are especially difficult to represent as ceasing to exist at the point of death. Bering has argued that due to the difficulty in imagining the cessation of our own mental states, the expectation of psychological immortality is the natural product of a default cognitive stance.

This stance is underpinned by a constraint of the imagination, that Bering called a simulation constraint. Bering argued (as did other scholars such as Freud and Nagel, many years prior) that it is impossible to conceive (i.e. to simulate) of ourselves as being "dead" and permanently lacking consciousness because we use mental states to represent all experiences. Bering often quotes Sartre's short story "The Wall," to illustrate this point. In the story, a group of prisoners believe that they are about to be shot dead by a firing squad, and one prisoner begins to speak. "Something's the matter … I see my corpse; that's not hard, but I'm the one who sees it, with my eyes. I've got to think … think that I won't see anything anymore, and the world will go on for the others. We aren't made to think that.[9]"

Indeed, trying to think about what it would be like to be dead seems almost impossible. Likewise, trying to think about what happens when other people are dead is also tricky, although some ideas about death seem to be easier to think about than others. This constraint does not mean that you cannot imagine what life would be like after you are dead. We are all capable of thinking about who would attend our funeral, but such a construal requires a first-person perceptive through which you envision these future events. As Justin Barrett put it, you may find it almost impossible to experience what it is like not to think consciously, so simulating what a dead person is not thinking is tough.[10]

Philosopher Shaun Nichols elaborated upon Bering's theory. Nichols proposed that thinking about death represents an imaginative obstacle. The paradox is this; we use our imagination to represent a future in which we do not exist, yet we hit a barrier of creating this representation because our mind wants to represent ourselves in that future in one way or another. The imaginative obstacle means that you cannot imagine a future in which you do not exist because this is a contradiction. When we try to imagine a time after our biological death, Nichols maintains, we hit this imaginative obstacle. Thus, according to Bering and Nichols, it is easier to represent your dead self, and correspondingly, dead others, as continuing to exist mentally—just elsewhere, whether in a different body or different realm.[11]

Bering's theory of a simulation constraint is based upon a philosophical theory, generally referred to as a simulation account, about how we reason about minds in general. This simulation account assumes that our understanding of other minds is not based on a theory we have about minds. In other words, we do not have to draw upon what we have theorized about people's beliefs, desires, intentions, goals, and so on. Instead, we arrive at an understanding of other people's minds through simulation or cognitive empathy—a more direct route, if you like, between reasoning about oneself and then applying this to others, without the need for a naïve theory. This account tends to draw upon explanations about how we reason about our death to explain how we then reason about the death of others. Correspondingly, much of Bering and Nichols' anecdotes used to support their theories draw from trying to imagine our death. Yet other theorists have focused on how we think about the death of others as the key to why afterlife beliefs are so easily facilitated. They tend to emphasize that humans reason about others in terms of a theory of other minds, instead of drawing directly upon our own experience. They are outlined in the next section.

Key points

- Bering argued that we have a simulation constraint when reasoning about our death. The limitation is that it is impossible to conceive of ourselves as being "dead" and permanently lacking consciousness because we use mental states to represent all experiences.
- Nichols elaborated on Bering's claim and proposed that thinking about death represents an imaginative obstacle. We use our imagination to represent a future in which we do not exist, yet our mind wants to represent ourselves in that future in one way or another.
- According to Bering and Nichols, it is easier to represent your dead self as continuing to exist mentally in the afterlife.

Folk-dualism

Bering proposed that people's inherent tendency for folk-dualism (also known as mind-body dualism) can contribute towards an explanation of why afterlife beliefs are so cross-culturally prevalent. Namely, that people reason as though minds and bodies are separate, and that minds can continue after biological death. The idea that people tend to reason as though they are intuitive mind-body dualists, and that these intuitions underpin beliefs about the afterlife, was first proposed by psychologist Paul Bloom.

Four claims underpin the theory of folk-dualism as outlined by Bloom. First, Bloom contends that we base our representations of people in the afterlife on representations of ordinary people, more generally. This claim is shared by most scholars in the cognitive science of religion. The next three points distinguish Bloom's view from other scholars in CSR and are more contentious. Second, Bloom contends that we naturally represent other people as having minds separate from bodies. He claims that we are predisposed to represent others as constituted by two independent and autonomous entities: material bodies and immaterial minds. Bloom proposes that although people are tracked fundamentally as objects— susceptible to the laws of physics so that they can be pushed, pulled, and so on—they are also represented as psychological beings, guided in their behavior by underlying mental states (e.g. beliefs, desires, intentions). This perceived psychological continuity enables others to attribute a continuous and numerical identity to people, even though they may undergo physical changes (e.g. grow older, gain weight, and so on). Naturally representing ordinary people as having minds separate from bodies explains why people think they can survive with intact psychological features even though they experienced bodily death.

Third, Bloom claims that people do not think that their identity is constituted by their physical bodies, but rather, by their psychological features. As Bloom put it (2004: 191), "we do not feel as if we are our bodies; we feel as if we occupy them.[12]" The fourth claim then explains why it is possible and plausible to imagine people in the afterlife occupying all sorts of different bodies—and how we can represent their psychology as intact, they are "the same person" as in life. What is common to all popular notions of the afterlife is that you—the things that make you who you are, whether you regard these as mental states or traits, such as thinking, remembering your past, or your unique personality or something else, continues after bodily death. The very definition of the afterlife is personal immortality. Bloom claims that what retains your identity is your mental state, not your physical embodiment. Bloom suggests that this even makes it possible for us to think about people in the afterlife as disembodied minds. Not only can we represent the mind and body as separate, but identity can reside solely in the mind. Thus, people can recognize that the body dies at the point of biological death, but yet intuitively reason as though the mind, which retains their identity, continues in the afterlife.

Many cognitive scientists of religion accept some version of this explanation of why ideas about the afterlife are acquired so easily, especially the idea that people can think about others as having minds and bodies. For instance, experimental cross-cultural research confirmed that people could easily reason about others in terms of persons and bodies, body dependent, and independent (i.e. mental) states.[13] Also, quantitative textual analyses on ancient Chinese texts revealed that authors referred distinctly to minds and bodies to conceptualize persons.[14] Further, one study of near-death experiences (NDE, where a person is either close to, or experiences clinical death) found that 58 percent of people felt as if they inhabited a new body at the time of the experience. Sometimes, they even reported lacking any body at the time of the experience.[15]

Figure 6.1 Folk-dualism is the intuition that bodies and minds are separate. Some researchers propose that this explains why ideas about life after death spread so rapidly. (Image credit: Denis Simonov/Shutterstock.com).

Anthropologist Michael Kinsella conducted ethnographic fieldwork of near-death experience groups in the US. He claims that many people articulate some version of mind-body dualism in their accounts and expectations of NDE.[16] I also found this to be the case when investigating people's reasoning about reincarnation. Specifically, I discovered that people have little difficulty representing themselves as occupying a new body but retaining their identity in another lifetime.[17]

Embodiment theories

More recently, CSR scholars have begun to question the explanatory power of the theory of folk-dualism. Some theorists propose a more nuanced account, and others outright reject the claim that people are intuitively represented as disembodied in the afterlife. We review these theories below.

Embodiment in the afterlife in some contexts

Religious studies scholar Istvan Czachesz argues that people are mind-body dualists by default. Yet in some theological representations of the afterlife, at least, the person is depicted as physically embodied and occupying the same body, especially when it emphasizes core tenets. For instance, in depictions of the afterlife, such as the Apocalypse of Peter, the same physical body is described in the resurrection as in life because it meshed with the idea that bodies contribute towards sin and are tormented in hell. In other words, the concept of punishment was more easily imagined as happening to the same person. Thus, people were able to accept that the body continued.[18] Of course, CSR makes the distinction between theological versions of the afterlife, and commonly held folk-representations of the afterlife, and seeks to explain mainly the latter. Yet, in some circumstances, such as thinking about our deceased loved one doing something in the afterlife or the possibility of punishment, we are more likely to evoke the idea of a physical body.

In my own research, I attempted to nuance the discussion concerning the role of the body in the afterlife. I found that even though people espoused a view of reincarnation where the deceased person was reborn into a *new* body when deciding who had been reborn as whom, they regarded distinctive physical similarities between a living and dead person as evidence that they were the same person. I proposed that even though people hold an explicit concept of reincarnation as entailing a new physical body when stakes on correct identification are high, people implicitly revert to habitual and reliable strategies they use every day to identify others. Namely, by their physical continuity, and especially, by distinctive physical features.[19] Thus, intuitive conceptions about the afterlife may be more easily overridden by other considerations and be more context-dependent than researchers have acknowledged.

Social embodiment in the afterlife

Philosopher Mitch Hodge challenges the assumption that people are represented in the afterlife as disembodied. Drawing upon cultural representations of the afterlife, he argues that we intuitively represent supernatural agents as embodied to some extent. Hodge is careful to delineate between embodiment in general, and social embodiment more specifically. He proposes that we do not represent people in the afterlife as wholly embodied, composed of internal organs, bones, defecating, or sleeping. Instead, we represent them as if they are socially embodied in the same way we imagine someone who is not within our present perceptual presence or how we would a fictional character, such as Sherlock Holmes.

For instance, when we think about loved ones at work, we imagine what they might be doing that is socially relevant to the job that they do. Talking on the phone or talking to a colleague, writing an email, and so on. We also represent the parts of their bodies that are necessary for that representation: a head, a mouth, eyes, arms, hands, ears, and so on. Likewise, when we think of loved ones in the afterlife, we represent the parts of their bodies that are necessary for that particular representation. We also represent those embodied characteristics that allow us to identify that representation as our loved ones in this life or another place (hair color, wearing glasses[20]).

Hodge argues that dualism is not the default intuitive stance when it comes to reasoning about the afterlife.[21] Often people are represented in the afterlife as having the same body as in their earthly existence. This view is supported by the findings of Harris and colleagues in their studies in Vanuatu, where participants reasoned as though people retained their biological processes and bodily parts in the afterlife.

Embodied people in the afterlife

As we discuss in Chapter 7 (Supernatural Agents), the anthropologist Pascal Boyer has proposed that we represent deceased loved ones in the afterlife fundamentally as still people.[22] He explains that this is because we use our existing concepts of people to understand and represent supernatural agents. Most scholars in CSR share this view including those we have reviewed thus far in the chapter. Scholars disagree, however, on what this intuitive view of persons entails. Drawing on Boyer's theory, psychologist Michael Barlev proposes that contra Bloom, the person concept contains representations of people's mental *and* physical properties that are likely not intuitively separate or separable.[23] Thus, according to Barlev, the default view of supernatural agents, such as God—but also by extension, an individual in the afterlife—is that of an embodied person. The theory that people use existing templates of people to represent God has received empirical support.[24] Still, this theory has not directly been tested for representations of people in the afterlife. It offers a

Figure 6.2 In specific contexts, the representation of people in the afterlife as physically embodied is as intuitive as the representation of people as psychologically immortal. (Image credit: Ure/Shutterstock.com).

direct challenge to the theory of folk-dualism as explaining how we represent deceased people in the afterlife.

Key points

- Bloom has proposed that people are intuitive mind-body dualists and that these intuitions underpin ideas about the afterlife. The mind and body are construed as separate entities, identity resides in the mind, and thus people are represented in the afterlife as disembodied minds.
- Many cognitive scientists of religion accept some version of this explanation of why ideas about the afterlife are acquired so easily. There is much support for the idea that we can think about other people as having minds and bodies and that in the afterlife, identity is associated with psychological continuity.
- Others, such as Barlev, Boyer, and Hodge, question whether dualism is the default intuitive stance when it comes to reasoning about the afterlife.
- Other research, such as that of Czachesz and White, implies that whether or not we employ the body in representations of the afterlife, it is more context-dependent than is typically acknowledged in standard accounts in CSR.

Psychological essentialism

Other researchers, including psychologists Maira Roazzi, Melanie Nyhof, and Carl Johnson, have questioned the claim that people assume that identity resides in the mind during life and in the afterlife. They suggest that this claim is perhaps an ethnocentric assumption, based on western Cartesian philosophy.[25] From cross-cultural empirical research, these scholars propose that children and adults have a tripartite view of persons, composed of a body, mind, and something akin to a soul or essence. This latter explanation is more aligned with the folk theory of psychological essentialism.

We encountered the theory of psychological essentialism in Chapter 5 (The Nature of the World). Psychological essentialism is an intuition that favors creationism as an explanation for the origins of the world, discovered by the developmental psychologist Susan Gelman.[26] To recap, psychological essentialism is a naïve (i.e. early developing, pre-scientific) theory about the identity of things, including category members. So, for instance, children will reason that tigers have a natural and immutable essence, a tiger-ness, that makes them roar, and stays the same even though the tiger can change its appearance (e.g. grows bigger). Children and adults tend to find this theory compelling when it comes to explaining what makes individuals within a category, such as people, the same over time.[27] For example, children reason as though they remain the same person even though they may change their appearance or grow older.[28,29]

Children and adults tend to view the mind as harboring mental properties of the person, such as their thoughts, memories, and preferences.[30] They also tend to reason that people who have changed mentally—gained knowledge, lost memories, etc.—are still the same person as they were before these changes.[31] As the mind may be the closest concept to the identity-retaining "essence," participants may choose it as more likely to continue.

Crucially, as psychologist Rebekah Richert and Harris discovered, when given the opportunity, participants tended to assign continued identity in life and the afterlife to the soul, not to the mind.[32] This finding is precisely what Astuti and Harris also discovered in the studies in Madagascar mentioned earlier in the chapter. In their studies, even though participants thought that the mind was more likely to continue than the body after death, they also reasoned that the spirit was more likely to continue than the mind or body.[33] One reasonable interpretation from these findings is that people reason about the afterlife as entailing personal immortality, and personal immortality tends to include psychological immortality but fundamentally ensures the survival of the person's soul or essence.

Key points

- Some scholars propose that children and adults do not have a dualistic view of the person as composed of mind and body. Instead, they have a tripartite view of persons, consisting of a body, mind, and something akin to a soul or essence.
- Gelman argues that people are psychological essentialists, perceiving individuals as having an immutable essence that retains their identity over dramatic physical changes.
- Other researchers have proposed that our inherent tendency towards imbuing people with immutable essences despite physical changes explains why we reason that people continue in the afterlife.
- Even though mental properties are also typically retained in depictions of people in the afterlife, the essence is not the same as the mind and is better described as a soul.
- In studies, participants choose the mind as more likely to continue than physical states, but when given the option, they chose the soul as the most likely to continue overall.

Theory of mind, emotional attachment, enduring mental models and offline social reasoning

Think for a second, if you will, about what happens when someone else dies. On the one hand, you can think about the corpse as the product of death. You know, at least at an explicit level, that the person is biologically dead—although this may take some time to sink in. On the other hand, you are also likely to find it extremely difficult to represent the person as psychologically dead, no matter how much time passes. How can this thinking, feeling person that you loved—well, stop thinking and feeling? While it is relatively easy to represent a dead person as no longer having biological processes, such as breathing, it seems comparatively more difficult to describe a deceased person as no longer having mental processes, such as thinking. One reason for this is likely to do with the fact that physical processes are more accessible than psychological processes. When a loved one or pet dies, we can physically observe that they no longer breathe, eat, or use the bathroom, etc., but we cannot physically see whether or not they are thinking, remembering or dreaming.

Theory of mind and representing the deceased as mentally active

Anthropologist Pascal Boyer (2001) has argued that dead bodies represent a contradiction in our thinking about persons. On the one hand, people explicitly understand that the physical body is inanimate, although we do not readily assume an inanimate person is dead. As psychologist Clark Barrett and colleagues have argued, the animacy system—i.e. the expectation that living things move—does not shut off whenever we see a motionless corpse.[34] After all, living entities have to sleep, and it is hardly surprising that sleep is used as a euphemism for death in many languages.[35] Typically, it takes time, and other cues of death, such as a cold body, to help us represent the person as not living. Yet this type of representation—of an immobile body—is more straightforward to comprehend than the corpse as a non-thinking person.

In his explanation, Boyer implies that our inbuilt theories about other peoples' minds (i.e. theory of mind) are responsible for the difficulty in accepting that corpses can no longer think. As we have discussed in previous chapters, theory of mind is a hypothesized cognitive ability. One theoretical account of this ability proposes that even from a young age, we automatically explain ourselves and other people's behavior regarding a theory of their beliefs, desires, intentions, and goals. We habitually track unobservable mental states for persons throughout our lifetime. It is difficult, almost impossible, to stop representing the person as psychologically active because they are inanimate.

Boyer proposes that thinking about a person as continuing psychologically in another realm is an unintended consequence (i.e. a by-product) of our tendency to think about people psychologically in this realm. That we have a theory of mind means that we always think about other people's mental states, and this tendency extends when we think about people even when they are dead. Similar representation systems may have been adaptive when the person is alive—for example, they help predict people's actions. They are, however, not adaptive in the context of death. In other words, representing a dead person as having desires, intentions, and goals has no benefits to our survival.

Emotional attachment and enduring mental models

Other related theories about grief have the potential to further our understanding of why belief in the afterlife is so cognitively attractive. Some scholars have proposed that some symptoms of grief, such as unconsciously expecting the person to appear in the vicinity, is viewed as a by-product of emotional attachment[36] and cognitive systems.[37] Emotional attachment motivates us to stay in close contact with people and to enable us to have close relationships with them. This tendency is one reason, for example, why young children do not like to be unexpectedly separated from their parents—think about the distress of a young child who lost his mother in a shopping mall. Cognitive systems also generate enduring mental models of others, so that out of sight does not mean out of mind, which may give rise to afterlife beliefs. These functions of attachment and enduring mental models are essential when the other party is alive—otherwise, maintaining close relationships would virtually be impossible—yet they are futile when the person is dead. In evolutionary terms, it does not benefit your survival to represent someone dead as continuing to exist in the afterlife.

Offline social reasoning and the deceased existing in another place

Bering has proposed another cognitive bias that seems to dovetail well with the cognitive systems offered by grief researchers, offline social reasoning.[38] In everyday contexts, out of sight does not mean out of mind. As our mental rosters are ill-equipped to update the list of social players in our world, and for excellent reasons—it would be cognitively taxing and evolutionarily maladaptive to do so. Our ability to represent others who are not physically present (i.e. offline social reasoning) also enables us to construe the dead as though they continue to exist. Offline social reasoning enables humans to think about people who are not present in our immediate vicinity. We can easily imagine what a family member whom we have not seen in many months, or even years, is doing at a given moment. We are thus also able to think about a person as existing in another place after death.

As Hodge rightly points out,[39] Another common aspect of afterlife beliefs is that death entails a journey and change of location. After death, people are often represented as beginning a journey where they physically move from this world to another place. In this journey, they may end up succumbing to perils, such as being devoured by a crocodile god, returning to a cycle of rebirth where they are reborn in another form, or being reunited with their maker. Despite differences in the details, the afterlife is typically represented by ordinary people as a place.

One apt illustration of this assumption is in the classic novel, *The Great Divorce*.[40] Readers often delight in reading about the recently dead who journey on a bus ride through various places. The passengers decide where to get off, including at a grey town, which turns out to be purgatory or hell, and beautiful countryside, which turns out to be the foothills of heaven. There is something perfectly reasonable about the idea that people travel to another realm when they die. Yet the concept of an afterlife could, in theory, be a state of mind rather than a physical location. In other words, when you think about it logically, there is no reason why a person would have to go anywhere after they die, what if the afterlife was just a feeling of being happy, satisfied, or at peace for example?

Hodge has proposed that the tendency to engage in offline social reasoning also explains why we quickly think about a deceased loved one doing something in another sphere of existence.[41] Harris adopts a similar view where he elaborates on the cognitive biases that may enrich the explanation of the results of the cross-cultural studies that he and colleagues conducted.[42] To recap, Harris and colleagues found that older children and adults have two parallel concepts of death that they adopt in different contexts. One is based on biology and often evokes a common secular idea of death; another is supported by ideas about the afterlife and evokes a religious concept of death.

In later works, Harris proposed that the religious concept of the afterlife is underpinned by a bias towards representing attachment figures as continuing to exist when they are not physically present and despite their prolonged absence. Harris contends that children use their memories of a loved one to simulate what they would be doing in another place when they are not physically present. This capacity requires some abilities that become consolidated in children, such as object permanence, retaining memories of a loved one, and being able to use those memories to imagine the person as existing elsewhere. When these maturing abilities mesh with highly accessible cultural ideas about life after death, older children extend this ability to imagine people in the afterlife in ways that also reflect culturally endorsed views.

Another observation worth noting is that we often assume that an afterlife is a similar place to the world we inhabit. Our intuitive assumptions inform representations of people in the afterlife about people. Yet representations of the afterlife as a place are also informed and constrained by human imagination and cognitive processing abilities. For instance, consider an afterlife that has four dimensions—or levels that we perceive to be the reality, such as height, width, depth, and time. This idea would be relatively easy to imagine since these dimensions surround our everyday experience of the world.

Yet consider entertaining the idea of an afterlife that consists of five, six, or even seven dimensions, measured by abstract notions such as their position in the world since the beginning of time. These ideas would be more difficult to spread without additional support at the cultural level because they are almost impossible to imagine. It is easy to understand why cultural ideas that endorse the view that a person goes to another realm when they die, much like this world, and continue to engage in everyday activities, spreads easily. In short, our imagination is not unbounded, but rather, constrained. Likewise, ideas about the afterlife that meet our intuitive expectations about the current world are more likely to be readily adopted.

Key points

- Boyer proposes that our intuitive theories about other peoples' minds (i.e. theory of mind) are responsible for the difficulty in accepting that dead people can no longer think.
- Harris and grief researchers propose that emotional attachment systems and enduring mental models of people also enable us to continue to think about the person.
- Bering has proposed that the ability to reason about someone doing something somewhere when he or she is not physically present (offline social reasoning) also explains why we can so easily imagine the person in another place after death.
- Hodge, Bering, and Harris have proposed that the tendency to engage in offline social reasoning also explains why we quickly think about a deceased loved one doing something in another sphere of existence.
- The afterlife is often represented as a place that is similar to this world. Our experiences of the world constrain ideas about the afterlife as a physical location.

Summary of intuitions that favor afterlife beliefs

- Cognitive scientists of religion have proposed that cognitive predispositions help to explain why ideas about the afterlife are cross-culturally recurrent, especially the idea that the mind or soul survives biological death, and that the person continues to exist in another physical location that is much like this world.
- Scholars have proposed many predispositions to explain the ease with which people endorse ideas about the afterlife. These include folk-dualism, psychological essentialism, simulation constraints, theory of mind, emotional attachment, enduring mental models, and offline social reasoning.

Participation 2: The cognitive foundations of ideas

Table 3.3 in Chapter 3 (Research Questions) provided examples of the cognitive foundations of religious ideas. Based on this table and this chapter:

1 Provide a brief definition of the following cognitive tendencies: (a) simulation constraints (b) folk-dualism (c) theory of mind (d) psychological essentialism (e) offline social reasoning, and (f) embodiment.

2 Explain (in a few sentences for each) how each bias enriches the understanding of (a) why people believe in an afterlife (b) why people represent the afterlife in similar ways.

So far, in the chapter, we have considered cognitive and contextual theories of afterlife beliefs, which are proposed by cognitive scientists of religion. As we cover in the final chapter of the book (Chapter 11: Conclusion), cognitive theories of religion are sometimes criticized for not endorsing emotional or motivational components of religious thought and experiences. In contrast to explanations about belief in the afterlife as a result of cognitive processes, motivational theories focus on the motivation of people to believe in the first place. For instance, terror management theorists see belief in an afterlife as a defense mechanism against the anxiety of death. In the next section, we consider theories that purport to explain the motivation for people to believe that life continues after biological death.

Who wants to live forever? Motivational theories of afterlife beliefs

Have you ever sat down and thought about your own death? Not just a fleeting thought, but thought seriously about what it would be like to die? For the materialists among you, perhaps you will find comfort in the fact that you will not know you are dead. Maybe not. At least in the Western world, where death is a taboo subject, and reminders of death are removed at every opportunity. We go to such efforts in the West to avoid the reality of our mortality. Recent research has shown that even many Tibetan monks in training, who deny that there is a permanent self, are petrified of death.[43] These observations bring us to the fundamental question, what's so scary about death?

Throughout the ages, scholars have conjectured why we fear death. Some people may fear how they will die; whether it will be unexpected and painful, others may lament upon the loss of social relationships in this world, their hopes, dreams, and memories, and the very loss of themselves. As the famous philosopher, Nagel put it, "The thought that the world will go on without you, that you will become nothing, is tough to take in.[44] "Fear of the unknown may also play a role in fostering the trepidation with which at least some humans face death. Yet consider the point made by Socrates (a philosopher in ancient Greece, who is widely regarded as one of the founders of Western philosophy) that those who think they know what death entails may also fear it. According to his student Plato, Socrates said that: "to fear death, gentlemen, is no other than to think oneself wise when one is not, to think one knows what one does not know. No one knows whether death may not be the greatest of all blessings for a man, yet men fear it as if he or she knew that it is the greatest of evils.[45]"

Many of the earliest psychological theories explained belief in the afterlife (and indeed, belief in religion in general) as man's response to this fear of death. Freud most famously proposed a version of this theory in the early twentieth century and most elaborated upon in his book *The Future of an Illusion*.[46] Freud's account included many historical claims about religion that have since been discredited, such as the idea that humans killed their original father and sought to replace him with a fictional God. Still, his view that the afterlife arose from the need to escape death remains influential in scholarly writings on the subject. It is a simple yet powerful idea. People are petrified of their own mortality and are motivated to assuage this fear, so they create the concept of an afterlife where they continue after biological death. They wish to escape death, and they fulfill these wishes by the creation of an afterlife; thus, their wishes are fulfilled. The afterlife is merely wish fulfillment.

Of course, there is no way of tracing the exact origins of afterlife beliefs, no decisive way of knowing whether fear of death motivated their initial creation. Yet a more empirically tractable question concerns whether death anxiety currently motivates belief in the afterlife (and likewise adherence to a religion in general). Freud's basic thesis was expounded upon by later theorists[47] and later re-emerged in a more sophisticated and contemporary form in social psychology as terror management theory (TMT).[48]

Belief in the afterlife as terror management

Terror management theorists seek to explain why people currently embrace specific ideas, including the afterlife. They claim that people are petrified of death as annihilation and are motivated by a self-preservation instinct. They manage this terror by embracing ideas that offer immortality (such as a belief in the afterlife), which relieves this fear. There is mixed empirical support for each of these sub-components of the theory. First, take the claim that humans are petrified of death. While few would doubt that self-preservation is instinctual (i.e. a zebra needs no encouragement to run from a lion) the existential fear of death in humans (i.e. the desire not to die in the abstract) is more difficult to prove. It turns out that when you ask people what they fear, death is typically mentioned less than ten percent of the time.[49] People are more concerned with current social and mundane fears.

Terror management theorists maintain that some fears, like terrorism, are ultimately explained by the fear of death. Other TMT theorists maintain that the fear of death is so extreme that people cannot think about it. According to these theorists, people suppress it, pushing the concern to the bottom of their consciousness. Thus, fear of death is not salient and inaccessible to explicit, higher-level reasoning, such as asking people questions about whether they fear death. TMT has been critiqued as being unfalsifiable. Whatever the outcome, it seems that some version of TMT wins; people are explicitly afraid of death, which they freely admit, or people are so scared of death that they disguise their fear of death.

Rather than asking if people fear death, some theorists have devised ingenious experiments to make the idea that one will die salient (i.e. noticeable or apparent) in the minds of participants. This reminder is then followed by measuring something that experimenters think is affected by a fear of death to see if making the realization that one will die more apparent has an impact. This effect occurs by merely reminding people of their own mortality, for example, getting them to think and write about death, or more subtly, by interviewing people in front of locations that remind them of death, such as the entrance to a cemetery[50] or a funeral home.[51]

One part of TMT has received some support. This is the claim that people manage terror by investing in things that seem to offer immortality. Yet most TMT theorists have examined the effects of mortality salience on what they call symbolic immortality, such as the means to symbolically live on after one's death, through, for example having children or writing a book or promoting the values of a religious group. Few researchers have examined the effects of mortality salience on literal immortality, which is directly escaping death through belief in an afterlife.

Although TMT theorists have not specified a prediction, according to the theory of TMT, we would expect a relationship between fear of death, the strength of religious belief, and belief in the afterlife. In other words, the more one fears their own destruction, the stronger they ought to believe in the existence of the afterlife. Yet the evidence for this relationship between fear of death and afterlife beliefs is mixed. Some studies have investigated the relationship between fear of death and belief in religion in general. Results were inconclusive. Researchers found that those who are religious are more, equally, or less afraid of death.[52,53] Many studies have found that making death more apparent strengthens religious belief for those who are already religious. Still, results are inconsistent when people are not religious.[54,55]

Psychologist Jonathan Jong and colleagues have argued that the problem with prior studies is that they are still dependent upon participants' self-report, which taps only into explicit reasoning. They conducted a study on mortality salience and judgments about supernatural entities (e.g. God).[56] Jong and collegues found that writing about one's death (i.e. mortality salience) did not strengthen explicit beliefs in supernatural entities. This was not the case, however, when they used a property verification task, which depended upon implicit processing.

In the property verification task, participants had to click "real" or "imaginary" as fast as they could on a computer screen when words about supernatural entities flashed on the screen. Those who wrote about their own death, regardless of religious belief, tended to be quicker at categorizing supernatural words as real, than those who feared death less. These findings suggest that explicit tasks may not be sensitive enough to tap into implicit processing concerning beliefs. That fear of death may compel people—well, New Zealand undergraduate psychology students at least—to believe in God. As the saying goes, "there are no atheists in foxholes," which suggests that in the height of anxiety, such as soldiers fighting in trenches during a war, people turn to religion for comfort. For now, the empirical question of whether fear of death compels people to believe in an afterlife remains open.

Key points

- TMT theorists claim that people are petrified of death as annihilation and are motivated by a self-preservation instinct to manage this terror by denying death or embracing ideas that offer symbolic immortality (such as writing a book) or literal immortality (such as a belief in the afterlife), which relieves this fear.
- TMT is often criticized for being unfalsifiable.
- Evidence for the relationship between fear of death and belief in an afterlife is, at best, inconclusive.
- Jong and colleagues have argued that the results of previous studies are mixed because researchers rely on specific tasks and consciously available ideas, which do not get at implicit processing and unconscious assumptions. Their research offers support for the claim that fear of death may compel people to believe in God.

The origins of fear of death

In addition to empirical objections, there are theoretical reasons for pausing to consider the explanatory power of TMT. Most obviously, the theory assumes that an afterlife is desirable, or at the least, less anxiety-producing than the thought of annihilation of oneself. Yet as anthropologists have long pointed out, conceptualizations of the afterlife are often not at all comforting. Jong and colleagues summarize a few of these include the Calvinist belief in a God who predetermines souls to salvation or damnation, the ancient Mesopotamian belief that people are thrown into a terrifying world filled with monsters, or the fire and brimstone preaching common in 18th Century Christian revivalist movements.[57]

Furthermore, doctrines and teachings often assume that people have to behave in ways that please the gods to attain entry into an afterlife like heaven. They also assume that another type of afterlife—such as hell—can seem even worse than biological death, may await them should they fail (eternal damnation, anyone?). Another possibility is that people are so petrified of death that they find life an appealing alternative in whatever form it is presented to them.[58]

So, what are the origins of this fear? Some scholars who study our fear of death claim that death anxiety is a uniquely human trait that may have arisen as a by-product of self-awareness. Thus "I know that I exist, and I know that I will die." It may also be potentially maladaptive in this form of existential anxiety. The motivation for self-preservation is quite obviously adaptive to survival, but all animals share this instinct. By contrast, terror management theorists would assume that if we fell prey to our imaginations, death anxiety would be crippling. For instance, occasionally, people—often those who have experienced the recent death of a loved one— have thanatophobia, a condition characterized by an obsessive fear of death. In severe cases, the sufferer ceases to function physically and emotionally. For instance, he or she may refuse to leave the house, suffer from anxiety attacks, become depressed, and unable to distinguish between reality and unreality.[59] TMT theorists maintain that people can deny this reality through the adoption of afterlife beliefs.

Key points

- TMT is sometimes criticized for assuming that an afterlife is more desirable than the thought of personal annihilation.
- TMT proposes that fear of death emerges as a by-product of self-awareness. Knowing we exist entails knowing that we will die.

Fear of death facilitates the spread of afterlife beliefs

Philosopher Shaun Nichols proposes a more reasonable theory to explain the relationship between the fear of death and the motivation to believe in an afterlife. Nichols does not focus on trying to explain the origins of afterlife beliefs, but rather, the prevalence of specific ideas about the afterlife within and across cultures. This focus is typical of CSR scholars, but Nichols's account is unique because he combines both motivational and cognitive factors.

Drawing on the epidemiological approach proposed by Dan Sperber (covered in Chapter 5: The Nature of the World), Nichols argues that motivationally attractive representations of the afterlife are better remembered and transmitted. Thus, in addition to sociocultural factors, human psychology can explain why specific ideas about the afterlife become prevalent. Taking a historical perspective, Nichols supports his claim by drawing from Abrahamic religions. He proposes that many failed descendants of Abrahamic religions do not preserve motivationally attractive elements, including the idea of an afterlife. For example, the Deistic view that God created the world with no guarantee of immortality (or divine justice for that matter), or in the case of early Judaism, the Sadducees' rejection of the existence of an afterlife. Nichols coded doctrines in Christianity, Judaism, and Islam as motivationally attractive or not, mainly based on Freud's writings. He found that motivationally appealing doctrines (including the idea of a harmonious afterlife) were more likely to persist into the descendant religion than motivationally neutral ideas.

This historical analysis is not without its weaknesses, however. For instance, it relies on Nichols' interpretation and does not take account of sociocultural factors, including past contact between traditions. Overall, this study does not provide evidence that the motivation to believe in an afterlife (preferably a pleasant one) causes people to believe or even causes religious doctrines to succeed. What Nichols is arguing, instead, is that motivationally attractive elements have a psychological advantage when they are introduced to a population. This advantage, when coupled with other sociocultural forces—such as wealth and cultural domination, make the doctrine more readily adopted, resilient to change, and more faithfully transmitted by ordinary people.

Key points

- Nichols combines cognitive and motivational factors to account for the success of some popular theological ideas about the afterlife.
- He draws on the epidemiology of representations theory by Sperber, and the ideas of TMT, to argue that motivationally attractive depictions of the afterlife are better remembered and transmitted.

Summary of motivational theories of afterlife beliefs

Many theorists have contemplated the question of why humans are motivated to believe in the afterlife. Freud tried to explain the origins of afterlife beliefs. While TMT theorists largely abandoned this endeavor of finding the origins of afterlife beliefs, they continue to adopt the basic argument that fear of death motivates people to believe that life continues after death. TMT has, however, received mixed empirical support, and it is uncertain whether it is the fear of death, or the denial of the fear of death, that causes people to adopt a belief in the afterlife. Shaun Nichols provides a more nuanced account of the role of death anxiety. His account holds that in addition to other social factors, religious doctrines that include an idea of life after death, and those that include particularly appealing versions of the afterlife, are more likely to be accepted by people and transmitted to others. It seems that what people want to happen after their death may well affect what they are likely to believe.

Participation 3: Afterlife documentary

Imagine that you have landed a new job as a documentarian. Your first assignment is to create a 30-minute documentary called "why do people believe in the afterlife?" Based on your background research of reading this chapter:

1. Prepare an outline. Include 3–5 main points the documentary will make, a list of people you will interview, and what images you will include.
2. Create a 5-minute voice-over narrative for the documentary. You may write this down, or record it on an electronic device, such as an iPhone.
3. In groups of 3–4 students, offer feedback on each member's outline and voice-over. Consider questions such as: Did they present the material

accurately? Did they misrepresent someone's work? Would ordinary people understand the claims they are making?

4 Revise your outline and voice-over to improve them, based upon the feedback you received.

Summary of motivational theories of afterlife beliefs

- TMT theorists explain belief in the afterlife as a product of people's fear of death as annihilation.
- Based on the self-awareness that we exist and will therefore die, and motivated by a self-preservation instinct, TMT claims that people manage this terror by embracing ideas that offer literal immortality.
- There is mixed empirical support for the theory, including a relationship between fear of death and belief in the afterlife. Jong maintains that this is due to methodological weaknesses of studies that tap into people's explicit reasoning about death.
- Others critique the underlying assumption in TMT that the afterlife is more desirable than the thought of personal annihilation.
- Nichols combines cognitive and motivational factors to account for the success of some popular theological ideas about the afterlife.

The epistemic implications of theories on the existence of the afterlife

As we discuss in Chapter 11 (Conclusion), a question that often follows from reading theories about the afterlife concerns their epistemic implications. In other words, what implications do cognitive, contextual, and motivational theories have for the truth, rationality, and justification of afterlife beliefs? Do they say whether belief in the afterlife is reasonable, justified or warranted? Also, do they prove or disprove the existence of the afterlife?

Most TMT theorists claim that, following Freud, a belief in the afterlife is a product of wishful thinking, it does not exist. By contrast, cognitive and contextual theories say little about these questions. First, it is essential to note that cognitive scientists of religion are not claiming that predispositions or enculturation thoroughly explain why people believe. Instead, they are proposing that mind and culture help explain why specific ideas about life after death (for example, the notion of psychological immortality in the afterlife) become popular and spread. The ease with which these ideas about the afterlife spread is unrelated to their truth value—consider string theory or evolutionary theory, which are profoundly counterintuitive yet scientifically upheld.

Of course, those outside CSR who are concerned about the truth value of religion may interpret these findings to mean something other than cognitive naturalness. They may propose, for example, that God causes people to believe in the afterlife or that people believe in the afterlife because it is true. Others may seek to explain belief away by reducing it to nothing but the mind (a form of ontological reductionism). For example, that religion is in the mind and, therefore, an illusion. Others may claim that people believe in ideas about life after death because others culturally endorse them. Yet CSR is not concerned with questions about whether or not the afterlife (or some version of it) exists. Cognitive scientists of religion propose that such issues are outside the scope of the psychological sciences. In their methods, at least, researchers remain agnostic to the possibility of an afterlife.

Chapter summary

There are many different psychological accounts of why people believe in life after biological death. For simplicity, these accounts can be divided up into the following categories: cognitive, contextual, and motivational theories. Cognitive scientists of religion have tended to propose accounts that belong to the cognitive and contextual types of approaches. These theories often posit psychological tendencies and constraints to explain the natural inclination to accept ideas about the afterlife. These tendencies and limitations include the inability to comprehend one's annihilation or absence, the tendency to see bodies, minds, and souls as separate, and the mind or soul as containing identity after the death of the physical body. Contextual theories attribute a more significant role to the cultural transmission of ideas about the afterlife to explain why people accept and believe in such ideas.

Cognitive theories concentrate more on the question of why ideas about the afterlife are recurrent across cultures. They focus less on the issue of why afterlife beliefs may differ, which are better accounted for by contextual theories. They also say less about why people have a commitment to these ideas, which may be better explained by motivational theories. Many early motivational theories can be traced back to Freud. These theories were concerned with explaining the origins of belief in life after death, for example, explaining why they emerged in the first place. By contrast, terror management theorists are more concerned with the question of why people currently believe in the afterlife, rather than the origins of such beliefs. Motivational theories claim that we believe in an afterlife because we are motivated to do so. Motivational theories may enhance the explanatory potential of cognitive theories of the afterlife. When coupled with cognitive biases that predispose humans to represent their continued existence, fear of annihilation, and fear of absence from the world are likely to increase the likelihood of endorsing ideas about the afterlife.

Chapter summary

- Cognitive scientists of religion have proposed that cognitive predispositions help to explain the inclination to believe in the afterlife. They also explain why specific ideas are cross-culturally recurrent, especially the idea that the mind or soul survives biological death, and that the person continues to exist in another physical location that is much like this world.
- Scholars have proposed many predispositions to explain the ease with which people endorse ideas about the afterlife.
- Contextual theories attribute a more significant role in the cultural transmission of ideas about the afterlife to explain why people accept and believe in such ideas.
- TMT theorists are also concerned with the question of why people currently believe in the afterlife, but they draw on reasons why people are motivated to believe.
- TMT claims that we believe in an afterlife because a self-preservation instinct motivates us to embrace ideas about life after death.
- Together, cognitive, contextual, and motivational theories may produce a more compelling explanation for why so people around the world believe in an afterlife. They also help to explain the stability and variance of ideas about the afterlife within and across cultures.

Discussion questions

1. To what extent do theories about psychological tendencies and constraints and cultural learning explain why people believe that life continues after death?
2. What are the main contributions of CSR to the study of the afterlife?
3. Freud's thesis confronts us with a fundamental question: is the afterlife what we want? Thinking about conceptualizations of the afterlife that you are familiar with; do you agree or disagree with this question?
4. Do you think motivational and cognitive theories are incompatible, or can they jointly explain why people believe in the afterlife?

Research case study: Reincarnation beliefs

In many places around the globe, biological birth does not mark a person's entrance into the world, but rather, their return to it from a previous life in another bodily form. Cross-cultural studies have recorded the presence of reincarnation beliefs in around 30 percent of world cultures, and approximately 20 percent of Americans believe that reincarnation is plausible. Why are ideas about reincarnation so recurrent?

Anthropologists have documented the diversity of forms that reincarnation beliefs and practices take around the globe. These include the relationship to one's ethical conduct (i.e. karma), whether and how one escapes the cycle of rebirth, and the functions of society (e.g. a system for the distribution of names, wealth, and even child-rearing practices). Traditional accounts explain the transmissive success of reincarnation beliefs by locating them in their historically situated sociocultural contexts. For example, people are more concerned with uncovering their past life identity than the identity of others in America because it suits a quintessentially modern, eclectic brand of New Age spirituality and religious individualism that has become immensely popular in the West. While insightful, these accounts say less about why ideas about reincarnation persist across cultures more generally.

I have adopted a cognitive approach to addressing the question of why the belief in reincarnation is cross-culturally recurrent. I researched reincarnation beliefs using systematic comparisons of archival, ethnographic records on reincarnation, cross-cultural studies with Jains in South India, and western adults with mixed religious beliefs, and interviews with US spiritual seekers who hold the conviction that they have lived before. Based on the results of my research, I proposed that by looking beyond the variation in local forms of reincarnation beliefs and practices, it is possible to determine similarities in basic ideas underpinning reincarnation. Drawing from theories in the social cognitive sciences, I argued that specific ideas about reincarnation are generated readily, remembered, and communicated in part because they meet cognitively optimal assumptions about what human survival entails and what constitutes evidence for it. There are thus natural foundations to reincarnation beliefs, and these foundations help explain their recurrence. These can be summarized by the following:

Personal immortality:

a The imaginative obstacle (i.e. the inability to readily conceive of our own, and others', death) may facilitate the idea that people survive death in the first place.
b The readiness to entertain reincarnation as a possibility for loved ones may be influenced by our ability to represent others who are not physically present (i.e. offline social reasoning). This tendency also enables us to describe the dead as though they continue to exist.
c As TMT theorists have claimed, there is also a motivational appeal to the idea that we are immortal. Fear of annihilation may drive the likelihood of endorsing beliefs about the afterlife. Even though some representations of reincarnation include the possibility of increased pain and suffering in the next lifetime, it may be easier—and more

psychologically appealing—to accept the potential of the self as existing and suffering than not existing at all. Such motivation also extends towards the ones we love. Given the social investments that go into relationships, people do not easily represent absent others as removed from their social world.

Practices designed to identify a reincarnated person by inspecting the appearance of newborn children may serve to fulfill a desire to be reunited with deceased loved ones.

Psychological immortality:

d People are conceptualized as surviving reincarnation mentally, just elsewhere, in a different body or a different realm. Conceptualizations of rebirth reflect the widespread assumption that people are constituted by minds, not bodies (i.e. folk-dualism).
e Research has shown that being in a hypothetical conscious state without memories appears especially difficult to imagine. I found that people assume that episodic memories (i.e. autobiographical events that one can recall having experienced at a particular place and time) survive reincarnation. Memories tell people something about themselves over time. They also enable the continuation of established relationships (i.e. if people do not remember you, then the connection has been irreparably damaged).

Embodied survival:

f Reincarnation also entails that the person occupies a new physical body after death. Yet, people assume that physical similarities between a living child and a dead person are evidence that the person has returned as a child. These physical similarities tend to be distinctive features such as unusual and rare birthmarks and skin irregularities. They provide a convenient (and reliable) means of evidence that they are the same person. People are employing the same default empirical devices as those used in the everyday social world to recognize people. Such features are convenient, unique, and easy to detect.

The afterlife is a place:

g Offline social reasoning is also likely to be partly responsible for the tendency for people to think about a deceased loved one doing something in another sphere of existence. The most accessible representation of the afterlife is that people return to where they originated (this world). Also, having the afterlife as the here-and-now enables the possibility of continued social relationships with the dead.

Conclusion

Ideas about reincarnation entail underlying assumptions: namely, that the essential identity and aspects of an individual exist apart from the body, survives biological death, and is reborn in another human form in this world. I argue that taking account of basic human tendencies to think about people in death and the afterlife, in addition to cultural and historical factors, can provide scholars with an enriched understanding of why reincarnation has become a widely endorsed concept. It also helps explain how and why it is used to determine the features of social systems of tribal and world religions.

Discussion questions

1 In your own words, summarize the claims the researcher is making.
2 What are the differences and similarities between this research and previous research on reincarnation?
3 What do you think demarks this research as typical of the CSR approach to religion?
4 Which of these aspects do you think best and least explain why the idea of reincarnation is popular?
5 What do you think are the real-world implications of this theory on how ordinary people and the media represent reincarnation?

Further reading

1 White, C., Kelly, B., and Nichols, S. "Remembering past lives: institutions about memory and personal identity in reincarnation." in *The Cognitive Science of Religion and its Philosophical Implications*, eds. Cruz, H. & Nichols, R., 169–196. London: Bloomsbury Academic, 2015.
2 White, C. "Who wants to live forever? Explaining the cross-cultural recurrence of reincarnation beliefs," *Journal of Cognition and Culture* 17, (2017): 419–436.
3 White, C. "The cognitive foundations of reincarnation." *Method and Theory in the Study of Religion* (2016): 1–23.
4 White, Claire, Michael Kinsella, and Jesse Bering. "How to know you've survived death: A cognitive account of the popularity of contemporary post-mortem survival narratives." *Method & Theory in the Study of Religion* 30, no. 3 (2018): 279–299.

Selected further reading

Articles

1 Harris, Paul L. *Children's Understanding of Death: From Biology to Religion.* Philosophical Transactions of the Royal Society (in Press).

Books

1 Bering, Jesse. *The Belief Instinct: The Psychology of Souls, Destiny, and the Meaning of Life.* New York: W.W. Norton & Company, 2012.
2 Bloom, Paul. *Descartes' Baby: How the Science of Child Development Explains What Makes us Human.* Manhattan: Random House, 2005.
3 Jong, Jonathan, and Jamin Halberstadt. *Death Anxiety and Religious Belief: An Existential Psychology of Religion.* New York: Bloomsbury Publishing, 2016.

Notes

1 Jesse M. Bering, "Intuitive conceptions of dead agents' minds: The natural foundations of afterlife beliefs as phenomenological boundary." *Journal of Cognition and Culture* 2, no. 4 (2002): 263–308.
2 Jesse M. Bering and David F. Bjorklund, "The natural emergence of reasoning about the afterlife as a developmental regularity." *Developmental Psychology* 40, no. 2 (2004): 217.
3 Jesse M. Bering, Carlos Hernández Blasi, and David F. Bjorklund, "The development of afterlife beliefs in religiously and secularly schooled children." *British Journal of Developmental Psychology* 23, no. 4 (2005): 587–607.
4 Natalie A. Emmons and Deborah Kelemen, "The development of children's prelife reasoning: Evidence from two cultures." *Child Development* 85, no. 4 (2014): 1617–1633.
5 Huang, Junwei, Lehua Cheng, and Jing Zhu. "Intuitive conceptions of dead persons' mentality: A cross-cultural replication and more." *International Journal for the Psychology of Religion* 23, no. 1 (2013): 29–41.
6 Paul L. Harris, and Marta Giménez, "Children's acceptance of conflicting testimony: The case of death." *Journal of Cognition and Culture* 5, no. 1 (2005): 143–164.
7 Rita Astuti and Paul L. Harris, "Understanding mortality and the life of the ancestors in rural Madagascar." *Cognitive Science* 32, no. 4 (2008): 713–740.
8 Watson-Jones, Rachel E., Justin T.A. Busch, Paul L. Harris, and Cristine H. Legare. "Does the body survive death? Cultural variation in beliefs about life everlasting." *Cognitive Science* 41, no. S3 (2017): 455–476.
9 Jean-Paul Sartre, *The Wall (Intimacy), and Other Stories.* Vol. 272. New York: New Directions Publishing, 1969, 8.
10 Justin L Barrett, *Why Would Anyone Believe in God?* Lanham, MD: AltaMira Press, 2004, 58.
11 Shaun Nichols, "Imagination and immortality: Thinking of me." *Synthese* 159, no. 2 (2007): 215–233.
12 Paul Bloom, *Descartes' Baby: How the Science of Child Development, Explains What Makes Us Human.* Manhattan: Random House, 2005, 191.
13 Emma Cohen, Emily Burdett, Nicola Knight, and Justin Barrett, "Cross-cultural similarities and differences in person-body reasoning: Experimental evidence from

the United Kingdom and Brazilian Amazon." *Cognitive Science* 35, no. 7 (2011): 1282–1304.

14 Edward Slingerland and Maciej Chudek, "The prevalence of mind-body dualism in early China." *Cognitive Science* 35, no. 5 (2011): 997–1007.

15 Bruce Greyson and Ian Stevenson, "The phenomenology of near-death experiences." *The American Journal of Psychiatry* (1980).

16 Michael Kinsella, "Near-death experiences and networked spirituality: The emergence of an afterlife movement," *Journal of the American Academy of Religion* 85, no. 1 (2017): 168–198.

17 Claire White, Michael Kinsella, and Jesse M. Bering, (In press) "How to know you've survived death: A cognitive account of the popularity of contemporary post-mortem survival narratives." *Method and Theory in the Study of Religion.*

18 Ivstan Czachesz, "Why body matters in the afterlife mind reading and body imagery in synoptic tradition and the apocalypse of Peter." In *The Human Body in Death and Resurrection*, ed. Tobias Nicklas, Friedrich Reiterer, and Joseph Verheyden. Berlin: DeGruyter, 2009, 391–411.

19 Claire White, "Cross-cultural similarities in reasoning about personal continuity in reincarnation: Evidence from South India." *Religion, Brain, and Behavior* 6, no. 2, (2016): 130–153.

20 Hodge, K. Mitch. "On imagining the afterlife." *Journal of Cognition and Culture* 11, no. 3–4 (2011): 367–389.

21 K. Mitch Hodge, "Descartes' mistake: How afterlife beliefs challenge the assumption that humans are intuitive Cartesian substance dualists." *Journal of Cognition and Culture* 8, no. 3 (2008): 387–415.

22 Boyer, Pascal. "Religious thought and behavior as by-products of brain function." *Trends in cognitive sciences* 7, no. 3 (2003): 119–124.

23 Barlev, M. On the ubiquity of beliefs in disembodied beings and on the default function integration of mind and body representations. Under review: *Cognitive Science.*

24 Barlev, Michael, Spencer Mermelstein, Adam S. Cohen, and Tamsin C. German. "The primacy of the embodied person concept in representations of disembodied extraordinary beings." Under review: *Perspectives in psychological science.*

25 Maira Roazzi, Melanie Nyhof, and Carl Johnson, "Mind, soul and spirit: Conceptions of immaterial identity in different cultures." *International Journal for the Psychology of Religion* 23, no. 1 (2013): 75–86.

26 Susan A Gelman, *The Essential Child: Origins of Essentialism in Everyday Thought.* New York: Oxford University Press, 2003.

27 Susan A Gelman, *The Essential Child: Origins of Essentialism in Everyday Thought.* New York: Oxford University Press, 2003.

28 Grant Gutheil and Karl S. Rosengren, "A rose by any other name: Preschoolers' understanding of individual identity across name and appearance changes." *British Journal of Developmental Psychology* 14, no. 4 (1996): 477–498.

29 Greta G. Fein, and Suzann Eshleman, "Individuals and dimensions in children's judgment of same and different." *Developmental Psychology* 10, no. 6 (1974): 793.

30 Corriveau, Kathleen H., Elisabeth S. Pasquini, and Paul L. Harris. "'If it's in your mind, it's in your knowledge': Children's developing anatomy of identity." *Cognitive Development* 20, no. 2 (2005): 321–340; Richert, Rebekah A., and Paul L. Harris. "Dualism revisited: Body vs. mind vs. soul." *Journal of Cognition and Culture* 8, no. 1 (2008): 99–115.

31 Blok, Sergey, George Newman, and Lance J. Rips. "Individuals and their concepts." In *Categorization Inside and Outside the Laboratory.* 2005: 127–149.

32 Rebekah A. Richert and Paul L. Harris, "Dualism revisited: Body vs. mind vs. soul." *Journal of Cognition and Culture* 8, no. 1 (2008): 99–115.

33 Astuti and Harris, "Understanding mortality," 713–740.

34 H. Clark Barrett and Tanya Behne, "Children's understanding of death as the cessation of agency: A test using sleep versus death." *Cognition* 96, no. 2 (2005): 93–108.
35 Marín-Arrese, Juana I. "To die, to sleep a contrastive study of metaphors for death and dying in English and Spanish." *Language Sciences* 18, no. 1–2 (1996): 37–52.
36 John Archer, "Grief from an evolutionary perspective." In *Handbook of Bereavement Research: Consequences, Coping and Care*, eds. Margaret S. Stroebe, Robert O. Hansson, Wolfgang Ed Stroebe, and Henk Ed Schut. Washington DC: American Psychological Association, 2001, 263–284.
37 Claire White and M.T. Fessler, (2018). "An evolutionary account of vigilance in grief." *Evolution, Medicine, and Public Health* 1, 34–42.
38 J. M Bering, "The cognitive science of souls: Clarifications and extensions of the evolutionary model." *Behavioral and Brain Sciences* 29, no. 5, (2006): 486–493.
39 K. Mitch Hodge, "Dead survivors, the living dead, and concepts of death." *Review of Philosophy and Psychology*: 1–27, (forthcoming).
40 C. S. Lewis. *The Great Divorce: A Dream*. San Francisco: Harper, 1946.
41 K. Mitch Hodge, "On imagining the afterlife." *The Journal of Cognition and Culture*, 11, (2011a): 367–389.
42 Harris, Paul. L. (2018). Children's understanding of death: From biology to religion. *Philosophical Transactions of the Royal Society B*, 373: 20170266.
43 Nichols, Shaun, Nina Strohminger, Arun Rai, and Jay Garfield. "Death and the self." *Cognitive Science* (2018): 1–19.
44 Thomas Nagel, *What Does it All Mean?: A Very Short Introduction to Philosophy*. Oxford: Oxford University Press, 1987, 93.
45 Plato, *Plato in Twelve Volumes*, Vol. 1 translated by Harold North Fowler; Introduction by W.R.M. Lamb. Cambridge, MA: Harvard University Press, 1966, 29.
46 Sigmund Freud. *The Future of an Illusion*. Peterborough: Broadview Press, 2012.
47 Ernest Becker. *The Denial of Death*. New York: Simon and Schuster, 2007.
48 Jeff Greenberg, Tom Pyszczynski, and Sheldon Solomon. "The causes and consequences of a need for self-esteem: A terror management theory." *Public Self and Private Self* 189 (1986): 189–212.
49 Jonathan Jong and Jamin Halberstadt, *Death Anxiety, and Religious Belief: An Existential Psychology of Religion*. New York: Bloomsbury Publishing, 2016, 93.
50 Eva Jonas, Immo Fritsche, and Jeff Greenberg, "Currencies as cultural symbols–an existential psychological perspective on reactions of Germans toward the Euro." *Journal of Economic Psychology* 26, no. 1 (2005): 129–146.
51 Tom Pyszczynski, Robert A. Wicklund, Stefan Floresku, Holgar Koch, Gerardine Gauch, Sheldon Solomon, and Jeff Greenberg, "Whistling in the dark: Exaggerated consensus estimates in response to incidental reminders of mortality." *Psychological Science* 7, no. 6 (1996): 332–336.
52 James M. Donovan, "Defining religion." In *Selected Readings in the Anthropology of Religion*. Westport: Greenwood Publishing Group, 2003, 61–98.
53 Paul Wink and Julia Scott, "Does religiousness buffer against the fear of death and dying in late adulthood? Findings from a longitudinal study." *The Journals of Gerontology Series B: Psychological Sciences and Social Sciences* 60, no. 4 (2005): 207–214.
54 Michael Osarchuk and Sherman J. Tatz. "Effect of induced fear of death on belief in afterlife." *Journal of Personality and Social Psychology* 27, no. 2 (1973): 256.
55 John W. Burling, "Death concerns and symbolic aspects of the self: The effects of mortality salience on status concern and religiosity." *Personality and Social Psychology Bulletin* 19, no. 1 (1993): 100–105.
56 Jonathan Jong, Jamin Halberstadt, and Matthias Bluemke, "Foxhole atheism, revisited: The effects of mortality salience on explicit and implicit religious belief." *Journal of Experimental Social Psychology* 48, no. 5 (2012): 983–989.
57 Jong, Halberstadt, and Bluemke, "Foxhole atheism, revisited," 7.

58 Van Tongeren, D.R., Pennington, A.R., McIntosh, D.N., Newton, T., Green, J. D., Davis, D.E., and Hook, J.N. (2017). "Where, o death, is thy sting? The meaning-providing function of beliefs in literal immortality." *Mental Health, Religion & Culture*, 1–15.

59 "Fear of Death Phobia: Thanatophobia," Fear Of, accessed April 2018, http://www.fearof.net/fear-of-death-phobia-thanatophobia/.

7 Supernatural agents

Ideas about gods, ghosts, goblins, ancestors, fairies, demons, and other agents are part and parcel of cultural discourse, and scholars have long been interested in these ideas. The cognitive science of religion (CSR) shares many aspects with earlier approaches to the study of religion. For example, nineteenth-century anthropologist Edward Tylor[1] likewise pondered where the belief in spiritual beings originated. Preceding Tylor, eminent scholars such as Spinoza and Hume proposed the theory that religious concepts, such as supernatural agents, tend to have a similar, human-like structure because we are most familiar with them. However, cognitive scientists of religion track the antecedents of ideas about supernatural agents using methods and theories from the evolutionary and social sciences, including how and when these ideas tend to emerge and develop in the minds of children, and how evolution shapes tendencies to represent supernatural agents in standard ways.

The definitional approach to supernatural agents in CSR is also distinctive. Key figures (including Durkheim, Evans-Pritchard, Lienhardt, Hallowell, Klass, and Saler) have long noted that the term "supernatural agents" is problematic. For example, the supernatural is often taken to mean variously "at odds with current science," "unnatural," "illusory," or sometimes simply "false." As discussed in detail later in this chapter, CSR mitigates definitional debates about what does and does not constitute supernatural agents by providing an evolutionary technical definition of the term. From this scientific perspective, the word "supernatural" could be replaced with another, and people would still explain recurrent phenomena. Indeed, in many non-western parts of the world, people do not use such terms. As we discussed in Chapter 2 (Core Assumptions) what matters for scientists who study religion are the underlying patterns, not the name assigned to them. Like the term "religion," "supernatural agents" are often invoked to characterize a common idea in the cultural environment.

Cognitive scientists of religion often begin studying representations of supernatural agents by selecting recurrent cultural concepts and then explaining similar features based upon their potential evolutionary origins, functions, and other psycho-social repercussions. In particular, CSR focuses on understanding three main aspects of reasoning about supernatural agents:

1 The antecedents of ideas about supernatural agents.
2 The role of social learning and cognitive biases in mature representations of supernatural agents cross-culturally.
3 The personal and broader social consequences of representing supernatural agents as part of the social world.

We consider the first two aspects (1 and 2 above) of reasoning about supernatural agents in this chapter and examine some personal and broader social consequences of these beliefs (3, above) in Chapter 8 (Morality).

Participation 1: Defining supernatural agents

1 Think about a supernatural agent. Write down the name.
2 What do you think makes this agent supernatural? Write down your answer in a few sentences.
3 Share and compare your answer with another student.
4 Together, come up with a new definition of supernatural agents based on your answers.

The acquisition and development of supernatural agent concepts

Most people around the world come to entertain ideas about agents with extraordinary features. Do young children find these ideas difficult or easy to represent? Moreover, what is the role of cognitive development in the acquisition of ideas about supernatural agents? Do they change their representations over time as they develop cognitively? Researchers in the socio-cognitive sciences have investigated these questions about the development of supernatural agent concepts (i.e. ontogeny) to understand better the role of cognition and culture in the origins of religious cognition.

Since the majority of studies conducted are with western children, researchers typically focus on how children represent the Judeo-Christian God. In particular, studies mostly concern how children represent God's mind, primarily as compared to other people's minds. Researchers converge on the idea that the tendency for concepts of extraordinary abilities emerge around preschool years but disagree over when and how children differentiate between the minds of ordinary humans and extraordinary agents, such as God. Cognitive scholars have proposed two main theories to account for children's understanding of God's mind; the preparedness account and the anthropomorphic account.

The preparedness account

Psychologists Justin Barrett and Rebekah Richert proposed a "preparedness" account of the development of god concepts. According to this account, the cognitive default of young children is that all intentional agents are supernatural agents. In other words, children find it relatively easy to represent ideas about an all-powerful God because they are psychologically predisposed (i.e. prepared) to represent minds as having super knowledge.[2,3] Theological concepts of God as omnipotent in Abrahamic monotheistic traditions are thus readily acquired by young minds that are cognitively predisposed to receive them. For instance, Barrett and Richert propose that children find it initially more straightforward to understand that God knows everything than understand that adults' knowledge is limited. The preparedness account predicts that children as young as three-years-old start by attributing super knowledge to all agents, including Mom and God, and only later in development come to be able to distinguish between the knowledge capabilities of different kinds of agents.

Barrett, Richert, and colleagues have interpreted the results of a series of developmental studies as providing evidence that children are cognitively predisposed to represent God's mind as infallible. However, they must learn that adults do not have unlimited knowledge. For example, studies have shown that children as young as three-years-old think that both God and humans have true beliefs.[4,5] At around elementary school age, children begin to distinguish God's mind (as knowing everything) from human minds (as having limited knowledge and holding false beliefs).[6] For example, in one study testing children's ability to determine who can hold false beliefs (known as a false belief study), children were shown a box of crackers that contained small rocks and asked what others would think is inside the box of crackers. Younger children, until around age five, understood that a human was more likely to falsely believe that the cracker box contained crackers than God because God would know that it contained rocks.[7] Additional cross-cultural research with Greek, Mayan, and Spanish children has also demonstrated that by around age five, children attribute more excellent and more accurate knowledge to God than humans.[8]

Some scholars have questioned Barrett, Richert and colleagues' interpretations of these studies, and whether the results provide support for the preparedness account of children's acquisition of ideas about extraordinary minds. One key question among critics is whether three and four-year-olds fail to attribute false beliefs to humans and god, or whether this is a consequence of this kind of experiment because the demands of that particular task are too complicated for young minds. In other words, the critical question here is why young children say that Mom and God know that the cracker box contains small rocks? One response is that children represent Mom and God as knowing everything (the preparedness account).

Another response (advocated by those who question the preparedness account) is that the task is too difficult for young children to understand and does not, therefore, accurately reflect their competence in representing the belief states of others. Indeed, some researchers have critiqued the use of false belief tasks altogether, claiming they are unreliable in indicating whether, and how, children take the perspectives of others more generally. In other words, these tasks do not detect an ability to ascribe mental states to others (known as mentalizing or theory of mind).[9,10] Some studies have shown that when probed with more straightforward tasks (e.g. looking time), three and four-year-old children and even 13-month-old children attribute false beliefs to persons.[11,12] However, some studies have failed to replicate these results of looking time studies with younger children (18-month-old). Other scholars propose that young children do not reliably form predictions based on false beliefs.[13,14] So, the results here are mixed.

Recent research using versions of false belief tasks have not found the developmental continuity reported by the preparedness theorists. For example, studies with children from the US, Germany, and Spain found that four-year-olds attributed ignorance both to humans *and* God.[15,16,17,18] Further evidence against the preparedness interpretation of findings with young children comes from the studies of developmental psychologist Jonathan Lane and colleagues. When asked to explain why God would know the real state of the world, three-year-olds often mentioned their knowledge, whereas five-year-olds often mentioned God's mental capacities.[19]

From these findings, Lane and colleagues proposed that young children's responses on false belief tasks do not represent an early bias towards an understanding of omniscience for agents, but rather, reflect egocentrism—the tendency to attribute what they know about reality to other agents. In other words, if children understand that the cracker box contains rocks, then they assume that other agents will also know that the cracker box includes rocks. Cognitive development is required for children to disambiguate how the world is, from how they and others perceive it, and very young children have difficulty understanding the distinction between appearances and reality. It is only later, at around age five, when children are exposed to sociocultural input about God's properties that they have the conceptual development to discriminate between their mind and extraordinary minds. This proposal is more akin to the anthropomorphism account of children's understanding of supernatural agents and we review it next.

The anthropomorphism account

The anthropomorphism account of children's concepts of God was first proposed in the 1920s by famous cognitive psychologist Jean Piaget. Anthropomorphism is the tendency to attribute human-like features to non-human things, and Piaget claimed that young children use human minds as templates to understand God's mind. Thus, they initially represent adults and God as having the same kinds of minds. That is to say, if children thought Mom knew everything, then God knew everything, but if they thought that Mom knew only some things, then they thought that God knew only some things.[20] This account has received experimental support. For example, research has found that young children (i.e. three to four-year-olds) attributed false beliefs to both humans and to God, which suggests that they may be attributing what adults know (and do not know) to what God knows.[21,22,23] Other scholars have proposed different interpretations of what is driving these results. As we discussed in the previous section, Lane and colleagues have suggested that children infer what ordinary and extraordinary agents know may be due not so much to anthropomorphism—i.e. what other people know generally, but to egocentrism—i.e. based on what they know.[24] One reasonable interpretation is that young children attribute knowledge to God that they possess but ignorance when they do not know the correct answer.[25]

Previous research in CSR has focused overwhelmingly on how children represent God's mental abilities, in particular, God's knowledge. A few studies do focus on how children think about other aspects of God, and results support and extend the anthropomorphism account. For example, psychologists Larisa Heiphetz and colleagues found that children tended to attribute the same kinds of moral beliefs to God as to humans. For example, both think that bad behaviors are morally unacceptable.[26] Consider further the work of cognitive scientist Andrew Shtulman. Shtulman investigated children's attribution of both psychological properties and biological and physical properties to different kinds of supernatural beings (e.g. angel, God, ghost). He found that five-year-old children do anthropomorphize supernatural beings.

Furthermore, young children also attributed as many human properties (both psychological and non-psychological) to fictional and religious beings, even

Figure 7.1 Anthropomorphism is the psychological tendency to attribute human-like features to non-human things, such as the god Zeus in Ancient Greek religion and mythology, who is often depicted as a human. (Image credit: Esteban De Armas/Shutterstock.com).

though they claimed to believe stronger in religious than fictional creatures. From these findings, it seems that young children do anthropomorphize God. However, this tendency is not something specially reserved for mental capacities or to the domain of religion but is part of a more general anthropomorphic tendency extended to all agents.

Psychologists Larisa Heiphetz and colleagues have synthesized current research to propose a developmental trajectory of God concepts that support the anthropomorphic account.[27] Their account contains four main stages of development:

1. Young children come to understand that others' minds can provide imperfect representations of the world and that adults are not all-knowing. Preschoolers also understand that they do not know everything and that some of their beliefs may be false.
2. As every human they encounter may have a limited mind, children initially represent God's mind as similarly limited.
3. As they increasingly understand that different minds may possess different beliefs (theory of mind), children may also come to understand God's mind as distinct from human minds.
4. The ability to understand a limitless mind (i.e. omniscience) is cognitively more complex and develops during early and middle childhood. This account proposes essential cognitive foundations to the representation of God. Children's initial concepts of God's mind are based on normal cognitive abilities that children use to conceptualize agents generally.

Heiphetz and colleagues further point to the cognitive naturalness of anthropomorphism. They contend that seeing God's mind as human-like (and therefore limited) does not require adult-like cognitive abilities or extensive experience, such as exposure to religious teachings, to emerge. This claim raises the question, what is the role of cultural learning in this version of the anthropomorphic account? According to the researchers, an understanding of God's omniscience can arise from social experience in addition to cognitive development. The anthropomorphic account holds that children are not cognitively predisposed towards extraordinary mental capacities. This anthropomorphic account is in contrast to the preparedness account. At a certain point in the theory of mind development, sociocultural input can facilitate an early appreciation of extraordinary minds. For instance, children who are raised in explicitly religious contexts and are more knowledgeable about God and tend to demonstrate an early appreciation of God's exceptional mental abilities.[28]

To date, there is more support for the anthropomorphic account of how children represent God than the preparedness account. In other words, it seems that young children initially represent all agents as limited and later learn that God is all-knowing. The version of the anthropomorphic account proposed by Lane and colleagues also suggests that this later developing understanding of God's mind (as limitless) does not entirely replace the earlier emerging anthropomorphic representations of God's mind (as limited). Instead, these representations of God's mind as human-like persist in adulthood and are elicited by implicit, rather than explicit measures. We discuss these claims in the next section.

Participation 2: Differences in theories

1. Divide up into groups of about 3–4 students. Work together as a group.
2. Briefly summarize the work so far in this chapter on children's concepts of supernatural agents, a few sentences for each theory is sufficient.
3. Explain differences in the claims that the researchers are making.
4. Consider why these differences exist (e.g. theoretical background, methods etc.).
5. Decide which theory you agree with most.

Key points

- Researchers have conducted much research on the question of how children represent God's mind in the Judeo-Christian tradition.
- Researchers agree that children tend to represent God's mind as extraordinary around preschool years but disagree over when and how they come to distinguish between God's mind and human minds.
- Two main theories have been proposed to account for children's understanding of God's mind; the preparedness account and the anthropomorphic account.
- The preparedness account proposes that children initially represent all agents as powerful and only later represent human minds as limited. By contrast, the anthropomorphic account suggests that children initially represent all agents as limited and only later learn that God is omniscient.

The representation of supernatural agent concepts in adults

The coexistence account

Abrahamic religions depict God as being omniscient, omnipotent, and omnipresent. The standard doctrine that God is limitless is, therefore, a theologically correct idea. Recall the discussion of theological correctness in Chapter 3 (Research Questions). To recap, when an idea is described as theologically correct by cognitive scientists of religion, it means that people describe an idea as it relates to official versions of the doctrine and widely reiterated among experts.[29] Indeed, many adults can distinguish between the capabilities of God and those of ordinary people when they have time to deliberate about what God is like. These reflective ideas are explicit representations of God and draw on system 1.

Explicit ideas often differ from people's implicit representations about God. People often elicit implicit ideas about God under conditions where they are not consciously aware or able to reflect, such as when they have to answer questions about God quickly.[30] The kind of off-the-cuff reasoning characteristic of implicit representations of God is also often a theologically incorrect representation.[31] Theological incorrectness occurs when people unconsciously distort the official doctrines of their belief systems to fit with their intuitive expectations. Research has shown that adults tend to represent God as anthropomorphic implicitly. In other words, they default to a cognitively natural default.

In one now-classic series of studies, psychologists Justin Barrett and Frank Keil elicited people's implicit and explicit representations of God. To test their inherent ideas about God, the experimenters told participants stories about God and then asked questions to test their comprehension and recall. For instance, in one vignette, participants heard about a boy who was drowning in a river, who prayed to God. God was currently answering another prayer and saved the boy. When asked to recall the story, many participants unconsciously distorted the stories in line with a more anthropomorphic God.

For example, in the story of the two people in need, they inferred that God first answered one prayer before attending to the drowning boy, just like an ordinary person would do. Following the narrative tasks, participants completed a questionnaire at their leisure, which tested their explicit beliefs about God. Even though most participants had unconsciously anthropomorphized God in the recall tasks, later, they professed to a theologically correct[32] God. In line with the accepted theology of Christianity, God was described as omnipresent and omnipotent and thus capable of answering two prayers simultaneously.[33]

Barrett and Keil explain these findings by proposing that people often possess two incompatible God concepts and deploy them in different contexts. They deduce that it seems easier to reason about an anthropomorphic God in everyday thought as a person who is relatable than a limitless, abstract entity. Of course, cultural learning plays a role in the representation of God concepts too, which has also been demonstrated empirically. For instance, Barrett and psychologist Brant Vanorman found that Reformed Christians who use images of God for worship tended to anthropomorphize God more readily than those who did not, suggesting a role for social reinforcement of anthropomorphic representations.[34]

Some scholars have criticized the design of the original Barrett and Keil study, suggesting that the language used in the narratives was anthropomorphic. Thus, participants may have been primed to think of God as human-like. For example, God was described as pushing a large stone, looking at the rock, listening to the birds, and enjoying the smell, which could have made participants more likely to reason about God as a person than if God was not described in anthropomorphic terms. Critics also claimed that there was no real-time pressure when recalling the narratives and answering questions. So, the experiments did not tap into implicit (and thus, intuitive) representations of God.[35,36,37]

Subsequent research has demonstrated that both children and adults tend to anthropomorphize representations of the monotheistic and Abrahamic God. This tendency is especially likely when reasoning about God's mind and when responding under time pressure, and this differs from how people reason explicitly about God's properties when they are not under pressure.[38,39,40,41] As discussed in Chapter 2 (Core Assumptions), CSR scholars use methods that require a quick response because these tend to access system 1 processing and reflect intuitive ideas, in this example, about God. Further, the effects that Barrett and Keil reported were also found using examples of Hindu gods with participants in India,[42,43] which suggests that anthropomorphizing gods is not merely a product of representing Christian deities.

Research by psychologist Michael Barlev and colleagues provides evidence for the anthropomorphic account and for Barrett and Keil's assertion that people have two incompatible concepts of God. The research by Barlev and colleagues also probes the nature of the representation of God concepts further, and they propose a coexistence model of how people represent God.[44] Specifically, the researchers were interested in the question of how adults possess two incompatible concepts of God as both a person with limits and a supernatural agent who is limitless.

Barlev and colleagues theorized that the idea of God as a person coexisted in the minds of believers alongside acquired Christian theology about God as supernatural. Based on this theory, they predicted that there might be interference or conflict between these representations when they are inconsistent. Indeed, they found evidence of this representational interference. For example, in one of their studies, the researchers asked participants to endorse or reject various statements about God under time pressure, which as you may recall, enables researchers to tap into system 1 processing (Chapter 2: Core Assumptions). The researchers presented participants with statements that they labeled in one of three ways. The first kind were consistent statements, valid for both theologically correct versions of God and persons (e.g. God has true beliefs). The second kind was statements false for both theologically correct versions of God and persons (e.g. all beliefs God has are false).

The third kind was inconsistent statements, and of most interest to the experimenters. Statements could be inconsistent in one of two ways. First, they could be inconsistent because they tended to be true for people but were false theologically (e.g. God has false beliefs). Second, they would be inconsistent because they tended to be false for people but true theologically (e.g. all beliefs that God has are correct). As Barlev and colleagues predicted, participants were less accurate and slower to respond to inconsistent versus consistent statements. In other words, participants found it more challenging to decide about God when there was a conflict between what was right for people and theologically correct for God, such as when God can do something that humans cannot. According to Barlev and colleagues, they found it more cognitively effortful to judge inconsistent statements because their minds had to reconcile between these inconsistent representations of God as a person and as a supernatural agent.

Furthermore, these differences in how participants responded to inconsistent statements were found when they were asked about God, but not when they were asked about a person who was a natural religious entity, such as a priest.[45] In other words, interference does not generalize to other natural religious entities based on the person-concept. Remarkably, in another series of studies, Barlev and colleagues found evidence of this interference effect in highly devout religious adherents.[46] This latter research shows further proof of representational coexistence. However, more importantly, it also provides evidence that the person template, which underlies the representation of God, cannot be revised despite decades of experience with formal Christian theology. In sum, the idea that God is human-like is deeply ingrained in the minds of modern American Christian adults.

The results of these studies help explain how and why people often tend to think of God's mind as human-like, and why these ideas persist despite the devotion to theological concepts of God, such as the idea that God is all-knowing, that are inconsistent with them. They also suggest that, like children, adults tend to anthropomorphize God in everyday contexts. Thus, young children's ideas about God often resemble those implicitly held by many adults. This finding brings us to the critical question of why people have an implicit bias towards anthropomorphizing God?

In the next section of this chapter, we consider two theories in the cognitive science of religion that purport to explain why anthropomorphic concepts of God emerged and proliferated in human culture; the cognitive constraint account and the hyperactive agency detection device (HADD or later, ADD). These accounts are complementary in the sense that they can contribute towards an understanding of why children's and adults' implicit concepts of God tend to be anthropomorphic.

Cognitive constraint account

Scholars in the cognitive sciences have long argued the case that humans cannot help but internalize versions of alternative worlds as at least partly based on the world around them, including the spread of extraordinary ideas.[47] For instance, psychologist Thomas Ward and religious studies scholar Thomas Lawson have argued that new ideas always have roots in modern ideas because of cognitive constraints on our imagination.

Cognitive constraints refer to the tendency for people to draw upon default inferences and assumptions. They further contend that ideas that are similar to our own experience are judged more likely to be true.[48] Indeed, research by Ward and colleagues have shown that people draw upon their existing knowledge of these conceptual domains to create and understand fictional ideas.[49] For example, in one study, the researchers found that about two-thirds of all participants brought to mind a specific animal as a template (e.g. an elephant) when imagining alien life forms.[50] Likewise, people retrieve ideas of apples and oranges when they conjure up imaginary fruit, or hammers and nails to think about imaginary tools.[51] Here, the crux of the explanations lies in cognitive heuristics.

Other, similar psychological explanations for the emergence of ideas about supernatural agents contend that anthropomorphism is a heuristic that minimizes cognitive load.[52] As children encounter many different beings such as animals and fictional characters in stories, working out each being's capacities would require a great deal of cognitive effort. Therefore, using templates of agents with which we are most familiar (i.e. humans) is a useful shortcut. Often, young children and adults use themselves as the agent template—an exceptionally efficient cognitive heuristic is to be egocentric in their representations of other agents.

Research suggests that people may be even more egocentric when reasoning about God's beliefs about important social and ethical issues than when estimating other people's beliefs.[53] Other studies have likewise demonstrated that people tend to attribute their views to moralistic agents in religious traditions. For instance, one study found the attribution of conservative or liberal views onto a contemporary Jesus according to whether participants were conservative or liberal American Christians. Thus, believers often use inferences about God's beliefs to guide their moral decision-making. However, they base God's beliefs mainly on their own beliefs in part because this is easier to represent.[54]

Although similar to these cognitive heuristic accounts, cognitive-evolutionary accounts of the emergence and spread of supernatural ideas are also distinctive because they make claims about universal features of the human mind and consider evolutionary factors that affect such ideas. More specifically, CSR scholars draw upon cognitive mechanisms, such as heuristics as proximate explanations (i.e. immediately responsible for causing the recurrent features of religion), but also draw upon the selection forces of evolution and thus consider the ultimate or distal cause of religious cognition as directing the emergence of cognitive templates in addition to social learning.

Specifically, scholars in CSR propose that cognitive constraints operate when we think about ordinary and extraordinary beings, including supernatural agents.[55] The anthropologist Pascal Boyer has highlighted the role of early emerging conceptual structures in explaining how people acquire ideas about supernatural agents.[56] His account is based on research that showcases that the mind naturally carves up the world as composed of certain types of things, most broadly including people, animals, plants, tools, artifacts, events, and so on, often referred to as intuitive ontologies. These ways of thinking are described as natural or intuitive because they are often under-determined by experience and appear much earlier than how a child's interactions with the world would predict. To describe ontologies as intuitive or natural does not mean that social learning is unimportant.

The role of social learning in cognitive constraint accounts

Social learning may explain why humans have biases towards certain kinds of things in the world in the first place. Take the research on plants by psychologists Annie Wertz and Karen Wynn to illustrate this point.[57] Their research underscores the importance of social learning to the development of food preferences in conjunction with cognitive predispositions shaped through evolution. When given the same information, namely, seeing an adult place something in his or her mouth, six and 18-month-old children selectively made inferences about edibility applied to plants but not artifacts. Given that humans have relied on plant resources throughout our evolutionary history, Wertz and Wynn deduced that human infants might possess particular social learning strategies that rapidly identify edible plants. These strategies would have enabled humans to survive and thrive in varied and changing environments.

Just like we think of plants but not artifacts as edible, Boyer has proposed that we intuitively think about other things in intuitive categories as having properties that differentiate them from others. In infancy, domain-specific learning mechanisms direct expectations of properties for each category. These assumptions about properties of things in our intuitive ontologies include folk physics (e.g. things move as a connected whole) folk biology (e.g. living things grow), folk psychology (e.g. agents have beliefs), and folk sociology (e.g. people who look alike have underlying similarities). These categories are, of course, broad, and other categories that have been proposed are more specific, including social categories such as "ownership[58]" and "cheater" in social exchange.[59] Scholars have proposed that people represent the world this way because it enables them to make generalizations that can be adaptive, like using plants for food.

The role of evolution in cognitive constraint accounts

Concepts about agents also make sense in light of evolution because humans carve up the world along lines that were relevant for the survival and reproduction of our species. For example, the anthropologist Clark Barrett found that young children tend to assume that an animate agent has intentions but not a sleeping one.[60] These biases are part of a constellation of adaptations for detecting, reasoning, and making decisions about intentional agents, which would have aided predator evasion and prey capture throughout our evolutionary history. However, we can also acquire concepts that were not targets of natural selection. Some scholars in CSR maintain that we draw inferences about extraordinary agents from our concepts of agents in general.

In evolutionary terms, these religious concepts exist within an actual domain (i.e. extraordinary agents) but not the proper domain (i.e. ordinary agents) of evolved mechanisms. As an illustration of these terms, consider a thirsty professional coming home from work and gulping milk from the carton in the refrigerator, discovering a few seconds later, to her horror, that the milk has gone sour. The event is likely to result in a feeling of disgust. For the next few days, every time she gets a whiff of milk, she feels nauseated. This tendency makes biological sense and has been shaped through disgust mechanisms in evolutionary history. The woman's learning system unconsciously calculates: if the milk was likely to make you sick, then it is best to avoid milk. Indeed, if the milk is still in the fridge, this calculation is sound. Thus, milk is the *proper domain* of the target cognitions and behavior. Imagine further that she decides to meet friends after work that evening for dinner, only to discover that the appetizer containing cheese also makes her feel nauseated. Both are a form of dairy, and her learning system unconsciously calculates: if the milk was likely to make you sick, then it is best to avoid dairy. Even though it is highly unlikely that the cheese in the restaurant has also gone bad, her system equates the two.

In the scenario just described, cheese is the *actual domain*; in other words, the domain where these ideas and behaviors are applied. Getting back to religious cognition, CSR scholars propose that humans have evolved a repertoire of assumptions about ordinary agents because they were adaptive. Thus, regular agents are like the milk in the previous example, the *proper domain* of target assumptions. We also readily apply these assumptions to concepts of supernatural agents, which, like the cheese, are the *actual domain* of target assumptions. As these assumptions evolved to derive adaptive benefits to the actual, but not the proper domain, these accounts are evolutionary **by-product** accounts. That is to say, the tendency to represent supernatural agents in the environment is an unintended consequence of the tendency to represent ordinary agents in the environment more generally.

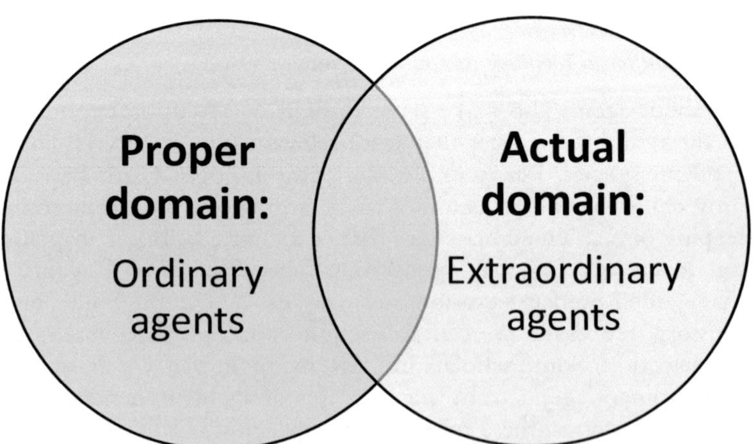

Figure 7.2 Evolutionary by-product accounts depict supernatural agent concepts as derived from the proper domain (i.e. ordinary agents in the environment) of evolved mechanisms.

These by-product accounts can be contrasted to adaptationist accounts. Adaptationist accounts explain the tendency to represent supernatural agents as shaped directly by natural selection because of their consequences. For example, social psychologist Ara Norenzayan and political scientist Dominic Johnson argue?that representations of omniscient and moralizing gods were culturally and/or genetically selected to promote cooperation in large groups.[61,62] We discuss these views in more detail in Chapter 8 (Morality).

While many cognitive scientists of religion maintain that we draw inferences about extraordinary agents from our concepts of agents in general, they disagree over the types of characteristics that are transferred from the concept of agency. For example, the body and/or mind. We review two versions of the cognitive constraints account below before turning to another kind of evolutionary account.

Embodied versus disembodied minds account

The most influential account to date in CSR to explain the representation of supernatural human agents is Boyer's version of the anthropomorphic account. Evolutionary scholars have argued that children rapidly come to develop theories about the properties of people, such as about their physicality, biology, and psychology, because it is adaptive for survival to do so, and they encounter people from the moment they are born. They have an early emerging "person template." Thus, Boyer and others have argued that supernatural agent concepts are just person concepts onto which extraordinary properties are loaded.[63,64] This tendency makes it easy for children and adults to represent similar features between the two, such as limited mental and perceptual abilities. It also makes people likely to distort the abilities of supernatural agents to conform to human agents, especially when they are under time constraints and have to make a decision quickly.

Psychologists Andrew Shtulman and Marjaana Lindeman have recently challenged this view. They have proposed that people's ideas about supernatural agents derive from their tendency to conceive of persons as disembodied minds. This view is similar to developmental psychologist Paul Bloom's folk-dualism view, reviewed in Chapter 6 (The Afterlife).[65] To recap, Bloom proposed that we naturally think of persons as constituted by minds and bodies. We represent bodies using one set of mental mechanisms for physicality, such as the idea that bodies are physical entities and move. We represent minds using another set that infers things like beliefs and intentions from behavior (i.e. mindreading). Bloom contends that we tend to think of bodies and minds as constituting persons, but because we use different mechanisms to represent people, we can separate their minds from their bodies. Bloom proposes that this separation in our representations of people gives rise to ideas about disembodied beings. In short, the representation of supernatural agents as disembodied minds is natural.

Drawing on this intuitive folk-dualism account, Shtulman and Lindeman argue that God is fundamentally represented not as a person but as an agent with a mind. They propose that when portraying God, people do not co-opt a person concept but rather, co-opt a disembodied mind concept. For instance, one study by Shtulman and Lindenman with Christian and Hindu adults demonstrated that participants attributed more psychological (i.e. mind-dependent) properties than physiological (i.e. body-dependent) properties to God.[66] They were also faster, more consistent, and more confident when applying psychological than physiological properties to God. Shtulman has argued that God is not represented as a person in general because God is not attributed equally to all person-like properties. Instead, God is construed as a particular agent with a mind upon default, and when people have time to further think about it, with a body.

Psychologist Michael Barlev has proposed that the folk-dualism account does not accurately depict how we intuitively represent people. He suggests that although representations of a person's psychology and physicality are not reducible to each other, they are also not intuitively separable. Instead, beliefs in disembodied minds like gods and spirits require cultural learning.[67] Barlev interprets the results of Shtulman and Lindeman according to the coexistence account that he (along with colleagues) have proposed to account for the fact that people have at least two representations of God. Specifically, Barlev contends that God is represented as an embodied person. He explains the differences between the types of properties attributed to God in the samples in Shtulman and Lindeman's studies (Finland, USA, and India) as acquired theology (e.g. Christianity and Hinduism) that co-exists alongside these embodied person representations.

Barlev and colleagues also conducted a series of experiments to determine whether people tended to adopt a disembodied or embodied mind concept when thinking about God.[68] The design of these studies was similar to the consistency statement studies by Barlev and colleagues described earlier in the chapter. To recap, participants read a series of statements about God and persons that were either true or false and had to decide between them. In line with the theory that people derive their concept of God from embodied persons, they found that participants were slower and less accurate to respond (i.e. they showed representational interference) on statements regarding God's physicality as well as psychology. They concluded from this research that the embodied person concept, as espoused by Boyer, more accurately reflects how people form representations of God.

Agency detection account

So far, we have reviewed the cognitive constraint account of the representation of supernatural agents. The second main evolutionary account that purports to explain why anthropomorphic concepts of God emerged and proliferated is that they are established in a more general tendency to perceive intentional agents in the environment. As we covered in Chapter 5 (The Nature of the World), following the work of classical scholars, the anthropologist Stewart

Guthrie made a cognitive theory of anthropomorphism central to a theory of religion.[69,70] Guthrie argued that anthropomorphism occurs as a perceptual and cognitive strategy. Namely, facing phenomena whose cause is unknown, people assume the most important possibility. For humans, that possibility is usually personal; in other words, we interpret beings as human-like (i.e. to anthropomorphize).

The crux of this cognitive theory is that when people face chronic uncertainty about the nature of the world, they are sensitive to the detection of intentional agency, such as a person, and are biased to attribute deliberate action as the cause of things and events. Guthrie supplemented these earlier anthropomorphic theories of religion by drawing upon Darwinian evolution to explain why this perceptual strategy originated.

Psychologist Justin Barrett simplified this broad anthropomorphic theory. He posited a mental tool that he called a hyperactive agency detection device (HADD).[71] The argument for the existence of HADD can be summarized as the following. As Guthrie noted, from an evolutionary perspective, the bias to detect agency in the environment is adaptive. Mistakenly interpreting a noise in a bush as a tiger when it is wind (a false positive) has no costs. Failing to detect a tiger in a bush when our ancestors heard a noise (a false negative) would have been detrimental to fitness, and this facilitated the development of belief in supernatural agents. Barrett proposed that in the modern environment, which contains more agents than the ancestral environment, anthropomorphism is triggered and produces beliefs in unseen agents who are assumed to be the cause of the stimuli. According to this account, the tendency to perceive intentional supernatural agents in the environment and draw on the same cognitive processes as human minds are a by-product of the tendency to see agents in the atmosphere more generally.

There have been debates in the literature over whether such a mechanism is hypersensitive in a way that leads to postulating superhumans. For instance, while the mechanism leads to false positives (i.e. detecting an agent where none exists),[72] some have contended that HADD served important functions in the Paleolithic, during which it was formed, where the environment was abundant with predators. By contrast, we face much less of the dangers of other agents in the modern environment. Presumably, over time, the costs of maintaining a constant state of vigilance, and these perceptual errors would have given rise to self-corrections to shut down the false positives when they occur. Thus, the role of HADD in generating or propagating supernatural agency is more complicated than Barrett initially proposed.[73,74] In response, Barrett began dropping the "H" from HADD, so that the device was characterized as actively interpreting agency in the environment, rather than hyperactive (i.e., ADD).

The issue surrounding the role of agent detection in the formulation of supernatural concepts, and even more controversial still, beliefs, remains. Overall, the tendency to conceive of agency in the environment as rooted in evolutionary origins complements existing evolutionary, developmental, and social accounts. While the tendency to conceive of intentional agency in the environment is insufficient as an exclusive explanation, in conjunction with accounts above, it contributes towards a more comprehensive explanation of the origins and spread of ideas about supernatural agents.

Key points

- Cognitive scientists of religion agree that in the Abrahamic traditions, adults' explicit representation of God mirrors theological doctrine, God is omniscient, omnipotent, and omnipresent. This representation often differs from adults' implicit representations of God as having limited capacities, which are elicited under conditions where adults are not consciously aware or able to reflect.
- CSR scholars disagree over the origins of these tendencies, although the two leading explanations themselves do not conflict with one another and can be accommodated into a single account.
- The conceptual constraints account holds that adults implicitly anthropomorphize God because they cannot help but draw from their intuitive ontology of persons when thinking about God.
- The active agency detection account holds that an agency detection mechanism is triggered in the modern environment, and it produces ideas about unseen agents who are assumed to be similar to humans and are the cause of the stimuli.
- Most cognitive accounts place an essential role in social learning, in conjunction with cognitive biases and development, for the emergence and persistence of ideas about supernatural agents.

Summary of the acquisition, development, and representation of supernatural concepts

- Cognitive scientists of religion conduct empirical research on the question of how children, primarily in Judeo-Christian traditions, come to represent God as omniscient.
- Developmental accounts maintain that when coupled with social learning about the nature of God, predispositions and cognitive development give rise to, or reinforce, children's developing concepts of God as super powerful.
- Cognitive scientists of religion also conduct empirical research on the question of how adults come to represent God's mind.
- Children's explicit representations of God often resemble adults' implicit representations. For both, God is human-like. The cognitive constraint account holds that this is because people draw on their intuitive ontologies of limited agents. Expectations that agents' knowledge is limited is based on interactions with agents throughout our evolutionary history and reinforced by the individual's current social experiences.

The spread of supernatural agent concepts: countering intuitive biases

There are countless examples of culturally successful supernatural agents in western culture. These include examples from religious traditions but also extend to fantasy novels, folktales, sci-fi movies, and legends. Cross-culturally recurrent ideas about other kinds of supernatural agents such as ghosts and witches are also remarkably human-like. Thinking about the types of supernatural agents that one could imagine, it is striking that only a few types, based on human-like features, recur across cultures. As Boyer put it, there is "a limited catalog of the supernatural.[75]" Cognitive scientists of religion are concerned with why this is so. As we covered in Chapter 1 (Introduction), cognitive scientist Sperber proposed a theory called "the epidemiology of representations," which at its core, maintained that some ideas are encoded, stored, and recalled better than others. Just like epidemiologists in medicine study, the incidence and distribution of disease, Sperber argued that social scientists could study the prevalence and distribution of ideas in culture. Today, CSR scholars are motivated to uncover the epidemiology of religious representations, and we review some of this research in this chapter.

Minimally counterintuitive concepts

So far, in the chapter, we have considered some intuitive biases that underlie the generation and transmission of supernatural agent concepts, such as a tendency to detect agency in the environment (ADD), attributing person-like features, such as minds and bodies, to supernatural agents. In this section, we will consider the claim that although supernatural agent concepts are rooted to some extent in our intuitive assumptions about agents, those that are widespread also deviate slightly from these intuitions. CSR scholars have argued that supernatural agents tend to have a special quality or combination of properties that make them counter some of our intuitive biases, they are minimally counterintuitive.

As Boyer noted, successfully transmitted supernatural agents tended to share two features. First, they tend to be like regular agents—i.e. like persons. That is to say, there is something relatable about them, and they seem on the face of it like ordinary people. Gods, ghosts, witches, and so on all appear remarkably human-like. Second, they have special properties, such as changing the physical landscape without touching it, causing illness to others with their mind, walking through walls, and so on, which provides them with extraordinary quality, making them supernatural.

Take the example of Superman. This fictional superhero is perhaps the most iconic American cultural supernatural agent of all time, rated the top comic book hero ever,[76] and boosting a movie empire spanning almost half a century.[77] On the one hand, Superman *is* Clark Kent, an ordinary 30-something-year-old American citizen raised on a farm and working as a newspaper journalist. He eats, sleeps, is motivated to avenge injustice, and even falls in love, just like the rest of us mere mortals. Superman has extraordinary powers and abilities. For example, he can fly, has super strength, super hearing, microscopic vision, and is invulnerable to most non-magical attacks. At least part of the explanation why Superman has become so successful among the American public is because of his relatability and paradoxically, his extraordinary powers. All good creative writers, consciously or unconsciously, realize that this paradox of humanness coupled with extraordinary qualities is the recipe for a successful supernatural agent concept. In the case of Superman, it is by no accident that he was depicted as more relatable (e.g. less aggressive), and more potent over time.[78]

Some scholars in CSR explain the social success of supernatural agents in religious traditions in much the same way they account for the spread of extraordinary concepts outside of religious domains. They describe the properties of supernatural agents as meeting some of our default expectations about the world while countering others. Specifically, supernatural agents seem much like regular agents and thus meet our inherent biases, assumptions, or predilections about agents generally. We have covered many of these so far in the chapter. Second, supernatural agents have exceptional quality, or a combination of properties, that makes them counter some of our inherent biases about agents; we refer to these as counterintuitive ideas, and we cover them here.

One classic view, found in the works of scholars such as Spinoza, Hume, and Feuerbach is that religious concepts, such as supernatural agents, tend to have a similar structure. Boyer based his technical version of this theory on classifying agents, including whether they meet intuitive assumptions about category members (e.g. people, animals, objects, and so on), and violate some of these assumptions in small ways,[79] such as a talking tree, a rock that eats, or an invisible cow. Supernatural agents violate our assumptions related to persons. For example, most people conceive God as a person with special cognitive powers.

By intuitive assumptions, Boyer refers to our naïve, folk theories of the world around us. He argued that this formula (minimal tweaking) ensures that these ideas have a transmission advantage over other ideas. Justin Barrett later characterized these types of religious concepts as "minimally counterintuitive," also referred to as MCI theory, which is a more formalized way of saying that the key to their success is that they minimally tweak our intuitive assumptions about the world. Through experiments, these scholars showed that ideas that met all intuitive expectations about a category member and those that violated too many intuitive expectations were not easily remembered and thus bad for transmission. However, people recall those that violated a few intuitive expectations more easily and as being suitable for cultural transmission.

Earlier in the chapter, we discussed work that charted our intuitive ontological assumptions. To recap, intuitive assumptions include categories of things in the world, such as persons, animals, and objects, and properties. These include spatiality and physicality in naïve physics (e.g. that things occupy a location in space and time); animacy in biology (e.g. self-propelled motion);

and mentality in folk-psychology (e.g. mental states), (see Table 7.1 for an extended list of properties). Boyer proposed this theory of counterintuitiveness to account for the popularity of religious concepts in general, although, in this chapter, we are concerned only with supernatural entities. To illustrate an example of how a supernatural agent concept violates our common assumptions about the person category, consider the standard representation of a ghost.

According to Boyer, the concept of ghosts is based on our naïve theories of persons. For example, they can think and have intentions and thus activate our naïve psychology for persons. The idea of ghosts violates a property in the domain of physics; they can permeate solid objects, such as walking through walls. This example contains a violation of our expectations of folk physics for persons. However, the concept of ghosts otherwise preserves the bulk of our expectations for persons and is, consequentially, a successful supernatural agent concept. If the concept has too many violations, then it becomes too complicated and challenging for people to remember and transmit. Consider a person created in a lab, is invisible, grows smaller with time, never dies, cannot move, only thinks on Tuesdays and can read minds. This concept would qualify as massively or maximally counterintuitive. It is unlikely to become famous when competing minimally counterintuitive concepts are equally available. It is just too difficult to understand and remember.

These examples bring us to the following question: why should concepts that minimally tweak our natural assumptions enjoy greater transmissive success as compared to those that do not? There have been some factors proposed to account for these effects. These proposals include the suggestion that some concepts are more distinctive than others. People pay more attention to counterintuitive stimuli than other stimuli, which results in thinking about them more to understand and process them. We are intrigued and motivated to make sense of something that we do not quite understand, whereas something too familiar evokes little interest. Something too complicated loses our interest.[80]

That unusual things and events are memorable is a basic information-theory finding that appears to make MCI theory redundant. However, Boyer and Barrett specifies that MCI concepts are successful *not* merely because they are bizarre or unusual as compared to what is acceptable in their culture or even based on their individual experiences. They are successful because they are

Table 7.1 Example of intuitive expectations sets.

Intuitive expectation set	*Properties assumed*
Spatiality	Occupy location in space and time
Physicality	Movement is continuous in space
Biology	Growth and development
Animacy	Self-propelled motion
Mentality	Mental states

counter to our intuitive expectations. As we covered earlier, intuitive assumptions are the basic, untutored explanations we have for the world, and they are pretty much shared by people everywhere. Thus, scholars have proposed that these naïve theories, and what qualifies as MCI concepts, are not dependent upon the culture and individual experience. In other words, what is an MCI concept in the United States is also an MCI concept anywhere else.

Evaluation of MCI theory

There has been mixed support for the theory that ideas that minimally tweak our assumptions are better remembered and more faithfully remembered. Some findings support the theories' predictions,[81,82,83,84] and provide evidence that children display a cognitive bias for minimally counterintuitive ideas.[85] Other research, however, has failed to support predictions.[86,87,88] In particular, theorists find it challenging to apply the counterintuitive label to real-world cultural concepts. Later, Barrett attempted to formalize what minimally versus maximally counterintuitive meant. This formula included:

1 Identifying the category of membership (e.g. golden retriever, cat).
2 Identifying the categories to which the member belonged (e.g. animates, persons) and the properties for that category (e.g. spatiality, biology, animacy, etc.).
3 Deciding whether there has been a transfer of a property (e.g. a rock that can reproduce would have transferred the property from the biology of reproduction).
4 Deciding whether there was a breach of naïve expectations, such as an invisible brick, which breaches the intuitive assumption that objects are visible.

Other steps that Barrett highlighted include coding the number of breaches and transfers (one point each). The exception to the one-point rule, according to Barrett, is that if multiple transfers come from the same expectation set, then they are to be considered a single instance. For example, a rock that thinks and is self-aware would be coded as one, not two points, because thinking and self-awareness are examples of mentality. It is possible to come up with some counterintuitive points for each example that represents how counterintuitive concepts are. In theory, those concepts that minimally tweak (i.e. transfer or breach only a few) expectations should enjoy greater transmissive success than those that maximally tweak them, or that include too few violations of expectations.[89]

Some researchers have pointed out what they perceive as weaknesses in MCI theory. Cognitive psychologist Afzal Upal has proposed that the theory underestimates the role of context. Upal draws from theories in cognitive science about how people represent concepts. He suggests that the context within which the idea is presented (e.g. the sentence, narrative), also makes it more or less memorable, especially views conflicting with what we expect based on our learned experience.[90] For example, people process some information (e.g. the sparrow has feathers) faster than others (e.g. canary has feathers) based in part on our learned mental models of the world around us (in this example, prototypes for birds and characteristics of birds). People expect to see certain words together with other words and in sentences, and Upal argues that the theory also ought to take this into account.

Anthropologist Maurice Bloch argues that MCI ideas lose their privileged status and distinctiveness when embedded in a culture. Then they become familiar, and they no longer enjoy memorability advantages. In contrast, new ideas are created with such advantages, yet they are not necessarily endorsed. The key to understanding why some religious concepts become widespread, he argues, is based on the cultural tradition; people accept the ideas passed on by those before them.[91] This view sharply contrasts with CSR proposal that we are cognitively predisposed to receive some ideas. Even though these intuitions can be revised in light of cultural input, cognitive science of religion scholars maintain that they are not entirely determined by it.

Anthropologist Ben Purzycki and psychologist Aiyana Willard have provided the most extensive critique of MCI theory to date. They contested the theory as an explanation of memory biases, challenging the very concept of intuitive and counterintuitive. For instance, they proposed that what is characterized as counterintuitive may become habitual to us, such as attributing mental states to animals.[92] Indeed, one difficulty with the application of MCI theory is the open question of what violations of core knowledge intuitions are. This issue is because of the remaining uncertainty in the developmental and cognitive literature on precisely what inferences are contained in each ontological category.[93] For example, if we ask, according to MCI theory, is a person with three eyes a violation? The answer depends entirely on whether our person concept specifies that a person can only have two eyes.

Thus, disagreement over what does and does not qualify as an MCI agent continues. Precision in MCI theory depends on precision in more basic theories in cognitive development, which we do not yet have. One major strength of the theory—albeit imperfect and developing— is that, unlike earlier theories in cognitive sciences (e.g. schemas), MCI theory makes claims about a universal mental organization. CSR scholars can make predictions about universals in religion, which is remarkable.

Participation 3: MCI theory

1 How does your definition of supernatural agents in the participation task at the beginning of this chapter compare to the MCI theory discussed above? Write your answer in a few sentences.
2 Use MCI theory to characterize the supernatural agent you named in the participation task at the beginning of this chapter. How many violations did your agent have? (Use Table 7.1). Which domains were the violations in? Write your answer in a few sentences or use bullet points.

Key points

- Cognitive scientists of religion explain the emergence of ideas about supernatural agents as based on inherent biases about agents, and the spread of ideas as also influenced by these biases.
- Ideas about supernatural agents based upon our intuitive ideas about persons but that deviate slightly from these intuitions enjoy a mnemonic advantage. They are known as minimally counterintuitive ideas.
- MCI theory is based on claims about universal features of the human mind. The strength of the predictions it generates depends upon the development of other theories about cognitive development, which makes it an imperfect and developing theory.

Cognitive explanations for the spread of supernatural agent concepts

The minimally counterintuitive theory is part of a broader agenda in the cognitive science of religion to identify cognitive biases that affect the generation and transmission of concepts, and by extension, beliefs. As we discussed in Chapter 1 (Introduction), because of the unique history of CSR, scholars emphasize the role of cognition in the generation of religious concepts. They tend to focus on the content of religious ideas (i.e. content biases) as helping to explain why some ideas spread more readily than others. This focus on the content of religious ideas has paved the way for both widespread criticisms and the refinement of existing theories.

Social learning and cultural context

Perhaps the broadest critique of explanations of the spread of religious ideas that focus on biases in their content is by psychologists Konika Banerjee and Paul Bloom. They argue that theories about cognitive biases, such as MCI theory, do not take adequate account of the role of social learning and culture in general, on the development of belief. They use the example of Tarzan, the boy who was raised by apes after his first birthday, to demonstrate the importance of social factors in the spread of a culturally widespread concept.

Banerjee and Bloom ask, would someone never exposed to cultural ideas such as God, come to believe in God? (Hereafter the Tarzan problem, see Table 7.2 for a summary of this and other challenges to MCI theory). The obvious answer is, of course, no. They interpret some theories, such as ADD, as implying that people independently come to believe in supernatural agents. In contrast, socialization is necessary to spread such ideas.[94] They propose that although intuitive biases may predispose children to accept some views over others, they must receive cultural input about the ideas to develop them. In sum, content biases are necessary, but not sufficient, to explain religious belief.[95]

Table 7.2 Summary of the role of social learning and context biases in the spread of religious ideas.

Label	*Question addressed by taking account of context and culture*
Tarzan problem	Why would Tarzan not believe in God?
Mickey Mouse problem	Why do people not treat all counterintuitive agents as Gods?
Zeus problem	Why do all people not worship the same Gods?

Of course, Banerjee and Bloom are right. As we have discussed throughout this book, religion is a socially constructed, human-made category, and so it does not come to humans independently from culture. Proponents of theories about content biases in CSR take issue with these claims as a misinterpretation of their theories. Their theories are primarily about the role of cognition in the transmission of cultural ideas. Transmission is always embedded in a culture. CSR scholars do not propose that content biases without social communication can lead to religious ideas. This proposal would be preposterous. Also, CSR scholars recognize that biases in the content of ideas (i.e. content biases) are insufficient to explain the emergence and distribution of supernatural agent concepts and people's commitment to them.

Other scholars have proposed modifications to enhance the specificity and, thus, predictive power of theories about content biases. They contend that the context within which religious ideas are transmitted ought to play a more significant role in cognitive explanations of why people commit and thus believe in ideas.[96] These cognitive biases are referred to as context biases, and they relate to the context within which ideas are transmitted. Take the spread of ideas about supernatural agents, for example. Content biases concerning how we represent agents, in general, may predispose people to express and transmit ideas about supernatural agents as invisible people who can read minds. Others propose that taking into account biases towards the context within which ideas are communicated, such as that children are typically exposed to ideas by reputable adults, and that they witness others pay commitment to these ideas through ritualized practice.

Context biases

Scholars first came to highlight the role of context biases through a series of articles that focused on explaining the transmission of god concepts. In a light-hearted article in 2008 titled "Why Santa Claus is not a god," Barrett outlined the features that successful god concepts share. He proposed five criteria that agents are:

1 Counterintuitive (i.e. violating intuitive assumptions).
2 Intentional (i.e. a being that deliberately and purposefully initiates action).
3 Possess strategic information (i.e. information about people that is important to their reputation and survival).

4 Able to act in the human world in detectable ways.
5 Capable of motivating behaviors that reinforce the belief.[97]

In the article, Barrett highlighted the reasons why Santa Claus, a culturally prominent figure in the modern west, especially among Christian subpopulations, is not worshipped as a God. He argued that Santa Claus might seem like a God in some ways, such as his strategic knowledge about whether children are good or bad at Christmas time, and thus motivating their behavior at this time of year. Barrett concluded, however, that Santa Claus falls short of being considered as a god because he is inconsistently represented as having his five criteria.

In response to this article, psychologist Will Gervais and anthropologist Joseph Henrich argued that Barrett's explanation for successful god concepts fell short of convincing.[98] They contended that representational content biases could not explain faith in gods. They posed two problems. First, despite meeting Barrett's criteria for a successful god concept, many counterintuitive agents are not worshipped or go out of fashion. For instance, why do children, with age, stop believing in Santa Claus even though his described content remains the same? Likewise, why do few adults believe that Mickey Mouse exists outside of the realm of fiction? They (and others) refer to the problem of why people believe in some counterintuitive concepts but not others as the Mickey Mouse problem.

The second problem concerns the question of why people do not believe in other people's gods? To illustrate, Gervais and Henrich drew upon the case of Zeus, who has many properties that make him a successful god concept (e.g., he is influential and morally imperative to people) see Figure 7.1. Zeus was once widely worshipped in Ancient Greece, yet today few believed in him. Gervais and Henrich refer to this problem as the Zeus problem. They proposed that contextual learning biases—which have also been shaped by evolution—can explain the commitment to specific minimally counter-intuitive agents and how widespread these concepts are, better than content biases alone. These context learning biases include (a) the tendency to take account of how many others tend to believe in a god, (b) how many people display their commitment to that god through behaviors, and (c) the reputability of the person who tells others about a god.

One endeavor of CSR has been to produce broad theories to explain general trends across the world between cultures. Principles of human cognition can be applied in different social contexts to explain religious cognition. For example, MCI theory predicts that all else being equal, minimally counterintuitive ideas will be easier to remember and transmit. Thus, they should be more widespread than maximally counterintuitive ideas. The ease of representation is a principle of transmission, but of course, part of the transmissive success of ideas also depends upon the context where they operate; in other words, all else is never equal. CSR scholars take account of this principle when they apply cognitive theories. For example, anthropologist Harvey Whitehouse explains how some rituals include repeating complex dogma often, such as reciting scripture or singing hymns. In this instance, because these traditions provide opportunities for rehearsal, and rehearsal aids memorability, doctrines that would have long been forgotten are passed on. That is to say, additional mechanisms may support the transmission of specific ideas.[99]

Likewise, theologian Hugh Nicholson has provided compelling accounts of the emergence of two counterintuitive theological doctrines. Namely, the Christian doctrine of consubstantiality (i.e. the Trinity, that the son is the same substance as the Father) and the Buddhist doctrine of non-permanence of self (i.e. that a person is irreducible to her or his physical and psychological constituents).[100] Although very different doctrines, Nicholson shows how they qualify as counterintuitive ideas because they violate our underlying assumptions about persons, for example, that a person can be multiple entities at the same time or that people are not continuous.

Nicholson explains how doctrines of the Trinity and no-self emerged and became widespread by arguing that these doctrines were created in part as a result of group conflict within and between religious traditions, where groups tried to maximize the uniqueness and contrast of their doctrines as compared to other accounts. For example, he argues that the no-self doctrine was driven by an effort to maximize the contrast with Brahmanical Hinduism, which held a doctrine of an unchanging and eternal self, very much akin to folk psychological assumptions that people have immutable essences. The very reason, therefore, that these newly created ideas (e.g. no-self) contrasted with previous ones (e.g., essential self) was because they were counter to intuitions about persons since those that met our intuitions tended to favor the most common views.

Nicholson is, of course, focusing on the creation and persistence of theological writing, not popular versions of those concepts. As he and others, such as philosopher Helen De Cruz have proposed, however, CSR can also explain the transmission of some theological concepts.[101] For instance, maximally counterintuitive doctrines may enjoy transmissive success. However, in popular renderings, people may espouse theologically incorrect versions of these ideas in their everyday thinking. For example, Christians assuming that Jesus and God are separate entities or Buddhists, assuming that there is a permanent self.[102]

To successfully explain the emergence and persistence of these theological concepts, therefore, requires multiple components. One is an understanding of intuitive biases and how they affect the transmission of ideas. Another is an understanding of the historical and contextual factors, such as group rivalry. These dual models (i.e. content and context) of religious cognition explain both the emergence and persistence of both formal theological doctrine and popular concepts in particular contexts. These critiques and refinements in MCI theory bring us to the broader question of the role that CSR scholars tend to attribute to social learning in their theories about how people represent supernatural agents

The role of social learning in the representation of supernatural agents

So far, in the chapter, we have reviewed theories that account for children's emerging concepts of God and adult representations of God. Each account highlights the interactive role of learning in a cultural context with cognitive predispositions to produce recurrent forms of God concepts. We have covered these intermittently throughout the sections but recap some of them here. Developmental theories of the emergence of God concepts present social learning as playing a vital role in the development of children's ideas about God. As developmental psychologist Paul Harris and colleagues have pointed out, children learn directly about God through the testimony of peers, parents, and religious leaders, all of whom reflect broader cultural ideas.[103,104]

Cultural input can strengthen children's early emerging intuitions about what God is like (i.e. the preparedness account) or reinforce an alternative view that differs from their intuitions (i.e. the anthropomorphism account). Whatever the nature of intuitions, scholars maintain that they are always affected by sociocultural input. On the anthropomorphic account, for example, when coupled with the development of other abilities, such as a theory of mind, in addition to exposure to information about a monotheistic God, children can conceptualize God as omniscient. Research has also demonstrated that social instruction impacts the developmental trajectory of ideas about God. For instance, Lane and colleagues discovered that children who are raised in explicitly religious contexts and are more knowledgeable about God tend to demonstrate an early appreciation of God's extraordinary mental abilities.

Likewise, CSR theories that purport to explain trends in mature concepts of God also assume a sociocultural component in the explanation. For instance, the cognitive constraint account claims that when coupled with the experience of agents as limited, cognitive predisposition towards anthropomorphism is strengthened in adults. When theological ideas about God as limitless are rehearsed, people develop specific concepts of God as such and draw upon these concepts in certain circumstances—such as when they have time to reflect. Research has also demonstrated that the level of rehearsal impacts the developmental trajectory of ideas about God. For instance, Barrett and Vanorman reported that believers who used images of God for worship tended to anthropomorphize God more readily than those who did not.

Some people may make the wrongful assumption that there is no role for social learning in evolutionary theories of how we develop common ideas about extraordinary agents. This mistake is often compounded by the fact that cognitive scientists of religion usually discuss how we are cognitively predisposed to think a certain way, or they use the term natural to describe these predispositions. As we discussed in the research on plants by Wertz and Wynn, experience—such as the reliance on plants throughout our evolutionary history, influences the emergence of cognitive biases, including learning strategies—such as the tendency to infer that plants are edible.

These biases are then reinforced through cultural exposure and direct instruction, such as seeing parents pick foods from a plant, or telling them that these things grow on plants and are edible. Specific ideas are described as natural for some reason. One reason, in this particular example, is because they are underdetermined by the current level of experience to the concept. Thus, other factors, such as cognitive biases shaped by evolution, are thought to be at play. The anthropologist Clark Barrett has provided a detailed account of how experience shapes the evolution of the mind, including our implicit and explicit ideas about aspects of the world in his book *The Shape of Thought*.[105]

Sometimes cognitive scientists of religion describe religious ideas as cognitively natural because they hinge upon intuitive biases that are reflected in implicit ideas about extraordinary agents. Again, this does not mean that social learning is not relevant in shaping how people come to represent God, what they believe, and how they behave in response to internalized concepts. For instance, the anthropologist Tanya Luhrmann showcased the crucial role of social learning through her extensive ethnographic and survey-based research with members of Vineyard Christian Fellowship in Chicago and Northern California. This charismatic denomination offers Pentecostal practices. Luhrmann explained how people come to believe in a God that they cannot physically see but who often speaks with them if they can learn how to listen.

Belief in an invisible but interactive God is not the result of merely receiving and accepting information but requires cognitive effort and practice.[106] It requires that an individual perceive God as in the environment, is able and willing to hear them and to engage in a conversation with them. Also, the belief requires that people be able to attune themselves to receive these messages. It is no wonder that people often have periodic doubts about their ability to speak with God. That some people articulate an idea about God as person-like may reflect both an inherent bias and widely accepted theological concept of God as anthropomorphic. As anthropologist Pascal Boyer explained, the act of achieving an intuitive grasp of the presence of God in your everyday environment, speaking directly to you, is difficult—even if it is accepted as true.[107]

In sum, theories in CSR purport to explain the emergence and persistence of ideas about supernatural agents. They are distinctive because they highlight the role of ordinary human cognition and evolutionary forces that shape religious cognition in addition to social learning. Social learning in the absence of cognitive processing is not necessary or sufficient to produce commonalities in representations of supernatural agents around the globe. The position adopted by CSR scholars thus contrasts with a strong version of a social learning account of the emergence of concepts of supernatural agents.

For instance, one version of this account proposes that children anthropomorphize God's mind because they have received instruction that both minds are similar and because of social interaction. Children's everyday social interactions with other people contribute to their developing understanding of God's mind as limited because they have learned that people's minds are limited.[108] A strong version of these ideas led to cultural determinism, the position that human behavior and modes of thinking are based exclusively on learning and social interaction in a particular culture. As you may recall from Chapter 1 (Introduction), CSR began in part as a response against cultural determinism to explain the emergence and spread of religious ideas. In short, such theories are mind-blind because they do not acknowledge or underspecify the role of human processing and predispositions and biases in shaping how people represent religious ideas.

Summary of the spread of supernatural agent concepts and evaluation of cognitive explanations for the emergence and spread of supernatural agent concepts

- CSR scholars have argued that culturally popular ideas of supernatural agents tend to counter some of our intuitive biases and are minimally counterintuitive.
- The minimally counterintuitive theory is part of a broader agenda in the cognitive science of religion to identify cognitive biases that affect the generation and transmission of concepts.
- Explaining the origins and spread of cognitive biases includes the context within which they are used. However, some scholars have proposed that CSR ought to emphasize these components of cognition more in their theories.
- CSR scholars maintain that cognitive biases are necessary but not sufficient to explain the emergence and spread of religious cognition, which requires both considerations about context and social learning.

Participation 4: Nature or nurture

Imagine that you have landed a new job as a journalist in a popular science magazine. Your first assignment is to create a one-page article called "Is belief in God the product of nurture or nature?" Based on your background research of reading this chapter:

1 Prepare an outline of your article. Include 3–5 main points that you will make, evidence that you will draw upon, and your conclusion.
2 Write the one-page article. You can also include visuals such as quotes, pictures, or charts.

3 In groups of two, offer feedback on another member's article. Consider questions such as: Did they present the material accurately? Did they misrepresent someone's work? Would ordinary people understand the claims they are making
4 Revise your outlines to improve them, based upon the feedback you received.

The philosophical implications of cognitive theories of supernatural agents

One important question concerns the implications of CSR explanations of religious cognition for the truth, rationality, or justification of such beliefs. Indeed, CSR theories do have implications for these types of questions. For instance, one suggestion is that religious concepts are much like ordinary concepts. This claim may help to shed light on the tendency of adherents to Abrahamic religious traditions to attribute human-like qualities to God in certain circumstances. As De Cruz and De Smedt point out, it may also explain why anthropomorphism remains a viable option in philosophical theology. For example, some schools of Islamic thought are based upon the idea that God has hands, eyes, and other attributes because it corresponds to a natural cognitive tendency.[109]

What does CSR say about whether supernatural agents exist? Some researchers have argued that cognitive scientists of religion should be more transparent about the ontological stance they take, and how it may affect their methodology.[110] For instance, in this chapter, we have discussed how people tend to represent God. Does this say anything about whether God is real, and if so, what God is like? Earlier philosophical theories of religion were explicit about the implications of their ideas, and indeed, a large part of historical natural theology was concerned with discovering what God was like. For instance, mid-nineteenth century anthropologist and philosopher Ludwig Feuerbach claimed that human-like agents begin in the imagination, which theologians then distort into God by proposing the existence of a "perfect" human.[111]

Such explicit renderings about the relationship between theoretical implications for the reality of God, or indeed other supernatural agents, are not typically found among cognitive scientists of religion. As Barrett and philosopher Roger Trigg point out, CSR scholars may have their ontological commitments about the truth-value of supernatural agents. However, cognitive theories and data do not directly address the issue of whether or not they are real.[112] Barrett and Trigg contend that as long as the methodology in scholarly work is neutral (i.e. their studies adhere to scientific guidelines, and their results are valid), then CSR scholars do not need to engage in such debates.

There are, however, indirect implications of these theories on debates about the truth-value of religious beliefs. Indeed, most cognitive scientists of religion have explicitly stated that their theories do not directly address the question of whether or not supernatural concepts are real. However, sometimes they do write as though a naturalistic theory of supernatural agent concepts makes a supernatural explanation superfluous.[113,114] For instance, one interpretation reads that if we can explain the emergence of ideas about supernatural agents as rooted in cognition—such as a by-product of agency detection (ADD) and our intuitive assumptions about agents—in cultural context, then we do not need to invoke a supernatural interpretation to explain religious cognition.

Others offer a more radical interpretation of the claim that religion is natural. Renowned militant atheists such as philosopher Daniel Dennett[115] and biologist Richard Dawkins[116] use the theories and findings of CSR to argue that religion is based on erroneous beliefs. For example, some have contended that if belief in supernatural agents derives from the tendency to detect agents in the environment when there are, in fact, none present, then the belief in such agents is based upon erroneous cognition. One counterargument is that agency detection is not erroneous if one considers the contexts within which it is activated (e.g. high uncertainty).[117]

Others have interpreted the claim that religion is natural as favoring the existence of God. The philosopher Michael Murray, for instance, argues for the possibility that God orchestrated our cognitive architecture so that humans were likely to detect supernatural agents, which, when coupled with religious beliefs, would be much more believable.[118] Others have argued along similar lines, that cognitive biases such as ADD are compatible with interpretations of the Christian doctrine of natural knowledge of God through our senses.[119] Other scholars in CSR take a middle-ground and are?open to the possible coexistence of both naturalistic and supernatural explanations.[120]

Participation 5: Defining cognitive tendencies

Table 3.3 in Chapter 3 (Research Questions) provided examples of the cognitive foundations of religious ideas. Based on this table and this chapter:

1 Provide a brief definition of the following cognitive tendencies (a) theory of mind, ToM, (b) hyperactive detective agency device, HADD, (c) anthropomorphism, and (d) folk-dualism.
2 Explain (in a few sentences for each) how each bias enriches the understanding of (a) why people believe in supernatural agents, and (b) why people represent supernatural agents in similar ways.

Key points

- Some have questioned the implications of cognitive theories on the truth-value of religion.
- These questions often arise from the claim that religion is natural.
- Like all religion scholars, CSR researchers have personal ontological commitments about religion but use scientific methodologies to study religion, which acts as checks and balances against biased research findings.
- The research findings of CSR do not support a position about the truth-value of religion. Instead, they are open to interpretation from others, and there are many and varied opinions.

Chapter summary

In this chapter, we have considered how ideas about supernatural agents develop and mature, and cognitive factors that affect the spread of these ideas cross-culturally. Cognitive science of religion scholars propose that understanding how cognitive systems support or discourage certain types of ideas is critical to understanding how religious concepts become widespread. According to these scholars, religious beliefs in supernatural agents need not be explained by any unique domain of thought, but rather, are likely to be the outcome of existing mechanisms that enable people to reason about themselves, and social agents more generally.

In the first half of this chapter, we considered some disagreements over the nature of these cognitive biases, especially concerning the question of whether the concept of God derives properties as compared to humans, agents, or minds. In the second half of this chapter, we considered the second half of the paradox for successful supernatural agent representations, especially gods, that they violate some of our intuitive expectations of persons. These biases can, however, only take us so far. To explain how and why people in different societies show commitment to specific supernatural agents, and not others, we need to take into account that they are learned concepts and the context within which they are communicated. Some scholars have pondered the philosophical and theological implications of these naturalistic theories and have come to different conclusions.

While this chapter has focused on the representation of God as a supernatural agent, in the other chapters of this book we also consider the representation of different types of supernatural agents, including reincarnated agents in Chapter 6 (The Afterlife), and witchcraft in Chapters 5 (The Nature of the World) and 8 (Morality). We also consider the role of cognitive factors in explaining the representation and spread of ideas about spirits in the case study for this chapter.

Research case study: Spirit possession

Many religious traditions contain ideas about possession, including Christianity, Buddhism, Hinduism, Islam, and many other southeast Asian and African traditions. Spirit possession usually entails episodes where bodies of people (referred to here as hosts) and minds (e.g. of hosts and spirits) change, merge, and compete for control, often during episodes, such as during rituals. Why is spirit possession so recurrent

Modern anthropological accounts of spirit possession attempted to capture the complexity and variability in particular sociocultural contexts, including local understandings of the phenomenon. They make few generalizations about spirit possession in general. By contrast, some of the earliest accounts of spirit possession provided general explanations of the phenomena. Cognitive anthropologist Emma Cohen characterizes two different types of accounts. The first are medicalist accounts. They reduce possession to temporary dissociative states, seek associations between trance and neurophysiological factors (such as calcium deficiency), and pathologize those who experience possession. The second is sociological theories.

They emphasize the emergence and spread of trance as a product of the forces of the broader social structure within which they are embedded, such as members of marginalized groups including racial minorities and women who participate in specific communities as an index of their subordinate status. There are issues with both types of accounts. Medicalist accounts pay little attention to the context within which possession occurs, nor do they consider the possibility that trance states can occur among healthy individuals. Sociological theories are vague and unverifiable. They say little about the mechanisms through which these states exert their effects (e.g. how does this work?), and competing hypotheses make the same predictions (e.g. is trance a display of power, or a display against power?)

Cognitive anthropologist Emma Cohen revisited and expanded upon the work of another anthropologist in the 1970s, Erika Bourguignon. Bourguignon was atypical at the time of her research because she conducted a cross-cultural analysis of almost 500 societies and attempted to categorize spirit possession into two types, based on the presence or absence of altered states of consciousness. Like Bourguignon, Cohen was interested in the distribution and the presence of certain types of spirit possession. Also, Cohen sought to (a) uncover the fundamental assumptions that underpin popular ideas about possession in different contexts, (b) identify general psychological tendencies that give rise to these assumptions, and (c) determine how these tendencies manifest themselves in culturally specific settings.

In 2002, Cohen spent 18 months conducting ethnographic fieldwork among Afro-Brazilian religionists in the Northern Brazilian city of Belém, among a group of around 60 people where spirit possession was often the focus of rituals. During her time, Cohen attended social gatherings, business meetings, healing, and ritual ceremonies and met with the group leader. She noticed that two forms of spirit possession emerged. When people talked casually about possession, they assumed that *the displacement* of the person occurred. In other words, the agency of the host (i.e. the person) was entirely replaced by an agent (i.e. the spirit), so that no trace of the host remains, and the agent completely controls the host's body.

However, the respected leader of the group (*pai-de-santo*) taught the laity about possession where the host *fused* identity with the agency of the spirit so that they merge during the episode. Much like lemon in a glass of water flavors the drink, the lemon and water can be separate but also fused entities to make a new taste. Cohen also noted that although some ethnographers and the popular media had recounted another type of possession—oscillation, where the agency and host fight for control during the episode (e.g. think of the movie, *The Exorcist*), this was seldom assumed in people's discussions. Most importantly, even though the theological concept of possession officially endorsed by the group was a fusion model of possession, people unconsciously assumed a displacement model, which contradicted the official teachings. In other words, people were endorsing the theologically incorrect version.

Cohen developed a theory about why the discrepancy between people's theological and everyday concepts was occurring. At the crux of her theory is the assumption that some ideas about minds and bodies are more straightforward to be remembered and faithfully communicated. Cohen proposed that people tend to attribute body behaviors to a single agent at one time. In other words, one mind controls one body. She dubbed this the "one-body-one-mind-principle." Thus, Cohen claimed, it is cognitively more accessible to represent spirit possession as entailing a complete displacement of the host's mind with the mind of a spirit (i.e. displacement model) than it is to represent the host's mind as merging with the spirit's mind in the host's body (i.e. fusion model).

In partnership with psychologist Justin Barrett, Emma Cohen did something atypical for an anthropologist: she conducted psychological experiments to test observations based on her field observations. Together, Cohen and Barrett tested the hypotheses about spirit possession with UK students, who, unlike the people of Belém, did not have experience with possession as a religious practice, and had been exposed to western media portrayals, which tend to adopt the oscillation model. In a series of studies, Barrett and Cohen investigated how the students described possession, identified possession from some possibilities, and how accurately they recalled the three concepts of spirit possession after they read about them. Across all studies, participants displayed a strong preference for the displacement model. Just like the members of the Afro-Brazilian group, UK students assumed that the mind displaces the body during a possession, rather than fusing with it, or fluctuating for control during episodes. They freely offered this model when describing possession, identified it among the other models as possession, and more accurately recalled the details of it than the other two models.

Cohen also wondered whether these findings could apply beyond the contexts of the UK and Brazil. She surveyed the ethnographic literature and found evidence for the displacement model of spirit possession in many different cultural contexts. From her research, Cohen proposed a cultural selectionist model of spirit possession. On this model, all else being equal, traditions that endorse a displacement model of possession will have a transmissive advantage over those that do not. Of course, all else is never equal, and Cohen emphasized the importance of investigating how our assumptions about minds and bodies are shaped and reinforced in different contexts, just like she did in the ethnographic component of her research.

Questions

1 In your own words, summarize the claims the researcher is making (include the terms displacement, fusion, and oscillation in your summary).
2 What are the differences and similarities between this research and previous research on spirit possession?
3 What do you think demarks this research as typical of the CSR approach to religion?
4 Read, summarize, and evaluate (i.e. say whether and why you agree or disagree with) the following critique of Cohen's work by sociologist Arnaud Halloy.

"Cohen focuses almost exclusively on what people think about spirit possession. However, if one wishes to take into account the process of possession, that is, how spirit possession is learned and how it evolves, such an overly 'representational' concept of cognition is prejudicial ... possession is lived through affects and precepts which, along with the conceptions of possession Cohen rightly identifies, are good candidates for explaining its wide success around the world.[121]"

Further reading

1 Cohen, Emma. *The mind possessed: The cognition of spirit possession in an Afro-Brazilian religious tradition*. Oxford University Press, 2007.
2 Cohen, Emma. "What is spirit possession? Defining, comparing, and explaining two possession forms." *Ethnos* 73, no. 1 (2008): 101–126.

3 Cohen, Emma, and Justin L. Barrett. "Conceptualizing spirit possession: Ethnographic and experimental evidence." *Ethos* 36, no. 2 (2008): 246–267.
4 Cohen, Emma, and Justin Barrett. "When minds migrate: Conceptualizing spirit possession." *Journal of Cognition and Culture* 8, no. 1 (2008): 23–48.
5 Cohen, E. "An author meets her critics. Around 'The mind possessed': The cognition of spirit possession in an Afro-Brazilian religious tradition" by Emma Cohen [Response to comments by Diana Espirito Santo, Arnaud Halloy, and Pierre Lienard]. *Religion and Society: Advances in Research* 1, No. 1 (2010): 164–176. www.berghahnjournals.com/view/journals/religion-and-society/1/1/air-rs010112.xml.

Discussion questions

1 Imagine that you had to create a new supernatural agent concept that would successfully spread. Based on the theories in this chapter, describe the characteristics of the agent.
2 Can you apply the formula of MCI theory to a supernatural agent concept? Is your agent MCI, based on this formula.
3 Do you agree or disagree that the Mickey Mouse, Zeus, and Tarzan problems are problems for MCI theory? Why?
4 Do you think that all CSR theories on the emergence and spread of supernatural agent concepts (e.g. anthropomorphism, HADD, MCI theory) have implications on whether these agents exist?

Selected further reading

Articles

1 Barrett, Justin L. "Theological correctness: Cognitive constraint and the study of religion." *Method & Theory in the Study of Religion* 11, no. 4 (1999): 325–339.
2 Heiphetz, Larisa, Jonathan D. Lane, Adam Waytz, and Liane L. Young. "How children and adults represent God's mind." *Cognitive Science* 40, no. 1 (2016): 121–144.

Books

1 Boyer, Pascal. *Religion Explained: The human instincts that fashion gods, spirits, and ancestors*. Random House, 2002.

Notes

1 Tylor, Edward Burnett. *Primitive culture: researches into the development of mythology, philosophy, religion, art, and custom.* Vol. 2. J. Murray, 1871.
2 Barrett, Justin L., Rebekah A. Richert, and Amanda Driesenga. "God's beliefs versus mother's: The development of nonhuman agent concepts." *Child Development* 72, no. 1 (2001): 50–65.
3 Richert, Rebekah A., and Justin L. Barrett. "Do you see what I see? Young children's assumptions about God's perceptual abilities." *The International Journal for the Psychology of Religion* 15, no. 4 (2005): 283–295.
4 Knight, Nicola, Paulo Sousa, Justin L. Barrett, and Scott Atran. "Children's attributions of beliefs to humans and God: Cross-cultural evidence." *Cognitive Science* 28, no. 1 (2004): 117–126.
5 Richert, Rebekah A., and Justin L. Barrett. "Do you see what I see? Young children's assumptions about God's perceptual abilities." *The International Journal for the Psychology of Religion* 15, no. 4 (2005): 283–295.
6 Barrett, Justin L., Rebekah A. Richert, and Amanda Driesenga. "God's beliefs versus mother's: The development of nonhuman agent concepts." *Child Development* 72, no. 1 (2001): 50–65.
7 Barrett, Justin L., Rebekah A. Richert, and Amanda Driesenga. "God's beliefs versus mother's: The development of nonhuman agent concepts." *Child Development* 72, no. 1 (2001): 50–65.
8 For a summary of these studies, see Heiphetz, Larisa, Jonathan D. Lane, Adam Waytz, and Liane L. Young. "How children and adults represent God's mind." *Cognitive Science* 40, no. 1 (2016): 121–144.
9 Bloom, Paul, and Tim P. German. "Two reasons to abandon the false belief task as a test of theory of mind." *Cognition* 77, no. 1 (2000): B25-B31.
10 Surian, Luca, and Alan M. Leslie. "Competence and performance in false belief understanding: A comparison of autistic and normal 3-year-old children." *British Journal of Developmental Psychology* 17, no. 1 (1999): 141–155.
11 Surian, Luca, Stefania Caldi, and Dan Sperber. "Attribution of beliefs by 13-month-old infants." *Psychological Science* 18, no. 7 (2007): 580–586.
12 Onishi, Kristine H., and Renée Baillargeon. "Do 15-month-old infants understand false beliefs?" *Science* 308, no. 5719 (2005): 255–258.
13 Powell, Lindsey J., Kathryn Hobbs, Alexandros Bardis, Susan Carey, and Rebecca Saxe. "Replications of implicit theory of mind tasks with varying representational demands." *Cognitive Development* 46 (2018): 40–50.
14 Perner, Josef, and Johannes Roessler. "From infants' to children's appreciation of belief." *Trends in Cognitive Sciences* 16, no. 10 (2012): 519–525.
15 Kiessling, Florian, and Josef Perner. "God–mother-baby: What children think they know." *Child Development* 85, no. 4 (2014): 1601–1616.
16 Lane, Jonathan D., Henry M. Wellman, and E. Margaret Evans. "Children's understanding of ordinary and extraordinary minds." *Child Development* 81, no. 5 (2010): 1475–1489.
17 Lane, Jonathan D., Henry M. Wellman, and E. Margaret Evans. "Sociocultural input facilitates children's developing understanding of extraordinary minds." *Child Development* 83, no. 3 (2012): 1007–1021.
18 Giménez-Dasí, Marta, Silvia Guerrero, and Paul L. Harris. "Intimations of immortality and omniscience in early childhood." *European Journal of Developmental Psychology* 2, no. 3 (2005): 285–297.
19 Lane, Jonathan D., Henry M. Wellman, and E. Margaret Evans. "Approaching an understanding of omniscience from the preschool years to early adulthood." *Developmental Psychology* 50, no. 10 (2014): 2380.
20 Piaget, Jean. *The child's conception of the world.* No. 213. Rowman & Littlefield, 1951.

21 Kiessling, Florian, and Josef Perner. "God–mother-baby: What children think they know." *Child Development* 85, no. 4 (2014): 1601–1616.

22 Lane, Jonathan D., Henry M. Wellman, and E. Margaret Evans. "Children's understanding of ordinary and extraordinary minds." *Child Development* 81, no. 5 (2010): 1475–1489.

23 Makris, Nikos, and Dimitris Pnevmatikos. "Children's understanding of human and super-natural mind." *Cognitive Development* 22, no. 3 (2007): 365–375.

24 Heiphetz, Larisa, Jonathan D. Lane, Adam Waytz, and Liane L. Young. "How children and adults represent God's mind." *Cognitive Science* 40, no. 1 (2016): 121–144.

25 Heiphetz, Larisa, Jonathan D. Lane, Adam Waytz, and Liane L. Young. "How children and adults represent God's mind." *Cognitive Science* 40, no. 1 (2016): 121–144.

26 Heiphetz, Larisa, Jonathan D. Lane, Adam Waytz, and Liane L. Young. "My mind, your mind, and God's mind: How children and adults conceive of different agents' moral beliefs." *British Journal of Developmental Psychology* (2018).

27 Heiphetz, Larisa, Jonathan D. Lane, Adam Waytz, and Liane L. Young. "How children and adults represent God's mind." *Cognitive Science* 40, no. 1 (2016): 121–144.

28 Lane, Jonathan D., Henry M. Wellman, and E. Margaret Evans. "Sociocultural input facilitates children's developing understanding of extraordinary minds." *Child Development* 83, no. 3 (2012): 1007–1021.

29 Barrett, Justin L. "Theological correctness: Cognitive constraint and the study of religion." *Method & Theory in the Study of Religion* 11, no. 4 (1999): 325–339.

30 Barrett, Justin L., and Frank C. Keil. "Conceptualizing a nonnatural entity: Anthropomorphism in God concepts." *Cognitive Psychology* 31, no. 3 (1996): 219–247.

31 Slone, Jason. *Theological Incorrectness: Why religious people believe what they should not.* Oxford University Press, 2007.

32 Boyer, Pascal. *Religion explained: The evolutionary foundations of religious belief.* New York: Basic Books, 2001.

33 Barrett, Justin L., and Frank C. Keil. "Conceptualizing a nonnatural entity: Anthropomorphism in God concepts." *Cognitive Psychology* 31, no. 3 (1996): 219–247.

34 Barrett, Justin L., and Brant VanOrman. "The effects of image-use in worship on God concepts." *Journal of Psychology and Christianity* (1996).

35 Shtulman, Andrew. "Variation in the anthropomorphization of supernatural beings and its implications for cognitive theories of religion." *Journal of Experimental Psychology: Learning, Memory, and Cognition* 34, no. 5 (2008): 1123.

36 Heiphetz, Larisa, Jonathan D. Lane, Adam Waytz, and Liane L. Young. "How children and adults represent God's mind." *Cognitive Science* 40, no. 1 (2016): 121–144.

37 Westh, Peter. "Anthropomorphism in God concepts: The role of narrative." *Origins of Religion, Cognition, and Culture (*2009): 396–413.

38 Shtulman, Andrew. "Variation in the anthropomorphization of supernatural beings and its implications for cognitive theories of religion." *Journal of Experimental Psychology: Learning, Memory, and Cognition* 34, no. 5 (2008): 1123.

39 Heiphetz, Larisa, Jonathan D. Lane, Adam Waytz, and Liane L. Young. "How children and adults represent God's mind." *Cognitive Science* 40, no. 1 (2016): 121–144.

40 Barlev, Michael, Spencer Mermelstein, and Tamsin C. German. "Core Intuitions About Persons Coexist and Interfere With Acquired Christian Beliefs About God." *Cognitive Science* 41, no. S3 (2017): 425–454.

41 Kelemen, Deborah. "Are children 'intuitive theists'? Reasoning about purpose and design in nature." *Psychological Science* 15, no. 5 (2004): 295–301.

42 Barrett, Justin L. "Cognitive constraints on Hindu concepts of the divine." *Journal for the Scientific Study of Religion* (1998): 608–619.
43 Chilcott, Travis, and Raymond F. Paloutzian. "Relations between Gauḍīya Vaiṣṇava devotional practices and implicit and explicit anthropomorphic reasoning about Kṛṣṇa." *Journal of Cognition and Culture* 16, no. 1–2 (2016): 107–121.
44 Barlev, M., Mermelstein, S., Cohen, A.S., and German, C.T. (2019). The Embodied God: Core intuitions about person physicality coexist and interfere with acquired Christian beliefs about God, the Holy Spirit, and Jesus. *Cognitive Science* 43, no. 9 (2019): e12784.
45 Barlev, Michael, Spencer Mermelstein, and Tamsin C. German. "Core intuitions about persons coexist and interfere with acquired Christian beliefs about God." *Cognitive Science* 41 (2017): 425–454.
46 Barlev, Michael, Spencer Mermelstein, and Tamsin C. German. "Representational coexistence in the God concept: Core knowledge intuitions of God as a person are not revised by Christian theology despite lifelong experience." *Psychonomic Bulletin & Review* (2018): 1–9.
47 d'Andrade, Roy G. *The development of cognitive anthropology*. Cambridge University Press, 1995.
48 Ward, Thomas B., and E. Thomas Lawson. "Creative cognition in science fiction and fantasy writing." (2009).
49 Ward, Thomas B. "Structured imagination: The role of category structure in exemplar generation." *Cognitive Psychology* 27, no. 1 (1994): 1–40.
50 Ward, Thomas B., Merryl J. Patterson, Cynthia M. Sifonis, Rebecca A. Dodds, and Katherine N. Saunders. "The role of graded category structure in imaginative thought." *Memory & Cognition* 30, no. 2 (2002): 199–216.
51 Ward, Thomas B., Merryl J. Patterson, Cynthia M. Sifonis, Rebecca A. Dodds, and Katherine N. Saunders. "The role of graded category structure in imaginative thought." *Memory & Cognition* 30, no. 2 (2002): 199–216.
52 See page 133 for a summary of theorists who support this view: Heiphetz, Larisa, Jonathan D. Lane, Adam Waytz, and Liane L. Young. "How children and adults represent God's mind." *Cognitive Science* 40, no. 1 (2016): 121–144.
53 Epley, Nicholas, Benjamin A. Converse, Alexa Delbosc, George A. Monteleone, and John T. Cacioppo. "Believers' estimates of God's beliefs are more egocentric than estimates of other people's beliefs." *Proceedings of the National Academy of Sciences* 106, no. 51 (2009): 21533–21538.
54 Ross, Lee D., Yphtach Lelkes, and Alexandra G. Russell. "How Christians reconcile their personal political views and the teachings of their faith: *Projection* as a means of dissonance reduction." *Proceedings of the National Academy of Sciences* 109, no. 10 (2012): 3616–3622.
55 De Cruz, Helen. "Religious concepts as structured imagination." *International Journal for the Psychology of Religion* 23, no. 1 (2013): 63–74.
56 Boyer, Pascal. *The naturalness of religious ideas: A cognitive theory of religion*. University of California Press, 1994.
57 Wertz, A. E., and Wynn, K. "Selective social learning of plant edibility in 6-and 18-month-old infants." *Psychological Science* 25, no. 4 (2014): 874–882.
58 Boyer, Pascal. "How natural selection shapes conceptual structure: Human intuitions and concepts of ownership." In *The conceptual mind. New directions in the study of concepts* (2015): 185–200.
59 Cosmides, Leda. "The logic of social exchange: Has natural selection shaped how humans reason? Studies with the Wason selection task." *Cognition* 31, no. 3 (1989): 187–276.
60 Barrett, H. Clark. "Adaptations to predators and prey." In *The handbook of evolutionary psychology* (2005): 200–223.

61 Norenzayan, Ara. *Big gods: How religion transformed cooperation and conflict*. Princeton University Press, 2013.
62 Johnson, Dominic. *God is watching you: How the fear of God makes us human*. USA: Oxford University Press, 2016.
63 Boyer, Pascal. "Religion explained: The evolutionary foundations of religious belief." New York: Basic Books, 2001.
64 Atran, Scott, and Ara Norenzayan. "Religion's evolutionary landscape: Counter-intuition, commitment, compassion, communion." *Behavioral and Brain Sciences* 27, no. 6 (2004): 713–730.
65 Bloom, Paul. *Descartes' baby: How the science of child development explains what makes us human*. Random House, 2005.
66 Shtulman, A., and Lindeman, M. "Attributes of God: Conceptual foundations of a foundational belief." *Cognitive Science* 40, no. 3 (2018), 635–670.
67 Barlev, M. and Shtulman, A. (under review). "Minds, bodies, spirits, and gods: Does widespread belief in disembodied beings imply that we are inherent dualists?" https://psyarxiv.com/e9cw4/.
68 Barlev, M., Mermelstein, S., Cohen, A.S., and German, C.T. "The Embodied God: Core intuitions about person physicality coexist and interfere with acquired Christian beliefs about God, the Holy Spirit, and Jesus. *Cognitive Science* 43, no. 9 (2019): e12784.
69 Guthrie, Stewart, Joseph Agassi, Karin R. Andriolo, David Buchdahl, H. Byron Earhart, Moshe Greenberg, Ian Jarvie et al. "A cognitive theory of religion [and comments and reply]." *Current Anthropology* 21, no. 2 (1980): 181–203.
70 Stewart, Elliott Guthrie. *Faces in the clouds: A new theory of religion*. New York: Oxford University Press, 1993.
71 Barrett, Justin L. *Why would anyone believe in God*. Walnut Creek: AltaMira Press, 2004.
72 Scholl, Brian J., and Patrice D. Tremoulet. "Perceptual causality and animacy." *Trends in Cognitive Sciences* 4, no. 8 (2000): 299–309.
73 E.g. see McKay, Ryan, and Charles Efferson. "The subtleties of error management." *Evolution and Human Behavior* 31, no. 5 (2010): 309–319.
74 Westh, Peter. "Anthropomorphism in God concepts: The role of narrative." *Origins of Religion, Cognition, and Culture* (2009): 396–413.
75 Boyer, Pascal. "Religious thought and behaviour as by-products of brain function." *Trends in Cognitive Sciences* 7, no. 3 (2003): 119–124.
76 *"IGN's top 100 comic book heroes > #1: Superman."* IGN Entertainment. Archived from the original on May 7, 2011. Retrieved May 27, 2011.
77 www.the-numbers.com/movies/franchise/Superman#tab=summary.
78 https://en.wikipedia.org/wiki/Superman#Personality.
79 Boyer, Pascal. *The naturalness of religious ideas: A cognitive theory of religion*. University of California Press, 1994.
80 Upal, M. Afzal. "Role of context in memorability of intuitive and counter-intuitive concepts." In *Proceedings of the Cognitive Science Society* 27, no. 27 (2005).
81 Barrett, Justin L., and Melanie A. Nyhof. "Spreading non-natural concepts: The role of intuitive conceptual structures in memory and transmission of cultural materials." *Journal of Cognition and Culture* 1, no. 1 (2001): 69–100.
82 Boyer, Pascal, and Charles Ramble. "Cognitive templates for religious concepts: Cross-cultural evidence for recall of counter-intuitive representations." *Cognitive Science* 25, no. 4 (2001): 535–564.
83 Upala, M. Afzal, Lauren O. Gonce, Ryan D. Tweney, and D. Jason Slone. "Contextualizing counterintuitiveness: How context affects comprehension and memorability of counterintuitive concepts." *Cognitive Science* 31, no. 3 (2007): 415–439.

84 Hornbeck, Ryan G., and Justin L. Barrett. "Refining and testing 'counter-intuitiveness' in virtual reality: Cross-cultural evidence for recall of counter-intuitive representations." *International Journal for the Psychology of Religion* 23, no. 1 (2013): 15–28.

85 Banerjee, Konika, Omar S. Haque, and Elizabeth S. Spelke. "Melting lizards and crying mailboxes: Children's preferential recall of minimally counterintuitive concepts." *Cognitive Science*, 37, no. 7 (2013): 1251–1289.

86 Gonce, Lauren O., M. Afzal Upal, D. Jason Slone, and D. Ryan Tweney. "Role of context in the recall of counterintuitive concepts." *Journal of Cognition and Culture* 6, no. 3 (2006): 521–547.

87 Tweney, Ryan D., M. Afzal Upal, Lauren O. Gonce, D. Jason Slone, and Kristin Edwards. "The creative structuring of counterintuitive worlds." *Journal of Cognition and Culture* 6, no. 3 (2006): 483–498.

88 Norenzayan, Ara, Scott Atran, Jason Faulkner, and Mark Schaller. "Memory and mystery: The cultural selection of minimally counterintuitive narratives." *Cognitive Science* 30, no. 3 (2006): 531–553.

89 Barrett, Justin L. "Coding and quantifying counterintuitiveness in religious concepts: Theoretical and methodological reflections." *Method & Theory in the Study of Religion* 20, no. 4 (2008): 308–338.

90 Upal, M. Afzal. "An alternative account of the minimal counterintuitiveness effect." *Cognitive Systems Research* 11, no. 2 (2010): 194–203.

91 Bloch, Maurice. "Are religious beliefs counter-intuitive." In *Radical interpretation in religion*, ed. N. Frankenberry. Cambridge University Press, [MB] 2002.

92 Purzycki, Benjamin Grant, and Aiyana K. Willard. "MCI theory: A critical discussion." *Religion, Brain & Behavior* 6, no. 3 (2016): 207–248.

93 Purzycki, Benjamin Grant, and Aiyana K. Willard. "MCI theory: A critical discussion." *Religion, Brain & Behavior* 6, no. 3 (2016): 207–248.

94 Banerjee, Konika, and Paul Bloom. "Would Tarzan believe in God? Conditions for the emergence of religious belief." *Trends in Cognitive Sciences* 17, no. 1 (2013): 7–8.

95 Gervais, Will M., Aiyana K. Willard, Ara Norenzayan, and Joseph Henrich. "The Cultural Transmission of Faith: Why innate intuitions are necessary but insufficient, to explain religious belief." *Religion* 41, no. 3 (2011): 389–410.

96 Henrich, Joseph, and Robert Boyd. "On modeling cognition and culture: why cultural evolution does not require replication of representations." *Journal of Cognition and Culture* 2, no. 2 (2002): 87–112.

97 Barrett, J.L. (2008). Why Santa Claus is not a god. *Journal of Cognition and Culture* 8, 149–161.

98 Gervais, Will M., and Joseph Henrich. "The Zeus problem: Why representational content biases cannot explain faith in gods." *Journal of Cognition and Culture* 10, no. 3 (2010): 383–389.

99 Whitehouse, Harvey. *Modes of religiosity: A cognitive theory of religious transmission.* Rowman Altamira, 2004.

100 Nicholson, Hugh. *The spirit of contradiction in Christianity and Buddhism.* Oxford University Press, 2016.

101 De Cruz, Helen. "Cognitive science of religion and the study of theological concepts." *Topoi* 33, no. 2 (2014): 487–497.

102 Berniunas, Renatas. "Folk psychology of the self and afterlife beliefs: The case of Mongolian Buddhists." Ph.D. diss., Queen's University Belfast, 2012.

103 Harris, Paul L., and Kathleen H. Corriveau. "Learning from testimony about religion and science." In *Trust and skepticism: Children's selective learning from testimony*. 2014, 28–41.

104 Harris, Paul L., and Melissa A. Koenig. "Trust in testimony: How children learn about science and religion." *Child Development* 77, no. 3 (2006): 505–524.

105 Barrett, H. Clark. *The Shape of Thought: How Mental Adaptations Evolve*. New York: Oxford University Press, 2015.
106 Luhrmann, Tanya M. *When God talks back: Understanding the American evangelical relationship with God*. Vintage, 2012.
107 Boyer, Pascal. "Why "belief" is hard work: Implications of Tanya Luhrmann's When God talks back." *HAU: Journal of Ethnographic Theory* 3, no. 3 (2013): 349–357.
108 Carpendale, Jeremy I.M., and Charlie Lewis. "Constructing an understanding of mind: The development of children's social understanding within social interaction." *Behavioral and Brain Sciences* 27, no. 1 (2004): 79–96.
109 De Cruz, Helen, and Johan De Smedt. *A natural history of natural theology: The cognitive science of theology and philosophy of religion*. MIT Press, 2014.
110 Näreaho, Leo. "The cognitive science of religion: philosophical observations." *Religious Studies* 44, no. 1 (2008): 83–98.
111 Feuerbach, Ludwig. *The essence of Christianity* trans. George Eliot [Marian Evans] (1854): 14.
112 Trigg, Roger, and Justin L. Barrett, eds. *The roots of religion: Exploring the cognitive science of religion*. Routledge, 2016.
113 Atran, Scott. *In gods we trust: The evolutionary landscape of religion*. Oxford University Press, 2004.
114 Boyer, Pascal. *Religion explained: The evolutionary foundations of religious belief*. New York: Basic Books, 2001.
115 Dennett, Daniel Clement. *Breaking the spell: Religion as a natural phenomenon*. New York: Penguin, 2006.
116 Dawkins, Richard. *The god delusion*. London: Bantam Press, 2006.
117 Murray, M.J. "Four arguments that the cognitive psychology of religion undermines the justification of religious belief." In J. Bulbulia, R. Sosis, E. Harris, R. Genet, C. Genet and K. Wyman eds. *The evolution of religion: Studies, theories, and critiques*. Santa Margarita, CA: The Collins Foundation Press, 2007.
118 Murray, M.J. (2007). "Four arguments that the cognitive psychology of religion undermines the justification of religious belief." In J. Bulbulia, R. Sosis, E. Harris, R. Genet, C. Genet and K. Wyman eds. *The evolution of religion: Studies, theories, and critiques*. Santa Margarita, CA: The Collins Foundation Press.
119 Clark, Kelly James, and Justin L. Barrett. "Reformed epistemology and the cognitive science of religion." *Faith and Philosophy* 27, no. 2 (2010): 174–189.
120 Barrett, Justin L. *Cognitive science, religion, and theology: From human minds to divine minds*. Conshohocken, PA: Templeton Press, 2011.
121 Cohen, E. (2010). An author meets her critics. Around "The mind possessed": The cognition of spirit possession in an Afro-Brazilian religious tradition" by Emma Cohen [Response to comments by Diana Espirito Santo, Arnaud Halloy, and Pierre Lienard]. *Religion and Society: Advances in Research* 1 No.1, 158, 164–176: www.berghahnjournals.com/view/journals/religion-and-society/1/1/air-rs010112.xml.

8 Morality

The connection between religion and morality has been debated for centuries.[1] In a famous dialogue that dates back to the fourth century BCE, Ancient Greek moral philosopher, Socrates, asked: "Is an action morally good because the gods command it, or do the gods command it because it is morally good?[2]" Many of the founders of the social scientists, including Emile Durkheim, have passionately weighed in on such questions by describing religion as a force that binds groups together and prevents immoral conduct. The idea that religion motivates selfless behavior to benefit others at a personal cost is central in debates about the evolutionary origins of religions. Today, debates about religion and morality continue to dominate academic and popular domains and highlight the complexity and controversy of issues.

Although scholars differ in how they conceptualize the term morality, it is used here in a broad sense to refer to standards or principles about right or wrong conduct. The chapter is organized into three sections. First, we will consider research on the question, where does morality come from? Next, we weigh up evidence about how religion affects moral decision-making and behavior in contemporary society. Here, we will discuss the results of social psychological research on prosociality and prosocial behaviors, actions intended to help others, such as honesty, cooperation, and generosity. Finally, we will turn to the contribution of research in the cognitive-evolutionary sciences on questions about the relationship between religion and morality.

Part 1: Where does morality come from?

One important question from a cognitive-evolutionary perspective concerns whether, and how, natural moral responses emerge in normally developing humans. As discussed in Chapter 3: Research Questions (Table 3.2), an understanding of ontogeny (how do traits related to morality develop in humans?) provides scientists with a proximate explanation of moral behavior. Correspondingly, one research task is to identify early emerging predispositions and biases towards moral behavior in children to locate the cognitive basis for moral tendencies.

The moral foundations of humans

Developmental psychologist Paul Bloom has also conducted much research on the question of the origins of moral behavior. Bloom's research contributes to a growing body of evidence that babies have what he refers to as a "naïve sense of morality." In the studies, babies demonstrate some rudimentary tendencies that we would expect to be necessary before full-blown culturally developed morality emerges. For instance, Bloom and members of his lab found that even six-month-olds differentiate between agents that help and hinder one another. For example, babies differentiate between helpful puppets that assist in pushing a ball up a hill and other puppets that hinder the ball by pushing it down the hill.

More remarkably, babies also show a preference for agents that display cooperative behavior. For example, when offered both puppets, they overwhelmingly displayed a preference for the puppet that pushed the ball up the hill—aka the good guy. When they develop language, 18-month-olds explicitly identify the pushing puppet as "the good guy." They also dispense justice by choosing to give the helping puppet, rather than the hindering puppet, a treat, and they prefer agents who do the same. In other words, babies have a strong preference for good over bad.

The research of developmental psychologists like Bloom reveals that this initial moral sense is biased towards members of our kind. Babies show a preference for members of their own group over others; they favor them and expect them to be more helpful than out-group members. Babies decide who is a member of the out-group mainly based on appearances, such as belonging to a different race, speaking a foreign language, and even by wearing a different colored T-shirt than them.[3]

Adults also have strong inclinations towards members of their in-group, and it seems that these inclinations emerge early. Such preferential treatment makes sense because in-group members are more likely to have shared interests and presumably to reciprocate acts of kindness, so ultimately favoring one's in-group is a wise investment. Research with babies is especially significant because it demonstrates that impartiality is not at the core of morality. Rather, in-group biases, which come to include religious affiliation, drive prosociality.

So, does religion make us moral? According to this research in developmental psychology, the answer is no. Nevertheless, Bloom is not advocating a simplistic view of the emergence of morality, and nor is he downplaying the role of religious socialization. Based on his research with babies, Bloom proposes that morality is ultimately a synthesis of the biological, cognitive, and cultural. In other words, fully developed morality is a combination of biological predispositions concerning aspects of human behavior.

These aspects include feeling the pain of others, cultural traditions (including religious socialization, which conspires with early inclinations to shape our sense of what is right and wrong) and learned experience and critical reflection. Bloom's studies fundamentally reveal that young children display the basic foundations of morality: the capacity and willingness to judge the actions of others, a sense of justice, and basic responses to altruism and nastiness. Bloom concludes that this basic moral apparatus is necessary for morality; without it, we would be nothing more than amoral agents, pursuing our self-interest. While Bloom acknowledges that the capacities of babies are minimal, he proposes that these capacities, rather than religious input, are necessary for morality.

Situated in an evolutionary-cognitive framework, Bloom suggests a cognitive basis for moral inclinations that are necessary, but not sufficient, for full-blown morality to develop. Research with children in contexts where ideas about what is moral differ would enhance what is known about ontogeny (i.e. how traits related to morality develop) by specifying the roles of cognitive biases and environmental inputs more precisely. Bloom's research suggests that these cognitive biases are based in part on identifying cooperative behavior (and others evolve for different reasons). Other scholars in CSR endorse a stronger version of this claim, known as the "morality as cooperation" theory. This is the theory that morality consists of a collection of biological and cultural solutions to the problems of cooperation recurrent in human social life, and some primatologists agree with this claim.

Key points

- Babies demonstrate some basic tendencies that we would expect to be necessary before full-blown culturally endorsed morality emerges, such as the capacity and willingness to judge the actions of others, a sense of justice, and primary responses to altruism and nastiness.
- Bloom concludes that this necessary moral apparatus is, in part, rooted in biological predispositions.
- These basic tendencies are necessary but not sufficient for moral systems of conduct to emerge.
- Fully developed morality also involves socialization, learned experience, and critical reflection.

The moral foundations of nonhuman animals

Some of the traits necessary for morality to develop are indeed also found in nonhuman animals, such as the great apes, dogs, elephants, dolphins, and whales. Animals provide a meaningful contrast to moral capacities, behaviors, and systems of conduct in humans. They enable us to understand the fundamental development of morality in humanity and to address the ultimate question from a phylogenetic perspective of where morality comes from?

There are hundreds of observations of animals engaging in helping behaviors in the media towards humans and each other. Consider the following report as an example. In June 2008, researchers in Ulsan, South Korea, spent a day following dolphins in the Sea of Japan. Late that morning, they noticed that around 12 dolphins were swimming very close together. Upon further inspection, they realized that one female dolphin was severely injured, wriggling, tipping from side to side, and turning upside down, as though her pectoral flippers were paralyzed. The small group of dolphins crowded around the injured female, diving beneath and supporting her from below. After about 30 minutes, the dolphins formed an impromptu raft: swimming side by side with the injured female on their backs, helping her to breathe and avoiding drowning. Eventually, the injured dolphin stopped breathing, and a handful of dolphins stayed touching the body until it sank out of sight.[4]

It is difficult not to be struck with emotion at this depiction of the group assisting their injured group member. However, most researchers who study nonhuman animals propose that they do not have morality in the human sense. In other words, other animals do not have a well-developed and reasoned sense of right and wrong as humans do. Instead, researchers propose that human morality incorporates a set of psychological tendencies and capacities that are older than our species. Historian of science, Michael Shermer, calls these tendencies and capacities premoral sentiments.

Shermer summarizes premoral sentiments that have been observed in nonhuman animals as the following:

> 'attachment and bonding, cooperation and mutual aid, sympathy and empathy, direct and indirect reciprocity, altruism and reciprocal altruism, conflict resolution and peacemaking, deception and deception detection, community concern and caring about what others think about you, and awareness of and response to the social rules of the group.[5]' This shopping list indeed points to the conclusion that the capacity for moral behavior is not uniquely human.

Many scientific studies also showcase the precursors to morality shared by humans and other mammals. For example, Capuchin monkeys display an understanding of fairness, refusing to cooperate when presented with unequal rewards for the same behaviors. This sense of fairness was famously demonstrated in an experiment by a primatologist, Frans de Waal, who has conducted extensive research on the moral capabilities of animals. In one study, two Capuchin monkeys were each housed in a self-contained cage, side-by-side, at de Waal's research facility.[6]

Both monkeys were trained to give a small token to a researcher through the bottom of the cage in exchange for a cucumber. On one occasion, however, the researcher changed the protocol and gave one monkey a grape, which is a preferred food, while the other monkey was still given a cucumber in exchange for the token. This new protocol was then repeated. Each time the researcher repeated the new protocol, the monkey with the cucumber, in witnessing his fellow monkey receive the delicious grape, became more agitated, grasping the bars in protest, looking to his fellow conspecific, and making a loud shrieking sound. In one trial, captured on video, the monkey who had only received the cucumber became so agitated that he forcefully threw the cucumber back at the experimenter in what appeared to be an act of protest.[7]

Notably, some of the traits necessary for morality to develop are found in our closest living relatives, chimpanzees, and bonobos. They share a common ancestor with humans who lived around 4–6 million years ago and can be viewed as the best available surrogate for this human ancestor and may offer us a glimpse into our evolutionary past. For instance, chimpanzees and bonobos will adopt and rear orphans as their offspring, and members of the group appear to mourn the death of elderly females.[8]

In addition to the similarity in human ancestral lineage, chimpanzees also mirror the social community size of early humans and are thus particularly apt for comparison to us. They live in groups that average around 50 individuals, which is likely to be similar to the size of early hunter-gatherer human groups in our ancestral history. Observational studies have showcased that chimpanzees often collaborate by forming political alliances, working with others to hunt as a team.[9] Chimpanzees also demonstrate reciprocity. For example, they are more likely to share meat following a hunt with individuals who previously groomed them.[10]

According to scholars such as Bloom, de Waal, and Shermer, religion does not make people moral. Drawing from hundreds of studies and observations, they argue that empathy, cooperation, and fairness are not distinctively human traits, nor are they the result of religious socialization in adults. Non-human animals and babies also demonstrate some of the untutored capacities that we would expect to find in moral beings, and so morality cannot come from religion. De Waal devotes an entire book, *The Bonobo and the Atheist: In Search of Humanism Amongst the Primates*,[11] to the argument that we do not get our morality from God. De Waal further argues that we do not even get our morality from careful philosophical reasoning about the conditions under which acts are good or bad, which are how some intellectual thinkers and new atheists propose that proper systems of morality emerge.

Most scholars in the evolutionary sciences concede that religion does not provide humans with an underlying moral system that they would not have otherwise had. Instead, it is more likely that religious prescriptions co-evolved as part of these tendencies that we already have, such as empathy and cooperative tendencies. In other words, religious dogma and philosophical thought piggybacked on what was already felt to be fundamentally right or wrong. This conclusion leads us full circle to the question of where morality comes from in the first place.

Key points

- Other animals do not have a well-developed and reasoned sense of right and wrong as humans do.
- However, non-human animals demonstrate some of the traits necessary for morality to develop, such as empathy, cooperation, and fairness.
- Premoral traits are not unique to humans and are not the result of religious teachings.

- Human morality incorporates a set of psychological tendencies and capacities that are older than our species.

The origins of morality

Scholars such as de Waal propose that the basic building blocks of morality, such as the fundamental sense of right and wrong, are felt in the bodies of babies and other mammals. As human adults, we often experience these kinds of bodily reactions to harm and suffering daily. Take, for example, the visceral response you may have in seeing a photograph of an abused child in a news report or watching an advertisement on television seeking donations to feed starving children in Africa. Many evolutionary scholars explicitly propose that morality emerged from the ancient roots of primate psychology, and they too endorse versions of the morality-as-cooperation theory.

Participation 1: The feeling of right and wrong

Close your eyes and imagine as vividly as you can a dog, child, or senior. If you choose someone you love, your reaction will be stronger, but you can use an image of a stranger. Once you have the image of them in your mind, imagine a teenage boy kicking them in the chest as hard as they can for no reason. Then open your eyes. How does your body feel? Is your heart pounding? Do you have sweaty palms? Has your breath become quicker than before? Did you grimace, clench your teeth, or feel a surge of adrenaline or a general feeling of unease? Whatever your reaction, it is unlikely that you would classify your response as making you feel "good." This general unpleasant feeling is what de Waal means when he says that our sense of right and wrong is felt in our bodies.

Popular authors and proponents of the view that morality is ultimately a product of our evolutionary history include de Waal, Shermer, and anthropologist Barbara King.[12] More specifically, these scholars view human decency as having grown out of primate sociality. Like many evolutionary scientists, they emphasize the benefits of group membership to humans and other social animals. Being part of a group enhances individual and group survival and provides more opportunities for reproduction than being alone. For example, groups are less vulnerable to attacks from outsiders than individuals and are more successful at finding food.

All social animals have had to modify or restrain behaviors for group living to be worthwhile. For instance, take social insects. Ant colonies can possess millions of individuals, and successful colonies include an ant sterile caste system, which significantly contributes to their success. Females serve the needs of the Queen, do not reproduce but instead raise their siblings. This system restricts competition for mating, which in turn facilitates cooperation, which is essential for the long-term survival of the colony.[13] On this account of morality, pre-moral sentiments such as empathy, sympathy, reciprocity, and altruism evolved as a means of restraining individual selfishness and building more cooperative groups, which ultimately led to the survival of the species.[14] This proclivity for parochialism helps to explain why babies display the strongest prosocial tendencies towards members of their kind, and non-human animals react strongest to behaviors that directly affect them.

Accounts that focus on primate sociality as the driver of moral sentiments may also explain why species differ in the degree to which they express them. Psychologist Michael Tomasello, who has spent much of his career studying the sociality of humans and animals, has proposed that humans are uniquely cooperative when compared to other animals because they are so dependent upon the group for survival. In short, he suggests that while many animals such as chimpanzees and bonobos are social and thus display some of the fundamental tendencies that underlie morality, humans are ultra-social and, therefore, best show the capacity for moral behavior.

Tomasello has conducted dozens of experiments that directly compare the cognitive and social abilities of both chimpanzees and human toddlers. His lab found that although toddlers and chimpanzees perform identically on physical tasks, like using a stick to retrieve food that is out of reach, they differ when it comes to the performance on social tasks, like learning how to solve a problem by imitating another person. In these social tasks, toddlers perform about twice as well as the apes. Children also out-perform chimpanzees in experiments where they have to work together to obtain a reward. Children are much more likely than their ape counterparts to collaborate with a partner.[15] Indeed, some of the earliest research with chimpanzees has shown that chimpanzees show no natural ability to work together. This reluctance occurs even when chimpanzees are trained to work together to obtain a reward.[16]

Tomasello pinpoints how, precisely, our evolutionary heritage contributed to this ultra-sociality in humans. He points to differences in the strategies for obtaining food when the two species diverged from their common ancestor around six million years ago as the key to understanding these fundamental differences. Chimpanzees, who eat mostly fruit, gather most food alone, whereas humans became collective foragers, working together to hunt big game when fruits and vegetables became scarce.

One effect of the need for humans to obtain food as a group was that they began to think of themselves as members of a larger unit whose members worked together for mutual gain. They were able to take the perspective of others and share intentions to reach shared goals. This ability gave rise to two components that are at the core of morality: sympathy, concern for other individuals, and fairness, the idea that everyone should get what he or she deserves. According to Tomasello, the enhanced ability to cooperate underpins the moral differences between humans and nonhumans. These arguments are versions of the "morality-as-cooperation" theory, which we visit in more detail later in the chapter.

In this section, we covered research suggesting that religion does not make people moral because the basic building blocks of morality are rooted in our evolutionary history as a social species. In other words, religion is not necessary for moral behavior. A more empirically grounded question is whether, and how, does religion impact ethical decision-making and behavior? For instance, does religiosity increase or decrease moral behavior? Scholars in the socio-cognitive sciences have proposed that when it comes to morality, there are both similarities and differences between how the religious and irreligious reason and act, and we cover this research in the next section.

Participation 2: Is morality possible without God?

Imagine that you have landed a new job as a journalist for an international religious newsletter. Your first assignment is to create a one-page article called "is morality possible without God?" Based on your background research of reading this chapter:

1 Prepare an outline of your article. Include 3–5 main points that you will make, evidence that you will draw upon, and your conclusion.
2 Write the one-page article. You can also include visuals such as quotes, pictures, or charts.
3 In groups of two offer feedback on another member's article. Consider questions such as: Did they present the material accurately? Did they misrepresent someone's work? Would ordinary religious people understand the claims they are making?
4 Revise your outlines to improve them based upon the feedback you received.

Key points

- Researchers propose that fully developed morality is ultimately a synthesis of the biological, cognitive, and the cultural, but that the basic apparatus for moral judgment and actions are found in our evolutionary heritage as social species.
- Morality-as-cooperation theory proposes that morality is a collection of biological and cultural solutions to the problems of cooperation, recurrent in human social life.
- Some scholars have proposed that religious dogma built upon what was already felt to be fundamentally right or wrong, which is why essential components of religious morality are similar.
- Religion is not necessary for morality, but different religions may encourage or enhance existing moralistic tendencies.

Summary of does religion make people moral?

- Research with babies and nonhuman animals have demonstrated that they possess basic underlying moralistic tendencies, even though they do not have a fully developed moral system of conduct like adult humans.
- The primary underlying moral apparatus in humans comes from their biological tendencies and cognitive-emotional reactions ultimately derived from their evolutionary heritage as a social species; many aspects of morality facilitated group living.
- Basic morality is not dependent upon cultural input, and it is possible to be moral without religious guidance. Thus, religion does not make people moral.
- Religious ethics are likely to have co-evolved with the development of moralistic tendencies in humans. Therefore, religious teachings about right and wrong share fundamental similarities.
- Moral guidelines derived from religious traditions play a role in developing and refining one's sense of right and wrong.

How does religion impact moral decision-making and behavior in contemporary society?

Holding questions about the ultimate origins of morality aside for now, another related question concerns how people reason in terms of what is right and wrong in contemporary society. Insights from moral philosophy and research in social psychology highlight the similarities and differences between theists and non-theists in the world today, and we review this research next. While a few studies have been conducted cross-culturally,[17] one limitation to keep in mind is that most research is in the modern western world. Comparisons between the two groups are divided into four key aspects in this section: (1) where people derive moral guidance, (2) what people care about, (3) whom people care about, and (4) why and when people act prosocially.

1 Metaethics: where people derive moral guidance

At the start of this chapter, we reviewed research suggesting that the fundamental building blocks of morality are part of our evolutionary heritage as a social species. Fundamental moral inclinations are deeply embedded in our evolved psychology and flourish naturally in the absence of religious indoctrination. As scholars such as Bloom have proposed, full-blown morality is ultimately a synthesis of the biological, cognitive, and cultural. Evolutionary processes and cognitive processing conspire to produce the fundamental building blocks of moral judgment. Yet fully developed morality is a combination of biological predispositions concerning aspects of human behavior, such as feeling the pain of others, and cultural traditions, including religious socialization. These predispositions conspire with early inclinations to shape our sense of what is right and wrong, along with learned experience and critical reflection. It is more likely that religious indoctrination concerning judgments of right and wrong co-evolved with these moral tendencies, emphasizing some rather than others, rather than contradicting them.

At the start of this chapter, we reviewed research suggesting that the fundamental building blocks of morality are part of our evolutionary heritage as a social species. Fundamental moral inclinations are deeply embedded in our evolved psychology and flourish naturally in the absence of religious indoctrination. As scholars such as Bloom have proposed, full-blown morality is ultimately a synthesis of the biological, cognitive, and cultural. In fundamental ways then, we would expect theists and non-theists to be morally similar. Indeed, this is the case. They seem to share core preferences for justice and compassion. For instance, all world religions agree on some basic principles regarding harm, and non-religious people tend to have similar ideas about harm and justice, such as the basic idea that torture or killing an innocent person is wrong. The philosopher Peter Singer points out the similarity in religious and non-religious dogma and philosophical writings, such as the notion of impartiality. This principle is found in many diverse religious and philosophical systems of morality from the golden rule in Christianity (i.e. do unto others as you would have done unto you) to the teachings of the renowned Chinese philosopher Confucius, and the political philosopher John Rawls's landmark theory of justice.

Nevertheless, theists and non-theists derive socialization and moral guidance from different sources, and in other ways, they differ. Most notably, theists and non-theists often use different criteria to determine which actions are immoral. The source of moral guidance and criteria used to establish moral judgment is commonly referred to as a metaethical style. Theists are often guided in their moral principles according to religious ethics, such as codes of conduct that are stipulated in holy books such as the Bible and Qur'an, oral and written traditions, and religious teachers. Many religious traditions have rules that reward obedience, such as the promise of seventy-two virgins in Islam. Many traditions also have punitive consequences for those who do not abide by and enforce religious codes of ethics, such as the Christian idea of the torment of hell.

Religious dogma tends to facilitate a type of rule-based objectivist morality, which stipulates that there is one right or wrong action, such as it is always wrong to commit adultery or kill. This rule-based objectivist morality is known in philosophy as deontological reasoning. Thus, religious people tend to believe that if two people differ on a moral issue, only one person can be right.[18] For believers, God is both the author of morality and the arbiter of justice. Thus, the sense of what is right is typically based on divine command, not only on consequences based on benefits or harm.[19] Although often religions share secular value frameworks, and as such, do consider things like the consequences of actions.

New atheists have claimed that this rule-based deontological style of reasoning based on ancient dogma deems religious ethics ill-equipped to determine moral values. They often draw upon the arguments of classic western thinkers such as Socrates who discussed the relationship between Greek gods and piety. The fundamental dilemma proposed is whether God's commandments are moral because he commands them or because they are moral. Whatever the answer, critics maintain that religion is an ineffective system to determine what is right. They point to problems with relativism, such as knowing which God is correct when two conflict in their moral stipulations.

There are also difficulties in interpreting scripture, such as making sense of moral commandments when they are taken out of cultural and historical context. For example, consider the custom of disgracing men with long hair in ancient Mediterranean cultures because it was a symbol of being subordinate to women (I Corinthians 11:14). Another primary criticism is that some moral commandments in religious texts seem to go against our most basic sensibilities. Consider the prescription to cut off the hand of a woman who seizes an attacker's genitals in defense of her husband (Deuteronomy 25:11–12),[20] or the advice for parents of a wayward son to bring him to the local elders to be stoned to death (Deuteronomy 21:18–21).

As the philosopher Ryan Falcioni summarizes it, on account of new atheists, religion is viewed as, at best, giving people bad reasons for doing good things, and at worst, bad reasons for doing bad things.[21] The late Christopher Hitchens, author of the book *God is Not Great: How Religion Poisons Everything*,[22] contends that there is no single act of moral goodness performed by a religious person that an irreligious person would not likewise perform, but without the reference to God. Hitchens, like Richard Dawkins, evolutionary biologist, and author of *The God Delusion*,[23] argues that religion motivates and justifies certain evils; it enables perpetrators to commit actions with a sense of righteousness that comes from assumed divine approval. According to these authors, religion adds justification to immoral acts.[24]

Theists are also less likely than non-theists to judge moral decisions as subjective or culturally relative, i.e. dependent upon context. This tendency is so strong that exposing most people to reminders of religion makes them perceive morality as more objective.[25] By contrast, the less religious people are, the more comfortable they are with ignoring abstract moral rules and basing decisions on consequences (consequentialism), especially based on principles of utilitarianism (the outcome that provides the most benefit to the largest number of people). The secular humanists herald consequentialism as a better system for determining what is right and wrong.

2 Moralizing spectrum: What people care about

Research in social psychology suggests that religious and non-religious people are guided in their moral decision-making by different values, and thus their moral concerns differ. Moral Foundations Theory (MFT), developed by the social psychologist Jon Haidt and colleagues,[26] is based on questionnaire data from thousands of people and explains how and why people differ in their moral decision-making across cultures and religious traditions. The gist of the theory is that our moral concerns can be divided up into five underlying values: (1) care-harm, (2) fairness, (3) in-group loyalty, (4) respect for authority, and (5) purity (i.e. the body is a temple and can be contaminated by thoughts and actions).

Haidt and colleagues propose that these values significantly influence but do not determine the types of moral systems that humans construct. Some cultures construct moral systems based on a few of these foundational values, such as the United States, which tends to focus narrowly on the first two individualizing moral foundations:[27] care and concern over harm and fairness. Other cultures use a broader array of values to determine their moral systems, such as in-group loyalty, respect for authority, and purity. Most people in western religious traditions endorse the first two foundational values: care and concern over harm, and fairness, in their moral decision-making. Yet, more religious people tend to moralize a broader range of actions beyond those about harm and injustice, including disobedience to authority, group disloyalty, and sexual impurity.[28] In short, the more religious a person is, the more likely they are to draw upon a broader spectrum of principles in their moral reasoning and to be moralistic.

Some scholars in CSR who favor of the morality-as-cooperation view have provided a critique of MFT theory. Anthropologist Oliver Curry points to both theoretical and empirical problems that he believes a fractionation method (discussed later in this chapter) can overcome.[29] First, MFT takes a cooperative approach to morality but it does not derive its domains from any underlying theory of cooperation. Thus, some domains that map onto cooperation, such as loyalty and authority, are likely to chart morality more reliably than others, such as care and purity. Second, the five foundations are too restrictive, and a seven-factor model based upon the recurrent problems of cooperation is the best available tool to map the moral landscape cross-culturally.[30] These include: helping kin, helping the group, reciprocating, being brave, deferring to superiors, dividing disputed resources, and respecting prior possession.

3 Moral discrimination: Whom people care about

Religions also tend to have value frameworks that serve to guide adherents in determining right and wrong. They include the Triple Gems of Jainism, Judaism's Halacha, Islam's Sharia, Catholicism's Canon Law, and Buddhism's Eightfold Path, among others.[31] Moral-based value systems increase in-group solidarity. They also increase the "otherness" of out-groups. As Jon Haidt observed, "morality binds and blinds,[32]" or as the saying goes, "one man's terrorist is another man's freedom fighter."

Social psychologist Azim Shariff has conducted many studies on the relationship between prosociality and religion. He explains the double-edged sword between in-group loyalty and religiously held values in particular, and he outlines how this effect is slightly different for theists and non-theists. Shariff draws on research demonstrating that theists direct their prosociality more parochially towards in-group members, whereas non-theists tend to be universal in scope. In other words, religious people tend to be more groupish at a local level. Theists are generally happier than non-theists because they feel part of a group, but they also actively, therefore, feel disconnected from the out-group.[33]

One line of reasoning explains why believers tend to be more discriminatory and why they are also more charitable to causes in their in-group, such as donating to their church. It is a two-sided coin. Theists tend to see those who share their religious views as one group, and atheists and those who do not share their beliefs as another out-group. Whereas non-theists, by contrast, tend to see one big universal constituency of people made up of lots of differences.

4 Moral motivation: Why and when people act prosocially

One important question concerns how religion changes people's behavior? In concrete terms, psychologists seek to determine whether religion increases prosociality, which is measured through aspects of behavior such as instances of generosity, cooperation, and honesty. Religious people report more prosocial behavior than non-religious people. A few surveys have supported these claims. Based on the number and amount of charitable donations made by religious folk.[34] Yet researchers have failed to confirm the effects of religiosity on prosocial behavior in controlled studies.

These experiments actually confirm that people say they are religious and suggest that religiosity increases the need for impression management. In other words, in these surveys, religious participants are engaging in socially desirable responding; they want to be perceived as more generous by others, and so they respond to these surveys as though they are. Other research provides a slightly different interpretation.[35] Believers do tend to be more charitable and prosocial than nonbelievers. However, much of this moral goodness is directed towards the religious in-group. These findings are hardly surprising given that religious values are powerful fuel for in-group solidarity.[36]

The motivation to demonstrate prosocial behaviors differs between theists and non-theists. Religious people are more charitable when primed with supernatural agent concepts, including God. This conclusion has been borne out by empirical results in hundreds of studies, obtained using experimental economic games, methods that allow for the exploration of decision-making in controlled social interactions involving opportunities for cooperation, punishment, trust, and generosity. For instance, in one series of studies, participants allocated more money to anonymous strangers when God concepts were implicitly activated than when neutral or no concepts were activated.[37]

One interpretation of this effect is that believers tend to be more vigilant of the fact that a social monitoring supernatural agent, like God, sees everything they do. Other research has shown that non-theists do not respond to these kinds of religious cues; they do not fret so much when they think that God could be watching them. Nonbelievers do, however, also demonstrate more prosocial behavior when they are primed with concepts relating to social institutions, such as the police and courts.[38] In other studies, experimenters found that even when participants were not consciously aware of eyespots, they donated more generously to anonymous strangers.[39]

Recent research has provided evidence that these supernatural priming effects extend to morally concerned non-agentic forces of karma. For instance, in one series of studies, participants from different religious and spiritual affiliations who believed in karma were more likely to share money with a stranger after thinking about karma than before. These effects were not found for participants

Figure 8.1 Watched people are nice people, even if they are not consciously aware that they feel they are being surveilled. For example, Buddha Eyes, also known as Wisdom Eyes, are painted on virtually every Buddhist shrine in Nepal. They are a reminder of the omniscience of a Buddha. (Image credit: filmlandscape/ Shutterstock.com).

who did not believe in karma.[40] These studies suggest that in addition to the fear of supernatural punishment, believers are also motivated to act prosocially to increase the likelihood of future good fortune.

Both religious and non-religious people are motivated to act prosocially by different social cues. For the religious, it is theistic cues of a watchful agent and even cues of karma.[41] For the irreligious, it is social institutions. All forms of social surveillance have the potential to punish wrongdoers, whether this is divine intervention, principles of supernatural justice, or an aspect of civil justice. Other research suggests that these effects only serve as a temporary increase in prosocial behavior, at the least, as long as the person thinks that he or she is under surveillance. This research may well explain the so-called "Sunday Effect" on people's behavior, such as less pornographic website traffic in religious metropolitan areas on Sundays.[42] Alternatively, even shorter duration, increased charitability among Marrakesh shopkeepers when the Muslim call to prayer (*adhan*) was audible but not when it was inaudible.[43] Likewise, secular institutions rely upon periodic reminders of justice, such as police presence and CCTV cameras, to ensure the civil obedience of citizens.[44]

Another intriguing finding is that non-religious people also view God as a kind of moral surveillance, keeping believers in check. So, disbelief in God signals a lack of monitoring.[45] For instance, believers in God are regarded by most as more moral and trustworthy than those who do not believe. A recent Pew survey found that the majority of respondents in almost 40 countries agreed that believing in God is essential to morality.[46] Rates of agreement were highest in Central Asia and West Africa, and the lowest in North America and Europe. However, even in the United States, where traditional religious affiliation has declined, the majority of people surveyed (53 percent) agreed that belief was necessary to be a good person.

Other polls suggest that theists are deeply mistrustful of atheists, and even atheists implicitly view theists as more trustworthy. For example, they see acts such as serial murder and incest as more representative of atheists than members of religious groups.[47] Furthermore, the religiously affiliated may view a particular religious affiliation as a precondition for morality. Believers are likely to trust only those who share their specific religious beliefs. Another recent survey by the Pew Research Centre found that half of Americans say that it is important for a President to share their religious beliefs.[48] It is by no accident that almost all U.S. presidents have been Christians, the dominant religion in the country.[49]

In sum, religion impacts moral decision-making in many important ways. Although theists and non-theists agree on some basic principles regarding harm and justice, they differ according to where they derive their moral guidance, their metaethical style of reasoning about morality, and what moral issues they care about. It is difficult to say with certainty whether theists are more prosocial than non-theists. Theists report higher levels of prosociality than nonbelievers, engage in more charitable behavior that tends to be directed towards other members of their religious group. Both religious and non-religious people are at least temporarily motivated to act prosocially based on the perception that they are being surveyed by a third party and can be punished for their behavior.

Key points

- Theists and non-theists share some core moral preferences such as justice and compassion.
- Theists and non-theists differ in key aspects of morality.
- Theists are more likely to employ deontological reasoning in their moral decision-making, apply a more extensive array of values such as respect for authority and purity in their morals, and act prosocially towards others who belong to their religious group—especially when they think that God is watching them.
- Non-theists are more likely to make moral decisions based on consequentialist principles, apply values concerning harm and fairness in moral decision-making, act prosocially towards other people—especially when they think that social institutions such as the police are monitoring them.

Case study: To what extent are religious beliefs responsible for Laney's actions?

Background

Questions about the role of religion in morality are apparent in legal debates over whether, and to what extent, beliefs influence those convicted of wrongdoing. On Mother's Day 2003, a Texas woman, Deanna Laney, stoned two of her children to death and seriously injured a third. She pleaded guilty by insanity to the killings of her sons; eight-year-old and six-year-old and causing severe injury to her 14-month-old.[50]

The Laney family were active members of the church community and Ms. Laney sang in the choir. A year earlier, she had told fellow churchgoers that the world was coming to an end and that God had told her to get her house in order. During the investigation, Laney explained to psychiatrists that she was driven to kill by a message from God and that they would rise again from the dead. In an interview, she said, "I felt like I obeyed God, and I believe there will be good out of this ... I feel like he will reveal his power, and they will be raised up. They will become alive again.[51]"

Laney said she understood God's will after watching one of her sons playing in her home. He turned to his mother and was holding a spear. After tripping over a stone in her garden, she said she understood that she was going to have to kill them by stoning. One doctor told the court that Laney had separated psychologically from the horror of her actions and felt that she was simply a woman on a divine mission carrying out the Lord's will.

Laney pleaded insanity in the killings. Five mental health experts were consulted on the case: two each by the prosecution and defense, and one by the judge. They concluded that she suffered from psychotic delusions and was unable to know right from wrong at the time of the killings.

Laney was committed to a State Hospital for eight years until her release in May 2012. She is subject to a list of conditions, including no unsupervised contact with minors and regular drug tests, to ensure that she takes the required medication.[52]

Assignment

- Imagine that you are the judge in this case. Based on the evidence above, and in your role as judge, write a one-page letter to the court, providing your decision on the four aspects of this case and justifying each response.

  1. Is Laney guilty of murder? (Yes/No/Unsure)
  2. Should she go to prison or be treated in a state hospital? (Yes/No/Unsure)
  3. To what extent do Laney's religious beliefs explain her actions? (5=Completely, 4=Very, 3=Unsure, 2=Somewhat, 1=Not at all).
  4. To what extent are Laney's religious beliefs responsible for her actions? (5=Completely, 4=Very, 3=Unsure, 2=Somewhat, 1=Not at all).

- Compare your justification for the rating in question 3 to another student who has answered differently and discuss your reasons.
- Compare your justification for the rating in question 4 to another student who has answered differently and discuss your reasons.

Part 3: Evolutionary-cognitive perspectives on the relationship between religion and morality

Researchers in the evolutionary cognitive sciences adopt a distinctive approach to questions about the relationship between religion and morality. For instance, cognitive scientists of religion often bypass the category of religion all together and instead carve up religious systems according to recurrent features across traditions, such as the notion of supernatural agency. These recurrent features are often part of the repertoire of evolved human tendencies, such as representing what another person is thinking (i.e. mentalizing), and modifying one's behavior in the presence of another agent.

Cognitive scientists of religion, therefore, tend not to discuss broad questions such as how religion impacts morality and instead focus on more specific issues such as the effect of thinking that a supernatural agent is monitoring a person on his/her behavior, and on the development of that society. Thus, another distinguishing feature of CSR is that researchers ask questions about the relationship between religion and morality at both the level of the individual and society. One consequence of the method of fractionating religion into recurrent features across traditions is that it showcases the fundamental building blocks of moral and religious systems, showcasing their natural foundations. Findings from CSR research usually point towards two broad conclusions, as outlined below.

1 Religion encourages prosocial behavior because it hinges upon our evolved tendencies

Components of religious systems are remarkably effective at ensuring that people follow the rules and cooperate, mainly because they are based upon natural tendencies that appear throughout our evolutionary history. For instance, social monitoring in religious traditions ensures compliance because they hinge upon our natural tendency to alter our behavior when we are monitored, especially when combined with the fear of punishment.

Religious systems also tap into intuitive ideas about immanent justice (covered in Chapter 5: The Nature of the World). For example, negative deeds are punished, and positive deeds are rewarded, even when there is no obvious causal link between the two.[53,54,55] These kinds of social monitors with the power to punish appear in many different forms throughout the world. For example, omnipotent agents such as the monotheistic God in Christian traditions;[56] the law of karma, adopted by the Vedic traditions of Hinduism, Buddhism, and Jainism;[57] and witchcraft.[58]

As we discussed in Chapter 3 (Research Questions), scholars in CSR disagree over the precise role of cultural evolution in the emergence and persistence of religious thinking and behavior. Crucially, the debate hinges upon the origins of the natural tendencies that make up religious systems. Specifically, whether they are by-products of cognitive machinery that evolved for reasons that have nothing to do with religion (e.g. agency detection device—ADD, encourages the detection of predators and prey). Or, whether religious ideas evolved because they became useful for individuals and groups in the course of cultural evolution (e.g. rituals enhance group solidarity).

Both adaptationist and by-product accounts have implications for the religion-morality debate. Common to both is a central role that cognitive biases and predispositions play in religious systems. There is a limited repertoire of psychological tendencies, shaped by our evolutionary history, which explains why many religious traditions have similar underlying components—including those that affect the endorsement of moral virtues and conformity. On the adaptationist account, however, the coexistence of recurrent features in moral and religious systems is driven by their benefits.

One example of an adaptationist account at the group-level is the theory of "Big Gods" described in the case study at the end of this chapter. This theory proposes that the cultural success of moralizing gods has been instrumental in ensuring the success of modern-day institutionalized religion. More specifically, ideas about powerful, all-knowing Gods is an important factor enabling the human transition from small-scale, kin-based groups to large-scale societies,[59] and it is also responsible for the stability of large-scale civilizations throughout history.

2 Religion is not the only route to behavior modification, but it is highly effective

While the effects associated with morality can be found in components that make up religious systems, religion is not unique at inducing these effects. For example, as we have previously discussed, the idea of a social monitoring agent, such as God, with the capacity to punish moral transgressions is effective at inducing compliance behavior in populations. Yet social monitoring in secular institutions, such as CCTV and the police, is another means of achieving this end.

Consider as a further illustration of the sharing of sacred values and participation in collective action in religious traditions. Sharing sacred values associated with a particular religion promotes in-group solidarity and derogation of perceived out-groups. Some primatologists have argued that moral behavior ultimately derived from the tendency of humans to be social. Specifically, collaboration and other prosocial tendencies enabled people to obtain benefits from group living. In other words, humans are inherently groupish. Thus, religious morality may well hinge upon the human tendency for parochialism.

One well-established finding is that moral-based values increase this propensity for in-group solidarity. The renowned sociologist Emile Durkheim noted this type of social cohesion in groups of people who believed in the same values and claimed that, especially when they acted together, there was a kind of "collective effervescence." Other research has suggested that groups performing synchronized actions are especially likely to feel bonded with one another.[60,61] It is therefore unsurprising that many religious traditions are replete with collective ritual actions entailing synchronized movements that enhance group cohesion.

Anthropologist Harvey Whitehouse proposes that certain kinds of rituals exploit the human tendency to benefit kin who share genetic relatedness preferentially. This tendency has evolved because it has clear evolutionary benefits, and humans are therefore attuned to recognize and preferentially treat others who are similar and share similar experiences. For instance, one reason why religious rituals serve to bond participants together is that they contain a range of kinship cues, such as similar costumes, headdresses, face paint, as well as similar movements that give rise to shared experiences.[62]

This groupishness and effervescence are not, of course, limited to groups who are affiliated by religious values. For example, Libyan revolutionaries justify fighting (which they perceive as morally righteous) because they regard their comrades as closer than brothers. This suggests that in addition to the effects of shared ritual action, the effect partly derives from an extension of evolved kinship systems to benefit family members.[63] Massive political rallies likewise maximize the effects of synchronized activity, which contributes to feelings of collective effervescence, such as the protests against the immigration ban in the U.S. during Trump's administration in 2017.

In sum, the components of religious systems exert effects on adherents, such as building solidarity, increasing out-group derogation, and modifying behaviors in response to potential supernatural punishment. Yet, these effects are not unique to religious systems and may be achieved through other means.

Key points

- CSR showcases the natural foundations of religious and moral systems.
- The CSR approach to studying the relationship between religion and morality is distinctive because it fractionates the category of religion into recurrent features, asks specific questions at measurable units of analyses, and investigates the effect of the relationship at the individual and societal level.
- Research on religion and morality in CSR points to two broad conclusions. First, religious systems and prosociality are underpinned by a limited number of predispositions and biases that can be traced back to our evolutionary history. Second, while religion is not the only means to ensure conformity, it is a highly effective means of behavior modification.

A new fractionation approach to religion and morality

Psychologist Ryan McKay and anthropologist Harvey Whitehouse propose a new approach to understanding the connection between religion and morality. Their work builds upon prior approaches in CSR by fractionating the category of religion (Chapter 2: Core Assumptions). They argue that morality must also be fractionated, and that prosociality—which is often used in social psychological studies as a proxy for morality—is an inadequate measure of morality.

McKay and Whitehouse's model involves two necessary procedures. First, the categories of religion and morality must be decomposed into theoretically grounded elements. Second, theorists ought to consider the complex interplay between cognition and culture in the development and expression of these elements. In short, researchers must first fractionate the categories of religion and morality and then establish connections between the components. These procedures are outlined in more detail below.

1 Researchers must fractionate the categories of religion and morality into theoretically grounded elements

We discussed how cognitive scientists of religion conceptualize religion in Chapter 2 (Core Assumptions). To recap, cognitive scientists of religion propose those general theories of what constitutes religion are unreliable and biased. Take the analogy of sport to help explain the fundamental problem they have with questions about religion. Imagine trying to answer the question of whether sport serves a particular function. It is true that in all cultures, people like to play and engage in exercise, but the differences in the configurations of these things across cultures are enormous. In some places, contests are competitive and draw in large crowds, in other places, they take the form of teams competing against one another, and in other places, the aim is for an individual to improve their physical skills. Where does sport begin and end?

As anthropologist Pascal Boyer puts it, the question is not worth pursuing, as it is a matter of terminology, not as a substantive understanding of what people do in these circumstances.[64] Likewise, asking whether religion makes one moral depends upon how one defines religion and morality. Since these are, like sport, not naturally occurring categories, they are defined based mainly on a person's viewpoint and experience, and in the modern west, what we consider as religious or moral most likely differs from how people in other parts of the world conceptualize these categories.

For these reasons above, cognitive scientists of religion take an alternative approach to study religion by fractionating religious systems into their constituent components. Key candidates to be explained are typically those that seem to recur across cultures, such as concepts of non-visible agents, punitive deities, continued consciousness in the afterlife, and ritualized behavior. The underlying assumption is that recurrent ideas and practices are underpinned by various psychological propensities that are reassembled in culturally contingent ways. For instance, ideas about places and people as having a purpose are based on the tendency for humans to engage in teleological reasoning. Assumptions that supernatural agents have minds are made possible by our capacity and inclination towards mentalizing agents generally.

McKay and Whitehouse have argued that we should study morality in much the same way CSR scholars research religion. Like religion, morality consists of many components. It can also mean different things to different people and labeling certain behaviors as moral or immoral may well depend upon judgments about the person, motivation, and situation. Scholars seem to circumvent the definitional problems of studying morality by investigating prosociality. Yet McKay and Whitehouse find this term equally unsatisfactory in its current usage. The standard social psychological usage focuses on pleasant, neighborly aspects of behavior such as generosity and trust. By contrast, evolutionary scholars tend to use the term prosociality to mean behavior that furthers the interests of a particular group (whether or not this disadvantages another group). Yet scholars are seldom explicit about what, precisely, their use of the term prosociality designates.

The lack of upfront conceptualizations is especially problematic because depending on which definition is used, the same behavior can be labeled either prosocial or not. For instance, murder and even genocide can be viewed as prosocial according to the evolutionary conceptualization of the term because they facilitate success in intergroup competition. Even more importantly, the term has implications for testing theories of religion and morality. For instance, harming an out-group member may be labeled as either prosocial or immoral and used to provide evidence for or against the hypothesis that religion enhances prosociality.

At the core of this new approach is the assumption that religion and morality are not unitary things, but rather, are multifaceted.[65] McKay and Whitehouse propose to fractionate both religion and morality in an attempt to understand the relationship between the two better. Unlike most other researchers, they do not assume that the relationship between religion and morality is unidirectional. Instead, they consider worthy of scholarship questions about which features of religion influence the expression of human virtues, and how moral representations amplify and constrain the activation of religious intuitions.

McKay and Whitehouse point out that the fractionation approach they propose works only when the elements are theoretically grounded in levels that account for the influence of both cognition and culture. They criticize other scholars for operationalizing religion or morality as purely psychological systems or cultural notions. For instance, recall the work of researchers such as Bloom and de Waal, who have investigated the precursors to morality in babies and other primates. These researchers have concluded that religion is not necessary for morality. Yet, they assume that morality is located in a set of evolved psychological mechanisms, for example, recall the discussions earlier in the chapter about the biological predispositions that underpin morality, such as feelings of empathy. Further, the same authors operationalize religion as a set of cultural notions; they do not seek out the potential psychological foundations. Work in CSR has demonstrated that although religion is culturally learned, to grasp such cultural concepts and transmit them to others is rooted in early emerging cognitive capacities and preferences.

On McKay and Whitehouse's account, the formation of religious and moral traits is a product of both cognitive-developmental and socio-historical processes. For instance, the capacity to empathize with others' pain may be located in the neural structures of infants' brains. However, environmental cues help shape these structures and culturally distributed norms about what is the right course of action in certain circumstances that affect their expression. Processes at each of these levels influence the nature and targets of empathy in society, influencing people's willingness to tolerate harming behaviors such as warfare and enslavement, for example. The same combination of cognition and culture is also valid for religious concepts. For example, the genetic capacity to process information about mental events may undergird developmental pathways for mind-body dualism. However, this tendency is also shaped and constrained by cultural concepts and their histories, such as notions of bodiless agents.

2 Establish connections between theoretically grounded elements of religion and morality

McKay and Whitehouse propose that understanding the relationship between religion and morality requires first unpacking these levels of influence for each concept and second specifying the levels at which the impact is hypothesized to occur. For instance, asking the question of how notions of bodiless agents impact the development of empathy at each level of explanation? Like others, such as Haidt, they propose a limited number of moral values based upon our evolutionary history.

McKay and Whitehouse also consider whether and how religions have selectively favored moral values of various kinds, and whether and how the evolutionary histories of religion and morality are related. For example, fairness is a good candidate as an element of morality in cultural systems because it can be tracked to concerns in our evolutionary past. Evolutionary psychologist Nicolas Baumard and colleagues have convincingly argued that the preference for fairness evolved to ensure mutually advantageous cooperative interactions in our ancestral past.[66]

McKay and Whitehouse propose that they can begin to ask whether, for example, there is a biologically evolved connection between a preference for fairness—regarded commonly as a moral virtue—and mentalizing capacities (a component of reasoning about supernatural agents). Research in CSR already suggests that the evolution of mentalizing abilities would have magnified the costs of violating norms of fairness. Being able to represent a supernatural agent as having a mind but being physically absent meant that one could also represent a third-party monitor to report one's cheating behavior.[67] McKay and Whitehouse have argued that these methods will provide the basis for more precise questions and answers to questions about the relationship between religion and morality and encourage future researchers to adopt them.

To recap, the theory of morality-as-cooperation proposes that morality consists of a collection of biological and cultural solutions to the problems of cooperation recurrent in human social life. We have come across versions of this theory earlier in the chapter, espoused by primatologists, developmental psychologists, and popular writers. CSR is distinctive, however, because researchers here have identified distinct problems of cooperation and their solutions, and they have formulated and tested predictions cross-culturally.

To date, this approach has proven fruitful and has provided data to support the theory of morality-as-cooperation. For instance, one research team at the University of Oxford, led by Dr. Oliver Curry, fractionated morality into seven specific forms of cooperative behavior. These included: helping kin, helping the group, reciprocating, being brave, deferring to superiors, dividing disputed resources, and respecting prior possession. The researchers predicted that these

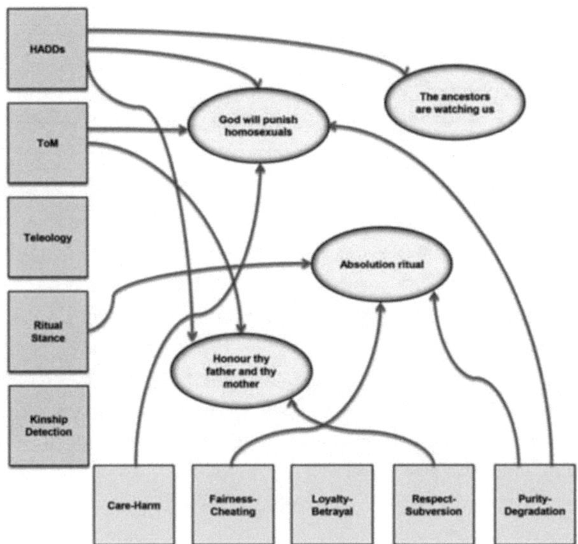

Figure 8.2 Whitehouse and McKay suggested breaking down claims about what constitutes morality into its components (e.g. as specified by Moral Foundations Theory, MFT) and religion and then ask if manifestations of religious constructs in different cultures actually combined those fractionated elements in various ways? For example, the proposition that "God will punish sinners" may evoke concerns over care and harm and resonate with intuitions. These may include events caused by agents in the environment (HADD) who have the ability to think (ToM). The relations depicted here are intended to be illustrative rather than exhaustive.[68]

seven cooperative behaviors would be considered morally good cross-culturally. Across 60 societies, they found that the moral valence of these behaviors was uniformly positive. This provides some evidence that the selected seven cooperative behaviors are plausible candidates for universal moral rules, and that morality-as-cooperation could provide a robust theory of morality across disciplines.[69] Researchers in the social-cognitive sciences continue to test the hypothesized relationships between religion and morality.[70]

Participation 3: The fractionation method

Chapter 2 (Core Assumptions) provides illustrations and examples of the fractionation approach to religion in CSR. Based on this chapter:

1 Provide a brief summary of how CSR researchers fractionate religion and morality.
2 Explain (in a few sentences for each) how this fractionation method enriches the understanding of religion and morality.

Key points

- McKay and Whitehouse criticize previous research on the relationship between religion and morality. For example, previous research assumes that religion and morality are unitary categories, fail to consider the role of cognition and culture in their expression and development, and investigates only the effect of religion on morality (and not vice-versa).
- McKay and Whitehouse propose a new approach to studying the relationship between religion and morality that has two steps.
- First, the categories of religion and morality are fractionated into theoretically grounded elements.
- Second, we can ask whether religious traditions found around the world produce constructs that connect these fractionated elements of religion and morality in various ways. This would allow scholars to establish whether and how the fractionated elements of religion and morality are or are not related.

Summary of how does religion impact moral decision-making and behavior?

- Members of the public assume that morality requires religion, and new atheists argue that religion is an obstacle to morality.
- The science of ethics movement proposes that science is the only way to determine what is right from wrong, but it has been met with skepticism from the broader scientific community.
- Research in social psychology has demonstrated that the relationship between religion and moral decision-making is more complicated than either the public or new atheists depict.
- There are both core similarities and important differences in how atheists and theists tend to reason about morality.
- Research in the cognitive science of religion showcases the natural foundations of these core similarities as rooted in our cognitive makeup and psychological heritage as group members.
- CSR scholars propose that a more sophisticated way to examine the relationship between religion and morality is to compare their elements and evolutionary history for possible connections and overlap.

Research case study: Religion as surveillance and moral enforcement

The basic observation that religion produces morally obedient citizens has been long advanced by scholars who are either proponents for or against religion, such as Voltaire and Marx, and those who have sought to understand the primary social functions of religion, such as Evans-Pritchard. Social psychologist Ara Norenzayan and colleagues draw upon experimental and cross-cultural data. They propose that powerful, omniscient interventionist deities are concerned with regulating the moral behavior of humans, for example, as found in monotheistic and polytheistic religions, which are a critical factor among several in the scaling up of cooperation in large-scale societies.

Norenzayan presents the following two observations and a connection between the two in the form of an argument. The first observation concerns the rapid rise in large-scale anonymous societies. For most of human history, people lived in small bands of foragers, yet today most humans live in large-scale anonymous societies. This change happened rapidly and recently, over the past 12,000 years. Even though humans and primates tend to cooperate with small groups, large-scale cooperation is unique to humans. Humans that cooperate often reap many more benefits than those who do not.

As an illustration, think for a moment of the many benefits to you by being a member of modern-day society. Nevertheless, such large-scale cooperation is also tricky without surveillance since cooperation relies to no small extent on trust, and not all people are trustworthy. As another simple illustration, consider any group project that you have been involved in, there always tend to be students who do not contribute much but get the same grade, aka social loafers. One way to monitor what people are doing and to ensure compliance with rules is through social surveillance, such as courts and police. Yet, these have developed somewhat recently and only for some places, especially more prosperous nations, although the administration of justice is also deemed unreliable and ineffective by many.

The second observation concerns the rise in moralizing gods. Throughout human history, in small-scale societies, gods, and other supernatural agents tended to have limited powers and limited moral concern. They demanded the right practice in behaviors, such as burial rites and sacrifice, but people represented these behaviors as linked to the selfish intention of the agents. Supernatural agents such as gods cared little about how people treated each other and mostly about how they were treated. Yet paralleling the rise in large-scale societies was the rise in so-called "Big Gods," omnipotent moralizing agents with the power to punish moral wrongdoers. Big Gods spread so successfully that the vast majority of the world's believers belong to religions with such gods.

The central argument proposed by Norenzayan and colleagues is that the spread of prosocial religions (i.e. religions that come with moral stipulations and consequences) over the last twelve millennia has been an important shaper of large-scale societies, characterized by cooperation and moral obedience among massive anonymous groups. As Norenzayan puts it, "watched people are nice people," and a range of naturalistic and lab experiments have demonstrated that the expectation of monitoring and accountability increases prosocial tendencies.[71] Although why we have these tendencies in the first place is another issue.

One compelling explanation is by evolutionary biologist Dominic Johnson, who argues that fear of supernatural punishment, like other forms of punishment, is not an accidental by-product of other evolved mechanisms but is, in fact, adaptive and has been favored by evolution for this reason.[72] Research has also demonstrated that people in societies, and societies, with Gods that are more moralizing, are even more cooperative.[73,74]

Norenzayan and colleagues are not proposing that religion, or even Big Gods, is necessary for abidance to rules and, more specifically, large-scale cooperation among strangers. Instead, they are proposing that Big Gods are a very efficient and successful means to achieve this. As we already mentioned, secular societies function well without religion as a source of moral authority and enforcement. However, they tend to rely on other forms of social policing (i.e. threats and reminders of law-enforcement). Of course, while Big Gods may be exceptionally efficient at inducing cooperation, religion has been (and in many parts of the world, still is) associated with morality in ways that ensure obedience to a set of rules as well as justifying punishment for wrongdoers.

Some scholars provide critiques and alternative accounts of the relationship between the rise of Big Gods and the parallel rise in large-scale societies as mainly due to the social monitoring effect of deities. Some have questioned the conceptual clarity of arguments based on divine punishment.[75] Others contend that the cultural prevalence of moralizing God concepts does not result from the fact that they promote cohesive behaviors among groups. For example, evolutionary psychologist Nicholas Baumard and colleagues propose that other features of the representation of god concepts make them memorable and transmissible. Such as applying the fairness or proportionality bias, the tendency to represent our actions and consequences as having proportionate consequences, to invisible agents. Baumard and colleagues also contend that the Big God's account underestimates the role of increased affluence in facilitating large-scale moralizing religions.[76] As we discuss in Chapter 10 (Rituals, Part 2), anthropologist Harvey Whitehouse and colleagues have argued that ritual practices were more important than the belief in moralizing gods to the initial rise of social complexity.[77] Norenzayan and colleagues have rebutted these claims, proposing that differences in how the data were prepared resulted in Whitehouse and colleagues' findings,[78] and so, the debate continues.

Questions

1 In your own words, summarize the claims the researchers are making.
2 What do you think demarks this research as typical of the CSR approach to religion?

3 Do you agree or disagree with the claims the author is making and the critiques?
4 What do you think are the real-world implications of this theory on debates about religion and morality?

Further reading

1 Norenzayan, Ara. *Big gods: How religion transformed cooperation and conflict*. Princeton University Press, 2013.
2 Norenzayan, Ara, Azim F. Shariff, Will M. Gervais, Aiyana K. Willard, Rita A. McNamara, Edward Slingerland, and Joseph Henrich. "The cultural evolution of prosocial religions." *Behavioral and Brain Sciences* 39 (2016).
3 Purzycki, Benjamin Grant, Coren Apicella, Quentin D. Atkinson, Emma Cohen, Rita Anne McNamara, Aiyana K. Willard, Dimitris Xygalatas, Ara Norenzayan, and Joseph Henrich. "Moralistic gods, supernatural punishment, and the expansion of human sociality." *Nature* 530, no. 7590 (2016): 327.

Chapter summary

The general public certainly assumes that religion makes people moral, and new atheists have argued that religion is likely to make people justify immoral actions. Yet, research in the social cognitive sciences presents a more empirically grounded, nuanced, and balanced picture of the relationship between religion and morality. Religious and irreligious people do tend to derive their morality from different sources, and they also tend to use different criteria to decide which actions are moral. Theists tend to view moral laws as derived from divine command. They also tend to be moral objectivists, reasoning that when two people argue about a position, only one person can be correct. By contrast, non-theists are subjective or culturally relative. They are more willing to base judgments on utilitarian thinking – less likely to consider whether a transgression would optimize welfare for the highest number of people but rather to look at principles to determine whether they are right or wrong rather than consequences. This finding has led some—such as secular humanists—to argue that weighing up the costs and benefits of such topics as abortion, war, world hunger, is a better moral system than just relying on principles.

Researchers in CSR have demonstrated that although there are significant differences, people who are religious and non-religious share a fundamental moral foundation concerning harm and fairness, a foundation that may well have predated religious doctrine and intellectualization. Humans and other mammals share basic moral apparatus, and the underlying sense of right and wrong may well have evolved from our history as a social species. Cognitive scientists of religion have also demonstrated that while religion is not necessary for morality, it is an effective behavior-modifying system whether religion is expressed as a powerful deity, principle of cause and effect, or the essence of witchcraft because ultimately watched people are nice people.

One question often asked is whether religion makes people moral? In other words, is religion necessary for morality? Research with babies and non-human animals has demonstrated that empirically it is possible to be moral without God. This research converges on the idea that fully developed morality is ultimately a synthesis of the biological, cognitive, and cultural. In other words, what we commonly think of as morality is ultimately a combination of biological predispositions, thoughtful considerations about things like the consequences of people's behaviors, and cultural norms—including socialization into religious traditions that stipulate what is right and wrong. On this account, moral guidelines derived from religious traditions play a role in judgments concerning right and wrong. However, the necessary underlying apparatus for morality is a concoction of biological, cognitive, and emotional tendencies derived from our evolutionary heritage. Elements of this concoction are thus part of early emerging tendencies in young children and non-human animals. Morality is therefore not dependent upon religiosity, nor is it even dependent upon cultural input, language, or even being human.

Discussion questions

1 Which view of morality do you most agree with? Why?
2 Do you think that atheists and theists are more alike, or different, on their views on morality?
3 What is the main contribution of CSR to the study of religion and morality?

Selected further reading

Articles

1 McKay, Ryan, and Harvey Whitehouse. "Religion and morality." *Psychological Bulletin* 141, no. 2 (2015): 447.
2 Norenzayan, Ara. "Does religion make people moral?" *Behaviour* 151, no. 2–3 (2014): 365–384.
3 Curry, Oliver Scott. What's Wrong with Moral Foundations Theory, and How to get Moral Psychology Right available at https://behavioralscientist.org/whats-wrong-with-moral-foundations-theory-and-how-to-get-moral-psychology-right/.

Books

1 Johnson, Dominic. *God is watching you: How the fear of God makes us human.* USA: Oxford University Press, 2016.

Notes

1 For a summary of some of these debates see Norenzayan, Ara. "Does religion make people moral?" *Behaviour* 151, no. 2–3 (2014): 365–384.
2 Plato. Euthyphro. Originally published c. 395 BCE.
3 Bloom, Paul. *Just babies: The origins of good and evil.* Broadway Books, 2013. A summary of some of this research is also here: www.nytimes.com/2010/05/09/magazine/09babies-t.html.
4 www.newscientist.com/article/dn23108-dolphins-form-life-raft-to-help-dying-friend/.
5 Shermer, Michael, and Dennis McFarland. *The science of good and evil: Why people cheat, gossip, care, share, and follow the golden rule.* Macmillan, 2004, 31.
6 See the paper: Brosnan, Sarah F., and Frans BM De Waal. "Monkeys reject unequal pay." *Nature* 425, no. 6955 (2003): 297, and the full talk https://www.npr.org/2014/08/15/338936897/do-animals-have-morals.
7 See here: www.youtube.com/watch?v=lKhAd0Tyny0.
8 De Waal, Frans, and Frans B.M. Waal. *The Bonobo and the atheist: In search of humanism among the primates.* W.W. Norton & Company, 2013.
9 Boesch, Christophe. "Cooperative hunting roles among Tai chimpanzees." *Human Nature* 13, no. 1 (2002): 27–46.
10 Hockings, Kimberley J., Tatyana Humle, James R. Anderson, Dora Biro, Claudia Sousa, Gaku Ohashi, and Tetsuro Matsuzawa. "Chimpanzees share forbidden fruit." *PLoS One* 2, no. 9 (2007): e886.
11 Waal, Frans B.M. *The Bonobo and the atheist: In search of humanism among the primates.* W.W. Norton & Company, 2013.
12 King, Barbara J. *Evolving God: A provocative view on the origins of religion.* University of Chicago Press, 2017.
13 Hölldobler, Bert, and Edward O. Wilson. *Journey to the ants: A story of scientific exploration.* Harvard University Press, 1994.
14 For further reading on this topic, see: De Waal, Frans. *Primates and philosophers: How morality evolved.* Princeton University Press, 2009; Hauser, Marc. *Moral minds: How nature designed our universal sense of right and wrong.* Ecco/HarperCollins Publishers, 2006; Tomasello, Michael. *A natural history of human morality.* Harvard University Press, 2016.
15 Herrmann, Esther, Josep Call, María Victoria Hernández-Lloreda, Brian Hare, and Michael Tomasello. "Humans have evolved specialized skills of social cognition: The cultural intelligence hypothesis." *Science* 317, no. 5843 (2007): 1360–1366.
16 Crawford, Meredith P. "The cooperative solving of problems by young chimpanzees." *Comparative Psychology Monographs* 14 (1937): 1–88.
17 E.g. Awad, Edmond, Sohan Dsouza, Azim Shariff, Iyad Rahwan, and Jean-François Bonnefon. "Universals and variations in moral decisions made in 42 countries by 70,000 participants." *Proceedings of the National Academy of Sciences* 117, no. 5 (2020): 2332–2337.
18 Piazza, Jared, and Justin F. Landy. "'Lean not on your own understanding': Belief that morality is founded on divine authority and non-utilitarian moral judgments." *Judgment and Decision Making* 8, no. 6 (2013): 639.
19 Piazza, Jared, and Paulo Sousa. "Religiosity, political orientation, and consequentialist moral thinking." *Social Psychological and Personality Science* 5, no. 3 (2014): 334–342.
20 See Falcioni pages 311–315, for a more detailed treatment of these arguments. (incomplete ref) Ch. 17 Ryan Falcioni edited volume (Phil Zuckerman) *Beyond Religion.*
21 (incomplete ref) Ch. 17 Ryan Falcioni edited volume (Phil Zuckerman) *Beyond Religion.*

22 Hitchens, Christopher. *God is not great: How religion poisons everything*. McClelland & Stewart, 2008.
23 Dawkins, Richard. *The god delusion*. Random House, 2016.
24 See the discussion with Dawkins, www.youtube.com/watch?time_continue=1630&v=nZp_cA60bN4.
25 Yilmaz, Onurcan, and Hasan G. Bahcekapili. "Without God, everything is permitted? The reciprocal influence of religious and meta-ethical beliefs." *Journal of Experimental Social Psychology* 58 (2015): 95–100.
26 For a summary of the theory, see Graham, Jesse, Jonathan Haidt, Sena Koleva, Matt Motyl, Ravi Iyer, Sean P. Wojcik, and Peter H. Ditto. "Moral foundations theory: The pragmatic validity of moral pluralism." In *Advances in Experimental Social Psychology* 47. Academic Press, 2013, 55–130.
27 Henrich, J., Heine, S.J., & Norenzayan, A. (2010). The weirdest people in the world? *Behavioral and Brain Sciences* 33, 61–83.
28 For a summary of this research, see Shariff, Azim F., Jared Piazza, and Stephanie R. Kramer. "Morality and the religious mind: Why theists and nontheists differ." *Trends in Cognitive Sciences* 18, no. 9 (2014): 439–441.
29 https://behavioralscientist.org/whats-wrong-with-moral-foundations-theory-and-how-to-get-moral-psychology-right/.
30 Curry, Oliver Scott, Matthew Jones Chesters, and Caspar J. Van Lissa. "Mapping morality with a compass: Testing the theory of 'morality-as-cooperation' with a new questionnaire." *Journal of Research in Personality* 78 (2019): 106–124.
31 Esptein, Greg M. *Good without God: What a billion nonreligious people do believe*. New York: HarperCollins, 2010, 117.
32 Haidt, Jonathan. "Moral psychology for the twenty-first century." *Journal of Moral Education* 42, no. 3 (2013): 281–297.
33 For a summary of this research, see Shariff, Azim F. "Does religion increase moral behavior?." *Current Opinion in Psychology* 6 (2015): 108–113.
34 Brooks, Arthur C. *Who really cares: The surprising truth about compassionate conservatism-America's charity divide-who gives, who doesn't, and why it matters*. Basic Books (AZ), 2007.
35 Sedikides, Constantine, and Jochen E. Gebauer. "Religiosity as self-enhancement: A meta-analysis of the relation between socially desirable responding and religiosity." *Personality and Social Psychology Review* 14, no. 1 (2010): 17–36.
36 Galen, Luke W. "Does religious belief promote prosociality? A critical examination." *Psychological Bulletin* 138, no. 5 (2012): 876.
37 Shariff, Azim F., and Ara Norenzayan. "God is watching you: Priming God concepts increases prosocial behavior in an anonymous economic game." *Psychological Science* 18, no. 9 (2007): 803–809.
38 Shariff, Azim F., and Ara Norenzayan. "God is watching you: Priming God concepts increases prosocial behavior in an anonymous economic game." *Psychological Science* 18, no. 9 (2007): 803–809.
39 Haley, Kevin J., and Daniel M.T. Fessler. "Nobody's watching?: Subtle cues affect generosity in an anonymous economic game." *Evolution and Human Behavior* 26, no. 3 (2005): 245–256.
40 White, Cindel J.M., John Michael Kelly, Azim F. Shariff, and Ara Norenzayan. "Supernatural norm enforcement: Thinking about karma and God reduces selfishness among believers." *Journal of Experimental Social Psychology* 84 (2019): 103797.
41 White, Cindel J.M., John Michael Kelly, Azim F. Shariff, and Ara Norenzayan. "Supernatural norm enforcement: Thinking about karma and God reduces selfishness among believers." *Journal of Experimental Social Psychology* 84 (2019): 103797.
42 Edelman, Benjamin. "Markets: Red light states: Who buys online adult entertainment?." *Journal of Economic Perspectives* 23, no. 1 (2009): 209–20.

43 Duhaime, Erik P. "Is the call to prayer a call to cooperate? A field experiment on the impact of religious salience on prosocial behavior." *Judgment and Decision Making* 10, no. 6 (2015): 593.
44 For example, see Pinker, Steven. *The better angels of our nature: The decline of violence in history and its causes*. Penguin UK, 2011.
45 Gervais, W.M., Shariff, A. F., and Norenzayan, A. (2011). "Do you believe in atheists? Distrust is central to anti-atheist prejudice." *Journal of Personality and Social Psychology* 101, No. 6, 1189–1206.
46 www.pewglobal.org/2014/03/13/worldwide-many-see-belief-in-god-as-essential-to-morality/.
47 Gervais, Will M. "Everything is permitted? People intuitively judge immorality as representative of atheists." *PloS One* 9, no. 4 (2014): e92302.
48 www.pewforum.org/2016/01/27/3-religion-in-public-life/.
49 www.pewresearch.org/fact-tank/2017/01/20/almost-all-presidents-have-been-christians/.
50 Retrieved Feb 2nd, 2020 from https://en.wikipedia.org/wiki/Deanna_Laney_murders#cite_note-Secrets-1.
51 Retrieved Feb 2nd, 2020 from www.independent.co.uk/news/world/americas/god-told-me-to-kill-boys-says-mother-54427.html.
52 Retrieved Feb 2, 2020 from https://www.kltv.com/story/18620253/deanna-laney-out-of-mental-institution/.
53 Baumard, Nicolas, and Coralie Chevallier. "What goes around comes around: The evolutionary roots of the belief in immanent justice." *Journal of Cognition and Culture* 12, no. 1–2 (2012): 67–80.
54 Jessica incomplete reference: White, Claire, Paulo Sousa, and Karolina Prochownik. "Explaining the Success of Karmic Religions."
55 White, Cindel, Adam Baimel, and Ara Norenzayan. "What are the causes and consequences of belief in karma?" *Religion, Brain & Behavior* 7, no. 4 (2017): 339–342; White, C.J.M., and Norenzayan, A. (2019). "Belief in karma: How cultural evolution, cognition, and motivations shape belief in supernatural justice." In J. M. Olson ed. *Advances in Experimental Social Psychology* 60: 1–63. doi:10.1016/bs.aesp.2019.03.001.
56 Norenzayan, Ara, Azim F. Shariff, Will M. Gervais, Aiyana K. Willard, Rita A. McNamara, Edward Slingerland, and Joseph Henrich. "The cultural evolution of prosocial religions." *Behavioral and brain sciences* 39 (2016).
57 White, Cindel, Adam Baimel, and Ara Norenzayan. "What are the causes and consequences of belief in karma?" *Religion, Brain & Behavior* 7, no. 4 (2017): 339–342.
58 Evans-Pritchard, Edward E. *Witchcraft, oracles and magic among the Azande*. Vol. 12. London: Oxford, 1937; Parren, Nora. "The (possible) cognitive naturalness of witchcraft beliefs: An exploration of the existing literature." *Journal of Cognition and Culture* 17, no. 5 (2017): 396–418.
59 Norenzayan, Ara, Azim F. Shariff, Will M. Gervais, Aiyana K. Willard, Rita A. McNamara, Edward Slingerland, and Joseph Henrich. "The cultural evolution of prosocial religions." *Behavioral and Brain Sciences* 39 (2016).
60 Lang, Martin, Daniel J. Shaw, Paul Reddish, Sebastian Wallot, Panagiotis Mitkidis, and Dimitris Xygalatas. "Lost in the rhythm: effects of rhythm on subsequent interpersonal coordination." *Cognitive Science* 40, no. 7 (2016): 1797–1815.
61 Miles, Lynden K., Louise K. Nind, and C. Neil Macrae. "The rhythm of rapport: Interpersonal synchrony and social perception." *Journal of Experimental Social Psychology* 45, no. 3 (2009): 585–589.
62 Saroglou, Vassilis. "Believing, bonding, behaving, and belonging: The big four religious dimensions and cultural variation." *Journal of Cross-Cultural Psychology* 42, no. 8 (2011): 1320–1340.

63 Whitehouse, Harvey, Brian McQuinn, Michael Buhrmester, and William B. Swann. "Brothers in Arms: Libyan revolutionaries bond like family." *Proceedings of the National Academy of Sciences* 111, no. 50 (2014): 17783–17785.
64 Boyer, Pascal. "Minds make societies: How cognition explains the world humans create." London: Yale University Press.
65 McKay, Ryan, and Harvey Whitehouse. "Religion and morality." *Psychological Bulletin* 141, no. 2 (2015): 447.
66 Baumard, Nicolas, Jean-Baptiste André, and Dan Sperber. "A mutualistic approach to morality: The evolution of fairness by partner choice." *Behavioral and Brain Sciences* 36, no. 1 (2013): 59–78.
67 Johnson, Dominic, and Jesse Bering. "Hand of God, mind of man: Punishment and cognition in the evolution of cooperation." *Evolutionary Psychology* 4, no. 1 (2006).
68 Taken from: McKay, Ryan, and Harvey Whitehouse. "Religion and Morality." *Psychological Bulletin* 141, no. 2 (2015): 447–473, with permission.
69 Curry, O. H., D. Mullins and Whitehouse, H. "Is it good to cooperate? Testing the theory of morality-as-cooperation in 60 societies." *Current Anthropology* 60, no. 1 (2019).
70 Personal communication with Harvey Whitehouse 11 August 2020.
71 See the summary on page 372. Norenzayan, Ara. "Does religion make people moral?" *Behaviour* 151, no. 2–3 (2014): 365–384.
72 Johnson, Dominic. *God is watching you: How the fear of God makes us human*. USA: Oxford University Press, 2016.
73 Johnson, Dominic DP. "God's punishment and public goods." *Human Nature* 16, no. 4 (2005): 410–446.
74 Purzycki, Benjamin Grant, Coren Apicella, Quentin D. Atkinson, Emma Cohen, Rita Anne McNamara, Aiyana K. Willard, Dimitris Xygalatas, Ara Norenzayan, and Joseph Henrich. "Moralistic gods, supernatural punishment, and the expansion of human sociality." *Nature* 530, no. 7590 (2016): 327.
75 Schloss, Jeff, and Murray, Michael. "Evolutionary Accounts of Belief in Supernatural Punishment: A Critical Review." *Religion, Brain & Behavior* 1, no. 1, (2011): 46–99.
76 Baumard, N., Hyafil, A., Morris, I. & Boyer, P. (2015) Increased affluence explains the emergence of ascetic wisdom and moralizing religions. *Current Biology* 25(1):10–15.
77 Whitehouse, Harvey, Pieter François, Patrick E. Savage, Thomas E. Currie, Kevin C. Feeney, Enrico Cioni, Rosalind Purcell, et al. "Complex societies precede moralizing gods throughout world history." *Nature* 568, no. 7751 (2019): 226–229.
78 Retrieved from here (forthcoming) https://psyarxiv.com/jwa2n/.

9 Rituals Part 1

How are rituals learned, represented, and transmitted?

In different parts of the world, people engage in acts that expend much time, effort, and resources without apparent benefits or inherent purpose. Catholics repeatedly kneel and bow in mass during worship, Muslims recite five daily prayers of Islam, and Apache boys lie motionless while being bitten by hordes of ants. Several questions typically follow these observations. What are rituals? What similarities underlie them? Why do people continue to learn and then repeat these behaviors across generations? Moreover, how can behavior of this kind be explained?

Ritual has long been the target of extensive scholarly inquiry, especially from the disciplines of anthropology and religious studies. For instance, German-born French anthropologist Arnold Van Gennep was the first to notice the regularity in what he called rites of passage. In these rites, initiates often go through a series of ordeals, for instance, to demark their transition from childhood to adulthood. Van Gennep characterized these types of rituals as having three phases: separation (from the group), liminality (a period in between the old and new status), and incorporation (return to the group with a new status). This theory helps to explain the typical components of transitional rituals, but it is of less utility explaining the features of rituals that occur more frequently in one's lifetime, such as the precise placement of items during table setting (the Seder table) during Jewish Passover.

Other classic theorists have focused on particular aspects of ritual, such as the transformative power of words in the ritual. Social anthropologist Stanley Tambiah[1] argued that the language, style, and performance used in rituals communicates something beyond surface-level meaning, and they serve different communicative purposes. For instance, many participants do not understand the meaning of the words they speak or hear in ritual. Indeed, in the case of Catholic exorcism, traditionally spoken in Latin, they may not even understand the language.

The cognitive science of religion (CSR) has advanced the scholarly understanding of rituals, including a general explanation of what they typically entail, and has generated testable hypotheses about broad features of rituals such as how and why rituals are learned, represented, and transmitted. CSR portrays rituals as natural behavior, bound by both cognitive and sociocultural constraints that have measurable psychological and social consequences. Cognitive scientists of religion are not primarily concerned with documenting the potential local meanings that can be attributed to the performance of rituals as were some earlier approaches to ritual in the late nineteenth and early twentieth centuries, such as symbolism. Instead, CSR scholars tend to focus on explaining why rituals take the distinctive forms that they do and with what consequences for group cohesion, scale, and structure.

What are rituals?

Participation 1: Examples of rituals

1. Think about a ritual that you have participated in or watched on television, perhaps a baptism, quinceañera, graduation, wedding, or funeral. What do you think makes this a ritual and not some other type of event? Write down your answer in a few sentences.
2. Next, think about three rituals that you know about and complete the table below.

#	*Name*	*Tradition or religion*	*Brief description of a ritual*
1			
2			
3			

3. Examine your list. What (if anything) do you think these rituals have in common? Write down your answer in a few sentences.
4. Share and compare your list with another student's list. Why do you think your responses are different or similar to the other student's? Write down your answer in a few sentences.
5. This method of sharing and comparing is often how scholars in ritual studies decide what qualifies as a ritual. What do you think are the advantages and disadvantages of this method? Write down your answer in a few sentences or use bullet points.

One way to define ritual is to gather up all instances where the term "ritual" has been applied in the literature and note what they have in common. This method of collecting and comparing is how many scholars in ritual studies have decided what qualifies as a ritual. It is also how scientists determine whether an instance belongs to a category in the natural world. For example, to determine whether something is an animal (such as a cat), simply compare the features of the example (a cat) against the common features of animals. We know that animals consume organic material, breathe oxygen, can move, can reproduce sexually, and so on because scientists have collected and compared them. Scientists can even divide up naturally occurring things into different kinds based upon their inherent properties (e.g. vertebrates), which makes it easier to study them.

Unlike participation task 1 that you completed, cognitive scientists of religion do not collect and compare other people's descriptions of rituals to come up with a definition because rituals are not naturally occurring entities. Instead, the term ritual is a socially constructed category. The label was initially employed to describe events from traditions that scholars were familiar with, and then extended to other institutions that seemed to share some features with these events.[2] Consequentially, scholars have collected instances based on some common features with some, but not all, events labeled as rituals. These problems may well explain the lack of scholarly consensus about what exactly constitutes ritual.

Therefore, CSR scholars—and some other anthropologists[3,4]—do not approach the study of ritual by collecting instances that scholars have labeled rituals (i.e. a top-down approach), but rather, begin to assemble instances of ritual as a type of behavior (i.e. a bottom-up approach). Cognitive scientists of religion also select instances of ritualized behavior and explain similar features, based upon their potential evolutionary origins, functions, and other psycho-social repercussions. It is important to note that from this cognitive perspective, you could easily replace the word "ritual" with another, and you would still explain recurrent phenomena. What matters are the underlying patterns, not the name assigned to them. Thus, CSR scholars approach the study of rituals in much the same way they study religion more broadly (as discussed in Chapter 2: Core Assumptions).

Based on the amalgamation of research, cognitive scientists of religion scholars have begun to delineate the criteria by which general behaviors qualify as rituals.[5] One compelling cultural evolutionary perspective holds that features of rituals were selected for because they promote high-fidelity transmission of behavioral group markers and inhibit individual-level innovation, ensuring group solidarity and survival over time.[6,7] The main features of ritualized behavior are outlined below.

1 Actions lack a physical-causal mechanism and rationale

One reason why cognitive scientists of religion construe rituals as a special kind of behavior is that the actions lack a physical-causal mechanism.[8] In other words, performers lack a direct physical explanation for the effect[9] of their acts. Across cultures, people have long relied on rituals for protective and problem-solving purposes, such as fending off malice, preventing or improving health and social problems such as asthma, AIDS, unemployment, and famine.[10] Even though rituals are intended to have particular effects on the world, they are not expected to do so by means that are transparent or even in principle, knowable based upon the laws of physical causality. In other words, we do not know or assume that we need to understand how particular actions produce intended outcomes in rituals.

For instance, why do people knock on wood to avoid adverse outcomes and not another kind of surface? Why do soldiers fire into the air to honor a fallen comrade and not some other action? From a physical-causal perspective, many activities in rituals seem arbitrary. They also seem to lack instrumental purpose, which is in stark contrast to how we usually behave in everyday contexts. For instance, if I am thirsty and reach for a glass of water, it becomes clear that the instrumental goal of my behavior is to quench my thirst. If I tap my forehead with my right hand three times, move the glass from one side of the table to the other, and then drink the water, then the first actions are disconnected to the overall goal of quenching my thirst. In other words, the behaviors are redundant to the goal.

Nevertheless, even when rituals are explained in the context of a particular belief, there is often no expectation of a direct causal connection between the actions and outcomes.[11] In other words, people lack a rationale for why they perform particular steps within the ritual sequence and are often unaware of how these actions produce the intended outcome according to physical laws. People's explanations for performing ritual actions in specific ways are often vague, circular, question-begging, mystery-ridden, and highly idiosyncratic.[12,13]

Think for a moment about how you would justify a conventional action to an alien from another planet, like common ways to greet people. The alien asks, why do you extend your hand when you encounter some people? You may google the question "why do people shake hands when they meet?" assuming that there is an explanation for this behavior that someone else knows. You may answer that it has always been done this way or that your ancestors performed this action, and so you do too, or even that it expresses pleasure to see someone. The alien may then ask why do you shake hands and not perform some other behavior? You may be dumbfounded or make up an explanation on the spot that sounds right. This lack of explicit rationale about the motivation behind ritual behaviors is why cognitive scientists do not spend their time exclusively trying to decipher local meanings of ritual behaviors.

On the first reflection, it may appear that the criteria of lacking a physical-causal mechanism and rationale is not all that special to rituals because we do not know how many behaviors that we perform every day produce outcomes. For instance, we often learn how to do things, such as flushing the toilet or driving to school, without knowing precisely how they work. In these instances, our actions are causally opaque because we lack a direct causal explanation for the effect.[14] We do not know precisely how pushing the handle down causes the water to flush, or how turning the key in the ignition causes the engine to start. Nevertheless, even though we may not know how everyday appliances work, we assume that there is a physical cause that experts like plumbers and mechanics understand. Ritual behaviors are causally opaque, but unlike other daily practices, it is not appropriate to expect there to be a physical-causal rationale for the procedures. Rather, rituals belong to a particular category of behaviors in a culture, often referred to as social conventions, such as clothing fashions and social etiquette.

2 Behaviors are rigid, repetitive, redundant, and disconnected from ordinary goals

Rituals are socially stipulated group conventions.[15] People often say that they perform the ritual because their ancestors did, and just like most conventions, they are motivated to reproduce the ritual as precisely as possible. Unlike habits and routines that may change over time, rituals tend to become highly standardized. People often stick strictly to a behavioral script.[16] This orthopraxy is often reinforced in many religious communities. For example, a Muslim must face Mecca during the five daily prayers, and a Jew must precisely place items of the Sedar table setting at Passover. Likewise, when even the smallest detail is omitted during the ritualistic slaughter of animals (common to Islamic and Judaic traditions), the performer may abandon the ritual altogether as it has failed to achieve the intended purpose.

As some anthropologists have noted,[17,18] rituals are full of actions that appear redundant and are often used repeatedly, and the exact number is crucial to the outcome of the ritual. This specificity contrasts with everyday behaviors where people do not repeat the same action, or they repeat a behavior because it produces a physical outcome, like stirring the coffee granules in boiling water until they are absorbed. Whereas in ritual, often, the number of repetitions is an end in itself and considered essential to the ritual's success. Another associated common feature of rituals is the rigidity of the particular objects required. For example, the seeds of a rare type of fruit, water from a specific river, relics from a dead person, etc. Consider how unacceptable it would be to a congregation if a Priest forgot to bring the stipulated holy water for baptism and used a bottle of mineral water instead.

Participation 2: Identifying ritual features

Read the following description of a ritual used to find a partner in Brazil:

> "Buy a new sharp knife and stick it four times into a banana tree on June 12th at midnight (i.e. Valentine's day in Brazil, Saint Anthony's day is on the 13th). Catch the liquid that will drip from the plant's wound on a crisp, white paper that has been folded in two. The dripping liquid captured on the paper at night will form the first letter of the name of your future partner.[19]"

Indicate which aspects of the ritual are:

a Rigid.
b Repetitive.
c Redundant and disconnected from ordinary goals.

Write down your answer to a, b, and c in a few sentences for each.

3 Ritualized behaviors do not stop when they fail to produce the intended outcome

Rituals are often performed to produce a result, yet when the outcome is not produced, people seldom stop performing the rituals in the future. This state of affairs is in stark contrast to ordinary behaviors, where people would stop doing something if it failed to produce the outcome they expected, like pressing the power button a limited number of times when the computer fails to start. Scholars have long noted this particular feature of rituals, and most famously documented by anthropologist Evans-Pritchard in his ethnography of witchcraft among the Azande in Central Africa during colonial times.[20]

One standard method of determining a past or future state of affairs among the Azande was to ask a question—for example, a man may want to know if his sick wife is going to die. Poison is administered to a fowl, the question is posed, and the fowl is observed to see whether it lives or dies; each outcome provided a different answer to the question. For instance, if the foul died, then the answer to the question would be yes, but if it survived, the answer would be no. Crucially, however, verdicts were not considered binding unless they were verified, and so the procedure would have to be repeated. However, often, the affirmative answer would contradict the first answer. Evans-Pritchard documented eight justifications for these contradictions, which often attributed human error to cause the outcome. For example, the amount of poison was not proportionate to the weight of the fowl. These justifications served to strengthen belief in the poison oracle efficacy.

More recently, CSR researchers Cristine Legare and André Souza demonstrated reasoning about ritual efficacy in the context of Brazilian simpatias rituals, which deal with life problems such as quitting smoking, asthma, and infidelity. While Evans-Pritchard derived his insights about the hidden logic of ritual through ethnographic participant-observation, Legare and Souza examined how people decided on the success of problem-solving rituals experimentally, integrating and applying cognitive psychological approaches to the study of ritual cognition.

Legare and Souza demonstrated that when the intended outcome of problem-based rituals does not occur, the performer is likely to blame incorrect steps of the ritual procedure and performance. For example, that he or she did not use enough poison, did not perform the ritual correctly or in the right order. The researchers empirically showcased that the more stipulations there are in a ritual, the more opportunities there are to blame something for the lack of efficacy other than concluding that the ritual does not work.[21] People unconsciously judge the effectiveness of ritual actions similarly to the way they judge the effectiveness of ordinary outcomes. In particular, the more specific action is, and the more steps are involved, the more likely observers are to intuitively assume that the actions have the potential to produce the outcome, even when they do not know how, precisely, this is achieved.

These principles of reasoning about actions may also help explain why people do not quickly abandon their cultural rituals. It also may explain why rituals contain many specificities and many steps. Procedural steps mark that something extraordinary is about to happen, and they protect the ritual from being judged ineffective. Thus, rituals with more procedural steps are likely to continue to be practiced and transmitted over time.

Participation 3: Commonalities in rituals

Review your answer to the question, "What (if anything) do you think these rituals have in common?" from the first participation task in this chapter. Compare your answer to the main features of ritualized behavior, as evidenced by systematic scientific CSR research in this section. Write in a few sentences (or bullet points) how they are similar or different.

Key points

- CSR construes ritual as a special kind of behavior rather than communicating a special meaning for the researcher to interpret according to the cultural context.
- Rituals are socially stipulated group conventions that often entail predefined behaviors that are rigid, formal, and repeated.
- People often lack a rationale for why they perform particular actions within the ritual sequence and are often unaware of how these actions produce the intended outcome according to physical laws.
- Unlike ordinary behaviors, rituals are not quickly abandoned when they fail to produce the intended outcome.

Summary of the main features of ritualized behavior, according to CSR:

1 Actions lack a physical-causal mechanism and rationale.
2 Behaviors are rigid, repetitive, redundant, and disconnected from ordinary goals.
3 Ritualized practices do not stop when they fail to produce the intended outcome.

How are rituals learned?

Rituals are a special kind of behavior that is often reproduced and passed on throughout generations. This fact begs the obvious question, how are rituals learned? People learn and imitate ritualized behavior without fully understanding how the actions physically bring about the end goal. They do so because they unconsciously understand that rituals are a special kind of action. Research in the developmental and cognitive sciences have suggested that the unique features of ritualized action behavior make them especially likely to be reproduced and transmitted. For instance, when people hear that behaviors are part of a traditional ritual, they assume that there is a "proper" way of doing something without explicit explanations as to why particular actions should be performed. Participants also designate the correct performance of ritual actions as desirable, heighten submission and respect for leaders, and affiliation with other participants. The result of this combination is high-fidelity imitation:[22] mimicking ritual behaviors as closely as possible.

Experimental research demonstrates that children's interpretation of behavior as instrumental or conventional (i.e. ritual practice) has wide-ranging implications for what children imitate, what they transmit to others, and how they reason about objects' functions. For example, cognitive scientists Csibra and Gergely[23] found that when communicated as though it were a ritual, infants imitated an adult switching on a light with their heads, not their hands. Yet when the action was repeated without cues that it was a ritual, infants used their hands to switch on the light, presumably because it was a more efficient means (pressing with the hand) to achieve the end goal (switching on the light).

Another series of studies have demonstrated that children's imitative fidelity is influenced by cues to interpret behavior as instrumental versus conventional.[24] For example, psychologists Clegg and Legare examined children's imitative behaviors in a necklace-making activity. They found that children in the conventional condition imitated with higher fidelity transmitted more of the modeled behavior and showed higher levels of functional fixedness than children in the instrumental condition.[25] Conversely, these and other findings suggest that we are attuned to replicate behaviors when they are part of a traditional ritual.

Research with children and adults has also demonstrated that the combination of causal opacity (i.e. lacking a direct physical explanation for the effect) and social stipulation of behaviors inhibits the tendency for individuals to change aspects of the ritual. Thus, people precisely replicate the behaviors involved in a ritual, what cognitive scientists refer to as high-fidelity cultural transmission over time.[26] As Legare and colleagues have argued, from an evolutionary perspective, given the variability and limitations of personal experience and intuition, and the cognitive effort involved in inferring intentions and goals, natural selection ought to favor a social learning strategy where we imitate ritual behaviors as closely as possible. In other words, what you know about the world is limited, and when uncertain about something, a sound strategy is to copy others whom you think know better. This copying strategy

Figure 9.1 Research in the evolutionary cognitive sciences has focused on uncovering the psycho-social foundations of children's imitative behavior in ritual, like the Jewish child praying at the Western Wall in Israel in the photo. (Image credit: SmadarSonyaStrauss/Shutterstock.com).

is especially likely when there is uncertainty in the environment, including potential hazards.[27]

The fidelity of imitative behaviors also increases when actual or threatened ostracism by the group is higher. For example, Legare and colleagues have demonstrated that young children who are excluded by their in-group are more likely to imitate the behaviors of the rituals than children who are included.[28] Thus, the threat of social exclusion and loss of status motivates engagement in ritual throughout development. Performing social-group conventions, such as ritual behaviors, may serve as a bid for re-inclusion into the group.[29,30,31] Throughout evolutionary history, social ostracism was akin to a death sentence, and social affiliation and one's reputation is likely to be one of the most motivating forces to explain the participation in cultural rituals today.[32] One only has to imagine the harmful and potentially detrimental reputational consequences a member of the community would suffer if they refused to participate in a traditional ritual. Consider, for example, the reputation of an American father who refused to help carry his adolescent son's coffin on his shoulder because it was uncomfortable.

The particular action sequences and meanings of rituals are learned. Scholars in CSR have proposed that children and adults can identify, learn, and replicate ritual behaviors with little effort because they understand that rituals are a specific kind of action. This understanding is not necessarily conscious. Just like the ability to create friction between the ground and our feet gives rise to walking, and the tendency to recognize and produce sounds gives rise to language, the acquisition and participation in rituals is possible with little direct, explicit instruction because of underlying mental systems.

Key points

- Rituals contain elements that inspire people to reproduce them as precisely as possible, even though they do not understand precisely how the actions physically cause the outcome.
- Even young children mimic behaviors that are less an efficient means to an end goal in rituals.
- Copying the behaviors of others, even without an understanding of the underlying mechanisms of their actions, can be advantageous because people often know something we do not.

How are rituals represented?

Before the 1990s, most accounts of ritual ignored the potential relationship between ritual and action representation. In the early 1990s, religious studies scholar E. Thomas Lawson and philosopher Robert McCauley first made the connection between the two, and their cognitive account of religious ritual inaugurated the cognitive science of religion.[33] Lawson and McCauley explained how the representation of ritual actions is handled by the same cognitive system that processes everyday actions. They further showcased how, just like an underlying language system enables speakers to produce and understand seemingly endless sentences in their language, people extrapolate many aspects of ritual based on the form the ritual takes.

The theory's roots began when E. Thomas Lawson was browsing a second-hand bookstore in the early 1970s and stumbled across a worn copy of Noam Chomsky's *Syntactic Structures* book. As he skimmed the book, Lawson was compelled by the central argument that Chomsky was making about language, and he could not help but notice the parallels to the study of rituals. In the book, Chomsky argued that humans everywhere have an innate capacity for linguistic knowledge. In contrast to empiricists' arguments that had come before, Chomsky was proposing that language was not acquired solely by experience but based upon a genetic component of language acquisition. This genetic component explained how children everywhere acquired language so quickly, relative to the input, and why languages tended to have similar syntactic rules. Lawson bought the book, showed it to his then-student Robert McCauley, and the two began formalizing a theory about how people represent rituals inspired by this competence theory of universal grammar.

Lawson and McCauley proposed that people have a tacit understanding of rituals based on their form. Like Chomsky, they traced this understanding to cognition, and more specifically, to a more general "action representation system," which they proposed operates in reasoning about all actions in the world.[34] Grammar contains certain kinds of words (nouns, verbs, adjectives), and words have different functions in a sentence (subject, verb, object). Likewise, all action contains "slots" or roles to make meaningful action. Specifically, the slot of agent or actor, the slot of patient or subject of the action, and the slot of an instrument(s) used in action. This is what they call the "action representation system."

One particular conceptualization of actions are rituals, where an actor acts on a patient ACTOR→ACT→PATIENT (See Figure 9.2). In other words, when you see a person or agent capable of goal-directed behavior (i.e. an actor) acting on another person, animal, object, etc. (i.e. the patient), via an instrument (e.g. water), you represent this action as a ritual. Much like your ability to speak a language without consciously noting the formal rules, you represent an action as a ritual when three aspects of action are completed. Just as language shared some common features, Lawson and McCauley were convinced that rituals shared common features too. In 1990, they published a theory about the lowest common denominator of rituals everywhere,[35] in other words, three elements (actor, act, patient) are the minimal requirements for a person to represent an action as a ritual. They later coined this theory Ritual Form Hypothesis (RFH).[36]

Key points

- We use the same cognitive capacities to represent rituals and actions more generally.
- According to RFH, ritual action involves an agent performing some action on a patient.
- This cognitive theory proposes that our understanding of ritual behaviors is not exclusively derived from cultural learning but is also based upon an inherent understanding of actions.

Figure 9.2 Basic representation of ritual actions.

Participation 4: What makes a ritual religious?

Think about a religious ritual that you have participated in. What do you think makes this a religious ritual? Write down your answer in a few sentences.

So far, in the chapter, we have considered the hallmark features of cultural rituals. Ritual Form Hypothesis (RFH), developed by Lawson and McCauley, proposes that we intuitively represent a ritual as a particular type of action, but what do people think demarks a religious ritual from other kinds of rituals? For example, how would you know whether an infant was being washed or baptized? Lawson and McCauley claimed that religious rituals are an elaboration of the basic system in Figure 9.1 ACTOR→ACT→PATIENT. In particular, they defined religious rituals as acts in which (1) someone (2) does something (3) to someone or something using an instrument (4) in order to bring about some non-natural consequence (5) by an appeal to superhuman agency, i.e. ACTOR→ACT→PATIENT→NON-NATURAL CONSEQUENCE→SUPERHUMAN AGENCY.

Religions often posit agents such as ancestors and gods as superior to humans. The crucial difference between ordinary action and religious ritual, according to RFH is the participation of agents that culture adds a nonhuman-like quality to (which they call "culturally postulated superhuman agents" or CPS-agents). According to Lawson and McCauley, all religious rituals are inevitably connected sooner or later with actions in which centrally postulated agents play a role and bring about some change in the religious world. Other kinds of religious events deviate from this structure, such as priests sacrificing goats or pilgrims circling shrines. While these activities may be parts of religious rituals, the activities themselves do not constitute religious rituals, according to RFH.

It is essential here to consider again the issue of how CSR defines ritual, posed at the start of the chapter. From this cognitive perspective, the word "ritual" could be replaced with another, and people would still represent these patterns as a distinct category of events. Just like changing the name for "language" does not stop people from understanding specific configurations of speech. What matters are the configurations, not the labels.

The Ritual Form Hypothesis (RFH) explains judgments about the frequency and efficacy of ritual as based on the ritual's form. The form includes whether the agent, action, or patient has a unique, counter-intuitive property (S-marker), a culturally postulated superhuman agent (i.e. CPS-agent) in the ritual, and where this agent fits into the formal structural description of the ritual action. For example, if the special marker is on the agent, and that agent is deemed close to the ultimate source of authority (e.g. a Priest, acting on behalf of God), then the ritual will be performed less frequently, and the consequences of the ritual are considered permanent. Whereas rituals with a special marker on the patient or instrument tend to be performed more regularly, and the implications of the ritual are less permanent. Likewise, frequency differs when the S-marker is in the actor position from when the S-marker is in the patient position.[37,38] Ordination of a soon-to-be-priest by an ordained priest means that the latter priest is acting with the power of God (S-marker in actor position). Whereas in a sacrifice to a god, the God is in the receiving position, not the acting position. The first ritual will occur only once, the latter many times.

Participation 5: Comparing ritual definitions

How does your definition of a ritual compare to the ritual form hypothesis? Write down your answer in a few sentences.

Key points

- According to RFH, all humans possess a basic conceptualization of actions.
- One conceptualization of actions is ritual, which involves an agent, action, and patient.
- Religious rituals are an elaboration of this ritual conceptualization.
- Religious rituals are acts in which (1) someone (2) does something (3) to someone or something using an instrument (4) in order to bring about some non-natural consequence (5) by an appeal to superhuman agency.

Participation 6: What makes religious rituals different from other rituals?

Compare your response to the participation task at the start of the section to how rituals are designated as religious in ritual form hypothesis. Write down your answer in a few sentences.

One outcome of RFH theory is the ability to label which kinds of events people would represent as rituals and to characterize the basic cognitive structure of religious rituals. The theory also generates testable predictions about our intuitions about aspects of religious rituals based on their features. Lawson and McCauley claim that we start to make all sorts of inferences about rituals in religious systems, even those that we have little information about.[39] These intuitions include many aspects of rituals. For example:

- Which rituals are performed only once (e.g. confirmation in the Catholic Church), and which are repeatable (e.g. the Eucharist, aka Holy Communion)?
- Which rituals are permanent (e.g. baptism) and which effects wear off naturally (e.g. pilgrimage to Lourdes)?
- Why some rituals are characterized by lots of stimuli and intense emotions (e.g. the Hindu festival Thaipusam) while others seem more humdrum affairs (e.g. Quaker prayer meeting).
- Which rituals are central, and which are peripheral?
- Which rituals permit substitutions, and which do not.

Some claims made by the ritual form hypothesis[40] include:

1 For a ritual to be effective, it must be performed by a qualified intentional agent.
2 In religious rituals, some actors, patients, and instruments (e.g. objects) are demarked as having special powers or qualities (i.e. an S-marker). As opposed to special patient and instrument rituals, special agent rituals (i.e. CPS rituals, such as when God acts) are regarded as having more permanence and are thus not repeatable. In particular, the theory proposes that rituals, where the S-marker is on the agent, are represented as exceptional types of rituals indeed. Consider agents such as Priests who are thought to be acting on behalf of God. These agents are termed "culturally postulated superhumans" (CPS) in RFH because they take the place of the ultimate religious authority in the ritual.
3 Typically, CPS agents can take the place of religious authority because they have been qualified to do so through some enabling rituals (e.g. ordination).
4 Special agent rituals have to convince participants that something profound is happening and thus will have more emotionally provocative stimuli (i.e. sensory pageantry) than other rituals in that religious system. When the ultimate source of religious authority or representatives of that authority are thought to act in the human world, then the rituals tend to be less frequent and more permanent.

These predictions make RFH an empirically tractable theory and set it apart from earlier anthropological theories that provide descriptions of what they propose people think religious rituals entail. Furthermore, with the help of other researchers, Lawson and McCauley set out to test these claims. Multiple studies with participants from a variety of mainstream religious traditions provided support for crucial predictions from the theory. These include judgments about when the correct performer (and intentions) were more important for the ritual outcome than the proper action, the level of sensory pageantry employed, and whether the ritual would be repeated or be reversed.[41,42,43,44]

Key points

- RFH provides testable predictions about our intuitions about aspects of religious rituals based on their features.
- These include the frequency of performance, the longevity of their effects and the level of sensory pageantry employed.
- Many of these claims have been empirically tested.

Summary of How are rituals learned and represented?

- Rituals are socially stipulated group conventions that often entail pre-defined behaviors that are rigid, formal, and repeated.
- Rituals contain elements that predispose children and adults to mimic behaviors that are a less efficient means to an end goal.
- Rituals are resilient to change.
- People unconsciously recognize rituals based on their intuitive understanding of actions, and religious rituals as a specific kind of ritual.
- People also generate intuitions about aspects of religious rituals based on their features.

How are rituals transmitted?

So far in the chapter, we have mainly considered how rituals are learned and represented. Next, we focus on how rituals are transmitted from one generation to the next. This question is vital because if rituals are not remembered, they will not be transmitted, and will cease to exist. One answer was proposed by the "Modes of Religiosity" (MOR) theory, developed by social anthropologist Harvey Whitehouse. MOR theory is concerned with the fundamental questions of how rituals are transmitted and how they relate to the scale and structure of the communities within which they are embedded.

Modes of religiosity (MOR)

Whitehouse's ethnographic fieldwork in Papua New Guinea in the 1980s originally inspired the Modes of Religiosity (MOR) theory (see the case study at the end of this chapter for more information). One group (the Pomio Kivung) was a large movement with highly repetitive rituals and public speeches. Smaller breakaway movements also popped up from time to time within the Pomio Kivung and consisted of emotionally intense rituals and ordeals. Whitehouse's theory purports to explain a set of general patterns of group formation in ritual groups around the world and across history.

Whitehouse observed that rituals tended to form into two characteristic patterns, and these patterns were also related to the transmission of religion and even socio-political organization.[45] Whitehouse called these two patterns "modes of religiosity.[46]" At the heart of MOR's theory is the claim that these differences are guided in part by the way crucial aspects of the religion are remembered and transmitted. Thus, memory systems constrain the types of rituals we see throughout religious communities. Characteristic of the CSR approach, MOR theory attributes a central role to human cognition.

Whitehouse described one mode as "doctrinal." Like the mainstream Pomio Kivung, the rituals in the doctrinal mode tended to entail low sensory pageantry and low levels of emotional arousal among the participants. Rituals tended to be performed frequently, emphasizing the repetition of doctrine, as well as the meanings of the rituals (exegesis). Based on research on memory processes in psychology at the time, Whitehouse surmised that these types of

Figure 9.3 Harvey Whitehouse's career began by carrying out immersive fieldwork in Papua New Guinea using conventional ethnographic methods. He later teamed with other researchers in adjacent fields and focused on uncovering the psycho-social foundations of rituals. Today, he carries out surveys and experiments alongside qualitative methods in the field, as depicted in the recent picture taken in a small village on the island of Tanna, Vanuatu. (Image credit: Veronika Rybanska).

ritual actions were encoded in implicit procedural memory even though doctrine and exegesis were stored in explicit memory systems. Think about driving a car or reciting a long poem; these tasks are complicated at first and require much concentration. However, eventually, they become effortless because you do them so often. Likewise, frequent repetition of ritual procedures, from genuflecting and self-crossing to collective chanting and marching, enables them to become sedimented in procedural memory. Meanwhile, the continual repetition of doctrines and narratives enable people to remember them in semantic memory as part of their long-term general knowledge. Consider Catholic mass in Ireland. If you ask any Irish Catholic what notable events happened at mass last week, they are probably more likely to scratch their heads. They will, however, be able to tell you what generally happens at mass each week and even recite scripture performed during rituals, such as The Rosary or Lord's Prayer, effortlessly (see Figure 9.4). Details of these more typical elements are often shared in semantic memory by large numbers of religious adherents.

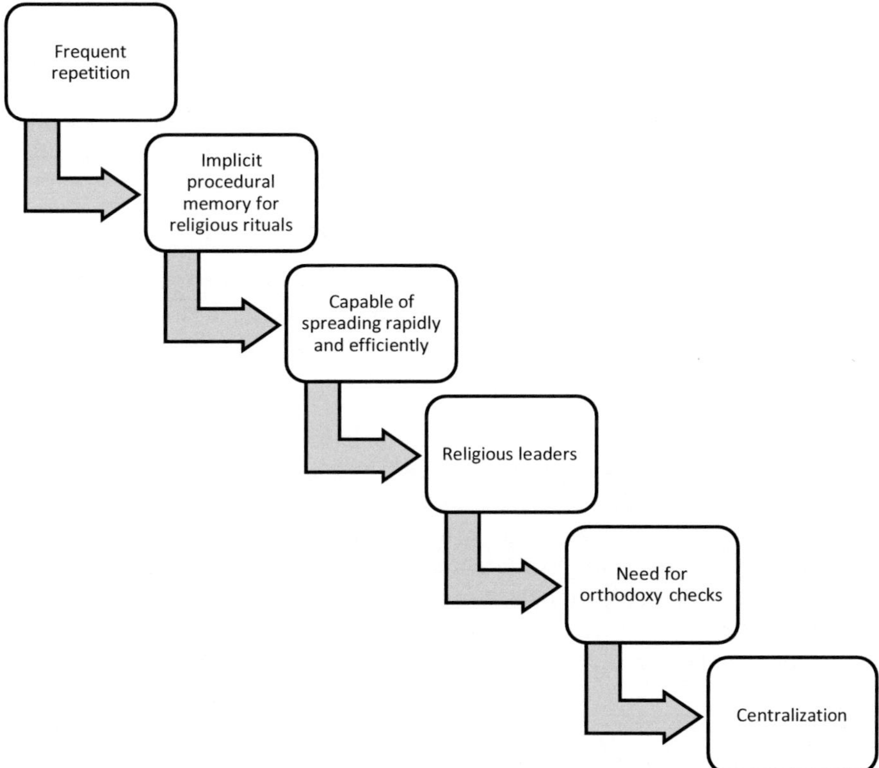

Figure 9.4 Example of how ritual frequency gives rise to other psycho-socio-political aspects in the doctrinal mode.

These cognitive features of the doctrinal mode have important consequences for cultural transmission. Since the doctrinal mode codifies religious teaching in oratory and text, it is capable of spreading rapidly and efficiently to large populations. Moreover, frequent repetition makes it easy to spot deviations from the orthodoxy stored in semantic memory. At the same time, reliance on implicit scripts for routinized rituals suppresses exegetical reflection, making innovation less likely. All these factors contribute to the stabilization of homogenized regional traditions.[47] However, since semantic memory for the group's identity markers is not anchored in personally lived experiences, doctrinal group alignments do not tap into a personal agency. Social psychologists refer to "identification" as a depersonalizing form of affiliation to the group, in which activation of the social identity makes the personal self less salient.[48]

Further, this combination of features also enables the emergence of specialist religious leaders and large anonymous communities with centralized authority. The emphasis on an elaborated body of teachings encourages the rise of experts and orators and the need for policing, although partly met by peer pressure and normative tightness, also fosters the emergence of priestly hierarchies. Figure 9.4, shows some of the ways in which all these different elements are connected.

The second mode, "imagistic" describes the splinter groups that Whitehouse witnessed in Papua New Guinea. This mode is characterized by the coalescence of different features than the doctrinal mode (see Figure 9.5). Rituals in the imagistic mode tend to be infrequent and are characterized by high sensory pageantry. These experiences are highly salient among the participants, which makes them stored as vivid, episodic flashbulb-like memories. Consider a meaningful, emotional, and infrequent event in your life, such as childbirth, marriage, perhaps a tragedy, or even where you were during a significant event, like when Princess Diana died in a fatal car crash in Paris or the 9/11 terrorist attacks against the U.S. You are likely to remember the details of the event, and with the case of painful personal experiences, primarily reflect that the events unfolded the way they did for a reason.

These kinds of personal experiences also have significant consequences for social cohesion. Whitehouse and colleagues have argued that the imagistic mode involves the establishment of personally salient episodic memories that come to form part of the essential autobiographical self. When such memories are shared with a group, it creates a fusion of personal and group identities, increasing group cohesion. Whitehouse further proposes that these kinds of salient rituals, which characterize the imagistic mode, are not accompanied by elaborate doctrine learned from elders or priests. Instead, they often lead people to privately reflect on the meaning of the ritual based upon their personal experiences.

Whitehouse calls this individualized process of meaning-making "spontaneous exegetical reflection" (SER). This pathway to religious knowledge discourages the emergence of centralized leadership and instead binds together small groups of people who have gone through the rituals together. Examples of these types of rituals include rites of passage—such as initiation rituals to

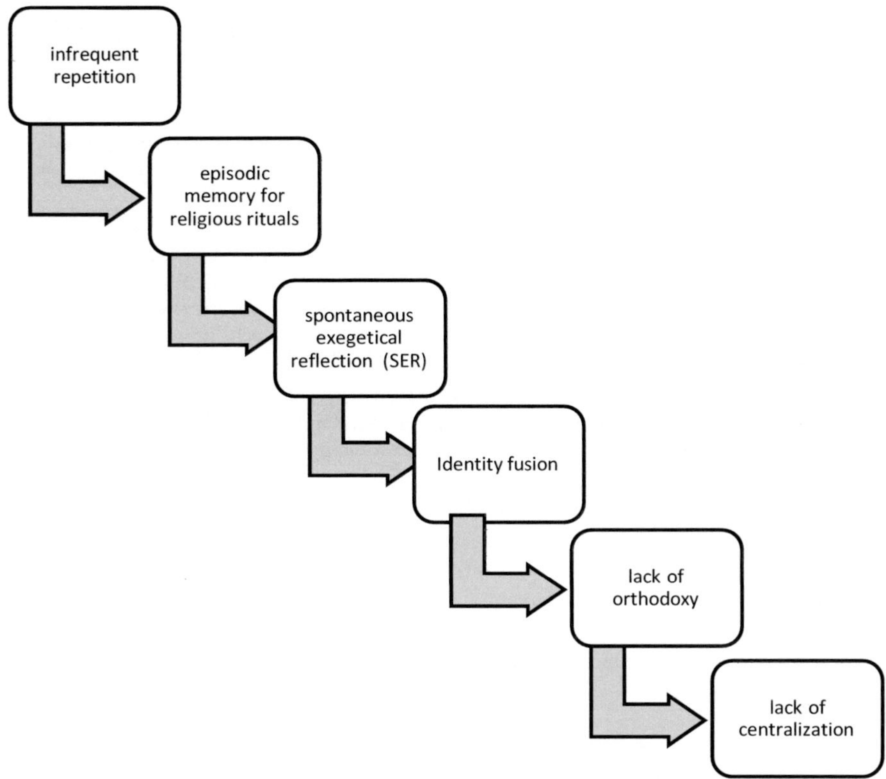

Figure 9.5 Example of how ritual frequency gives rise to other psycho-socio-political aspects in the imagistic mode.

demark a change in people's social status, common in small-scale traditional societies.[49] These rituals typically include traumatic ordeals, such as extended periods of isolation, piercing, burning, and scarification.[50]

Modes of Religiosity (MOR) theory and Ritual Form Hypothesis (RFH)

You may have noticed some overlap between the claims about rituals in this section by Modes of Religiosity (MOR) theory and Ritual Form Hypothesis (RFH) that we covered in the previous section. Much of CSR in the late 1990s and early 2000s was dominated by these two theories of religious rituals and their implications for the understanding of ritual transmission. MOR and RFH share many underlying assumptions, but they differ on a few crucial predictions. One key difference is that MOR emphasizes the *frequency* of ritual performance as the key to understanding the diversity of rituals. In other words, rituals tend to cluster into two forms (i.e. doctrinal and imagistic modes) that

Table 9.1 Summary of some of the central claims of modes of religiosity (partly based on the more extensive summary by Justin Barrett[51] and Whitehouse[52]).

#	*Doctrinal mode*	*Imagistic mode*
1	Frequent repetition of doctrinal information activates semantic memory for religious teaching and implicit memory for routinized ritual procedures.	Infrequent repetition with high sensory pageantry rituals creates episodic memories for events.
2	Implicit memory for rituals reduces individual reflection and innovation regarding the meaning of ceremonies, increasing acceptance of authoritative interpretations (i.e. orthodoxy).	Episodic memory for rituals generates spontaneous exegetical reflection (SER), which means that people have idiosyncratic and different understandings of the rituals.
4	Larger bodies of knowledge required of participants and the presence of religious leaders/authority are mutually reinforcing.	Diversity of understanding the meanings of rituals discourages central leadership.
5	The presence of religious leaders/teachers helps to enforce orthodoxy.	Lacking central leadership and lack of orthodoxy are mutually reinforcing.
6	The presence of orthodoxy checks in a religious community encourages the centralization of power structures.	Participants in rituals with high sensory pageantry tend to experience intense social cohesion and identity fusion.
7	Semantic memory for religious teachings encourages anonymous communities.	Strong social cohesion and episodic memories for rituals encourage exclusive religious communities.
8	Religious leaders can facilitate the spread of the tradition to other populations (e.g. via proselytism and missionization).	Religious traditions based on locally shared ritual experiences are hard to spread.

differ in frequency because they are constrained by mnemonic factors (i.e. how people tend to remember and transmit religion).

By contrast, RFH proposes that the ritual *form* is the independent variable that underpins frequency, namely the reference to, and place of the special S-marker, especially the presence and location of the CPS agent in the structure of the ritual. In short, the S-marker determines the frequency. There are also differences in the scope of the theories. While RFH explains how humans represent and constrain rituals, especially where a superhuman agent is evoked in the ritual structure, the modes theory includes broader predictions about the consequences of varying the frequency and emotionality of collective rituals for the scale and structure of social groups.

Participation 7: Levels of analyses

1 In Chapter 4 (Methods) we discussed methodological pluralism and interdisciplinary research paradigms (Table 4.1, Table 4.2, and Figure 4.3).
2 Re-read Chapter 9, and read the case study at the end of this chapter also.

3 Summarize the different kinds of research methods used (e.g. developmental, historical, experimental).
4 Outline the different levels of analyses (e.g. psychological, cultural).
5 Share and compare your answer to another student's.

Research case study: Modes of Religiosity (MOR) theory of religious transmission

Social anthropologist Harvey Whitehouse formalized his theory of "modes of religiosity" based on two years of ethnographic fieldwork in Papua New Guinea in the late 1980s.[53] Whitehouse noticed that there were two different types of religious activity and transmission in the Pomio Kivung, a religious movement in East New Britain Province, encompassing thousands of people in many villages. Pomio Kivung followers would frequently gather to perform rituals and listen to preachers reiterate laws. Yet there were also smaller splinter groups that periodically emerged every five years or so in particular villages and then dissolved. The rituals of these splinter groups were much more emotionally intense and quite often unpleasant.

When he returned to the libraries of Cambridge, Whitehouse discovered that the patterns he had observed in Papua New Guinea were not unique. It seemed that rituals in other parts of the world also tended to conform to two characteristic patterns. These ritual patterns were also related to the transmission of religion and even socio-political organization.[54] As we discussed earlier in the chapter, Whitehouse dubbed one package of ritual elements as "imagistic" and the other "doctrinal," and these two packages of rituals and associated socio-political features Modes of Religiosity (MOR).[55]

Like other generalizing theories about religion and socio-political organization in the social sciences, MOR is ambitious. MOR theory is, however, distinctive compared to other theories about religious dynamics that are broad in scope for at least seven reasons:

1 MOR fractionates the category of ritual into distinct, empirically tractable components

Like other CSR approaches, MOR theory fractionates the category of ritual into distinct cognitive and behavioral patterns that appear cross-culturally, such as causally opaque action, and euphoric and dysphoric arousal. These components can be investigated independently and empirically as having particular psycho-social effects, such as on cohesion and cooperation.

2 MOR attributes a central role to human cognition in the formation of religious practices

Like other theories in the cognitive science of religion, MOR attributes human psychology with a critical role in underpinning religious forms. For instance, at the heart of MOR is the theory that the differences in two characteristic packages of rituals and socio-political features of communities are guided in part by the way crucial aspects of the religion are recalled and transmitted. Memory systems constrain the types of rituals we see throughout religious communities. In the doctrinal mode, frequent repetition of doctrinal information activates semantic memory for religious teaching and implicit memory for routinized ritual procedures. In the imagistic mode, infrequent repetition with high sensory pageantry rituals creates episodic memories for events.

3 MOR specifies the mechanisms connecting ritual participation with identity fusion in the imagistic mode and identification in the doctrinal mode

Most social scientists endorse some version of the claim that participating in collective rituals promotes social cohesion, yet lack an explanation of how, precisely, participation gives rise to social solidarity. Later formulations of MOR theory also emphasized the effect of rituals on measurable forms of group alignment. For example, Whitehouse and colleagues have shown how those with shared collective identity who undergo emotionally intense (e.g. painful rituals) may experience the fusion of personal and group identities, resulting in a visceral sense of oneness with the group. Identity fusion results from specific kinds of rituals typically found in kin-like groups around the world, from tribes in Papua New Guinea to Libyan insurgents and Muslim fundamentalists in Indonesia.[56]

By contrast, doctrinal modes of ritual practice promote shared social norms through instruction, are stored in semantic memory, and result in intuitions of shared group membership and trustworthiness based on identification, a depersonalizing form of group alignment. These later formulations are where current research inspired by MOR has focused, and we will turn to this in more detail when we consider the group-level effects of ritual participation in the next chapter.

4 MOR generates testable hypotheses concerning the relationships between psychological and social-level variables

Like many anthropological theories, MOR was inspired by ethnographic insights based upon Whitehouse's first-hand experience of participant observation in Papua New Guinea. However, unlike most social anthropologists, Whitehouse used his ethnographic observations to generate a set of testable hypotheses. He attempted to explain the underlying patterns in divergent modes of religiosity in Papua New Guinea and other places around the world by partnering with psychologists and other scientists to develop and test these hypotheses experimentally, comparatively, and longitudinally.

5 Many aspects of MOR have received empirical support from a variety of methodologies

Whitehouse and other researchers have tested the purported relationships in MOR theory, and many aspects of the theory have received support. Support includes data derived from neurophysiological studies[57,58] and psychological experiments with children[59,60,61] and adults.[62] For example, concerning the connection between sensory pageantry, emotional arousal, memory, and perceived ritual efficacy. For instance, experiments with adults have demonstrated that high arousal rituals do tend to generate spontaneous exegetical reflection (SER) about the meaning of the rituals.[63]

Broader claims about the association between socio-political conditions that facilitate different forms of religion are understandably more difficult to test. Whitehouse invited archaeologists and historians to consider how detailed case studies might support or refute his theories. These attempts at goodness-of-fit between MOR and real-world data have been met with mainly positive reviews[64,65] ethnographic,[66] archaeological and historical records,[67,68,69,70] and data from computer simulation modeling has provided some support.[71] Building on these quantitative methods, further evidence for core predictions of the theory continues to appear.[72,73]

6 MOR is adaptable in response to data

MOR qualifies as a scientific theory because it is responsive to change based upon empirical findings. For example, due to scholarly feedback, MOR has undergone many clarifications and modifications. For instance, based on historical data, the modes are presented as less discrete and more continuum-like than was initially proposed.[74]

7 MOR is grounded in an evolutionary account

MOR draws upon individual and group-level evolutionary processes to explain the recurrent features of religion. For instance, based upon a selectionist model, the theory assumes that memorable rituals are more likely to survive than those that are not. Evolutionary theory also underpins other aspects of MOR. For instance, one explanation for identity fusion in imagistic ritual experiences focuses on evolved coalitionary psychology and tribal instincts. Namely, groupmates with whom we share important life events are perceived as "psychological kin" because the human brain is predisposed for sacrificial behavior towards close kin. This strategy is genetically adaptive, yet in specific contexts, such as shared ritual experiences, we unconsciously misattribute the strategy to non-kin, where it facilitates pro-group behavior irrespective of genetic relatedness.

Questions

1 In your own words, summarize the claims of Modes of Religiosity theory (MOR).
2 Compare and contrast the Modes of Religiosity theory (MOR) to Ritual Form Hypothesis (RFH) in the previous section. Note similarities and differences between them. You can use bullet points, diagrams, sentences, or anything else that helps you answer the question.
3 What do you think demarks this research on rituals as typical of the CSR approach to ritual?
4 What are the implications of MOR on the religion-as-irrational thesis proposed by new atheists (covered earlier in the chapter)?
5 What do you think are the real-world implications of MOR theory on explaining rituals around the world?

Further reading

1 Whitehouse, Harvey. *Modes of religiosity: A cognitive theory of religious transmission*. Rowman Altamira, 2004.
2 Whitehouse, Harvey, Jonathan A. Lanman "The ties that bind us: Ritual, fusion, and identification." *Current Anthropology* 55, no. 6 (2014): 1–22.
3 Atkinson, Quentin D., and Harvey Whitehouse. "The cultural morphospace of ritual form: Examining modes of religiosity cross-culturally." *Evolution and Human Behavior* 32, no. 1 (2011): 50–62.
4 Whitehouse, Harvey, and James Laidlaw, eds. *Ritual and memory: Toward a comparative anthropology of religion*. Vol. 6. Rowman Altamira, 2004.

Discussion questions

1 Go through this chapter again and note down all of the contributions of CSR to the study of ritual.
2 Read the section in this chapter again, "What are rituals?" and compare it to the section in "What is religion?" in Chapter 2: Core Assumptions. How are they similar or different? Write down your answer in a few sentences.
3 Imagine that you entered a competition to teach kids a new ritual. The winner is judged by the number of children who successfully perform the behavior. Based on what you have learned in this chapter, describe

the features of the action, and describe what you would tell the children about the behavior.

4 Do you think that all CSR theories on rituals (e.g. RFH, MOR) have implications on whether or not they work? Write down your answer in a few sentences.

Chapter summary

Rituals are a trademark of human behavior. Although they are not unique to religion, rituals are especially common among religious communities. CSR has shed light on many important questions, including questions of what demarks a ritual from other actions, what people think makes a ritual religious, and how psychological and social factors explain why rituals are similar and different. Scholars have also tackled the crucial questions of how rituals are learned, represented, and transmitted. When taken together, research and theories in CSR help to demonstrate that rituals are not for the naïve or religious fanatics, but that these behaviors are a product of being human.

Selected further reading

Articles

1 Atkinson, Quentin D., and Harvey Whitehouse. "The cultural morphospace of ritual form: Examining modes of religiosity cross-culturally." *Evolution and Human Behavior* 32, no. 1 (2011): 50–62.

2 Legare, Cristine H., and André L. Souza. "Evaluating ritual efficacy: Evidence from the supernatural." *Cognition* 124, no. 1 (2012): 1–15.

3 McCauley, Robert N. "Ritual, memory, and emotion: Comparing two cognitive hypotheses." In *Religion in mind: Cognitive perspectives on religious belief, ritual, and experience*, ed. J. Andresen, Cambridge: Cambridge University Press, Ch. 5, 114–151.

Books

1 McCauley, Robert N., and E. Thomas Lawson. *Bringing ritual to mind: Psychological foundations of cultural forms*. Cambridge University Press, 2002.

Notes

1 Tambiah, Stanley Jeyaraja. "The magical power of words." *Man* 3, no. 2 (1968): 175–208.

2 Stocking, George W. *After Tylor: British social anthropology, 1888–1951*. Madison: University of Wisconsin Press, 1995.

3 Humphrey, Caroline, and James Laidlaw. *The archetypal actions of ritual: A theory of ritual illustrated by the Jain rite of worship*. USA: Oxford University Press, 1994.
4 Rappaport, R. A. *Ritual and religion in the making of humanity*. Cambridge, U.K., New York: Cambridge University Press, 1999.
5 Liénard, Pierre, and Pascal Boyer. "Whence collective rituals? A cultural selection model of ritualized behavior." *American Anthropologist* 108, no. 4 (2006): 814–827.
6 Watson-Jones, Rachel E., and Cristine H. Legare. "The social functions of group rituals." *Current Directions in Psychological Science* 25, no. 1 (2016): 42–46.
7 Legare, Cristine H., and Mark Nielsen. "Imitation and innovation: The dual engines of cultural learning." *Trends in Cognitive Sciences* 19, no. 11 (2015): 688–699.
8 Whitehouse, Harvey. "The coexistence problem in psychology, anthropology, and evolutionary theory." *Human Development* 54, no. 3 (2011): 191.
9 E.g. see Legare, Cristine H., and Rachel E. Watson-Jones. "The evolution and ontogeny of ritual." In *The handbook of evolutionary psychology*, 2015.
10 Legare, Cristine H., Rachel E. Watson-Jones, and Andre L. Souza. "A cognitive psychological account of reasoning about ritual efficacy." In *Advances in religion, cognitive science, and experimental philosophy*, 2016, 85.
11 Sørensen, J. *A cognitive theory of magic*. Lanham, MD: Rowman Altamira Press, 2007.
12 E.g. Bloch, Maurice. "Symbols, song, dance, and features of articulation: Is religion an extreme form of traditional authority?" *European Journal of Sociology/Archives Européennes de Sociologie* 15, no. 1 (1974): 54–81; Boyer, Pascal. *Religion explained: The evolutionary origins of religious thought*. No. 170. Basic Books, 2001.
13 Sperber, Dan. (1975). *Rethinking Symbolism*. (A.L. Morton.). Cambridge, UK: Cambridge University Press.
14 E.g. see Legare, Cristine H., and Rachel E. Watson-Jones. "The evolution and ontogeny of ritual." In *The handbook of evolutionary psychology*, 2015.
15 Legare, Cristine H., and André L. Souza. "Evaluating ritual efficacy: Evidence from the supernatural." *Cognition* 124, no. 1 (2012): 1–15.
16 Herrmann, Patricia A., Cristine H. Legare, Paul L. Harris, and Harvey Whitehouse. "Stick to the script: The effect of witnessing multiple actors on children's imitation." *Cognition* 129, no. 3 (2013): 536–543.
17 E.g. Tambiah, Stanley Jeyaraja. "A performative approach to ritual." In *Proceedings of the British Academy London* 65 (1979): 113–169.
18 E.g. Humphrey, Caroline, and James Laidlaw. *The archetypal actions of ritual: A theory of ritual illustrated by the Jain rite of worship*. Oxford University Press, USA, 1994.
19 Scharf, R. (2010, February 18). "How to get a husband the Brazilian way." http://deepbrazil.com/2010/02/18/how-to-find-a-husband-the-brazilian-way/.
20 Evans-Pritchard, E.E. *Witchcraft, oracles, and magic among the Azande* (Vol. 12). London: Oxford, 1937.
21 Legare, Cristine H., and André L. Souza. "Evaluating ritual efficacy: Evidence from the supernatural." *Cognition* 124, no. 1 (2012): 1–15. Cited in Legare, Cristine H., and André L. Souza. "Evaluating ritual efficacy: Evidence from the supernatural." *Cognition* 124, no. 1 (2012): 1–15.
22 Whitehouse, Harvey. "The coexistence problem in psychology, anthropology, and evolutionary theory." *Human Development*, 54: 191–199.
23 Csibra, Gergely, and György Gergely. "Natural pedagogy." *Trends in Cognitive Sciences* 13, no. 4 (2009): 148–153.
24 Legare, Cristine H., Nicole J. Wen, Patricia A. Herrmann, and Harvey Whitehouse. "Imitative flexibility and the development of cultural learning." *Cognition* 142 (2015): 351–361.
25 Clegg, Jennifer M., and Cristine H. Legare. "Instrumental and conventional interpretations of behavior are associated with distinct outcomes in early childhood." *Child Development* 87, no. 2 (2016): 527–542.

26 Legare, Cristine H., and Mark Nielsen. "Imitation and innovation: The dual engines of cultural learning." *Trends in Cognitive Sciences* 19, no. 11 (2015): 688–699.
27 Henrich, Joseph, and Francisco J. Gil-White. "The evolution of prestige: Freely conferred deference as a mechanism for enhancing the benefits of cultural transmission." *Evolution and Human Behavior* 22, no. 3 (2001): 165–196.
28 Watson-Jones, Rachel E., Harvey Whitehouse, and Cristine H. Legare. "In-group ostracism increases high-fidelity imitation in early childhood." *Psychological Science* 27, no. 1 (2016): 34–42.
29 Watson-Jones, Rachel E., Harvey Whitehouse, and Cristine H. Legare. "In-group ostracism increases high-fidelity imitation in early childhood." *Psychological Science* 27, no. 1 (2016): 34–42.
30 Legare, Cristine H., and Rachel E. Watson-Jones. "The evolution and ontogeny of ritual." In *The handbook of evolutionary psychology*, 2015: 1–19.
31 Legare, C.H., H. Whitehouse, N.J. Wen, and P.A. Herrmann. "Imitative foundations of cultural learning." *Cognition* (2012).
32 Gruter, Margaret, and Roger D. Masters. "Ostracism as a social and biological phenomenon: An introduction." (1986): 149–158.
33 Lawson, E. Thomas, and Robert N. McCauley. *Rethinking religion: Connecting cognition and culture*. Cambridge University Press, 1990.
34 Lawson, E. Thomas, and Robert N. McCauley. *Rethinking Religion: Connecting cognition and culture*. Cambridge University Press, 1990.
35 Lawson, E. Thomas, and R. McCauley. "Rethinking religion: Connecting culture and cognition." Cambridge: Cambridge University Press, 1990.
36 McCauley, Robert N., and E. Thomas Lawson. *Bringing ritual to mind: Psychological foundations of cultural forms*. Cambridge University Press, 2002.
37 Whitehouse, H. "Theoretical challenges." In Whitehouse, H. *Modes of religiosity: A cognitive theory of religious transmission*. Walnut Creek, CA: AltaMira Press, 2004.
38 McCauley, R.N. "Ritual, memory, and emotion: Comparing two cognitive hypotheses." In *Religion in mind: Cognitive perspectives on religious belief, ritual, and experience*. Ed. J. Andresen, Cambridge: Cambridge University Press, 2001.
39 McCauley, Robert N., and E. Thomas Lawson. *Bringing Ritual to Mind: Psychological foundations of cultural forms*. Cambridge University Press, 2002.
40 Barrett, J.L. "Bringing data to mind: Empirical claims of Lawson and McCauley's theory of religious ritual." In T. Light and B. C. Wilson eds., *Religion as a human capacity: A festschrift in honor of E. Thomas Lawson*. Leiden: Brill, 2004.
41 Barrett, J.L. "Smart gods, dumb gods, and the role of social cognition in structuring ritual intentions." *Journal of Cognition and Culture* 2 no. 3 (2002): 183–193.
42 Barrett, J.L., and Lawson, E.T. "Ritual intentions: Cognitive contributions to judgments and ritual efficacy." *Journal of Cognition and Culture* 1, no. 2 (2001): 183–201.
43 Malley, B., and Barrett, J.L. "Can ritual form be predicted from religious belief? A test of the Lawson-McCauley hypothesis." *Journal of Ritual Studies* 17, no. 2 (2003): 1–14.
44 Sørensen, J.P., Liénard, P., and Feeny, C. "Agent and instrument in judgments of ritual efficacy." *Journal of Cognition and Culture* 6, nos. 3–4, (2006): 463–482.
45 Whitehouse, H. *Arguments and icons: Divergent modes of religiosity*. Oxford: Oxford University Press, 2000.
46 Whitehouse, H. *Modes of religiosity: A cognitive theory of religious transmission*. Walnut Creek, CA: AltaMira Press, 2004.
47 Whitehouse, Harvey. *Arguments and icons: Divergent modes of religiosity: Divergent modes of religiosity*. Oxford: Oxford University Press, 2000.
48 Whitehouse, Harvey and Jonathan A. Lanman "The ties that bind us: Ritual, fusion, and identification." *Current Anthropology* 55, no. 6 (2014): 000–000.
49 Van Gennep, Arnold, and Gabrielle L. CAFFEE. *The rites of passage*. Translated by Monika B. Vizedomand and Gabrielle L. Caffee, et al. Routledge & Kegan, Paul, 1960.

50 For further examples, see Whitehouse, Harvey. "Rites of terror: Emotion, metaphor, and memory in Melanesian initiation cults." *Journal of the Royal Anthropological Institute* (1996): 703–715.
51 Barrett, J.L. "In the empirical mode: Evidence needed for the modes of religiosity theory." In H. Whitehouse and R. N. McCauley eds., *Mind and religion: Psychological and cognitive foundations of religiosity*. Walnut Creek, CA: AltaMira Press, 2005.
52 Whitehouse, Harvey. *Modes of religiosity: A cognitive theory of religious transmission*. Rowman Altamira, 2004, 66–70.
53 Whitehouse, H. *Inside the cult: religious innovation and transmission in Papua New Guinea*. Oxford: Oxford University Press, 1995.
54 Whitehouse, H. *Arguments and icons: Divergent modes of religiosity*. Oxford: Oxford University Press, 2000.
55 Whitehouse, H. *Modes of religiosity: A cognitive theory of religious transmission*. Walnut Creek, CA: AltaMira Press, 2004.
56 Whitehouse, Harvey. "Dying for the group: Towards a general theory of extreme self-sacrifice." *Behavioral and Brain Sciences* 41 (2018).
57 Apps, Matthew A.J., Ryan McKay, Ruben T. Azevedo, Harvey Whitehouse, and Manos Tsakiris. "Not on my team: Medial prefrontal cortex responses to ingroup fusion and unfair monetary divisions." *Brain and Behavior* 8, no. 8 (2018): e01030.
58 Cho, Philip S., Nicolas Escoffier, Yinan Mao, April Ching, Christopher Green, Jonathan Jong, and Harvey Whitehouse. "Groups and emotional arousal mediate neural synchrony and perceived ritual efficacy." *Frontiers in Psychology* 9 (2018): 2071.
59 Watson-Jones, Rachel E., Cristine H. Legare, Harvey Whitehouse, and Jennifer M. Clegg. "Task-specific effects of ostracism on imitative fidelity in early childhood." *Evolution and Human Behavior* 35, no. 3 (2014): 204–210.
60 Watson-Jones, Rachel E., Harvey Whitehouse, and Cristine H. Legare. "In-group ostracism increases high-fidelity imitation in early childhood." *Psychological Science* 27, no. 1 (2016): 34–42.
61 Legare, Cristine H., Nicole J. Wen, Patricia A. Herrmann, and Harvey Whitehouse. "Imitative flexibility and the development of cultural learning." *Cognition* 142 (2015): 351–361.
62 Kapitány, Rohan, Christopher Kavanagh, Harvey Whitehouse, and Mark Nielsen. "Examining memory for ritualized gesture in complex causal sequences." *Cognition* 181 (2018): 46–57.
63 Richert, R., Whitehouse, H., and Stewart, E. eds. *Memory and analogical thinking in high-arousal rituals*. Walnut Creek, CA: AltaMira Press, 2005.
64 Whitehouse, H.; Martin, L.H. *Theorizing religions past: Historical and archaeological perspectives*. Walnut Creek, CA: AltaMira Press.
65 Whitehouse, Harvey, and James Laidlaw, eds. *Ritual and memory: Toward a comparative anthropology of religion*. Vol. 6. Rowman Altamira, 2004.
66 Atkinson, Quentin D., and Harvey Whitehouse. "The cultural morphospace of ritual form: Examining modes of religiosity cross-culturally." *Evolution and Human Behavior* 32, no. 1 (2011): 50–62.
67 Hodder, Ian, ed. *Religion in the emergence of civilization: Çatalhöyük as a case study*. Cambridge University Press, 2010.
68 Whitehouse, Harvey, Camilla Mazzucato, Ian Hodder, and Quentin D. Atkinson. "Modes of religiosity and the evolution of social complexity at Çatalhöyük." *Religion at work in a Neolithic society* (2014): 134–158.
69 Gantley, Michael, Harvey Whitehouse, and Amy Bogaard. "Material Correlates Analysis (MCA): an innovative way of examining questions in archaeology using ethnographic data." *Advances in Archaeological Practice* 6, no. 4 (2018): 328–341.
70 Whitehouse, H.; Martin, L.H. *Theorizing religions past: Historical and archaeological perspectives*. Walnut Creek, CA: AltaMira Press.

71 Whitehouse, Harvey, Ken Kahn, Michael E. Hochberg, and Joanna J. Bryson. "The role for simulations in theory construction for the social sciences: Case studies concerning divergent modes of religiosity." *Religion, Brain & Behavior* 2, no. 3 (2012): 182–201; Whitehouse, Harvey, Jonathan Jong, Michael D. Buhrmester, Ángel Gómez, Brock Bastian, Christopher M. Kavanagh, Martha Newson et al. "The evolution of extreme cooperation via shared dysphoric experiences." *Scientific Reports* 7 (2017): 44292.

72 Gantley, Michael, Harvey Whitehouse, and Amy Bogaard. "Material correlates analysis (MCA): An innovative way of examining questions in archaeology using ethnographic data." *Advances in Archaeological Practice* 6, no. 4 (2018): 328–341.

73 Whitehouse, Harvey, Pieter François, Patrick E. Savage, Thomas E. Currie, Kevin C. Feeney, Enrico Cioni, Rosalind Purcell, et al. "Complex societies precede moralizing gods throughout world history." *Nature* 568, no. 7751 (2019): 226.

74 Whitehouse, Harvey, and James Laidlaw, eds. *Ritual and memory: Toward a comparative anthropology of religion*. Vol. 6. Rowman Altamira, 2004.

10 Rituals Part 2

What are the functions of rituals?

Rituals are puzzling aspects of human behavior because they continue across generations with little change, often evoke powerful emotions and commitments, and yet the reasons why people perform them are not always obvious, even with contextual information. For example, consider the initiation system of the *Orokavia* of northern Papua, which includes periods of isolation for participants for up to seven years. During this time, they must not be seen or heard beyond their place of confinement, on pain of death. Other aspects of the ritual include being blindfolded by hoods, and herded together in the village, brutally attacked by senior men.[1] How can ritual behavior of this kind be explained? What function, if any, do rituals like this serve in human social groups?

A long tradition of research in the anthropological and sociological literature argues that rituals survive despite their costs because they serve important individual and social functions, such as reducing anxiety, promoting shared beliefs, and creating social cohesion. However, they lack precise and testable hypotheses concerning the mechanisms connecting ritual participation with group cohesion and cooperation.[2] The cognitive science of religion (CSR) builds upon, expands, and refines these earlier functionalist explanations of ritual behavior. CSR scholars often research evolutionary, biological, psychological, and cultural forces that shape ritual behavior. Some scholars can even propose and pinpoint fundamental mechanisms that mediate the relationship between ritual participation and outcomes. They observe and measure these outcomes using a variety of tools in diverse contexts, such as experiments in the laboratory and physiological measurements of local people in field sites around the world.

In this chapter, we consider the benefits of ritual from functionalist perspectives, which include, but are not limited to, research in the cognitive-evolutionary sciences. The functions of rituals in this chapter are divided into two types, effects on the individual and the group. In the real world, these two types of benefits are not mutually exclusive. A ritual can affect the person as an individual and also as a member of a group. This division is employed in the chapter because it helps to explain the different kinds of theories that social scientists employ.

What do rituals do for the individual?

Individuals often engage in their own idiosyncratic form of ritualistic behavior. In a casino, for example, people often perform rigid routines around gambling. They may insist on being in a particular seat, arrange their slot boards a certain way on the table, and even perform some seemingly arbitrary action—like kissing coins before putting them into the slot machine. Another arena where individuals often perform idiosyncratic ritualistic behaviors is in sports. Some players eat only certain foods before a game, sleep in particular clothes and even wear specific underwear. These behaviors are observed even among experts. Many world-famous athletes engage in pregaming rituals, such as now-retired major league baseball player Nomar Garciaparra, who relentlessly strapped and unstrapped his gloves before a game.[3] Interestingly, observational studies suggest that better performers tend to exhibit more ritualistic behavior.[4]

These ritualistic behaviors continue to a large extent because of the effects they have, even if people are not consciously aware of them. Rituals serve critical psychological functions, such as the reduction of anxiety in the face of uncertainty, emotional regulation, and the improvement of mental well-being more generally. Especially when the stakes are high, and the outcome is uncertain, ritual behavior gives people a sense of control over their environment.

One of the earliest descriptions of the association between anxious uncertainty and rituals is the observations of fishing behaviors among the Trobriand Islanders in Melanesia in the early 1900s by one of the most important 20th-century anthropologists, Bronislaw Malinowski. Malinowski observed that the extent to which Trobriand fishermen engaged in rituals was associated with the unpredictability of the terrain and the likelihood of obtaining fish. When the men fished in the calm waters of a lagoon, they did not perform any rituals. Yet when the men fished in turbulent, shark-infested waters, and when the likelihood of catching fish was highly uncertain, they performed rituals for their safety and protection. Malinowski asserted that rituals functioned to relieve people of their anxiety over uncertainty when the outcome was beyond human control[5] and important.

Malinowski's work remains the cornerstone of anxiety reduction explanation of ritual behavior. However, until relatively recently, quantitative evidence for these conjectures was scarce. Research in the psychological sciences has now begun to emerge to support these claims. For instance, research has found a relationship between the extent to which athletes and fishermen engage in rituals and the unpredictability of their jobs.[6,7] Psychologists have also reported that participating in a set of ritualized behaviors after writing about the death of a loved one increased people's feelings of control and lessened their feelings of grief, whereas sitting in silence did not.[8] Other researchers have reported the emergence of rituals among diverse populations facing uncontrollable conditions. These populations include gamblers, consumers, test-taking students, targets of warfare, puzzle solvers, and athletes.[9] Other research with nonhuman animals and young children has found that once you introduce unpredictability to the environment, spontaneous ritual behavior emerges.[10]

Anthropologists Pascal Boyer and Pierre Lienard greatly enhanced the anxiety reduction account of ritual by taking into account the cognitive mechanisms involved in ritualized behavior. They explained features that people intuitively recognize as ritualized.[11,12] These behaviors include:

- Compulsion: it would be dangerous not to act.
- Rigidity: adherence to a particular way of acting.
- Goal-demotion: action-sequences performed are divorced from their common goals.
- Internal repetition and redundancy: repeated enactments of identical sequences within the same ritual.
- A restricted range of themes: such as pollution and purification, danger and protection, order, and boundaries.

Boyer and Lienard's model of ritualized behavior explains behaviors that are found in childhood, features of obsessive-compulsive disorder, and many collective cultural behaviors. They propose that perceived threats (such as psychological distress and contamination) activate mental security systems, which results in security-related behavior.[13] Boyer and Lienard's theory, like many in CSR also evokes evolutionary considerations. Specifically, Boyer and Lienard propose that ritualized behavior spontaneously emerges because it triggers an evolved "Hazard Precaution System" geared towards the detection of and reaction to inferred fitness threats. Throughout human history, these threats to our survival were ubiquitous, and include predation, intrusion by strangers, contamination, contagion, social offense, and harm to offspring. Anxiety is lowered by subjectively containing it through scripted action. In particular, rituals tend to be parsed into smaller steps. Participants focus on the activity they are performing, not on the goal of each behavior, which swamps working memory. Thus, attention is readily deployed towards the concern to perform the actions correctly. These behaviors eliminate unwanted thoughts. These effects are at least temporary, while the acts are performed, and so the actions are repeated over and over in a bid to reduce anxiety.

Boyer and Lienard argue that ritualized behavior is a by-product of the activation of systems that are triggered in response to perceived danger in the environment (e.g. hazard precaution). Their account suggests that we perform rituals, especially when this precaution system is activated and that rituals are compelling because of their temporary anxiety-relieving effects. Furthermore, the authors propose an evolutionary account of the spread of cultural rituals. They claim that all else being equal, these rituals that activate the Hazard Precaution System will be more attention-grabbing and compelling in comparison to other types of rituals, and thus will tend to be transmitted.[14]

Experimental and observational research in CSR supports the anxiety reduction aspect of Hazard Precaution theory. For instance, religious studies scholar Martin Lang and colleagues found support for the first crucial step in this anxiety-reduction process, that ritual is a natural response to anxiety. More specifically, they found that anxiety significantly predicted the number of movements participants made while cleaning an object. The task involved cleaning an object and the time spent cleaning.[15] Lang and colleagues explained these findings in light of the entropy reduction model of ritual. Specifically, to cope with uncertainty, participants adopted familiar and predictable behavioral sequences and performed them repetitively to gain a sense of predictability and control over the situation.

Naturalistic studies of religious women in Israel during the 2006 Lebanon War by evolutionary anthropologist Richard Sosis and colleagues also support these claims about the relationship between ritual and anxiety.[16] Sosis and colleagues found that psalm recitation was associated with lower rates of anxiety among women who remained in the north during the war, and who faced the uncertainty of warfare. The researchers also found no relationship between this recitation ritual and stress among women who relocated outside the war zone and had additional stressors that they could control, such as finding new schools. Sosis and colleagues proposed that psalm recitation reduces anxiety caused by the uncontrollable conditions of war, but it is ineffective at combating more mundane, controllable stressors. In sum, according to these accounts, ritualized behavior results in regained feelings of control or containment of anxiety in the face of potential hazards.

More recently, in a controlled field study among the Marathi Hindu community in Mauritius, Xygalatas, and colleagues demonstrated that ritual actually does reduce anxiety.[17] In their research, 75 participants first experienced anxiety induction through public speaking. They were asked to either perform their habitual ritual in a local temple (ritual condition) or sit and relax (control condition). The results revealed that participants in the ritual condition reported lower perceived anxiety after the ritual treatment. Crucially, they also displayed lower physiological anxiety, which was assessed as heart-rate variability. This research provides experimental vindication of Malinwoski's anecdotal insights and Sosis' correlational evidence about the role of ritual behavior on anxiety reduction. Other scholars have asserted that rituals serve similar functions for the social group, and we will turn to these group-level functionalist theories next.

Participation 1: Personal rituals

1 Make a note of any personal rituals that you perform, for example, before an exam, such as using the same pen or equipment, sitting in the same seat, or arranging your papers and pens in a particular way.
2 Which theories covered so far in this chapter help to explain your behavior? Write your answer in a few sentences.

Summary of What do Rituals do for the individual?

- Ritualistic behaviors often continue because of the unconscious effects they have on the performer.
- Rituals serve critical psychological functions, such as the reduction of anxiety in the face of uncertainty.
- Hazard Precaution Theory proposes that ritualized behavior emerges when the mind detects threats in the environment. By performing habitual behaviors repeatedly people gain a sense of control over the situation.
- According to Hazard Precaution Theory, ritualized behavior is a by-product of the activation of threat detection systems.

What do rituals do for the group?

Anthropologists have long noted that rituals confer tangible benefits to the social group. Importantly, these benefits exceed their costs, which helps to explain why people engage in such time-consuming, elaborate, and often expensive practices. The postulated benefits of rituals include reaffirming the social order, reinforcing core group values, and redefining social relationships at a time of social uncertainty and change.[18] Yet, the evidence for these functionalist theories is limited. It is almost exclusively observational, depends mainly upon ethnographic case studies, and the mechanisms that drive these effects are underspecified. For example, theories propose that rituals promote solidarity, but do not specify how. Other anthropological theories of ritual focus on explaining the local details of rituals embedded in specific contexts and are thus less effective as a means to explain the effects of rituals in other contexts.

Cognitive scientists of religion often adopt an evolutionary approach to explain why people perform cultural rituals. From one evolutionary perspective known as behavioral ecology, ritual behaviors appear at first to be especially perplexing. Behavioral ecologists note that humans and other animals have limited resources. Time and energy spent doing one activity detract from other activities that people could be doing, including those that contribute to their survival, such as foraging for food or mating. Yet living in groups is an adaptive problem. Throughout human history, living in groups has been essential to our survival as a species. Our ancestral past was characterized by small nomadic groups that were entirely dependent on each member to survive. It discouraged predators, allowed for coordinated caretaking of children and food collection and preparation, and aided technological innovation, to name a few. Yet group-living also has many challenges.

On the one hand, to reap the benefits of living in a group, you have to cooperate. Yet how do you know whom to trust? Members of groups often cheat or engage in social loafing—they are free-riders because they reap the rewards of the group without equivalent contributions. For example, think about a student in your group project who did next to nothing and got the same grade as you. Throughout our evolutionary history, it was crucial to survival to have group members who were loyal to the group and who cooperated. Some CSR theorists propose that rituals evolved to solve this problem of whom to trust. Specifically, they argue that rituals serve to identify group members, enable people to demonstrate their commitment to the group's values, facilitate cooperation between group members, and increase social cohesion.[19]

Social cohesion

One way to increase trust is to facilitate social cohesion among groups of people. Sociologist Émile Durkheim famously proposed that collective rituals produce a feeling of belonging, assimilation, and create a sense of collective unity[20] that he called "collective effervescence."

Think about a Christian evangelical megachurch worship service, a faith-healing ritual, or political rallies. The type of electricity and exaltation generated by the closeness of people in these rituals is what Durkheim meant by the term collective effervescence. Durkheim's claim has initiated a plethora of research in the social sciences. Many studies demonstrate an association between group ritual participation and positive social outcomes such as social cohesion and cooperation.[21] These associations suggest but do not prove that ritual participation causes social cohesion. Further, Durkheim's theory does not say much about the mechanisms through which collective effervescence occurs. Recent research by CSR scholars provides crucial data to refine this theory.

Consider again the Modes of Religiosity theory (MOR) that we covered in the last chapter. To recap, social anthropologist Harvey Whitehouse encountered two different types of movements during his fieldwork in Papua New Guinea, and he proposed that the patterns he observed applied to different contexts around the world. One of these modes is the imagistic mode. This mode is characterized by infrequent rituals, high sensory pageantry, and emotional arousal, episodic recall, and strong social cohesion. Examples of these types of rituals include rites of passage—such as initiation rituals to mark a change in people's social status, common in small-scale traditional societies,[22] just like the initiation system of the *Orokavia* of northern Papua described at the beginning of this chapter. These rituals typically include traumatic ordeals, such as extended periods of isolation, piercing, burning, and scarification.[23]

Whitehouse recently turned his attention to understanding one aspect of the imagistic mode in more detail. He was especially interested in understanding how imagistic rituals promote strong, relational bonds with in-group members. Drawing from social psychological theories, Whitehouse and colleagues proposed that intense and arousing group rituals involve the establishment of personally salient episodic memories that come to form part of the essential autobiographical self. When such memories are shared with a group, it creates the conditions for participants to fuse their personal identities with the group. In other words, the boundary between personal and group identity becomes porous. For instance, for a fused revolutionary insurgent, making their battalion salient would also activate their personal identity.

Whitehouse proposes that these imagistic rituals exploit the tendency to fuse with kin.[24] Feeling connected to and protecting kin is a sound adaptive strategy for the survival of one's genetic material. These kin connections are based in part upon shared experiences with family members. Rituals that create intense emotions as part of shared physiological experiences endowed with similar meanings may well recreate these feelings in a short period, and indeed, between us and non-genetic kin (see Figure 10.1).

This fusion of individual and group identities has significant consequences for group cohesion. For example, when another group member is threatened, it prompts the same defensive reactions as a personal attack or attack on one's kin. Highly fused individuals are more likely to fight, sacrifice, and die for their group than those who simply identify as a member of the group.[25]

Consistent with this, a series of studies found that encouraging fused persons to focus on shared core characteristics of members of their country increased their endorsement of making extreme sacrifices for their country, whether participants were from China, India, the United States, or Spain.[26]

Whitehouse and colleagues have also conducted investigations that test the imagistic pathway to fusion. They have used data from controlled psychological experiments and ethnographic, archaeological, and historical records[27] to explain the dynamics of social cohesion in a broad range of groups, including among martial arts practitioners[28] and soccer fans,[29] sectarianists in Northern Ireland,[30] and those affected by the Boston bombing.[31] For example, in one study, the researchers surveyed Libyan revolutionary battalion members who fought against Gaddafi's regime in 2011. They found that the civilians-turned-fighters were very highly fused with their fellow fighters.[32] Furthermore, many frontline fighters reported feeling more fused with their battalion than their family. One interpretation of these findings is that fighting together, and other emotionally intense experiences associated with frontline combat, may have fostered and strengthened fusion within the group. Whitehouse and colleagues propose that their theory of identity fusion can explain other forms of self-sacrifice. These include suicide terrorism, gang-related violence, and other forms of extreme pro-group action.[33]

Anthropologist Dimitris Xygalatas and colleagues' research on rituals has further refined the understanding of the relationship between rituals and social cohesion. Xygalatas' research is distinctive because of his methods. Often psychologists conduct quantitative experiments in the lab—and are

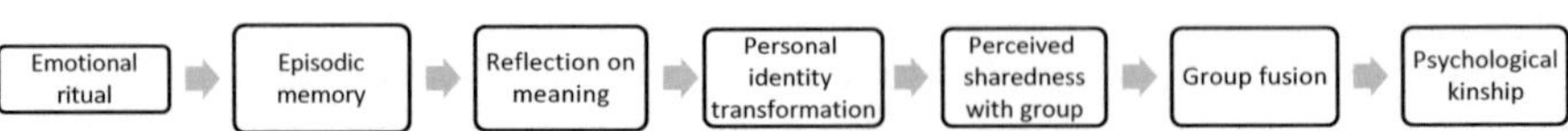

Figure 10.1 Pathways to group fusion.[34]

accused of lacking real-world applicability. Anthropologists do qualitative research in a geographical area of interest, are accused of lacking control over their study and in ritual studies, assuming people know why they perform rituals. Xygalatas combines the best of these two methods by conducting quasi-experimental studies (often including physiological monitoring) in naturalistic field settings. In other words, after spending time getting to know the people and gaining their trust, he brings the lab and equipment to the people he is interested in understanding. This methodology includes videotaping sacred ceremonies, distributing questionnaires before and after peak ritual events, and village communities have even permitted his research team to hook them up to heart rate monitors, motion detectors, and health monitors.

Most of Xygalatas' research focuses on extreme rituals such as those involving fire-walking and body piercing.[35] These rituals often last for days and include many bloody ordeals, including self-mutilation, by covering the body in hooks or inserting large objects through the mouth. They are labeled as extreme and dysphoric rituals by Xygalatas and colleagues because of the exceptionally high levels of physiological arousal that they have recorded during participation, indicating stress and pain.[36,37]

Figure 10.2 CSR scholars are interested in the effects of participating in high-intensity rituals, like the extreme piercing in Phuket, Thailand, as part of the Phuket Vegetarian Festival or Nine Emperor Gods Fest. Inflicting and experiencing pain in a ritual setting may serve psychological and social functions. (Image credit: Phuketian.S/Shutterstock.com).

Extreme rituals are particularly interesting because people engage in these painful, costly rituals when they could be doing other things with their time. In one series of studies, Xygalatas and colleagues found that people donated more money to their temple after participating in a high-intensity Hindu ritual compared with a low-intensity ritual. Furthermore, the level of experienced pain correlated with the amount of donation.[38] These findings suggest that rituals that induce suffering lead to a stronger sense of group cohesion.

Much like the runners' high experienced in a marathon, Xygalatas and colleagues propose that ritual participants may well experience a firewalkers' high.[39] This state is characterized by physiological changes (i.e. the endogenous release of opioids) that offset pain but also makes them happier, ecstatic, and more amenable to bonding with their fellow participants. Indeed, people who participate in exhausting ritual ordeals report the same feelings of euphoria and bliss as marathon runners do. Yet, what about people who observe but do not participate in communal rituals? Do they receive any benefits?

In another series of studies, Xygalatas and colleagues examined the heart rates of people during an annual ritual in Spain. At the rural village of San Pedro Manrique, a fire-walking ceremony takes place at midnight on the summer solstice in an area built specifically for the ceremony, which accommodates 3,000 spectators, around six times the number of people in the village. Before the ceremony, those who will fire-walk are accompanied by fellow villagers who proceed throughout the village. The ceremony culminates in the fire-walk, which lasts around half an hour. One by one, the participants walk across a seven-meter bed of red-hot coals (with surface temperatures of 677°C!), usually carrying a loved-one on their backs.

The Xygalatas team found that performers had exceptionally high (often dangerously high) heart rates. Even more impressive, related spectators (but not unrelated ones) had synchronized heart rates during the ritual. When the researchers mapped the social network of the area, they found that social proximity predicted physiological synchrony. In other words, people's heart rates synchronized more closely with those of their friends and relatives during the ritual, even if they were not interacting directly with them. It seems that rituals are likely to strengthen the bonds between people via shared physiological states. Yet this effect is most potent between those who already hold an affiliation. It does not generalize to strangers.[40]

Research by developmental and cross-cultural psychologist Legare and colleagues supports this interpretation of the relationship between in-group members, ritual actions, and social cohesion, and we covered some of this research in the previous chapter.[41] For example, in one series of studies, researchers examined the impact of ritual participation versus another activity on children's in-group and out-group affiliation.[42] The researchers found that the experience of participating in a ritual, rather than group activity alone, increases in-group affiliation. The results provide insight into the early developing preference for in-group members and are consistent with the proposal that rituals facilitate in-group cohesion. They also suggest that humans are psychologically prepared to engage in ritual as a means of in-group affiliation. Other theories in CSR further extend these findings.

Key points

- A long tradition of research in the anthropological and sociological literature argues that collective rituals enable participants to affiliate with group members by creating a sense of collective unity.
- Cognitive scientists of religion extend and refine these theories by adopting an evolutionary approach to explain why people perform cultural rituals.
- Research in CSR has further refined the understanding of the relationship between rituals and social cohesion using data from controlled psychological experiments, quasi-experimental field experiments, and the ethnographic, archaeological, and historical records.
- Researchers in CSR have examined the physiological, psychological, and social mechanisms through which group affiliation occurs in rituals.

Costly signaling

Costly signaling theory may explain the function of ritualized behaviors in human social groups. The starting point of this theory is the observation that many rituals include costly practices. These costs take many forms, such as calories, time, pain, and money. Costly signaling theory construes some costly actions, especially those that have the additional properties of being honest and hard to fake, as sending a message to the receiver. The message includes information about reliability (i.e. honesty) of the signal and promoting trustworthiness of members of the group, ultimately facilitating group cooperation and survival.

Versions of costly signaling theory explain the occurrence of honest, hard-to-fake signaling behaviors in many domains, including conspicuous consumption in market economics and animal behavior. Perhaps the most famous example of the latter is the peacock's tail. Peacock females (i.e. peahens) cannot judge a male's genetic quality directly, so they attend to signals that the males provide. Males advertise their genetic condition by their bright feathers and long flamboyant tails. These features are costly—they are energetically expensive to produce and maintain, and the bird is more noticeable to predators—but their costliness ensures their reliability.

Another often-cited example of costly signaling in behavioral ecology is stotting behavior (i.e. continuously jumping high) by gazelles when approached by predators, such as lions, in their natural habitat. This behavior sends a signal to the predator about the animal's speed and energy. The gazelle is effectively saying to the lion, "don't waste your time chasing me; I will get away." This behavior discourages the predator, who selects a non-stotting target. In return, the gazelle is free from the demands of being pursued by the predator.

Figure 10.3 A running Springbok jumping high in South Africa. (Image credit: Johan Swanepoel/Shutterstock.com).

Evolutionary anthropologists and archaeologists have argued that natural selection has favored high-cost behaviors as a mechanism of honest signaling in human contexts. In cultures where the costs of dishonest signaling are high, receivers will tend to interpret costly actions as honest signaling. For example, if organizing a social event such as a feast requires massive coordination efforts, then a successful feast could provide evidence of the host's social support and status.

Sosis has extended the costly signaling theory to explain the function of ritualized behaviors in human social groups, of which there are many examples. Consider ultra-Orthodox Jews who spend hours per day worshipping at the Western Wall in Jerusalem. Or, the Shiite Muslims in Karbala, Iraq, who beat their backs with chains to mark the killing of one of their saints. Or young Christian men in Bulgaria who dive into icy waters to retrieve the crucifix to mark the feast of Epiphany Monday. Sosis notes that many ritual behaviors are also hard-to-fake and costly, consuming participants' time, energy, and commitment.[43] These behaviors may serve as a communicative signal that the performer is a genuine cooperator and, therefore, a trustworthy member of the group. In other words, some rituals promote group cohesion by requiring members to engage in behavior that is too costly to fake. They also prevent free-riders from joining the group.

Sosis has provided naturalistic, historical, and experimental support for aspects of this costly signaling theory. For instance, he found that communities such as 19th-century religious communes that required more commitments from their members (e.g. ritual attendance, resource sharing), tended to have more trust between group members compared to those that had fewer responsibilities.

They also tended to survive longer.[44] Sosis found a similar pattern on extant communes in Israel known as kibbutzim, where religious kibbutzim exhibited greater trust and cooperation between members than secular kibbutzim.[45]

Likewise, research by anthropologist Montserrat Soler supports the claim that ritual effectively predicts willingness to cooperate with other group members and that others are more likely to then cooperate. Soler studied adherents of Candomblé, an African diasporic religion organized in autonomous congregations primarily located in low-income urban areas in northeast Brazil. She found that those who reported higher levels of religious commitment behaved more generously in a public goods economic game and experienced more cooperation within their religious community.[46] Other researchers have found that low-status individuals seek costlier forms of ritual participation. For example, they put more needles through their bodies,[47] and people who engage in costlier rituals reap more cooperative benefits.[48]

Costly signaling theory has the potential to explain why many people in religious communities participate in costly ritual behavior. Yet signaling systems are complex. Not all signals are honest, or hard-to-fake, and not all honest and hard-to-fake signals are costly. To understand the function of a signal, therefore, necessitates an understanding of the situation, including aspects such as the context, signaler's attributes, receiver's interpretations, and responses, and signal costs.[49] To investigate the function of a signal in a ritual requires expert knowledge of the culture, which anthropologists are especially equipped to provide.

Key points

- Many rituals include behaviors that are costly and judged by others as a reliable signal of commitment to the group.
- One consequence of performing costly ritual behaviors is that it distinguishes participants as genuine cooperators.
- Research supports this account of the relationship between practices and group affiliation in rituals.

Credibility enhancing displays (CREDs)

Evolutionary anthropologist Joseph Henrich has proposed an additional group-level function that ritual participation serves. Namely, it increases the credibility of the performer, which in turn means that the ideas and behaviors of the group are more likely to spread and survive.[50] Henrich starts with the following problem: people are biased to follow the ideas and practices of prestigious people in a group, yet how do we know that we can trust that what people say is their sincere belief? Acting and failing to act on an idea serve as crucial markers of true faith to others. For instance, if I tell you that the blue mushrooms are not poisonous, but during a ritual ceremony, I do not eat them, then my behavior would make you doubt my sincere belief.

Conversely, if I did eat the blue mushrooms, then you would be more likely to accept that the mushrooms were not poisonous. We take exceptionally costly actions to entail and lend credence to beliefs, especially when those beliefs are said to be sincerely held religious convictions, for example, the Ten Commandments in the Bible. Consider further suicide attacks and martyrdom in religious traditions such as Al Qaeda, Hamas, or Hezbollah. The act of dying for your beliefs communicates both commitments to the faith and the strength of belief in the afterlife. These behaviors are influential communicative acts. In short, actions speak louder than words. In this sense, costly rituals can be credibility enhancing displays (CREDs) of one's commitment to the values and ideals of the group.

The history of group dynamics demonstrates why skepticism about whom to trust would be inherent when people unite. The history of groups has been marred with scandal, including, but not limited to, those committed by religious leaders. Consider, for example, the 2017 case of Pentecostal church leaders in Rwanda who were arrested for the mismanagement of church finances.[51] By contrast, consider ascetic leaders who donate their money to charity and live humbly. If both leaders preach the value of social responsibility, you are, of course, more likely to believe and transmit the belief system of the person who "walks the walk." For instance, anthropologists Manvir Singh and Joseph Henrich found that shamans who observe costly prohibitions are regarded as more cooperative, greater believers, and more supernaturally powerful than others.[52]

Researchers in CSR have also begun to investigate what happens to a person's faith when they detect religious hypocrisy. Social anthropologist Jon Lanman and colleagues have proposed that failing to act in line with stated beliefs or acting in a way that contradicts those beliefs constitutes credibility undermining displays (CRUDs). These undermining displays, Lanman argues, help to explain the rejection of religion.[53] However, disengagement from religion may well depend on other factors, such as the extent to which the individual was entrenched in the belief system.[54] Recent research on the U.S. Catholic clergy abuse scandals supports these claims. For instance, the scandals result in a significant and long-lasting decline in religious participation in the zip code where the scandal occurs, and in charitable contributions for the Catholic church more generally.[55]

The theory of CREDs is related to costly signaling but is also distinct from it. Costly signaling communicates something that already exists (i.e. your commitment to values) through behaviors such as fasting, abstinence, and participation in painful rituals. Ritual practices are time-consuming and elaborate and act as credibility enhancing displays for those performing them, which provide salient behavioral manifestations of commitment and foster the cultural transmission of these commitments to others.[56] If I do something based on my belief, then you are also likely to copy that behavior and accept that my faith is true.

Key points

- Actions speak louder than words.
- People risk social ostracism for not participating in rituals.
- Ritual actions enhance the credibility of the performer.
- Credible leaders and participants are more likely to spread their ideas and behaviors successfully.
- Those who fail to act in accord with their stated beliefs discourage others from believing what they say.

Social complexity

Scholars in CSR have suggested that aspects of religion functions enable the rapid expansion and increasing complexity of societies.[57] One explanation (that we covered in Chapter 7: Supernatural Agents), is known as the "moralizing gods" hypothesis. This hypothesis proposes that the belief in morally concerned supernatural agents culturally evolved to facilitate cooperation among strangers in large-scale societies. This purported effect is partly due to the principle that "watched people are nice people." When people believe God is watching, for instance, they are less likely to breach normative rules.[58] One challenge to this moralizing gods hypothesis comes from Whitehouse and colleagues. They place ritual, not details of beliefs about deities, as a critical variable facilitating the complexity and expansion of society.

Consider again the Modes of Religiosity theory (MOR) that we covered in the last chapter. To recap, at the core of MOR theory is a hypothesis about the causal links between ritual performance and features of social morphology, such as the scale, structure, and cohesiveness of ancient groups. Recently, Whitehouse and colleagues have investigated causal links between ritual performance in the doctrinal mode, (characterized by frequent rituals, low sensory pageantry, and semantic recall, and the evolution of social complexity) and the evolution of social complexity using systematic comparisons of archaeological and historical data around the globe.

Whitehouse and colleagues' findings challenge the moralizing gods hypothesis because they propose that moralizing gods follow, rather than precede substantial increases in social complexity.[59] Whitehouse and colleagues argue that doctrinal rituals, by contrast, play a crucial role in the rise of agriculture and the initial emergence of large-scale civilizations, by facilitating the standardization of religious traditions across large populations.[60,61] Their results suggest that ritual practices were more important than the belief in moralizing gods to the initial rise of social complexity even if moralizing gods may have subsequently helped much larger-scale empires to flourish and spread. Both the moralizing gods hypothesis and MOR theory accord a central role to aspects of religion in shaping the emergence and survival of modern societies.

Participation 2: Evolutionary theories of rituals

1 Refer back to Tables 3.4 and 3.6 in Chapter 3 (Research Questions) for accounts of the origin and function of religion.
2 Go through this chapter again and list all theories about the origins and functions of rituals. Label the accounts as by-product or adaptations and specify who benefits (individual, group).
3 Compare your answer to another student's and note whether you arrived at the same, or different, conclusions.

Key points

- CSR scholars have proposed relationships between religion and expansion and the increasing complexity of society.
- The moralizing gods hypothesis proposes that belief in moralizing gods played a causal role in the emergence of large-scale, complex societies.
- Research by Whitehouse and colleagues challenges the moralizing gods hypothesis and instead proposes that doctrinal rituals served to enable large-scale, complex societies.

Summary of What do rituals do for the group?

- Rituals serve critical social functions, such as reducing anxiety, promoting shared beliefs, and creating social cohesion in groups.
- People are psychologically prepared to engage in ritual as a means of in-group affiliation.
- Ritual participation creates a sense of collective unity through multiple means.
- Costly behaviors showcase a commitment to the group and promote trust.
- Ritual behaviors enhance the credibility of the performers.
- Those who do not participate in ritual risk being outcast from the social group.
- Some scholars argue that doctrinal rituals facilitate the rise and spread of complex societies.

Research case study: Mortuary rituals

Mortuary practices are among the most ubiquitous features of human cultural traditions, and they highlight the extent to which people engage in ritualistic behaviors. Even early modern humans in the Paleolithic era did not merely discard their dead, but deliberately buried them deep in the ground, manipulated their bodies into certain positions, accompanied with flowers, tools, and other artifacts. The ethnographic record evidences the dazzling array of conventional practices undertaken when a member of the community dies. The number of different mortuary practices is apparent in the treatment of the corpse before disposal. Bodies are washed, anointed, dismantled, clothed, wrapped, viewed extensively, embraced, shouted at, danced over, among other practices. How can we understand these behaviors?

Anthropologists have long documented rich accounts of mortuary practices. They have traditionally tended to focus on how rituals are practiced in particular regions, explaining unique aspects of these practices regarding the meanings they hold for people, such as shared ideas about the process of death and identity of the dead and the afterlife. Classical anthropological theories contend that mortuary rituals are a product of shared insights about the self, process of death, the identity of the dead in the afterlife, and the identity of the living. The researcher aims to decode such meanings. Yet mortuary practices are functionally opaque; that is to say, there is no apparent physical-causal relationship between the actions and the goal. Just like other rituals, people's explanation for actions following a death is often vague. Like most collective rituals, they do not convey coded meanings except in the vaguest sense. Despite archaeological and cross-cultural findings on mortuary burials, for instance, there is little consensus over the extent to which—if at all— practices are related to afterlife beliefs.

Other explanations about why people perform mortuary rituals have looked beyond the details of local belief systems to explain their recurrence throughout history and across cultures. Along with anthropologists Daniel Fessler and Maya Marin, we systematically compared ethnographic accounts of mortuary practices in a global database. We did this by having Research Assistants collect excerpts of rituals from the database. Then other researchers completed a questionnaire about aspects of the rituals, enabling them to quantify and statistically analyze the results.

We found that there were similarities. For instance, most often the bereaved (e.g. kin) participated in the preparation of the corpse. They tended to engage in moderately intimate tactile contact with the body (i.e. whether they viewed them, touched them), and members of the existing community—but not members of other communities, attended the ritual. From these findings and drawing from evolutionary insights and clinical research, which suggest that seeing and touching the corpse is the most effective means to realizing the person is dead, my colleagues and I conducted a series of interviews with people who had been recently bereaved. We investigated the possibility that people who had seen the corpse were less likely to mistakenly see or hear the person in the environment because they had cognitively processed the person as dead, just like they would be participating in mortuary rituals.

This research supports and extends functionalist theories, which claim that rituals serve important individual and group functions following the death of a group member. Based on the studies of myself and my colleagues, we proposed that by exposing the bereaved to the corpse, mortuary rituals have benefits to the individual. Specifically, they shorten and regulate the period of grief-induced disability, regain feelings of control in the face of both psychological threat (i.e. distress) and actual threat (i.e. contamination danger posed by corpses). As rituals are typically communal, and often expensive, they also serve important social functions. They help the bereaved individual to identify group members who can support them.

Additionally, they enable the bereaved individual and others to demonstrate their commitment to the group via costly signaling (especially those who handle the corpse). They also facilitate the formation of new social bonds that are essential to psychological well-being (and survival in our ancestral past). This research suggests that mortuary rituals are not for the dead but serve the living.

Questions

1 In your own words, summarize the claims the researchers (White and colleagues) are making.
2 Based on your experience of mortuary rituals (or those you have seen on TV), do you agree or disagree with these claims?
3 What are the differences and similarities between this research and previous research on mortuary rituals?
4 What do you think demarks this research as typical of the CSR approach to religion?
5 What do you think are the real-world implications of this theory on modern funerary practices?

Further reading

1 Murray, D., Fessler, Daniel M.T., Kerry, N., White, C. and Marin, M. (2017). "The kiss of death: Three tests of the relationship between disease threat and physical contact within traditional cultures." *Evolution and Human Behavior* 38, no. 1, 63–70.
2 White, Claire, Maya Marin, and Daniel M.T. Fessler. "Not just dead meat: An evolutionary account of corpse treatment in mortuary rituals." *Journal of Cognition and Culture* 17, no. 1–2 (2017): 146–168.
3 White, C. and Fessler, Daniel M.T. "An evolutionary account of vigilance in grief." *Evolution, Medicine, and Public Health* 1 (2018): 34–42.
4 White, C. Mortuary Practices. In Barrett, Justin L. (Ed.) *Oxford university handbook on the cognitive science of religion*. Oxford University Press, 2021.

Chapter summary

Scholars have tackled the crucial question of why people perform rituals. In this chapter, we have covered some functions that rituals serve, often based on evolutionary considerations. These include theories about how rituals serve to facilitate social groups, which were essential for our survival as a species. When taken together, research and theories in CSR help to demonstrate that rituals are not for the naïve or religious fanatics, but that these behaviors are a product of being human.

Discussion questions

1. Think about a time that you or another person you know have been socially isolated, such as being ignored or not included in a group activity, or imagine such an event. Consider how you felt, or how you would feel. Do you think that these feelings would motivate you to participate in rituals that promote the group's beliefs? Explain in a few sentences.
2. Which theory of rituals covered in the last two chapters do you find the most compelling? Why? Answer in a few sentences.
3. What are the main contributions of CSR to the study of ritual? Explain in a few sentences.
4. What are the assumptions of evolutionary theories of ritual? For example, do some propose that cultural rituals evolved because of their fitness-enhancing effects (i.e. an adaptation)? Alternatively, cultural rituals are a by-product of something else? Answer in a few sentences.

Selected further reading

Articles

1. Henrich, Joseph. "The evolution of costly displays, cooperation, and religion: Credibility enhancing displays and their implications for cultural evolution." *Evolution and Human Behavior* 30, no. 4 (2009): 244–260.
2. Sosis, Richard. "Religious behaviors, badges, and bans: Signaling theory and the evolution of religion." In *Where God and science meet: How brain and evolutionary studies alter our understanding of religion* 1 (2006): 61–86.
3. Watson-Jones, Rachel E., and Cristine H. Legare. "The social functions of group rituals." *Current Directions in Psychological Science* 25, no. 1 (2016): 42–46.

Books

1. Xygalatas, Dimitris. *The Power of Rituals*. Profile Books (forthcoming 2021).

Notes

1 Whitehouse, Harvey. "Rites of terror: Emotion, metaphor and memory in Melanesian initiation cults." *Journal of the Royal Anthropological Institute* (1996): 703–715.
2 Whitehouse, Harvey, Jonathan A. Lanman, Greg Downey, Leah A. Fredman, William B. Swann Jr, Daniel H. Lende, Robert N. McCauley et al. "The ties that bind us: Ritual, fusion, and identification." *Current Anthropology* 55, no. 6 (2014): 1–22.
3 http://articles.latimes.com/2006/sep/30/entertainment/et-nomar30.
4 Foster, David J., Daniel A. Weigand, and Dean Baines. "The effect of removing superstitious behavior and introducing a pre-performance routine on basketball free-throw performance." *Journal of Applied Sport Psychology* 18, no. 2 (2006): 167–171.
5 Malinowski, Bronislaw, and Robert Redfield. *Magic, science and religion and other essays: Selected, and with an Introduction by Robert Redfield*. 1948.
6 Malinowski, Bronislaw, and Robert Redfield. *Magic, science and religion and other essays: Selected, and with an Introduction by Robert Redfield*. 1948.
7 Whitson, Jennifer A., and Adam D. Galinsky. "Lacking control increases illusory pattern perception." *Science* 322, no. 5898 (2008): 115–117.
8 Norton, Michael I., and Francesca Gino. "Rituals alleviate grieving for loved ones, lovers, and lotteries." *Journal of Experimental Psychology: General* 143, no. 1 (2014): 266.
9 For a list of this research, see Sosis, Richard, and W. Penn Handwerker. "Psalms and coping with uncertainty: Religious Israeli women's responses to the 2006 Lebanon War." *American Anthropologist* 113, no. 1 (2011): 40–55.
10 Skinner, B.F. "'Superstition' in the Pigeon." *Journal of Experimental Psychology* 38 (1948): 168–172.
11 Boyer, P., and Liénard, P. (2006). "Why ritualized behaviour? Precaution systems and action parsing in developmental, pathological, and cultural rituals." *Behavioral and Brain Sciences* 29, 595–613.
12 Rappaport, Roy A. *Ritual and religion in the making of humanity*. Vol. 110. Cambridge University Press, 1999.
13 Boyer, Pascal, and Pierre Liénard. "Precaution systems and ritualized behavior." *Behavioral and Brain Sciences* 29, no. 6 (2006): 635–641.
14 Why do they spread? Liénard, P., and Boyer, P. "Whence collective rituals? A cultural selection model of ritualized behavior." *American Anthropologist* 108, no. 4 (2006): 814–827.
15 Lang, Martin, Jan Krátký, John H. Shaver, Danijela Jerotijević, and Dimitris Xygalatas. "Effects of anxiety on spontaneous ritualized behavior." *Current Biology* 25, no. 14 (2015): 1892–1897.
16 Sosis, Richard, and W. Penn Handwerker. "Psalms and coping with uncertainty: Religious Israeli women's responses to the 2006 Lebanon War." *American Anthropologist* 113, no. 1 (2011): 40–55.
17 Lang, M., J. Krátký, and D. Xygalatas. "The role of ritual behaviour in anxiety reduction: An investigation of Marathi religious practices in Mauritius." *Philosophical Transactions of the Royal Society B* 375, no. 1805 (2020): 20190431.
18 E.g. Durkheim, Émile. *The elementary forms of religious life* (1912, 1995); Goody, Jack. *Death and the ancestors: A study of the mortuary customs of the LoDagaa of West Africa*. Routledge, 2013; Hertz, Robert. "A contribution to the study of the collective representation of death." *Death and the right hand. 1901. Reprint.* R. Needham and C. Needham eds. Glencoe, Illinois: The Free Press, 1960; van Gennep, Arnold. *The rites of passage*. 1909. Reprint, Paris: 1960.
19 Watson-Jones, Rachel E., and Cristine H. Legare. "The social functions of group rituals." *Current Directions in Psychological Science* 25, no. 1 (2016): 42–46.
20 Durkheim, Émile. *The elementary forms of the religious life*. New York: Free Press, 1915.

21 Hobson, Nicholas M., Juliana Schroeder, Jane L. Risen, Dimitris Xygalatas, and Michael Inzlicht. "The psychology of rituals: An integrative review and process-based framework." *Personality and Social Psychology Review* (2017): 11.
22 Van Gennep, Arnold, and Gabrielle L. Caffee. *The rites of passage*. Translated by Monika B. Vizedomand and Gabrielle L. Caffee, et al. Routledge & Kegan Paul, 1960.
23 For further examples, see Whitehouse, Harvey. "Rites of terror: Emotion, metaphor, and memory in Melanesian initiation cults." *Journal of the Royal Anthropological Institute* (1996): 703–715.
24 Whitehouse, Harvey, Jonathan A. Lanman, Greg Downey, Leah A. Fredman, William B. Swann Jr, Daniel H. Lende, Robert N. McCauley et al. "The ties that bind us: Ritual, fusion, and identification." *Current Anthropology* 55, no. 6 (2014): 000–000.
25 Whitehouse, Harvey. "Dying for the group: Towards a general theory of extreme self-sacrifice." *Behavioral and Brain Sciences* (2018): 1–64.
26 Swann Jr, William B., Michael D. Buhrmester, Angel Gomez, Jolanda Jetten, Brock Bastian, Alexandra Vazquez, Amarina Ariyanto et al. "What makes a group worth dying for? Identity fusion fosters perception of familial ties, promoting self-sacrifice." *Journal of Personality and Social Psychology* 106, no. 6 (2014): 912.
27 Whitehouse, Harvey, Jonathan A. Lanman, Greg Downey, Leah A. Fredman, William B. Swann Jr, Daniel H. Lende, Robert N. McCauley et al. "The ties that bind us: Ritual, fusion, and identification." *Current Anthropology* 55, no. 6 (2014): 000–000.
28 Kavanagh, Christopher M., Jonathan Jong, Ryan McKay, and Harvey Whitehouse. "Positive experiences of high arousal martial arts rituals are linked to identity fusion and costly pro-group actions." *European Journal of Social Psychology* 49, no. 3 (2019): 461–481.
29 Newson, Martha, Michael Buhrmester, and Harvey Whitehouse. "Explaining lifelong loyalty: The role of identity fusion and self-shaping group events." *PloS one* 11, no. 8 (2016).
30 Jong, Jonathan, Harvey Whitehouse, Christopher Kavanagh, and Justin Lane. "Shared negative experiences lead to identity fusion via personal reflection." *PloS one* 10, no. 12 (2015).
31 Buhrmester, Michael D., William T. Fraser, Jonathan A. Lanman, Harvey Whitehouse, and William B. Swann Jr. "When terror hits home: Identity fused Americans who saw Boston bombing victims as 'family' provided aid." *Self and Identity* 14, no. 3 (2015): 253–270.
32 Whitehouse, Harvey, Brian McQuinn, Michael Buhrmester, and William B. Swann. "Brothers in Arms: Libyan revolutionaries bond like family." *Proceedings of the National Academy of Sciences* 111, no. 50 (2014): 17783–17785.
33 Whitehouse, Harvey. "Dying for the group: Towards a general theory of extreme self-sacrifice." *Behavioral and Brain Sciences* 41 (2018).
34 Adapted from, Whitehouse, Harvey. "Dying for the group: Towards a general theory of extreme self-sacrifice." *Behavioral and Brain Sciences* 41 (2018).
35 E.g. Fischer, Ronald, and Dimitris Xygalatas. "Extreme rituals as social technologies." *Journal of Cognition and Culture* 14, no. 5 (2014): 345–355.
36 Xygalatas, Dimitris, Uffe Schjoedt, Joseph Bulbulia, Ivana Konvalinka, Else-Marie Jegindø, Paul Reddish, Armin W. Geertz, and Andreas Roepstoff. "Autobiographical memory in a fire-walking ritual." *Journal of Cognition and Culture* 13, no. 1–2 (2013): 1–16.
37 Xygalatas, D., S. Khan, M. Lang, R. Kundt, E. Kundtová-Klocová, J. Kratky & J. Shaver. Effects of extreme ritual practices on health and well-being (forthcoming).
38 Xygalatas, Dimitris, Panagiotis Mitkidis, Ronald Fischer, Paul Reddish, Joshua Skewes, Armin W. Geertz, Andreas Roepstorff, and Joseph Bulbulia. "Extreme rituals promote prosociality." *Psychological Science* 24, no. 8 (2013): 1602–1605.

39 Fischer, Ronald, Dimitris Xygalatas, Panagiotis Mitkidis, Paul Reddish, Penny Tok, Ivana Konvalinka, and Joseph Bulbulia. "The fire-walker's high: Affect and physiological responses in an extreme collective ritual." *PloS one* 9, no. 2 (2014): e88355.

40 Xygalatas, Dimitris, Panagiotis Mitkidis, Ronald Fischer, Paul Reddish, Joshua Skewes, Armin W. Geertz, Andreas Roepstorff, and Joseph Bulbulia. "Extreme rituals promote prosociality." *Psychological Science* 24, no. 8 (2013): 1602–1605; Fischer, Ronald, Dimitris Xygalatas, Panagiotis Mitkidis, Paul Reddish, Penny Tok, Ivana Konvalinka, and Joseph Bulbulia. "The fire walker's high: Affect and physiological responses in an extreme collective ritual." *PloS one* 9, no. 2 (2014).

41 Watson-Jones, Rachel E., Harvey Whitehouse, and Cristine H. Legare. "In-group ostracism increases high-fidelity imitation in early childhood." *Psychological Science* 27, no. 1 (2016): 34–42; Legare, Cristine H., and Rachel E. Watson-Jones. "The evolution and ontogeny of ritual." *The handbook of evolutionary psychology* (2015): 1–19; Legare, C.H., H. Whitehouse, N.J. Wen, and P.A. Herrmann. "Imitative foundations of cultural learning." *Cognition*, (2012).

42 Wen, Nicole J., Patricia A. Herrmann, and Cristine H. Legare. "Ritual increases children's affiliation with in-group members." *Evolution and Human Behavior* 37, no. 1 (2016): 54–60.

43 Sosis, Richard. "The adaptive value of religious ritual: Rituals promote group cohesion by requiring members to engage in behavior that is too costly to fake." *American Scientist* 92, no. 2 (2004): 166–172.

44 Sosis, Richard, and Eric R. Bressler. "Cooperation and commune longevity: A test of the costly signaling theory of religion." *Cross-Cultural Research* 37, no. 2 (2003): 211–239.

45 Sosis, Richard, and Bradley J. Ruffle. "Religious ritual and cooperation: Testing for a relationship on Israeli religious and secular kibbutzim." *Current Anthropology* 44, no. 5 (2003): 713–722.

46 Soler, Montserrat. "Costly signaling, ritual, and cooperation: Evidence from Candomblé, an Afro-Brazilian religion." *Evolution and Human Behavior* 33, no. 4 (2012): 346–356.

47 D. Xygalatas, P. Maňo, V. Bahna, E. Kundtová-Klocová, R. Kundt, and J. Shaver (forthcoming) Social status and costly signaling in an extreme ritual.

48 Bird, Rebecca Bliege, and Eleanor A. Power. "Prosocial signaling and cooperation among Martu hunters." *Evolution and Human Behavior* 36, no. 5 (2015): 389–397.

49 Barker, Jessica L., Eleanor A. Power, Stephen Heap, Mikael Puurtinen, and Richard Sosis. "Content, cost, and context: A framework for understanding human signaling systems." *Evolutionary Anthropology: Issues, News, and Reviews* 28, no. 2 (2019): 86–99.

50 Henrich, Joseph. "The evolution of costly displays, cooperation, and religion." *Evolution and Human Behavior* 30, no. 4 (2009): 244–260.

51 http://ktpress.rw/2017/05/pentecostal-leaders-face-jail-for-mismanaging-church-finances/.

52 Singh, Manvir, and Joseph Henrich. "Why do religious leaders observe costly prohibitions? Examining taboos on Mentawai shamans." *Evolutionary Human Sciences* 2 (2020).

53 Lanman, Jonathan A. "The importance of religious displays for belief acquisition and secularization." *Journal of Contemporary Religion* 27, no. 1 (2012): 49–65.

54 Turpin, H., Lanman, J., and Andersen, M. "CREDs, CRUDs, and Catholic scandals: Experimentally examining the effects of religious paragon behavior on co-religionist belief." *Religion, Brain, and Behavior* (2018).

55 Bottan, Nicolas L., and Ricardo Perez-Truglia. "Losing my religion: The effects of religious scandals on religious participation and charitable giving." *Journal of Public Economics* 129 (2015): 106–119.

56 Henrich, Joseph. "The evolution of costly displays, cooperation, and religion: Credibility enhancing displays and their implications for cultural evolution." *Evolution and Human Behavior* 30, no. 4 (2009): 244–260.

57 Whitehouse, Harvey, Pieter Francois, and Peter Turchin. "The role of ritual in the evolution of social complexity: Five predictions and a drum roll." *Cliodynamics: The Journal of Quantitative History and Cultural Evolution* (2015).

58 Norenzayan, Ara, Azim F. Shariff, Will M. Gervais, Aiyana K. Willard, Rita A. McNamara, Edward Slingerland, and Joseph Henrich. "The cultural evolution of prosocial religions." *Behavioral and Brain Sciences* 39 (2016).

59 Whitehouse, Harvey, Pieter François, Patrick E. Savage, Thomas E. Currie, Kevin C. Feeney, Enrico Cioni, Rosalind Purcell et al. "Complex societies precede moralizing gods throughout world history." *Nature* 568, no. 7751 (2019): 226–229.

60 E.g. Hodder, Ian, ed. *Religion in the emergence of civilization: Çatalhöyük as a case study*. Cambridge University Press, 2010.

61 Atkinson, Quentin D., and Harvey Whitehouse. "The cultural morphospace of ritual form: Examining modes of religiosity cross-culturally." *Evolution and Human Behavior* 32, no. 1 (2011): 50–62.

11 Conclusion

> *The standard assumption in the social sciences and humanities has been that only social and cultural methods can explain social and cultural facts. Of course, the possibility of a cognitive science of religion depends upon showing that cognitive explanations of social-cultural facts are not only possible but have already happened.*
>
> (Lawson, 2000[1])

The cognitive science of religion (CSR) began in earnest with a handful of scholars who wanted to "science up" the study of religion. Today, scholars of many disciplinary backgrounds contribute to the scientific understanding of religion. Over the past two decades or so, CSR has made tremendous progress in understanding the cognitive basis of religious ideas and behaviors, such as:

- Gods and other supernatural agents.
- The design and origin of the natural world.
- Life before, or after, death.
- Beliefs about supernatural causes of illness.
- The origins of the natural world, a creator deity.
- The forms and functions of prayer.
- Teleological reasoning about life events.
- Assumptions about continued existence in the afterlife.
- Representations of the self and others during spirit possession.
- Ideas about continued personal identity in reincarnation.
- The relationships between religiosity and prosociality.
- The recurrent features of rituals, ritualized actions, and their representation.
- Religious activity that occurred before the emergence of state societies.

These findings also have practical implications outside of academia, including among laypeople and religious devotees. These include:

- Best practices for educating children about science and religion.
- Showcasing the positive individual and group effects of ritual performance.
- Informing debates and policy on sacred values, self-sacrifice, and religious conflict.

- Providing data to enrich conversations about the relationship between religion and morality.
- Highlighting how religious tolerance can be made easier by showcasing the similarities in religious traditions and spiritual movements.
- Increasing religious tolerance by countering popular misconceptions that religious people are irrational and that scientists are rational.
- Explaining how and why religion endures throughout history and across cultures.
- Accounting for the prevalence of atheism.

As CSR expands, so too does the number of scholars, methods, and approaches. Scholars often cite examples of projects to explain what CSR entails. These examples include research on our sensitivity toward detecting human-like beings in the environment; the minimally counterintuitive (MCI) theory of religious transmission (ADD); and discrepancies between theological correctness—ideas based upon the official theological doctrine of a given tradition—and theological incorrectness—deviations from official religious dogma, which often emerge during real-time cognitive processing. These examples showcase a small, yet important spectrum of what CSR has to offer. As this book demonstrates, the breadth of research deemed as falling under the scope of CSR runs wide.

Today, newcomers remain as committed to the central tenets of CSR as early pioneers. These commitments include attributing an active role of the human mind in the acquisition, processing, and transfer of religious ideas and behaviors, and the importance of a scientific approach to religion. Many theories, even those regarded as central to CSR, have been challenged and revised in light of new evidence. Prominent examples include:

- The extent to which theories concerning transmission biases such as agency detection device (ADD, formerly HADD, the cognitive system deemed responsible for detecting human-like beings in the environment[2]) explain belief in supernatural agents.
- The extent to which theories concerning transmission biases such as minimally counterintuitive theory (MCI, that all else being equal, concepts that minimally tweak our intuitive assumptions about the world will be remembered more accurately and transmitted) explain belief in supernatural agents.[3]
- The relationship between theological correctness and folk concepts of religion.[4]
- The cognitive mechanisms and structure of common representations of the afterlife and supernatural agents.[5]

In addition to testing and revising established theories in CSR, new theories are being proposed and debated. For example, the explanation for "Big Gods" by psychologist Ara Norenzayan and colleagues, which concerns the relationship between the cultural prevalence of moralizing gods and the transition to large-scale societies[6] (see Chapter 8: Morality). Some theorists interpret these changes as undermining CSR. In contrast, others argue that the continuous revision of theories is not a weakness, but rather, the hallmark of a genuinely scientific approach to the study of religion. For instance, in disagreements, the burden of proof is upon scholars to defend and provide evidence for their theory among alternatives. As psychologist Justin Barrett (2011: 232) put it, reassessment emphasizes "empirical fortification and/or falsification of claims" in CSR.[7]

The culture of CSR has, however, changed since it was established as a subfield. Early pioneers had a strong foothold in the philosophy of science. While they fought for the possibility of hypothesis testing, they had less experience in experimental methods than many who have joined the ranks today. Consequentially, CSR now enjoys more rigorous methodologies and a plethora of experimental techniques.

The demographic makeup of cognitive scientists of religion has also changed. For instance, the early scholars in CSR were predominantly male. Today, more female scholarship is included in publications, and some pioneers have made a concerted effort to redress this balance. For example, the *Journal of Cognition and Culture*, edited by E. Thomas Lawson, featured an issue titled "New Voices in Cognition and Culture," which included exclusively female authors.[8] Overall, however, women remain underrepresented. For example, a 15-chapter book outlining what CSR has achieved to date *Religion Explained: The Cognitive Science of Religion After Twenty-Five Years* contains two female co-authors and 21 male contributors.[9] Likewise, even though much insightful and robust empirical research on children's developing religious cognition has been conducted by female scholars (e.g. see Chapters 5 and 7), they remain notably absent from many overviews on the cognitive science of religion in journals and books. Likewise, a more concentrated effort is needed to provide opportunities and represent scholars from ethnic minorities in the subfield.

The overall aims of CSR have also shifted. Fresh from the cognitive revolution and inspired by developments in linguistics, CSR began with the idea that the study of religion could reach the same predictive power of the natural sciences, and that religion could be explained through precise mathematical models. CSR has moved towards a more balanced bio-cultural approach to explain religion through a combining what is known about evolution, brain, cognition, and culture,[10] with evolution as the unifying conceptual framework.

This more balanced approach has shifted CSR towards stronger forms of interdisciplinarity. For instance, much early work in the subfield was produced by individual scholars, whereas today, the team-based research paradigm is common. Furthermore, this approach is now less opportunistic and reflects more of a coordinated attempt to integrate specific methodologies and research cultures.

There is now a more concentrated effort to combine both the values of scientific measurement with contextual sensitivity. CSR continues to foster an integrative culture of collaboration from scholars both in the humanities and sciences and across methodologies. CSR scholars need both well-designed studies cross-culturally replicated in contexts where researchers have extensive knowledge about local populations (or collaborate with those who hold such knowledge). These skills are essential to all scholars studying human activity. As anthropologist Dimitris Xygalatas puts it, "the process may be an upward climb, but the view from the top is worth all the sweat.[11]"

In this chapter, we review the philosophical, theological, and practical implications of the approach, including whether CSR theories speak to questions about whether or not religion (or a specific religion) is true. Finally, we turn to a critical evaluation of the approach, including misconceptions of CSR, key strengths and limitations, and future directions.

Key points

- CSR has grown exponentially over the past two decades and continues to expand.
- We now understand more about the cognitive basis of religious ideas and behaviors.
- CSR research also has practical implications.
- CSR continues to adopt different methods, revise theories, and challenge findings within the social-cognitive sciences, including those previously upheld in CSR.

Philosophical and theological implications of CSR

Since the 1990s the number of empirical projects in CSR has grown exponentially. As research has grown, so too has the amount of attention paid to the implications of the approach. In this section, we review these implications.

Philosophical and theological questions in response to CSR research

The philosopher Justin McBrayer has provided an overview of the philosophical and theological issues that often arise as a result of theories and research in CSR.[12] He divides these into three categories, outlined below:

1 The nature and success of explanations of religion in CSR

The first type of issue concerns the nature and success of explanations of religion in CSR. We have already covered some of these throughout this chapter and in Chapter 1 (Introduction). They include questions about whether, and how, research supports theories about religion (e.g. does research support an MCI theory of religious transmission?[13] Is the belief in "Big Gods" adaptive?[14]), the type of conclusions reached (e.g. can we conclude that religion is intuitive or natural?[15]), and the nature and success of empirical explanations of religion in general (e.g. what are the strengths and weaknesses of a reductionist account of religion?[16])

2 Metaphysical implications of explanations of religion in CSR

The second type of issue concerns the metaphysical implications of explanations of religion in CSR. These include implications for the nature of humanity and the nature of the divine (e.g. does research reveal a bias towards some conceptions of the divine?) Philosophers of religion, in particular, have begun to consider these implications in detail.[17] For instance, philosopher Helen De Cruz and colleagues have applied the findings of CSR to an array of important issues. These issues include the compatibility of CSR findings with philosophers of religion, who have often made claims about the nature of religion (including the naturalness of religion) and how religious thought relates to other beliefs. For instance, the question of whether religious and scientific theories are compatible.[18]

CSR has focused mostly on the content biases that underlie the successful transmission of religious concepts. One claim by De Cruz is that there is more continuity between cross-culturally widespread religious ideas and official theological beliefs than recognized. Therefore, CSR also has implications for the acquisition and transmission of theological beliefs that ought to be further explored.[19]

3 Epistemic questions about the implications of CSR explanations of religion for the truth, rationality, or justification of religious beliefs

The third type of implication is epistemic. They include questions about the implications of CSR explanations of religion for the truth, rationality, or justification of religious beliefs: especially the question of whether religious beliefs are reasonable, justified, or warranted.[20] These types of issues have attracted the most attention from outside of CSR. For instance, in their popular books on religion, philosopher Daniel Dennett[21] and evolutionary biologist Richard Dawkins[22] cite the work of CSR as supporting the conclusion that religion is part of an irrational cognitive delusion that should be eradicated, even though these ideas about religion are not part of the research agendas of CSR scholars. Further, adding fuel to the fire, CSR scholars often attract broad readership with controversial questions and phrases as titles, such as "Is God an accident?[23]" "Religion is natural,[24]" *Religion explained,*[25] and *Born believers.*[26] The content of these works portrays a more careful treatment of such issues, but casual readers seldom have the patience to digest these more nuanced points.

Key points

Three kinds of philosophical and theological issues arise from CSR:

1 The nature and success of explanations of religion in CSR.
2 Metaphysical implications of explanations of religion in CSR.
3 Epistemic questions about the implications of CSR explanations of religion for the truth, rationality, or justification of religious beliefs.

Religious and theological implications of CSR

At least three responses stem from CSR research to questions about the relationship between CSR and religious belief in general:

1 Typically developing humans everywhere are likely to engage in religious concepts and activities

One basic claim is that religion is cognitively natural. That is to say, the predispositions that give rise to cross-culturally recurrent religious ideas and practices arise with minimal instruction and, once introduced, spread rapidly. This "naturalness-of-religion" thesis (coined by Justin Barrett[27]) implies that popular religion is at the heart of human activity, and typically developing humans everywhere are likely to engage in religious concepts and activities. By contrast, atheism does not emerge as easily since it goes against the grain of our inherent biases. When it does, it evokes much more cognitive effort to sustain consistency in ideas about the world. Thus, it is harder to sell than theism.[28] New research on atheism in the future, such as the "Understanding Unbelief" program by sociologist Lois Lee and anthropologist Jon Lanman in the UK is likely to build upon and refine these claims. The same can be said of some theological concepts that are complex and based on ideas that counter our intuitions, and indeed of many scientific concepts.[29] The level of difficulty and likelihood of acquisition and transmission of an idea or behavior does not determine which is true.

2 Religion is here to stay

A related issue is the relevance of CSR to secularization theory. Broadly speaking, secularization theory predicts that societies will transform from close identification with religious values and institutions toward nonreligious values and institutions. Historically, secularization theory has not borne out. Rather, religion has changed rather than dissipated. For example, more people in the U.S. now identify as spiritual but not religious than previously documented, and affiliates of organized world religions have declined in this context.

Findings from CSR speak to predictions about the future of religion. Specifically, they render the hypothesis that religion is going to go away implausible. First, the definition of religion in CSR is more inclusive of ideas and practices beyond the "big five" traditions, so while the number of people affiliated with institutionalized forms of religion may decline, this does not equate to the disappearance of religiosity. From the perspective of the evolutionary cognitive sciences, religion, as broadly construed, is here to stay because humans have a psychological propensity to engage in such ideas and behaviors.

3 The cognitive science of religion cannot determine whether religion is true or false

The third response from cognitive scientists of religion on the relationship between CSR and religious beliefs comes from the methodological framework employed to study religion. Cognitive scientists of religion abide by the commitment to methodological naturalism, which is the basic idea that only the "human side" of religious ideas and experiences can be studied in naturalistic terms. CSR scholars are interested in understanding how and why humans respond to ideas that are deemed religious, rather than decipher whether or not those ideas are true or false (i.e. ontological status).

Researchers naturally have their commitments and dispositions towards religion. In CSR, these dispositions are many and varied. Even though some scholars may offer their personal opinions on the reality of religion in their writings, this does not mean that CSR, in general, supports their opinion. Most importantly, when scholars conduct research, they bracket personal opinions. Research in CSR is guided by methods in science in much the same way that it governs other research outside of religious domains. Some doubt that a scientific study of religion will always be subject to the influence of religious concerns,[30] while others have argued that a non-confessional and scientific approach to the study of religion in CSR is not only possible but has already occurred.[31]

The general stance of CSR on whether or not religion is true

CSR does not support any doctrinal view or a particular religion. That the approach is neutral about religion may be disappointing to those who want to undermine religion or provide scientific support for their beliefs. To date, most scholars in CSR engaged in deriving primary research do not engage extensively in debates about the relationship between their theories and findings to the truism of religion (there are, of course, exceptions to this[32]), although they often include qualifiers. For example, cognitive scientists of religion often point out that the goal of the research is to uncover human tendencies that predispose us to religion. However, predispositions are not antithetical to the existence of religious phenomena, such as supernatural agents, and nor do they provide evidence that phenomena do exist. For example, Barrett has argued that cognitively natural beliefs are "epistemically innocent until proven guilty.[33]" Similarly, others clarify that evolutionary theories speak to the question of the adaptive function of religion, which is separate from questions about the existence of religious phenomena.

1 Controversy in the neurosciences and evolutionary sciences

Researchers in the neurosciences and evolutionary sciences have been confronted with questions about whether a natural explanation of religious cognition makes a difference to the epistemic status of religious belief. Some misinterpret neuroscientific findings to mean that religion is "all in the mind," and therefore, a cognitive delusion or false belief. Others presume (or indeed, fear) that CSR is essentially "explaining religion away," with the associated claim that a natural explanation of religion makes the existence of anything supernatural superfluous.[34] Others have interpreted the idea that religion is natural and rooted in our evolutionary heritage as meaning that religion is true. As anthropologist Pascal Boyer (2008: 1038) put it, "some people of faith fear that an understanding of the processes underlying belief could undermine it. Others worry that what is shown to be part of our evolutionary heritage will be interpreted as good, true, necessary, or inevitable.[35]"

These interpretations are often compounded by sensationalist accounts of work conducted by researchers in the study of religion. Such accounts are often referred to as "neurotheology.[36]" Most notably is the idea that there is a specialized area of the brain dedicated to religious experience, often referred to as the "god spot" (based on the findings of Michael Persinger's helmet studies),[37] and that finding the source of religious experience negates the need for any other account. As neuropsychologist Uffe Schjoedt remarks, since religious behavior encompasses widely different thoughts and practices, it must be assumed to have different content and corresponding mental correlates. The aim of the neuroscientific research, as Schjoedt rightly points out, is to describe the basic neural processing employed by participants in religious practices,[38] not to localize God. Likewise, as Barrett points out, such research says next to nothing about whether religious beliefs are warranted or not.[39]

Researchers in CSR have, however, acknowledged that a theistic and antitheistic reading of research is possible. However, such readings require much more precise and sophisticated work than sweeping generalizations. One important consideration is that the approach is diverse regarding the theories of the mind and the evolutionary origins and functions of religion, and therefore it is practically impossible to be informed about CSR and conclude that CSR provides support for or against the reality of religious beliefs. It is possible, however, to take individual cognitive and evolutionary theories within CSR and to compare and contrast their potential implications. This type of treatment is best achieved with precision and insight and likely to be the focus of future scholarly work.

Summary of philosophical and theological implications of CSR

There are three types of philosophical and theological issues that often arise as a result of theories and research in CSR:

1 The nature and success of explanations of religion in CSR.
2 Metaphysical implications of explanations of religion in CSR, such as implications for the nature of humanity and the nature of the divine.
3 Epistemic questions about the implications of CSR explanations of religion for the truth, rationality, or justification of religious beliefs.

At least two responses follow from CSR research to questions about the relationship between CSR and religious belief in general:

- Normally developing humans everywhere are likely to engage in religious concepts and activities.
- The cognitive science of religion cannot determine whether religion is true or false.

CSR does not support any doctrinal view or a particular religion. That the approach is neutral about religion. Research in the neurosciences and evolutionary sciences have been especially plagued with questions about whether a natural explanation of religious cognition makes a difference to the epistemic status of religious belief. These interpretations are often compounded by sensationalist accounts of work conducted by researchers in the study of religion. Researchers in CSR have, however, acknowledged that a theistic and anti-theistic reading of research is possible. This type of treatment may be the focus of future scholarly work.

Evaluation, implications and future directions

Over the past two decades or so, CSR has made many advancements in the study of religion. However, many important questions about religion remain. In what follows, we review the strengths and limitations of the approach and the potential future directions that the approach could take.

The role of evolution in religion

As discussed in Chapter 1 (Introduction), evolutionary processes capture the ultimate mechanisms. Many contemporary scientists consider accounting for them as necessary for developing a more comprehensive explanation of religion. However, the evolutionary approach to religion is still relatively new. It began to influence a cognitive approach to religion following the publication of *The Adapted Mind* in 1992[40] by evolutionary scholars Barkow, Tooby, and Cosmides. Most assume that evolutionary sciences are, or should be, essential to a cognitive explanation of religious phenomena and that understanding the evolutionary causality behind the origins of ideas and behaviors of the executive committee leads to a better explanation of religion overall. For instance, in 2020 members of the Executive Committee voted to change the name of the organization "The International Association for the Cognitive Science of Religion" (IACSR) to "the International Association for the Cognitive *and Evolutionary* Sciences of Religion (IACESR)".

1 Disagreements over the unit of selection and mechanisms of cultural change in evolutionary accounts

Many cognitive scientists of religion differ according to their endorsement of particular theories and research on the evolutionary origins of religious ideas and behaviors, including the unit of selection—i.e. genetics, individuals, groups, and mechanisms of cultural change.

Recently, scholars have proposed that CSR be situated more firmly within existing frameworks of cultural evolution. These frameworks emphasize that human thinking and behavior are powerfully shaped both by genetic and cultural inheritance (also known as "dual-inheritance theory[41]" or gene-culture coevolution).

At the crux of these arguments is the case that cognitive biases (as shaped by our evolutionary heritage and contemporary environments) alone do not explain the spread of religious ideas and behaviors. Scholars must account for context biases (which are also shaped by our evolutionary heritage and contemporary environments). In short, human cognition is the result of dual inheritance from interacting genetic and cultural streams of evolution. One advantage of the dual-inheritance theory as a framework for studying religion is that it deals with more complex interactions between cognitive and cultural phenomena. Nevertheless, it also incurs the cost of research designs, having to take into consideration a more abundant number of possibilities.

2 Disagreements over the origin, function, and role of evolution in religion

There is also an ongoing debate about the origin, function, and exact role of evolution in religious ideas and behaviors—notably whether it enhanced survival. The dominant position in the field historically has been that religious beliefs and behaviors are a by-product of cognitive processes and behaviors that evolved for other purposes.[42] More recently, however, a growing number of scholars are challenging this view. They propose that religious beliefs and behaviors evolved due to their (historical and current) adaptive advantages to individuals and groups because of the psychological and material benefits,[43] such as extending human cooperation and coordination.[44] These debates are likely to continue over the coming years. Theories about the role of evolution in religious thought and behavior are likely to be both articulated and revised in light of new data.

3 The difficulty in deciphering between competing evolutionary accounts

One problem that confronts evolutionary scientists is difficulty in testing their theories and competing hypotheses. To date, one of the most reliable means of testing evolutionary theories is through systematic, cross-cultural studies. They afford researchers the opportunity to investigate whether and how intuitive responses emerge. Intuitive responses are likely to be based on universal mechanisms, constraints, traits, etc., which may have been selected for during evolution.

The implications of such results for the study of religion would be magnified when data is derived from outside western cultures, suggesting that findings are not a product of Judeo-Christian or WEIRD traditions (i.e. Western, Educated, Industrialized, Rich, and Democratic). CSR has derived fewer data from western samples than compared to the rest of the behavioral sciences. Nevertheless, there is still a need for more cross-cultural data to make claims about how humans typically tend to think and behave, and to compare and contrast these from different cultural inputs.[45] Future research addressing the role of cognitive biases in the context of Eastern traditions, such as the work in CSR of religious studies scholar Edward Slingerland and colleagues[46] and psychologist Melanie Nyhof and colleagues,[47] would be especially fruitful.

4 Future research possibilities in evolutionary studies of religion

Other avenues to test evolutionary theories include simulation modeling. This is where researchers are developing large-scale agent-based models to predict and explain religious dynamics both past and present (such as the Institute for the Bio-Cultural Study of Religion's "Modeling Religion Project"; Masaryk University's "Generative Historiography of Religion Project"). Another promising development is the emergence of new databases specifically tailored for questions concerning cognition, the environment, and religion, such as the Historical Database of Sociocultural Evolution[48] and the Database of Religious History (DRH), which is collecting quantifiable data directly from historians and other specialists.[49]

In the future, even closer ties between the evolutionary sciences and CSR are likely to be forged. As theories about evolutionary processes and the relationship between evolution and cultural processes develop (recent noteworthy examples include books by anthropologists Clark Barrett[50] and Joseph Henrich[51]), theories in the cognitive science of religion are likely to follow suit. One promising avenue of research is on religion and mental health. Traditionally, the psychology of religion has been concerned with questions of individual differences and the health outcomes of belief. Yet, research and theories are not typically formulated with modern evolutionary theory in mind.

By contrast, religious studies scholar Joseph Bulbulia has accumulated research (informed by evolutionary theory) on the beneficial impact of religious participation on human health and well-being.[52]

Key points

- The evolutionary approach to religion is still relatively new.
- There are disagreements in evolutionary approaches.
- They include disagreements over:
  - The unit of selection and mechanisms of cultural change in evolutionary accounts.
  - The origin, function, and role of evolution in religion.
- It is sometimes difficult to adjudicate between different evolutionary accounts, but this is likely to change in the future as new methods and data become available.

The mind and models of cognition

As we covered in Chapter 1 (Introduction), CSR began with a handful of scholars who were influenced by a modular view of the mind (i.e. that the mind is composed of innate neural structures or modules, which have distinct established evolutionary functions). This idea was proposed by evolutionary scholars Barkow, Tooby, and Cosmides in *The Adapted Mind* in 1992.[53] Even though CSR has been critiqued for endorsing a nativist (i.e. that ideas are hardwired at birth), modular view of the mind, there are disagreements over the models of cognition involved in religious thought—which includes whether, and to what extent, the mind is modular. These debates are likely to continue.

Some scholars, such as philosopher Mitch Hodge,[54] have called for greater consideration of the view of the mind and the type of cognitive processing that arises from empirical results on topics such as the structure and mechanisms involved in belief in the afterlife. Others have considered the more basic question of how narrowly or broadly cognition is construed in CSR in general. Whether it consists of internal rules and representations (i.e. in the head); or, also includes a broader concept where cognition is regarded as embodied (i.e. in the body), extended, and distributed (i.e. across minds in the environment, often referred to as situated or distributed cognition).[55] These latter formulations focus on the interaction between brain, body, and environment in the formation of and reception to, ideas and behaviors. For instance, religious studies scholar Armin Geertz has argued that CSR has been focused on a narrow view of cognition as individual minds and has overlooked the role of the body and environment.[56]

Geertz has proposed a biocultural theory of religion, which is based on an expanded view of cognition that is anchored in the brain and body, dependent upon culture, and extended and distributed beyond individual minds.[57] For instance, techniques used in religious practices often manipulate the body, such as kneeling, standing and dancing in rituals, inducing drugs or fasting, and enduring painful ordeals. Geertz proposes that understanding which manipulations are at play in religion, and how they implement cultural values, alter emotional states, and interact with cognitive processing can enrich our understanding of religion. Religion is embedded, enacted, extended, and embodied, and CSR scholars are striving to examine each of these aspects.

Geertz is not the only scholar to propose broadening the scope of cognition and culture in CSR. Anthropologist Benjamin Purzycki has argued that CSR needs to take more account of cultural factors in shaping religious representations. He considers the interaction of individuals and their environment as an ecological system, focusing, for example, on how people represent supernatural agents when they face local problems.[58]

Key points

- There are disagreements in CSR and the socio-cognitive sciences more generally over the models of cognition involved in religious thought.
- Recently, CSR scholars have called for more attention to be paid towards the models of cognition in religious thought.

Methods and theories underlying the scientific study of religion

Scholars in traditional approaches to the study of religion have differed in their responses to CSR. Their reception has ranged along a continuum—from enthusiasm to skepticism, and antagonism. As we covered in Chapter 1 (Introduction), the history of CSR makes some resistance to the approach from some corners almost inevitable. As religious studies scholar E. Thomas Lawson (2000: 47) put it, "A cognitive approach to … religion is capable of arousing intense suspicion … the standard assumption in the social sciences and the humanities has been that only social and cultural methods can explain social and cultural facts." The approach started by challenging some of the most fundamental assumptions that were standard fare in the study of religion at the time, including cultural determinism and cultural relativism.

One criticism that is often associated with those who commit cultural relativism is that CSR tries to "explain away" the specialness of religion, or as we have covered previously in this chapter, fears that cognitive approaches reduce religious experience to the mind. As we discussed in Chapter 1 (Introduction), religion was often construed among scholars as sui generis (i.e. unique) and could not be reduced or compared to anything other than itself. At the heart of these critiques is a reaction against reductionism. To a greater extent, a reaction against a scientific approach to the study of religion since reductionism is a cornerstone of the scientific method. Cognitive scientists of religion have proposed that explanations of religion are necessarily reductive.[59]

As we discussed in Chapter 1 (Introduction), CSR engages in the form of methodological reductionism that first fractionates religion to study the different components, while acknowledging the complexity and interaction of many levels and not reducing an explanation of religion to any one level. There is often an underlying assumption in critiques of CSR that scholars are proposing a form of ontological reductionism. This type of reasoning can be identified in writing as preceded with a "nothing but" phrase. That religion is "nothing but" supernatural agents is "nothing but" the processes of the human mind. As scholars in CSR point out, especially philosopher Robert McCauley,[60] this is a misunderstanding of the approach. Others, such as religious studies' scholar Edward Slingerland, have implied that the misconception may also partially stem from a fear that explaining religion away makes the study of religion from those outside of science redundant. This view is not shared by cognitive-evolutionary scholars who research CSR.[61]

Key points

- CSR is sometimes met with enthusiasm and by others with skepticism among those trained in traditional approaches to the study of religion.
- Some religious scholars assume that CSR scholars employ ontological reductionism.

The conceptualization of religion in CSR

As discussed in Chapter 2 (Core Assumptions), another critique that sometimes emerges from scholars of religion is that CSR does not have a clear conceptualization of religion because scholars do not engage in extensive debates about what does or does not constitute religion.[62] As discussed, such debates over how to define religion have characterized the study of religion since the field's inception, and CSR scholars take a bottom-up approach to characterizing and investigating religious phenomena. It is a truism that, to date, CSR has focused most on explaining common representations of, and responses to, supernatural agents over other recurrent features of religious systems. The focus to date is likely a product of two factors.

First is the influence of scholars such as anthropologist Stewart Guthrie. Second is the ubiquity and accessibility of the phenomena and the comparative ease with which scholars can investigate these phenomena. This focus has been interpreted as endorsing a Tylorian minimalist view of religion *as* supernatural agents. It is often coined as Tylorian because of the association with the classical scholar, Edward Tylor, who proposed that religion was the belief in supernatural agents and that people came to their convictions about religion by cold, laborious processes of thinking. However, this view does not adequately characterize the approach. First, CSR researchers have addressed many other phenomena falling under the category of religion, including those captured in this book. Indeed, some have studied phenomena that may be considered outside of what mainstream scholars would classify as religion, such as magic[63] and even atheism.[64] Second, as discussed in more detail below, CSR proposes that religious ideas and behaviors emerge as culturally transmitted ideas that people find intuitively plausible, not the high-level conscious deliberation of the individual about the truth value of different religions.

Religious belief

A related question that we have encountered throughout the book is whether, and to what extent, CSR explains belief. As discussed in Chapter 2 (Core Assumptions), CSR construes beliefs as reflective elaborations on intuitions about the world. They emerge in part due to their foundation on ideas and behaviors that people find intuitively plausible and inherently appealing, and because they have been culturally transmitted.

CSR has veered away from explaining the process of belief formation for individuals within a particular tradition. Likewise, the approach has been more concerned with explaining why and how general trends in religion emerge cross-culturally than those that differ from those trends (i.e. statistical outliers), and how individuals differ from one another. Research on explaining individual differences in religiosity is more characteristic of the work conducted in the field of psychology of religion. Nevertheless, recent research in CSR does account for individual predictors of tendencies that underpin religious beliefs, such as the detection of agency in the environment.[65]

Historically, however, CSR has focused more on explaining the acquisition and transmission of religious beliefs in groups of people rather than explaining differences between individuals. This endeavor requires an understanding of both intuitive cognitive processes and the socio-cultural and historical environment within which ideas about religion are communicated.

Debates still abound on what the precise nature of religious beliefs entail, such as whether they are factual beliefs influenced by processing fluency,[66] or are attitudes of a different type altogether.[67] As psychologists Cristine Legare and Susan Gelman have suggested, one truism is that beliefs are often immune to argumentation and refutation.[68] As the anthropologist Tanya Luhrmann has noted, understanding the socialization and learning processes are crucial to explaining how people come to believe, such as the articulated belief among some contemporary American evangelicals that God can speak to them.[69] Ideas like these are not a matter of merely receiving and accepting information but rather, require complex cognitive processes, in this case, to perceive God as around, able and willing to hear and engage in a conversation with believers. As anthropologist Pascal Boyer put it, "belief is hard work,".[70]

The contribution of CSR to understanding belief is the clarity with which scholars distinguish between propositional beliefs and intuitions. As early pioneers of CSR proposed, religious representations are much more compelling, attention-grabbing, and memorable when they are associated with intuitive content. As cultural transmission is a selective process, ideas that are based on intuitions about the world have a competitive advantage, which can explain why they become widespread. However, beliefs that build upon these intuitive ideas, and counterintuitive ideas, may also have a competitive advantage over other ideas in the culture based on additional cognitive and socio-cultural factors. As anthropologist Harvey Whitehouse showcased in his theory of religious dynamics, known as Modes of Religiosity, MOR (see Chapter 9: Rituals Part 1), these include the extent to which ideas are repeated, and behaviors are performed (which enhances recall) and the extent to which prestigious individuals (e.g. elders, religious leaders) accept and promote such ideas.

Key points

- CSR has grown exponentially over the past two decades and continues to expand.
- We now understand more about the cognitive basis of religious ideas and behaviors.
- CSR research also has practical implications.
- CSR continues to adopt different methods, revise theories, and challenge findings within the social-cognitive sciences, including those previously upheld in CSR.

The role of cognition and culture in explaining religion

Theories and research within CSR differ in the extent to which they embrace both cognition and culture to explain the transmission of religious ideas and beliefs. As outlined in Chapter 1 (Introduction), CSR aimed to redress the balance in the study of religion, which was skewed in favor of idiosyncratic and interpretative accounts by including explanatory, scientific reports. Cognitive scholars did not want to hijack the study of religion but rather to integrate research in the sciences to understand better and explain religion. The emphasis placed on explanatory endeavors may have led some to the conclusion that CSR neglects the role of the socio-cultural environment and historical factors in affecting the forms and transmission of religious ideas and beliefs, but this is an unfair characterization.

As outlined in Chapter 1 (Introduction) of this book, cognitive scientists of religion did not perceive culture as hovering above cognition or cognition as isolated from culture. Scholars have demonstrated a deep commitment to understanding how cognitive biases manifest themselves in particular socio-cultural contexts. This commitment is achieved by drawing on their specialist knowledge and often spending extended periods in the field conducting ethnographic research. Examples of this type of research are mentioned throughout this book.

While their general theories are outlined, due to word constraints, the richness of their contextual observations and considerations are not portrayed, although these can be found in their manuscripts. These include detailed ethnographic accounts of how religion is expressed in particular contemporary traditions, including: Chapter 7 (Supernatural Agents) anthropologist Emma Cohen on spirit possession in an Afro-Brazilian religious tradition, *The Mind Possessed*[71] (Cohen, 2008); Chapter 9 (Rituals Part 1) Harvey Whitehouse's account of rituals and religious dynamics in Papua New Guinea *Inside the Cult*[72] (Whitehouse, 1995); anthropologist Brian Malley's work with North American fundamentalist Baptists[73] (Malley, 2004); and anthropologist Dimitris Xygalatas' account of fire-walking rituals in Northern Greece, *The Burning Saints: Cognition and culture in the fire-walking rituals of the Anastenaria*[74] (Xygalatas, 2014).

A more reasonable and evidence-based claim is that, on the whole, CSR has contributed more to understanding the role of cognition in the transmission of ideas and beliefs than on the part of socio-cultural and historical contexts in shaping them. Such a stronghold in cognition in CSR is inevitable given the motivation of early pioneers to redress the balance in cultural studies towards cultural explanations of religion. Indeed, perhaps the greatest insight of CSR is that religion is shaped and constrained by implicit, panhuman intuitions about the way the world works, and that these intuitions derive from many distinct psychological systems.

As we discussed in Chapter 7 (Supernatural Agents), many scholars in CSR have proposed that cognitive biases are necessary, but not sufficient, to explain belief formation. Some have extended this claim to recommend that the general model of transmission potential—such as minimally counterintuitive theory (MCI)—needs to take account of context biases, including the cultural context, to provide a more comprehensive explanation of religious beliefs. Few would doubt this. However, many theories (such as MCI) are general models intended to provoke further research by applying them to specific contexts with an understanding of the cultural and historical context within which religious ideas are communicated.

Researchers have already made headway in specifying how cognitive biases that predispose humans towards religious belief interact with each other, their relationship to cultural input, and how they are accounted for by individual differences. For instance, psychologist Aiyana Willard and social anthropologist Ara Norenzayan investigated the relationship between cognitive tendencies such as mentalizing, mind-body dualism, teleological thinking, anthropomorphism, and cultural exposure to religion to predict belief in God, paranormal beliefs, and belief in life's purpose.[75]

The results of Willard and Norenzayan's analyses demonstrated in more precise terms how these tendencies relate to one another and the direction of influence. For example, they concluded that cognitive biases come first and are followed by beliefs and not the other way around. They also reported results that would be expected of cultural explanations of religion, such as greater exposure to religious attendance predicts more belief in God. However, they also reported other unexpected findings. For example, the relationship between Christianity and anthropomorphism suggested that high rates of Christianity in a community might suppress anthropomorphic tendencies in individuals. In the future, research that addresses similar questions and interaction effects of individual differences, cognitive biases, and cultural input is likely to provide a much more specific explanation of religion.

Key points

- Theories and research within CSR differ in the extent to which they embrace both cognition and culture to explain the transmission of religious ideas and beliefs.
- CSR has contributed more to understanding the role of cognition in the transmission of ideas and beliefs than on the part of socio-cultural and historical contexts in shaping them. However, they also take account of the cultural context in their explanations.
- Researchers have showcased how cognitive biases interact with each other, their relationship to cultural input, and how they are accounted for by individual differences.

The role of experience, the body, emotions, and motivation in religious belief and behavior

Some scholars have argued that CSR ought to engage more with the role of affect to explain belief acquisition, experience, and processing of information about religion.[76] Historically, the field of psychology of religion has engaged extensively in the relationship between affective processing and religious concepts (especially towards the Christian God), and some classic CSR theories, such as minimally counterintuitive theory (MCI), take little account of emotional processing.[77] However, cognitive scientists of religion do not treat people like emotionless computers, and many CSR theories have focused on motivational and affective aspects of religiosity. These include the behavioral effects of fear of supernatural punishment,[78] emotional commitments required in some ritual displays,[79] the alleviation of anxiety in ritual performance,[80] the mnemonic and cohesive impact of emotional arousal,[81] and the motivational attractiveness of particular depictions of life after death as contributing towards their transmissive success.[82]

This engagement with motivational and affective aspects of religiosity is set to continue. For example, scholars have proposed a revised explanation of the tendency to engage in anthropomorphic reasoning across cultures depending on individual dispositions and the cultural environment. One prediction from this model is that people who desire social contact and affiliation, and those in cultures with exposure to anthropomorphic representations (such as computers and electronic devices) will tend to anthropomorphize nonhuman agents.[83] The results of studies testing these predictions will clarify the role of motivation and affect in cognitive processing, both between individuals and across cultures.

Key points

- Historically, CSR has engaged less extensively in the relationship between affective processing and religious concepts than other approaches, such as the psychology of religion.
- CSR now engages more with the role of affect and religion than previously, and this is set to continue.

Phenomenology of religious experience

Many venerated figures in the study of religion, most notably William James, have brought attention to the fact that religious belief is also based on religious experience. Religious belief is a metacognitive process (i.e. thinking about thinking), and individual experiences also feature in how one thinks about beliefs. As anthropologist Tanya Luhrmann rightly highlights, people pay attention to specific events and experiences and code them as significant (and disattend to others) partly as a result of popular ideas in the cultural milieu.[84] In addition to the underlying cognitive scaffolding of intuitions that CSR scholars have showcased, belief formation is also based on personal experiences and those that are deemed meaningful. So, what does CSR have to say about experience and belief?

Historically, CSR has had less to say about the phenomenology of religious experience. In other words, what it feels like for an individual to experience an episode of possession, or to sense the presence of a loved one who has recently died. However, this is changing. Some scholars have incorporated recent theories in the cognitive sciences to address religious experiences. The most notable is religious studies scholar, Ann Taves, in her foundational book on religious experience *Religious experience reconsidered: A building-block approach to the study of religion and other special things*,[85] and in subsequent work on religion.[86] Along with others, including the anthropologist Michael Kinsella and psychologist Tamsin German and members of the Religion, Experience, and Mind Lab Group at UC Santa Barbra, Taves and colleagues are undertaking a mixed-methods study on near-death experiences (NDEs) and the role of shared experiences in the formation of new social movements.[87]

The "Quantifying Religious Experience Project" at the Institute for the Bio-Cultural Study of Religion's lab at Boston University (led by philosopher and theologian Wesley Wildman) will make significant headway in understanding religious experiences.[88] This project aims to investigate the phenomenology of religious experiences across traditions (e.g. the Catholic nun's experience of God through contemplative prayer, the Hindu's feeling of the presence of Shiva). Crucially, the project does not rely on narrative accounts of beliefs. Narrative accounts are notoriously imprecise as a basis of comparison between experiences across religious traditions. Instead, researchers will compare experiences using the latest techniques in cognitive psychology and quantitative research, such as an inventory of consciousness that is culturally independent. This research, and others like it, will lead to a better understanding of the experiential dimensions of cognitive processing and the processes by which people come to attribute meaning to their experiences.

One potential area of collaboration in the future is between descriptive accounts of individual experiences and neuroscientific findings on brain activation to enrich the understanding of religious experience. Most research on religious experiences has taken place among those versed in the neurocognitive sciences, where researchers are employing the latest brain imaging technologies to understand the neural correlates activated in religious cognition and experiences. There is a growing interest among neuroscientists in how ritual, trance, meditation, and other altered states of consciousness affect brain functioning and development. Here, neuroscientist Patrick McNamara has done much to showcase the subject in an informed manner to a general audience.[89]

Some exciting new findings are now coming out of these methods in CSR research. For instance, Schjoedt and colleagues have made headway in uncovering the basic neural processing employed by participants in religious practices. For example, they found differences in brain activation when believers and non-believers listened to some speakers, including a reputable Christian known for his healing powers. Only Christians showed significant differences in brain activation when they listened to the renowned Christian healer, most notably, Christians who rated the healer as more charismatic had less brain activation than those who rated the leader as less charismatic. In other words, the more charismatic they regarded the leader, the more passively they listened to the speaker. Schjoedt and colleagues concluded that they suspend or hand over their critical faculty to the trusted person. Further, the suspension of downregulation of neural activity in these brain regions may be an earmark of followers' susceptibility to charismatic authority.[90]

Consider another example, discussed in Chapter 10 (Rituals Part 2). Anthropologist Dimitris Xygalatas and colleagues studied fire-walking rituals in a small Spanish village of San Pedro Manrique. They measured the relationship between firewalkers' and spectators' heart rates. One important finding was that arousal levels between ritual performers and spectators were similarly high for people who knew each other, but dissimilar among ritual performers and strangers. These findings have implications for synchrony in arousal, empathic arousal in social relationships, and social cohesion during religious rituals. For example, they demonstrated that the effects of arousal are mainly a product of existing social relations and not exclusively on mirroring and empathy. These insights were only possible using a combination of physiological measures, relationship mapping, and self-report measures. This research is radically interdisciplinary, and future studies in CSR, which combine ethnographic research, scientific methods, and technologies, are likely to be equally insightful.

Key points

- Religious belief is also based on religious experience.
- Historically, CSR has had less to say about the phenomenology of religious experience, but this is changing.

Summary of evaluation, implications, and future directions

1 The role of evolution in religion

Most cognitive scientists of religion consider an evolutionary approach as essential to a cognitive explanation of religious phenomena. They disagree over the unit of selection, mechanisms of cultural change and the origin, function, and precise role of evolution in religion. These debates will continue over the coming years, and theories about the role of evolution in religious thought and behavior will be articulated and revised in light of new data. In the future, even closer ties between the evolutionary sciences and CSR are likely to be forged.

2 The mind and models of cognition

CSR began with a handful of scholars who were influenced by a modular view of the mind. Currently, there are disagreements over the models of cognition involved in religious thought—which includes whether, and to what extent, the mind is modular. These debates are likely to continue. Some have called for considerable attention over the view of the mind and the type of cognitive processing that is implied by theories in CSR. In the future, more consideration is likely to be given to discussions of the mind, as well as theories that consider embodied and extended cognition and the ecological environment in shaping religious thought and behavior.

3 Methods and theories underlying the scientific study of religion

CSR engages in the form of methodological reductionism that first fractionates religion in order to study the different components while acknowledging the complexity and interaction of many levels and not reducing an explanation of religion to any one level. Some feel threatened by scientific approaches to religion and make the assumption that CSR endorses ontological reductionism. However, this is a misunderstanding of the approach.

4 The conceptualization of religion in CSR

Another critique that sometimes emerges from scholars of religion is that CSR does not have a clear conceptualization of religion. CSR scholars do not propose a general theory of religion but take a bottom-up approach to characterize and investigate religious phenomena.

5 Religious belief

A related question is whether, and to what extent, CSR explains belief. CSR has veered away from explaining the process of belief formation for individuals within a tradition. It has been primarily concerned with explaining why and how general trends in religion emerge cross-culturally than those that differ from those trends, and how individuals differ from one another. The main contribution of CSR to understanding belief is the clarity with which scholars distinguish between propositional beliefs and intuitions.

6 The role of cognition and culture in explaining religion

CSR has contributed more to understanding the role of cognition in the transmission of ideas and beliefs than on the role of socio-cultural and historical contexts in shaping them. CSR scholars acknowledge that cognitive biases are necessary, but not sufficient, to explain belief formation. An understanding of contextual biases is also required. In the future, research that addresses interaction effects between individual differences, cognitive biases, and cultural input is likely to provide a much more specific explanation of religion.

7 The role of experience, the body, emotions, and motivation in religious belief and behavior

Some scholars have proposed that CSR ought to engage more with the role of affect to explain belief acquisition, experience, and processing of information about religion. Cognitive scientists of religion do not treat people like emotionless computers, and many CSR theories have focused on motivational and affective aspects of religiosity. This engagement with motivational and affective aspects of religiosity is set to continue.

8 Phenomenology of religious experience

Historically, CSR has had less to say about the phenomenology of religious experience. However, this is changing. New research will lead to a better understanding of the experiential dimensions of cognitive processing and the processes by which people come to attribute meaning to their experiences.

Chapter summary

CSR is a progressive research program, and researchers have proposed many—often diverse—theories about different religious phenomena. Despite differences in the details, all champion the promise of the methods and theories, and findings of the cognitive sciences to produce insight into religion, and all maintain that religious thought and action harness ordinary forms of cognition. Although tremendous progress has been made towards understanding the cognitive basis of religious ideas and behaviors, there is still much work to be done. CSR has proposed that science can explain religion. However, it does not pretend to exhaustively explain everything that might be called religion (provocative book titles aside) and acknowledges that all explanations of religion are partial explanations. Research in the cognitive sciences has only scratched the surface of the vast repertoire of the cross-culturally recurrent phenomena that have been deemed as "religious." In many ways then, research findings are the start, rather than the endpoint, of explaining religion.

Discussion questions

1 What do you think are the main strengths of CSR?
2 Which criticisms of CSR do you agree and disagree with? Why?
3 Do you think CSR has any implications for whether religious concepts (such as supernatural agents) exist? Why?
4 Can you think of any practical implications of CSR not addressed in this chapter?

Selected further reading

Articles

1 Cohen, Emma, Jonathan A. Lanman, Harvey Whitehouse, and Robert N. McCauley. "Common criticisms of the cognitive science of religion—answered." *Bulletin of the Council of Societies for the Study of Religion* 37, no. 4 (2008): 112–115.

2 McBrayer, Justin. "Explanations of religion". In *Oxford Bibliographies in Philosophy,* Duncan Pritchard ed., 2018.

Books

1 Barrett, Justin L. *Cognitive science, religion, and theology: From human minds to divine minds.* Templeton Press, 2011.

2 De Cruz, Helen, and Johan De Smedt. *A natural history of natural theology: The cognitive science of theology and philosophy of religion.* MIT Press, 2014.

Notes

1 Lawson, E. Thomas. "Towards a cognitive science of religion." *Numen* 47, no. 3 (2000): 338–339.

2 E.g. Willard, Aiyana K. "Agency detection is unnecessary in the explanation of religious belief." *Religion, Brain & Behavior* 9, no. 1 (2019): 96–98.

3 E.g. Willard, Aiyana K., Joseph Henrich, and Ara Norenzayan. "Memory and belief in the transmission of counterintuitive content." *Human Nature* 27, no. 3 (2016): 221–243.

4 E.g. De Cruz, Helen. "Cognitive science of religion and the study of theological concepts." *Topoi* 33, no. 2 (2014): 487–497.

5 E.g. Hodge, K. Mitch. "Descartes' mistake: How afterlife beliefs challenge the assumption that humans are intuitive Cartesian substance dualists." *Journal of Cognition and Culture* 8, no. 3–4 (2008): 387–415.

6 E.g. Baumard, Nicolas, and Pascal Boyer. "Empirical problems with the notion of 'Big Gods' and of prosociality in large societies." *Religion, Brain & Behavior* 5, no. 4 (2015): 279–283.

7 Barrett, Justin L. "Cognitive science of religion: Looking back, looking forward." *Journal for the Scientific Study of Religion* 50, no. 2 (2011): 229–239.

8 "New Voices in Cognition and Culture." *The Journal of Cognition and Culture* 17, 5 (2017).

9 Martin, Luther H., and Donald Wiebe, eds. *Religion explained? The cognitive science of religion after twenty-five years.* Bloomsbury Publishing, 2017.

10 Xygalatas, Dimitris. "Bridging the gap: The cognitive science of religion as an integrative approach." In *Evolution, cognition, and the history of religion: A new synthesis,* Brill, 2018, 255–272.

11 Xygalatas, Dimitris. "Bridging the gap: The cognitive science of religion as an integrative approach." In *Evolution, cognition, and the history of religion: A new synthesis,* Brill, 2018, 255–272, 265.

12 McBrayer, Justin. "Explanations of religion." In *Oxford Bibliographies in Philosophy,* Duncan Pritchard ed., 2018.

13 Purzycki, Benjamin, and Willard, Aiyana. "MCI theory: A critical discussion." *Religion, Brain & Behavior* 6, no. 3 (2015): 207–248.

14 Schloss, Jeff, and Murray, Michael. "Evolutionary accounts of belief in supernatural punishment: A critical review." *Religion, Brain & Behavior* 1, no. 1 (2011): 46–99.

15 Pyysiainen, Ilkka. "Religion-naturally: Religion, theology, and science." In *Is religion natural?* Evers, Dirk et al. London: T&T Clark International, 2012, 67–84.

16 Slingerland, Edward. "Who's afraid of reductionism? The study of religion in the age of cognitive science." *Journal of the American Academy of Religion* 76, no. 2 (2008): 375–411.

17 E.g. Van Eyghen, Hans, Rik Peels, and Gijsbert B. Van den Brink. *New developments in the cognitive science of religion: The rationality of religious belief.* 2018.
18 De Cruz, Helen, and Johan De Smedt. *A natural history of natural theology: The cognitive science of theology and philosophy of religion.* MIT Press, 2014; De Cruz, Helen, Ryan Nichols, and James R. Beebe, eds. *Advances in religion, cognitive science, and experimental philosophy.* Bloomsbury Publishing, 2017.
19 De Cruz, Helen. "Cognitive science of religion and the study of theological concepts." *Topoi* 33, no. 2 (2014): 487–497.
20 E.g. Jong, Jonathan, and Visala, Aku. "Evolutionary debunking arguments against theism, reconsidered." *International Journal for Philosophy of Religion* 76: 243–258.
21 Dennett, Daniel Clement. *Breaking the spell: Religion as a natural phenomenon.* Vol. 14. Penguin, 2006.
22 Dawkins, Richard, and Lalla Ward. *The god delusion.* Boston: Houghton Mifflin Company, 2006.
23 Bloom, Paul. "Is God an accident?" *Atlantic Monthly* 296, no. 5 (2005): 105.
24 Bloom, Paul. "Religion is natural." *Developmental Science* 10, no. 1 (2007): 147–151.
25 Boyer, Pascal. *Religion explained: The human instincts that fashion gods, spirits, and ancestors.* Random House, 2002.
26 Barrett, Justin L. *Born believers: The science of children's religious belief.* Simon and Schuster, 2012.
27 Barrett, Justin L. "Exploring the natural foundations of religion." *Trends in Cognitive Sciences* 4, no. 1 (2000): 29–34.
28 https://www.nature.com/articles/4551038a.
29 E.g. see McCauley, Robert N. *Why religion is natural and science is not.* Oxford University Press, 2011.
30 Martin, Luther H., and Donald Wiebe. "Religious studies as a scientific discipline: The persistence of a delusion." *Journal of the American Academy of Religion* 80, no. 3 (2012): 587–597.
31 E.g. see Slingerland, Edward. "Back to the future: A response to Martin and Wiebe." *Journal of the American Academy of Religion* 80, no. 3 (2012): 611–617; McCauley, Robert N. "A cognitive science of religion will be difficult, expensive, complicated, radically counter-intuitive, and possible: A response to Martin and Wiebe." *Journal of the American Academy of Religion* 80, no. 3 (2012): 605–610; Taves, Ann. "A response to Martin and Wiebe." *Journal of the American Academy of Religion* 80, no. 3 (2012): 601–604.
32 Notably Justin Barrett. E.g. Barrett, Justin L., and Roger Trigg. *The roots of religion: Exploring the cognitive science of religion (Ashgate Science and Religion Series).* Ashgate Publishing Group, 2014.
33 E.g. Barrett, Justin L. *Cognitive science, religion, and theology: From human minds to divine minds.* Templeton Press, 2011.
34 Van Eyghen, Hans. "Two types of 'explaining away': Arguments in the cognitive science of religion." *Zygon* 51, no. 4 (2016): 966–982.
35 Boyer, Pascal. *Religion explained.* Random House, 2008, 1038.
36 "Neurotheology: A science of what?" In McNamara, P. ed. (2006) *Where God and science meet, Volume 2, The neurology of religious experience.* Westport, Connecticut: Praeger: 81–104.
37 E.g. see www.independent.co.uk/news/science/belief-and-the-brains-god-spot-1641022.html.
38 Schjoedt, Uffe. "The religious brain: A general introduction to the experimental neuroscience of religion." *Method & Theory in the Study of Religion* 21, no. 3 (2009): 310–339.
39 Barrett, Justin L. "Is the spell really broken? Bio-psychological explanations of religion and theistic belief." *Theology and Science* 5, no. 1 (2007): 57–72.

40 Barkow, Jerome H., Leda Ed Cosmides, and John Ed Tooby. *The adapted mind: Evolutionary psychology and the generation of culture.* USA: Oxford University Press, 1992.

41 Henrich, Joseph, Robert Boyd, and Peter J. Richerson. "Five misunderstandings about cultural evolution." *Human Nature* 19, no. 2 (2008): 119–137; Henrich, Joseph, and Richard McElreath. "Dual-inheritance theory: The evolution of human cultural capacities and cultural evolution." In *Oxford handbook of evolutionary psychology*. 2007.

42 E.g. see Boyer, Pascal. "Cognitive constraints on cultural representations: Natural ontologies and religious ideas." In *Mapping the mind: Domain specificity in cognition and culture* (1994): 391–411.

43 E.g. see Wilson, David Sloan. *Darwin's Cathedral: Evolution, religion, and the nature of society*. University of Chicago Press, 2010.

44 E.g. see Bulbulia, Joseph. "Religious costs as adaptations that signal altruistic intention." *Evolution and Cognition* 10, no. 1 (2004): 19–38.

45 Henrich, Joseph, Steven J. Heine, and A. Noranyazan. "The weirdest people in the world." *Behavioral and Brain Sciences*, 2010.

46 Slingerland, Edward, Ryan Nichols, Kristoffer Neilbo, and Carson Logan. "The distant reading of religious texts: A 'big data' approach to mind-body concepts in early China." *Journal of the American Academy of Religion* (2017): lfw090.

47 Roazzi, Maira Monteiro, Carl N. Johnson, Melanie Nyhof, Silvia Helena Koller, and Antonio Roazzi. "Vital energy and afterlife: Implications for cognitive science of religion." *Paidéia (Ribeirão Preto)* 25, no. 61 (2015): 145–152.

48 Turchin, Peter, Harvey Whitehouse, Pieter Francois, Edward Slingerland, and Mark Collard. "A historical database of sociocultural evolution." *Cliodynamics* 3, no. 2 (2012).

49 Slingerland, Edward, and Brenton Sullivan. "Durkheim with data: The database of religious history." *Journal of the American Academy of Religion* 85, no. 2 (2017): 312–347.

50 Barrett, H. Clark. *The shape of thought: How mental adaptations evolve*. Oxford University Press, 2014.

51 Henrich, Joseph. *The secret of our success: How culture is driving human evolution, domesticating our species, and making us smarter*. Princeton University Press, 2015.

52 Bulbulia, Joseph. "Nature's medicine: Religiosity as an adaptation for health and cooperation." *Where God and science meet* 1 (2006): 87–121.

53 Barkow, Jerome H., Leda Ed Cosmides, and John Ed Tooby. *The adapted mind: Evolutionary psychology and the generation of culture*. USA: Oxford University Press, 1992.

54 Hodge, Mitch K., Sousa, Paulo and White, Claire (manuscript in preparation). Proposed cognitive mechanisms and representational structures of afterlife beliefs: A review.

55 E.g. see Donald, Merlin. *A mind so rare: The evolution of human consciousness*. W.W. Norton & Company, 2001; Hutchins, Edwin. *Cognition in the wild*. MIT Press, 1995.

56 Geertz, Armin W. "Too much mind and not enough brain, body, and culture: On what needs to be done in the cognitive science of religion." *Historia Religionum* 2, no. 2 (2010): 1000–1017.

57 Geertz, Armin W. "Brain, body and culture: A biocultural theory of religion." *Method & Theory in the Study of Religion* 22, no. 4 (2010): 304–321.

58 Purzycki, B.G., and McNamara, R.A. "An ecological theory of gods' minds." In De Cruz, Helen, and Nichols, Ryan eds. *Advances in religion, cognitive science, and experimental philosophy*. New York: Continuum, 2016, 143–167.

59 E.g. Slingerland, Edward. "Who's afraid of reductionism? The study of religion in the age of cognitive science." *Journal of the American Academy of Religion* 76, no. 2 (2008): 375–411; cf to Van Slyke, James A. *The cognitive science of religion*. Routledge, 2016.

60 McCauley, Robert N. "Explanatory pluralism and the cognitive science of religion: Or why scholars in religious studies should stop worrying about reductionism." In *Mental culture: Classical social theory and the cognitive science of religion* (2013): 11–32.
61 Slingerland, Edward. "Who's afraid of reductionism? The study of religion in the age of cognitive science." *Journal of the American Academy of Religion* 76, no. 2 (2008): 375–411.
62 E.g. Dawes, Greg, and James Maclaurin, eds. *A new science of religion*. Routledge, 2012.
63 Sørensen, Jesper. *A cognitive theory of magic*. Rowman Altamira, 2007.
64 Lanman, Jonathan. "On the non-evolution of atheism and the importance of definitions and data." *Religion, Brain & Behavior* 2, no. 1 (2012): 76–78.
65 Barnes, Kirsten, and Nicholas J.S. Gibson. "Supernatural agency: Individual difference predictors and situational correlates." *International Journal for the Psychology of Religion* 23, no. 1 (2013): 42–62.
66 Levy, Neil. "Religious beliefs are factual beliefs: Content does not correlate with context sensitivity." *Cognition* 161 (2017): 109–116.
67 Van Leeuwen, Neil. "Religious credence is not factual belief." *Cognition*, 133, no. 3 (2014): 698–715.
68 Legare, Cristine H., and Susan A. Gelman. "Bewitchment, biology, or both: The co-existence of natural and supernatural explanatory frameworks across development." *Cognitive Science* 32, no. 4 (2008): 607–642.
69 Luhrmann, Tanya M. *When God talks back: Understanding the American evangelical relationship with God*. Vintage, 2012.
70 Boyer, Pascal. "Why 'belief' is hard work: Implications of Tanya Luhrmann's When God talks back." *HAU: Journal of Ethnographic Theory* 3, no. 3 (2013): 349–357.
71 Cohen, Emma. *The mind possessed: The cognition of spirit possession in an Afro-Brazilian religious tradition*. Oxford University Press, 2007.
72 Whitehouse, Harvey. *Inside the cult: Religious innovation and transmission in Papua New Guinea*. Oxford University Press on Demand, 1995.
73 Malley, Brian. *How the Bible works: An anthropological study of evangelical Biblicism*. Rowman Altamira, 2004.
74 Xygalatas, Dimitris. *The burning saints: Cognition and culture in the fire-walking rituals of the Anastenaria*. Routledge, 2014.
75 Willard, Aiyana K., and Ara Norenzayan. "Cognitive biases explain religious belief, paranormal belief, and belief in life's purpose." *Cognition* 129, no. 2 (2013): 379–391.
76 Gibson, N.J.S. "Once more, with feelings: The importance of emotion for cognitive science of religion." In *The evolution of religion: Studies, theories, and critiques* (2008): 271–277.
77 E.g. related, see Upala, M. Afzal, Lauren O. Gonce, Ryan D. Tweney, and D. Jason Slone. "Contextualizing counterintuitiveness: How context affects comprehension and memorability of counterintuitive concepts." *Cognitive Science* 31, no. 3 (2007): 415–439.
78 E.g. Johnson, Dominic, and Jesse Bering. "Hand of God, mind of man: Punishment and cognition in the evolution of cooperation." *Evolutionary Psychology* 4, no. 1 (2006); Norenzayan, Ara. *Big gods: How religion transformed cooperation and conflict*. Princeton University Press, 2013.
79 Atran, Scott. *In gods, we trust*. New York: Oxford University Press, 2002.
80 Liénard, Pierre, and Pascal Boyer. "Whence collective rituals? A cultural selection model of ritualized behavior." *American Anthropologist* 108, no. 4 (2006): 814–827.
81 McCauley, Robert N., and E. Thomas Lawson. *Bringing ritual to mind: Psychological foundations of cultural forms*. Cambridge University Press, 2002; Whitehouse, Harvey. *Modes of religiosity: A cognitive theory of religious transmission*. Rowman Altamira, 2004.
82 Nichols, Shaun. "Is religion what we want? Motivation and the cultural transmission of religious representations." *Journal of Cognition and Culture* 4, no. 2 (2004): 347–371.

83 Epley, Nicholas, Adam Waytz, and John T. Cacioppo. "On seeing human: A three-factor theory of anthropomorphism." *Psychological Review* 114, no. 4 (2007): 864.
84 Luhrmann, Tanya. "Talking back about When God talks back." *HAU: Journal of Ethnographic Theory* 3, no. 3 (2013): 389–398.
85 Taves, Ann. *Religious experience reconsidered: A building-block approach to the study of religion and other special things*. Princeton University Press, 2011.
86 Taves, Ann. *Revelatory events: Three case studies of the emergence of new spiritual paths*. Princeton University Press, 2016.
87 Related, see: Kinsella, Michael. "Near-death experiences and networked spirituality: The emergence of an afterlife movement," *Journal of the American Academy of Religion* 85, no. 1 (2016): 168–198.
88 See: www.ibcsr.org/index.php/activitites/current-activities/495-the-quantifiying-religious-experience-project.
89 E.g. see McNamara, Patrick. *The neuroscience of religious experience*. Cambridge University Press, 2009.
90 Schjoedt, Uffe, Hans Stødkilde-Jørgensen, Armin W. Geertz, Torben E. Lund, and Andreas Roepstorff. "The power of charisma—perceived charisma inhibits the frontal executive network of believers in intercessory prayer." *Social Cognitive and Affective Neuroscience* 6, no. 1 (2010): 119–127.

Glossary

Adaptationist	Explaining the evolution of traits in terms of their adaptive function or survival value.
Adaptive	In evolution, a heritable trait that serves a specific function and improves an organism's fitness or survival.
Anthropomorphism	The tendency to attribute human-like properties, including mental states and characteristics, to nonhuman things.
Axiomatic	Self-evident or unquestionable.
Big Gods	Omnipotent moralizing agents with the power to punish moral wrongdoers.
Black box	A system in which both the input and output are observable, but the processes that occur between them are unknown or not observable.
Blank slates	The mind in its hypothetical primary blank or empty state before receiving outside impressions.
Bottom-up	A bottom-up approach is the piecing together of systems to give rise to more complex systems.
By-product	In evolution, a secondary and sometimes unexpected or unintended result.
Causally	How one thing causes another; by way of cause and effect.
Causally opaque	There is no clear or direct physical causal mechanism to explain the relationship between an action and its effect.
Coexistence model	Accommodating and reconciling multiple explanations for the same kind of event or outcomes.

Cognitive biases	A form of thinking that occurs when people are processing and interpreting information in the world around them.
Cognitive constraints	Limitations to what we can imagine.
Cognitive revolution	An intellectual movement that began in the 1950s as an interdisciplinary study of the mind and its processes, which became known collectively as cognitive science. The relevant areas of interchange were between the fields of psychology, anthropology, and linguistics using approaches developed within the then-nascent fields of artificial intelligence, computer science, and neuroscience.
Collective effervescence	A sociological concept coined by Émile Durkheim. According to Durkheim, a community or society may, at times, come together and simultaneously communicate the same thought and participate in the same action.
Compatible account	Accounts of the world are consistent or viewed as such.
Conflict account	Accounts of the world are incompatible or viewed as such.
Consequentialism	Basing decisions on consequences, such as based on principles of utilitarianism (the outcome that provides the most benefit to the largest number of people).
Conspicuous consumption	Spending money on and acquiring luxury goods and services to publicly display economic power— the income or the accumulated wealth of the buyer.
Content biases	The transmission potential of concepts based on their content.
Context biases	Contextual effects on the transmission of concepts.
Correlation	The degree of a relationship (usually linear) between two variables, which may be quantified as a correlation coefficient.
Creationism	The belief that the universe was created by divine intervention.
Credibility enhancing displays	Performing actions as a means to convince individuals of commitment to belief systems.
Cultural determinism	The theory or premise that individual and group characteristics and behavior patterns

	are mainly produced by a given society's economic, social, political, and religious organization.
Cultural relativism	The view that attitudes, behaviors, values, concepts, and achievements must be understood in the light of their cultural milieu and not judged according to the standards of a different culture. In psychology, the relativist position questions the universal application of psychological theory, research, therapeutic techniques, and clinical approaches, because those used or developed in one culture may not be appropriate or applicable to another.
Cultural selection theory	The study of cultural change modeled on theories of evolutionary biology. It proposes that some cultures will have a transmissive advantage.
Deontological reasoning	Rule-based objectivist morality, which stipulates that there is one right or wrong action, such as it is always wrong to commit adultery or kill.
Dependent variables	The outcome is observed to occur or change after the occurrence or variation of the independent variable in an experiment, or the effect that one wants to predict or explain in correlational research. Dependent variables may or may not be related causally to the independent variable.
Descriptive	Describing.
Displacement Theory	The theory that increasing scientific knowledge supplants religious ideas.
Distal	The most distant, or ultimate, causal explanation of an event.
Domain-general	A cognitive ability, such as general intelligence or speed of information processing, that influences performance over a wide range of situations and tasks.
Domain-specific	A cognitive ability, such as face recognition that is specific to a task and under control of a specific function of the mind, brain, or both. Domain-specific systems or modules or learning mechanisms direct expectations of properties for each category. These assumptions about properties

	of things in our intuitive ontologies include folk physics (e.g. things move as a connected whole), folk biology.
Dual-process in psychology	A dual-process theory provides an account of how thought can arise in two different ways, or as a result of two different processes. Often, the two processes consist of an implicit (automatic), unconscious process, and an explicit (controlled), conscious process.
Emergent properties	Emergence occurs when an entity is observed to have properties its parts do not have on their own. These properties or behaviors emerge only when the parts interact in a wider whole. For example, life, as studied in biology, is an emergent property of chemistry.
Enculturation Hypothesis	The process by which people learn the requirements of their surrounding culture and acquire values and behaviors appropriate or necessary in that culture.
Environment of Evolutionary Adaptedness	The conditions and properties of the external world in which evolutionary adaptations occur.
Epidemiology of representations	The theory that some ideas are encoded, stored, and recalled better than others. Just like epidemiologists in medicine study, the incidence and distribution of disease, Sperber argued that social scientists could study the prevalence and distribution of ideas in culture.
Epistemological	Relating to the theory of knowledge, especially with regard to its methods, validity, and scope, and the distinction between justified belief and opinion.
Ethnocentrism	Evaluation of other cultures according to preconceptions originating in the standards and customs of one's own culture.
Ethnographic research	A qualitative method where researchers observe and/or interact with a study's participants in their real-life environment.
Evolution by Natural Selection	Species change over time and give rise to new species that share a common ancestor.
Evolutionary psychology	An approach to psychological inquiry that views human cognition and behavior in a

	broadly Darwinian context of adaptation to evolving physical and social environments and new intellectual challenges. It differs from sociobiology mainly in its emphasis on the effects of natural selection on information processing and the structure of the human mind.
Exegesis	Critical interpretation or explanation.
Explanatory accounts	Accounts that serve to explain, which includes to account for the reason or cause of a phenomenon.
Explanatory pluralism	The view that the best form and level of explanation depends on the kind of question one seeks to answer by the explanation, and that in order to answer all questions in the best way possible, we need more than one form and level of explanation.
Extinctivists	The position that a person does not survive biological death.
Fairness or proportionality bias	The tendency to represent actions and consequences as having proportionate consequences.
Folk Biology	The cognitive study of how people classify and reason about the organic world.
Folk concepts	Common sense ideas.
Folk-dualism	The intuition that minds are separate and independent from bodies.
Free-riders	People who reap the benefits of living in a group without contributing.
Galton's problem	The problem of drawing inferences from cross-cultural data due to the effects of historical contact between societies.
Hazard Precaution System	A cognitive system proposed by Boyer and Lienard geared towards the detection of and reaction to inferred fitness threats.
High-fidelity imitation/transmission	Accurately copying/mimicking a behavior.
Hyperactive agency detection device (HADD)	A tendency towards agency detection that becomes hyperactive and leads to the over-attribution of agency in the environment and as being the cause of stimuli in the environment.
Hypotheses	The generation of testable predictions.

Immanent Justice Reasoning	A belief that good things happen to good people and, conversely, that bad things happen to bad people.
Immortalists	The position that a person survives biological death.
Implicit	Implied though not plainly expressed or not conscious.
Independent variables	The variable in an experiment that is individually manipulated or is observed to occur before the dependent, or outcome, variable, in order to assess its effect or influence. Independent variables may or may not be causally related to the dependent variable.
Integrated Causal Model (ICM)	Posed by Cosmides and Tooby to describe evolutionary psychology, which took account of the evolution of the human mind and its interaction with the environment.
Integrated thinking	Natural and supernatural explanations of a single phenomenon are combined in a precise fashion.
Intelligent Design	An intelligent cause best explains the universe and living things.
Interpretive	An approach to describing data.
Intuitive ontological categories	Acquired at the earliest stages of conceptual development constitute an intuitive ontology. This is a limited set of expectations concerning particular domains of experience, such as persons, animals, and human-made objects.
Intuitive processes	Often called System 1 or "non-reflective," thoughts that are quick, automatic, and implicit (i.e. we are not consciously aware of them).
Karma	The sum of a person's actions in this and previous states of existence viewed as deciding their fate in future existences.
Kibbutzim	A collective community in Israel that was traditionally based on agriculture.
Kinship detection and identity fusion	The ability to recognize and calibrate kinship, and by extension, fuse identity with imagined kin.

Knowledge-deficit hypothesis	People do not endorse ideas because they do not understand them.
Language Acquisition Device (LAD)	A hypothetical faculty used to explain a child's ability to acquire language. In Noam Chomsky's view, the LAD contains significant innate knowledge that actively interprets the input. Only this can explain how a highly abstract competence in language results from a relatively deprived input.
Literal Immortality	Directly escaping death through a belief in the afterlife.
Maximally Counterintuitive Ideas	Ideas that violate many intuitive assumptions, making them difficult to understand and remember.
Materialist	A philosophical position that existence is explainable solely in material/physical terms.
Maturationally natural	Tendencies that emerge early in development with little instruction.
Mentalizing	The tendency to regard individuals as intentional and self-directed agents.
Metaphysical	The nature of the world.
Metarepresentational	Representations of representations, often known as thinking about thinking.
Methodological naturalism	The study of the natural universe.
Methodological pluralism	Adopt a range of methods to answer research questions.
Minimally counterintuitive ideas	Ideas that minimally tweak intuitive assumptions about the world.
Modularity	A view of the mind as composed of innate neural structures or modules which have distinct established evolutionary functions.
Monotheistic	The belief in one God.
Multidisciplinary research	Scholars address problems from different disciplinary perspectives.
Naïve	Intuitive, pre-scientific theories about the world.
Nativist	The view that ideas are hardwired at birth.
Natural	Observable and empirically verifiable phenomena of the physical or material world.
Naturalness-of-Religion Thesis	The theory that religion emerges from ordinary cognition.

Natural theology	Theology or knowledge of God based on observed facts and experience apart from divine revelation.
New atheists	Authors of early twenty-first century books promoting atheism.
Non-falsifiable	Cannot be proven false.
Offline Social Reasoning	The ability to represent others who are not within our immediate perceptual presence.
Ontogeny	The origination and development of an organism (both physical and psychological, e.g. moral development), usually from the time of fertilization of the egg to adult. The term can also be used to refer to the study of the entirety of an organism's lifespan.
Ontological reductionism	The belief that reality is composed of a minimum number of kinds of entities or substances. This claim is usually metaphysical, and is most commonly a form of monism, in effect claiming that all objects, properties, and events are reducible to a single substance.
Ontological status	Deciphering whether or not something is true or false.
Operationalized	Express or define something in terms of the operations used to determine or prove it.
Orthopraxy	Correct conduct in religion.
Parochialism	Focusing on small sections of an issue rather than considering its wider context.
Phenomenology	The study of structures of consciousness as experienced from the first-person point of view.
Phylogeny	The evolutionary history and relationships among or within groups of organisms
Pluridisciplinarity	Researchers who borrow methods, concepts, and theories from one another.
Polytheistic	Belief in or worship of more than one God.
Postmodernism	Is generally characterized by an attitude of skepticism, irony, or rejection toward what it describes as ideologies associated with modernism, often criticizing Enlightenment rationality. Postmodern thinkers frequently describe knowledge claims

	and value systems as contingent or socially-conditioned, describing them as products of political, historical, or cultural discourses and hierarchies.
Poverty of the stimulus	The argument from linguistics that children are not exposed to rich enough data within their linguistic environments to acquire every feature of their language. This is considered evidence contrary to the empiricist idea that language is learned solely through experience.
Practical rationality	Involves the individual who considers ends, and on some systematic basis, decides what the best means or course of action to pursue in order to achieve these ends is. This form of rationality can be considered to be pragmatic in that it provides individuals with a way of pursuing practical ends.
Practiced naturalness	Tendencies that emerge automatically through consistent training.
Primed	In the experimental paradigm, a target stimulus is processed in the context of a stimulus previously encountered.
Probabilistic models	Predictions based on probability distribution.
Promiscuous Teleology	When teleological reasoning extends to things that were not made for and did not exist for a purpose.
Propositional	Relating to, consisting of, or based on propositions, such as beliefs.
Prosociality and prosocial behaviors	Actions intended to help others, such as honesty, cooperation, and generosity.
Proximate	The closest causal explanation of an event.
Proximate mechanisms	The immediate cause of something.
Psychological Essentialism	The tendency to reason that species have a fixed essence or innate being.
Psychological mechanisms	Evolved psychological mechanisms (EPM) are also known as psychological adaptations and are responsible for the particular set of behaviors that humans or animals have in response to various evolutionary circumstances. EPMs are generally tuned to respond to specific adaptive problems.
Public goods economic game	A standard experimental economics game. In the basic game, subjects secretly choose

	how many of their private tokens to put into a public pot. The tokens in this pot are multiplied by a factor (greater than one and less than the number of players, N), and this "public good" payoff is evenly divided among players. Each subject also keeps the tokens they do not contribute.
Rationalism	The belief that reason is the chief source and test of knowledge.
Reductionism	The strategy of explaining or accounting for some phenomenon or construct by claiming that, when properly understood, it can be shown to be some other phenomenon or construct, where the latter is seen to be more straightforward, more basic, or more fundamental. The term is mainly applied to positions that attempt to explain human culture, society, or psychology in terms of animal behavior or physical laws. In psychology, a common form of reductionism is that in which psychological phenomena are reduced to biological phenomena so that mental life is presented as merely a function of biological processes.
Reflective processes or explicit thinking	Often called System 2, thinking in a slow, deliberate and explicit way.
Relativism	Any position that challenges the existence of absolute standards of truth or value. What is considered correct will depend on individual judgments and local conditions of culture, reflecting individual and collective experience. Such relativism challenges the validity of science except as a catalog of experience and a basis for ad hoc empirical prediction.
Religion-as-irrational thesis	The belief that people who endorse religion are irrational.
Rites of passage	A ceremony or event marking an important stage in someone's life, especially birth, puberty, marriage, and death.
Ritual Form Hypothesis	A theory by Lawson and McCauley explaining why people form similar cognitive representations of ritual.

Science-as-rational thesis	The belief that people who endorse science are rational.
Sensory pageantry	Stimuli (e.g. sounds, sights) that impact the senses and induce emotional arousal.
Simulation Constraint	A concept that states it is impossible to imagine ourselves devoid of any mental states.
Social loafing	Exerting less effort to achieve a goal when he or she works in a group than when working alone.
Socially desirable responding	The tendency to respond to present oneself in the most positive light.
Socially embodied	Representing a person as embodied in a socially appropriate way.
Socially stipulated	Demanded by society.
Socialization	The process of learning to behave in a way that is acceptable to society.
Spandrel	A characteristic that is a by-product of the evolution of some other characteristic, rather than a direct product of adaptive selection.
Splinter groups	A small organization that has broken away from a broader tradition.
Standard Social Science Model (SSM)	Posed by Cosmides and Tooby to describe the dominant explanatory model in cultural studies, which included philosophies such as cultural determinism.
Statistical analyses	The interpretation of numerical facts and data using mathematical theories of probability.
Sui generis	Unique, or within a class of its own.
Supernatural	Phenomena that violate, operate outside of, or are distinct from the realm of the natural world or known natural law.
Supplication, or petitioning	The action of asking or begging for something earnestly or humbly.
Symbolic Immortality	The ability for one to live on after one's death through producing offspring or the cultural or societal means one leaves behind.
Tacit	Understood without being stated.
Taxonomical	Concerned with the classification of things, especially organisms.
Teleology	A bias towards seeing things in the world as having a purpose and being made for that purpose.

Terror Management Theory (TMT)	A psychological theory that describes the management of the "terror" that occurs through the knowledge that death is inevitable.
Thanatophobia	The fear of death and dying.
The Blank Slate Hypothesis	The mind contains no implicate or innate traits.
The Epidemiology of Representations	Or, cultural epidemiology provides a conceptual framework for explaining cultural phenomena by how mental representations get distributed within a population.
Theologically correct	When ordinary ideas are consistent with a theological idea.
Theologically incorrect	When ordinary ideas are inconsistent with a theological idea.
Theory of Mind (ToM)	The understanding that others have intentions, desires, beliefs, perceptions, and emotions different from one's own and that such intentions, desires, and so on, affect people's actions and behaviors.
Thick descriptions	In qualitative research, the delineation and interpretation of observed behavior within its particular context so that the behavior becomes meaningful to an outsider. The researcher not only accurately describes observed behavior or social actions but also assigns purpose, motivation, and intentionality to these actions by explaining the context within which they took place; thick description conveys the thoughts and feelings of participants as well as the complex web of relationships among them.
Top-down	A top-down approach is the opposite of a bottom-up approach. You start with the complex system, or definition of the problem to be solved and then find means to test it.
Ultimate mechanisms	A distal cause, often referred to as the ultimate cause to explain an event.
Universal grammar	A theoretical linguistic construct positing the existence of a set of rules or grammatical principles that are innate in human beings and underlie most natural languages. The concept is of considerable

interest to psycholinguists who study language acquisition and the formation of valid sentences.

WEIRD traditions — Western, Educated, Industrialized, Rich, and Democratic.

Index